Urbanization in Tropical Africa:
An Annotated Bibliography

Bibliographies
and
Guides
in
African Studies

James C. Armstrong
Editor

Urbanization in Tropical Africa:
An Annotated Bibliography

ANTHONY M. O'CONNOR

G.K.HALL &CO.
70 LINCOLN STREET, BOSTON, MASS.

572 805

This publication is printed on permanent/durable acid-free paper
MANUFACTURED IN THE UNITED STATES OF AMERICA

To Gus Caesar, teacher extraordinary

Contents

Contents

Preface

Tropical Africa is still the least urbanized part of the world, but it is of particular interest for comparative urban studies, since nowhere else are cities now experiencing such rapid growth. The population of some African cities is rising by almost 10 percent annually, and many have doubled in size over the past ten to fifteen years. This means that it is possible in Africa to see "cities in the making" in a way that is hardly possible elsewhere. Within the field of African Studies there is much to be said for a continuing emphasis on the rural areas, since the great majority of the people still live there; yet the cities also merit attention, since their economic and political importance is quite out of proportion to their size. Indeed, now that all the countries have made the transition to (at least nominal) political independence, the most significant change that they are experiencing is perhaps the rapid expansion of their cities and towns. There seems, therefore, good reason for the spate of academic literature currently appearing on African urbanization and for an attempt to document it in a bibliography such as this.

For parts of the world where most people are city-dwellers, a comprehensive urban bibliography would be impracticable, since it would have to include almost all the literature on all aspects of life. For African countries such a compilation might be more realistic, but even here the range of relevant material is very wide, including, for instance, most that has been written on emerging elites, on trade unions, or on industrial development, as well as much in the fields of law, education, and so on. The two major existing bibliographies on African urbanization, both published in 1972 (items 0.0.1, 0.0.6), did indeed cover a wide range; but the scope of the present work is more limited. Its focus is on studies concerned specifically with urbanization processes and with cities and towns as entities, aiming to include most of the social science literature with these concerns published between 1960 and 1979. Most of the works listed fall broadly within the disciplines of sociology, demography, geography, and urban planning, but others are drawn from history, economics, and political science. Public administration and labor organization are two topics that are generally not covered, partly because they are the subjects of other African bibliographies produced by G. K. Hall & Co.[1] Migration is also the subject of another recent bibliography (item 0.0.9), and so references in this field have been confined to those with a clear urban component. It has been suggested that a particularly unfortunate omission is that of novels set in African cities, but the compiler did not feel competent to judge which of these should be included.

Some of the comprehensive bibliographies on individual cities or countries already in existence include many more items than are listed here, not only because they include additional topics, such as education or medicine, but also because they cover brief items in newspapers, etc., and much unpublished material. For this larger-scale work this would have been neither appropriate nor feasible. Items such as unpublished discussion papers of research institutions or undergraduate and Masters' dissertations have thus not normally been included: but as complete a listing as possible of relevant doctoral theses has been provided. For many cities substantial planning reports have been prepared, but generally for very limited circulation: decisions on which of these to include have inevitably been somewhat arbitrary, depending in part on how much material has been produced on any given city that is more readily available.

The time period covered is confined to that since 1960, partly in a further attempt to keep the project to manageable proportions and partly because all earlier work is already noted in other bibliographies. The concern here is therefore essentially with postcolonial Africa. A note is made of earlier studies only where they remain of particular value for understanding the present situation, or where little or nothing has been published more recently on an individual town. A further general limitation is to works in English or French, although a few items of particular importance in German and Portuguese have been added. The compiler's command of languages has not been sufficient to permit coverage of material in Russian, Japanese, Arabic, or Yoruba!

The vast majority of the literature relates to specific countries or cities, and the arrangement is therefore basically geographical, with an alphabetical list of works on each country being followed by lists for each major urban center within that country. The countries have been grouped regionally largely because of the existence of a number of studies relating to West Africa and East Africa as a whole, and lists of these precede the individual country lists for each region. The first 180 items are the minority that are concerned with Africa or tropical Africa in general, and these have been

1. E. S. Asiedu, Public Administration in English-speaking West Africa: an annotated bibliography. G. K. Hall, Boston, 1977.

   G.R. Martens, African Trade Unionism: a bibliography. G. K. Hall, Boston, 1977.

subdivided by topic, inevitably very arbitrarily as explained in the Introduction.

Within each section the pre-1960 studies, those in languages other than English or French, and the unpublished theses have been appended rather than integrated in order to emphasize that these lists are highly selective, whereas the main lists aim to be as comprehensive as possible. The compiler would be glad to know of any major items that have been inadvertently omitted and hereby offers apologies to the authors concerned.

The quality of the material covered obviously varies enormously, but nothing has been excluded on these grounds. In fact there is probably little that is actually erroneous, or even grossly mislead-ing, while something can be learned even from the poorest pieces. It has certainly not seemed appropriate to attempt to pass judgement on the individual items in a volume of this nature.

All the items that are annotated have been seen and the majority read, albeit rather quickly in many cases. References that I have not been able to trace personally have been marked with an asterisk. The bulk of the work has been undertaken in the libraries of the University of London, including those of University College, the London School of Economics, the Institute of Commonwealth Studies, and especially the School of Oriental and African Studies. Indeed, it has only been ready access to the S. O. A. S. library that has made the task feasible. Further material has been traced at other libraries in London, notably the British Library, and those of the Overseas Development Institute and the Royal Geographical Society, and elsewhere in Britain, notably at the Institute of Development Studies; and also at the libraries of the Sorbonne, the Centre d'Etudes Africaines and the Centre d'Etudes Documentaires sur l'Afrique in Paris. Within Africa, much use has been made of the libraries of Fourah Bay College in Freetown, the University of Ibadan, and the University of Dar es Salaam. Sincere thanks are due to the staff of all these libraries, as well as to scores of colleagues and students who have contributed in one way or another to this publication. I am also most grateful to Annabel Swindells for much assistance with the typing, and to Sarah Skinner who drew the endleaf maps.

Introduction

The Pre-1960 Literature

Around the close of the colonial period the level of urbanization in tropical Africa was very much lower than it is today. No
city had over a million inhabitants, and the total urban population
of the region was only fifteen to twenty million, compared with forty-
five to fifty million in 1980. However, the lack of relevant literature at that time was even more remarkable. The number of books and
periodical articles on tropical African towns and cities published
by 1960 was less than one eighth of the number in existence by 1979,
so that one may justifiably speak of a recent explosion of publications in this field.

A large proportion of what had been written by 1960 was not
widely available, taking the form of either government reports or
unpublished conference papers. The few major studies that had ap-
peared in book form were nearly all concerned with individual cities.
Sociological studies included those of Michael Banton in Freetown,
Georges Balandier in Brazzaville, F. Grevisse in the former
Elisabethville, and Aidan Southall and Peter Gutkind in Kampala,
while urban politics was the focus of a study of Luanshya by A. L.
Epstein, who worked with Max Gluckman at the Rhodes-Livingstone
Institute in Lusaka.

Geographical monographs included those on Cotonou by J. Lombard,
on Elisabethville by Alice Chapelier, and on Libreville by Guy
Lasserre, but there was nothing comparable in English. There were a
few volumes reporting on government-sponsored social surveys, such as
that by Kofi Busia on Sekondi-Takoradi and that by Ione Acquah on
Accra, and also official planning reports, such as those for Accra
and Nairobi. In comparison with the situation today, the lack of
any academic work on Kenya's urban centers is remarkable, but even
more so is the dearth of any publications on the cities of Nigeria,
which were already far larger and more numerous than those in most
other countries. It was certainly on Zaire (then the Belgian Congo)
that the urban literature was most abundant, especially since that
country figured prominently in the only major attempt at a comparative

survey of urban development across a large tract of Africa produced
by the Belgian geographer, Jacques Denis.

The Post-1960 Literature in General

It was in the early 1960s that the trickle of publications on
African cities rapidly became a torrent, as researchers swarmed in
from overseas and as new universities opened throughout the continent.
By the end of the decade there were twenty to thirty books appearing
each year, along with hundreds of relevant papers in a wide range of
journals. There is now also one journal devoted specifically to the
subject, appearing in the 1960s as African Urban Notes and now in a
more polished form as African Urban Studies, edited by Ruth Simms
Hamilton at Michigan State University.

A few individuals have published prolifically throughout this
period. Outstanding among these are Peter Gutkind of McGill
University, Akin Mabogunje of the University of Ibadan, Josef Gugler,
Kenneth Little, David Parkin, Margaret Peil, and Pierre Vennetier.
About fifty other writers have produced either one or two major monographs or a series of valuable papers, but a notable feature of the
literature is the vast number of people who have made just one or two
minor contributions.

Even a quick glance through this bibliography would indicate
that, however narrowly defined, urbanization in tropical Africa is a
vast topic. The great majority of the writing on the subject is therefore still focused upon individual countries or cities, although, as
the relative numbers of items noted in later sections would imply,
the extent of the literature varies greatly from country to country
and from city to city and shows only a very weak correlation with
their respective sizes. There have been remarkably few attempts at
comparisons between individual countries or cities, and there is
surely scope for much more work of this nature, within Africa or even
beyond, since it might reveal considerably more about urban processes
than a similar effort devoted to single case studies.

Most of the writing that has been concerned with more than one
country has considered Africa as a whole, tropical or "Subsaharan"
Africa, or the group of states so widely recognized as "West Africa,"
which has no real equivalent elsewhere on the continent. The works
dealing with all or most of Africa are listed in the first section
of the bibliography and amount to about 10 percent of the total, but
even some of these are largely collections of case studies. The
distinction between general discussions and case studies is of course
not always a clear one, for there are some contributions that focus
upon an individual city but in the context of Africa as a whole, or
as an example of an issue that is also discussed in more general terms.
These have here normally been listed under the specific country or
city, but their number is in fact remarkably small: the majority of

writings are quite specific as to place, and even many of the so-
called case studies say little or nothing about the more general
situation to which they are supposed to relate.

As mentioned above, the number of specific as to place studies
varies very greatly from country to country and from city to city.
The dominant position of Nigeria is notable, but perhaps should not
be surprising, since the country has about a quarter of the total
population of tropical Africa and also has a particularly long history
of urbanization. Its capital, Lagos, is one of the two largest cities
of tropical Africa, while it has at least forty other urban centers
with over 50,000 inhabitants.

Although smaller in absolute terms, the volume of literature
on urbanization in Kenya, and on Nairobi in particular, is much
larger in relation to population numbers, reflecting both the interest
aroused by the rapid contemporary growth there and a favorable research climate for both expatriates and Kenyan social scientists.
Ghana, Ivory Coast, and Senegal are also very well represented even
in relation to their quite substantial urban populations, whereas the
literature on the cities of Zaire and Ethiopia does not reflect their
size and importance.

The countries whose urban centers have received little attention include Mali and particularly Guinea in the West, where research,
at least by outsiders, has certainly not been encouraged; and also
Malawi and particularly Somalia on the eastern side of the continent.
There has been a similar dearth of writing on the urban centers of
Angola and Mozambique, even if work in Portuguese is included. Some
relevant material on these countries has probably been overlooked,
but here too political conditions have been much less favorable for
study than in countries such as Kenya and Senegal, though it would be
of great interest to know what the end of Portuguese rule has meant
for Maputo and Luanda.

The balance within the literature towards country and city
studies is one reason for the basic arrangement of this bibliography
by place rather than by topic: but another is the near-impossibility
of separating specific topics within the broad field of urbanization.
It would be very convenient to be able to identify a group of studies
on unemployment or on squatter settlement, but the realities of urban
life are such that these topics are hardly separable from the total
system of which they are a part. Some attempt at classification has
been adopted for the items on all or most of Africa, but in such
cases as papers examining the relationship between migration and unemployment the allocation has inevitably been somewhat arbitrary.
The same would apply to studies of squatter settlements, since these
have their physical, demographic, social, economic, and political
aspects, and since, in any case, while sometimes seen as "marginal"
to the city, they may be in many respects closely integrated with
its various other parts.

Introduction

Existing Bibliographies

Reference has already been made in the Preface to the two
major bibliographies on African urbanization in existence, both published in 1972. The larger of the two was prepared under the direction of Pierre Vennetier to coincide with a symposium on African
urbanization held at the Centre d'Etudes de Géographie Tropicale in
Bordeaux. The other was prepared by Hyacinth Ajaegbu for the
International African Institute in London. Together they provide a
very comprehensive listing of works published up to 1971, but neither
is in any way annotated. Bibliographies on urbanization in a number
of individual countries have also been produced, although none is
either really satisfactory or really up-to-date; and for some countries there are national bibliographies that have specific sections
on urbanization, though more often the relevant items are scattered
among topics such as economy or administration.

Wide-Ranging Studies

The most comprehensive individual surveys of urbanization in
tropical Africa so far undertaken are those by the French geographer
just mentioned, Pierre Vennetier, and by the German geographer,
Walther Manshard, the former adopting a systematic approach while
the latter surveys the region city by city. The nearest equivalents
in English are the synthesis by William Hance in his study covering
population in general, as well as migration and urbanization, and the
review of economic, social, and political aspects of African urbanization by William and Judith Hanna. A useful set of symposium papers
edited by Horace Miner was published in 1967, but undoubtedly the
greatest contribution to the literature on African urbanization to
date was provided by the publication in two volumes of the proceedings of the Bordeaux symposium. Most of the individual papers dealt
with particular cities, but some viewed tropical Africa as a whole,
while overviews of various themes were provided by the rapporteurs of
several sessions.

Among the studies dealing with West Africa as a whole the
broadest, though with a clear sociological emphasis, is that of Josef
Gugler and William Flanagan, while a rare example of a volume span-
ning eastern and central Africa is an interdisciplinary collection
of papers arising from the 1972 Lusaka seminar of the International
African Institute and edited by David Parkin. Among individual
studies on a national scale the most outstanding is certainly that
on Nigerian urbanization by Akin Mabogunje, while a notable study of
the distinctive group of "traditional" Yoruba cities in southwestern
Nigeria is that by Eva Krapf-Askari. Books on particular cities, each
covering many aspects but each with a different emphasis, have been
produced by René Gouellain on Douala, Andrew Hake on Nairobi, George
Kay and Michael Smout on Salisbury, Assane Seck on Dakar, and Elliott
Skinner on Ouagadougou. Geographical studies of smaller towns include

those of the old Senegal town of Saint-Louis by Camille Camara and
the new Mauritanian capital, Nouakchott, by Jean-Robert Pitte, and
that of Benin City in Nigeria by Andrew Onokerhoraye, whose doctoral
thesis must hold the record among those listed here for the number
of papers produced from it. Although the great majority of city
studies are in English or French, others include German studies of
Kano by Christopher Becker and Kampala by Karl Vorlaufer and one of
Luanda in Portuguese by Ilia do Amaral.

Finally, multidisciplinary volumes have been prepared on a
number of cities, sometimes including papers of very uneven quality
and sometimes thrown together in a rather haphazard manner. Three
particularly useful collections of this type are those published on
Ibadan in 1967 (Fyfe and Jones), on Freetown in 1968 (Lloyd,
Mabogunje, and Awe), and on Dakar also in 1968 (Sankalé and others).
The main example to appear more recently is the 1975 volume on Lagos,
edited by A. B. Aderibigbe, but several others are said to be in
preparation.

History

The substantial volume of literature on African history
naturally includes discussion of the evolution of its towns and cities,
and much relevant material incorporated in studies at both continental
and national levels may have been overlooked in compiling this bibliography. The only book devoted specifically to the history of urbanization and tropical Africa as a whole is that by Richard Hull, but
several national and individual city studies are concerned primarily
with the past rather than the present. These include Wesley Johnson's
work on Senegal towns, volumes on Lagos by Michael Echuero, by Patrick
Cole, and by Pauline Baker, and on Elizabethville (now Lubumbashi) by
Bruce Fetter, and the accounts of the origins and early growth of
Salisbury by George Tanser. Others have been noted, perhaps rather
arbitrarily, elsewhere in this review under a systematic heading.

Migration and Demography

The rapid but differing rates of population growth in African
cities result from a combination of natural increase, which is uni-
formly high at about 3 percent a year, and in-migration, which adds
a further 6 or 7 percent for some cities, yet is insignificant in
others. Very little has been written for Africa in general on the
demographic structure of the urban population or on rates of natural
increase; but migration has received more attention, sometimes in
relation to the issue of rising unemployment as in writings by Josef
Gugler and Michael Todaro. However, most of the literature, including all that in French, relates to individual countries, or, as in
the case of Mansell Prothero's syntheses, concerns population movement as a whole.

Introduction

Among the national studies in English, the most outstanding is perhaps that by John Caldwell resulting from a major research project on movement to the towns of Ghana. Others also of much value have been produced by Helmuth Heisler on Zambia, by Simeon Ominde on Kenya, and more recently by Richard Sabot on Tanzania. These, together with comparable works in French by Raymond Deniel on movement to Abidjan, and by both Abdoulaye Diop and Bernard Lacombe on movement to Dakar, could provide an excellent foundation for comparative studies. There are, of course, many more brief papers on rural-urban migration, and when other types of movement are taken into account the total volume of literature is very large, as the bibliography prepared by William Gould clearly indicates.

Ethnicity and Social Structures

The extent of migration into African cities and the complexity of the migration patterns produce urban populations of great ethnic diversity, and ethnicity is a highly significant factor in the social structure of most cities. It forms the basis of many voluntary associations, but there are other important types of association that cut across ethnic boundaries, while narrower kinship and family ties are of course also important. These topics have received attention on a continental, as well as national, scale from sociologists such as Josef Gugler, Kenneth Little, and Aidan Southall. Kenneth Little has also given particular attention to the particular roles of women in African towns, while Peter Gutkind has written extensively on social relationships and social change. As in the case of migration, work by African writers and work in French is concentrated to a larger extent on individual countries.

The number of sociological studies on individual African cities is now quite substantial, and not even all those of book length, published since 1960, can be mentioned here. Studies that concentrate particularly on ethnicity include those of Merran Fraenkel in Monrovia, Suzanne Bernus in Niamey, Enid Schildkrout in Kumasi, Abner Cohen in Ibadan, and David Parkin in Kampala. Studies of social relationships include those of Claude Meillassoux in Bamako, Marion Kilson in Accra, Jean-Marie Gibbal in Abidjan, Leonard Plotnicov in Jos, Dan Aronson in Ibadan, Peter Marris in Lagos, Peter Lloyd in both of these cities, Valdo Pons in Stanleyville (now Kisangani), David Parkin in Nairobi, David Jacobson in Mbale, and Hortense Powdermaker in Luanshya, together with the collection of papers on social networks in urban Zambia edited by Clyde Mitchell. Other works focus on particular groups of urban residents such as industrial workers, e.g., those by Richard Jeffries on Sekondi-Takoradi, by Margaret Peil on Ghana in general, by Adrian Peace on a Lagos suburb, and by Ralph Grillo on Kampala; and the women of particular cities are the focus of attention in works by Colette Lecour Grandmaison on Dakar, Deborah Pellow on Accra, Jeanne-Francoise Vincent on Brazzaville, Margaret Strobel on Mombasa, and Ilsa Schuster on Lusaka.

Introduction

Politics and Administration

Clearly there is no sharp division between social relationships
and political life, and for African cities the writings of Peter
Gutkind provide a notable link between the two. Nearly all the other
writers on African urban politics have dealt with individual countries
or cities, and many of these studies concern both political and social
relationships and so differ little from some of those mentioned above.
Examples include the work of Annik Osmont on Dakar, Howard Wolpe on
Port Harcourt, John Paden on Kano, Jean La Fontaine on Kinshasa,
Marc Ross on Nairobi, and Peter Harries-Jones on Luanshya. Other
portions of the literature might be broadly classified as dealing
with urban administration, but even this is not a clearly defined
topic, and such studies range from those of urban policy in Ivory
Coast by Michael Cohen and in Rhodesia (as it then was) by Eric
Gargett to the broad review of metropolitan government in Lagos by
Babatunde Williams and Anne-Marie Walsh and the micro-study of the
changing nature of the Nairobi City Council by Herbert Werlin.

Economy and Employment

The urban economy in Africa has received far less academic
attention than urban society, and writings on it for Africa as a
whole are of a very scattered and disparate nature, though with unemployment emerging, very appropriately, as a major theme. The
desperate problem of un- and under-employment has brought several
International Labor Organization (ILO) missions to Africa and these
have produced useful studies of Abidjan and Lagos, together with
better-known country reports on Sudan, and especially Kenya, which
provide valuable material on the cities. The most substantial of the
studies on the economic activities of particular groups are perhaps
those of traders in Ghana by Peter Garlick, in Brazzaville by Roland
Devauges and in Lusaka by Andrew Beveridge and Anthony Oberschall,
while the most detailed analysis of the whole economic structure of
a town is certainly that of Cape Coast by J. Hinderink and J.
Sterkenburg. A distinct group of works is concerned with the function of many African towns as ports, notably the East African study
by Brian Hoyle and the series of case studies from around Tropical
Africa edited by Brian Hoyle and David Hilling.

The Physical Structure of the Cities

A rapidly growing body of literature is concerned with the
physical structure of African cities and the physical planning problems arising from their rapid expansion, and a notable subgroup is
concerned specifically with housing. Again boundaries are not sharp,
for as noted above much work on squatter settlements, whether detailed
case studies, such as those in Tanzania by Richard Stren and in Zambia
by David Pasteur, or continental syntheses, such as that by Margaret

Introduction

Peil, covers their social and political aspects; while some of the studies from an architectural viewpoint such as that of Susan Denyer cover both urban and rural housing. Substantial volumes ranging widely across Africa have been produced by the United Nations, while case studies on housing include both university research publications, such as Richard Stren's further monograph on Mombasa, and government reports, such as that by Richard Martin on Lusaka.

Several of the wide-ranging geographical studies mentioned earlier include an analysis of the morphology of the cities under examination, and there are some, such as those by Harm de Blij on Dar es Salaam and Mombasa, which are primarily concerned with this. One notable study in depth is that of the Dagoudane-Pikine suburbs of Dakar by Marc Vernière. Two other types of publication might be mentioned here: first, monumental planning reports, such as those by B. A. W. Trevallion on Kano and by Max Lock and partners on Kaduna, and also many that are less widely available (or in some cases virtually secret!), which may be as valuable for their surveys of existing patterns as for their plans; and second, atlases, such as that produced for Khartoum by El Sayed El Bushra or the lavishly-produced Atlas de Kinshasa.

Urban Systems

A small proportion of the literature on African urbanization deals not with structures and systems within cities, but with national or even international systems of cities. Some of this arises from concern about the degree to which urban growth in many countries is concentrated in a single major city, especially if a disproportionate share of the country's scarce resources are invested there. This topic receives some, but perhaps too little, attention in many national development plans and is discussed in various geographical studies that are concerned with patterns of regional development as a whole rather than merely their urban component. Several of these are summarized in two volumes edited by Salah El-Shakhs and Robert Obudho, one covering many aspects of urbanization and planning and one rather more focused on the evolution of urban systems. A notable national survey of towns as service centers within a hierarchy is that of Ghana by David Grove and Laszlo Huszar. Several papers on the urban system of Zaire have been written by Leon de Saint-Moulin, while an interesting comparison of the urban systems of Cameroon and Ivory Coast has been produced by Anne-Marie Cotten and Yves Marguerat.

Conclusion

Twenty years ago the literature on urbanization in tropical Africa was extremely limited in extent, and much of this was in rather inaccessible government documents or conference reports. In comparison, there is today a great abundance, including many readily

Introduction

available books and many more articles in widely circulating journals,
in addition to the further government documents, unpublished seminar
papers, and Masters' theses not listed here. Yet in terms of both
topics and areas the coverage is very uneven, while the African urban
situation is in a state of rapid change: as a result, the scope for
further studies, both area-specific and comparative, is still immense.

Periodicals

Periodicals yielding three or more items in English or
in French, 1960-1979

Number of Items	Periodical title and place of publication
20	Africa (London)
3	African Affairs (London)
5	African Environment (Dakar)
9	African Social Research (Lusaka)
11	African Studies Review (Waltham, Mass., U.S.A.)
81	African Urban Studies, formerly African Urban Notes (East Lansing, Michigan, U.S.A.)
3	American Anthropologist (Washington, D.C.)
8	Annales de l'Université d'Abidjan (Abidjan)
5	Annals of the Association of American Geographers (Washington, D.C.)
5	Anthropological Quarterly (Washington, D.C.)
14	Bulletin de l'IFAN (Dakar)
6	Bulletin of the Ghana Geographical Association (Accra)
29	Cahiers d'Etudes Africaines (Paris)
32	Cahiers d'Outre-Mer (Bordeaux)
9	Cahiers Economiques et Sociaux (Kinshasa)

Periodicals

15	Cahiers ORSTOM, Série Sciences Humaines (Paris)
20	Canadian Journal of African Studies (Montreal)
16	Civilisations (Brussels)
6	Comparative Studies in Society and History (London)
7	Cultures et Développement (Louvain)
7	East African Geographical Review (Kampala)
4	East(ern) African Economics Review (Nairobi)
5	Economic Bulletin of Ghana (Accra)
5	Economic Development and Cultural Change (Chicago)
6	Economic Geography (Worcester, Mass., U.S.A.)
18	Ekistics (Athens)
3	Erdkunde (Bonn)
3	Espace Géographique (Paris)
3	Ethiopian Geographical Journal (Addis Ababa)
7	Ethiopian Observer (Addis Ababa)
3	Etudes d'Histoire Africaine (Kinshasa)
4	Etudes Maliennes (Bamako)
7	Etudes Zairoises, formerly Etudes Congolaises (Kinshasa)
3	Genève-Afrique (Geneva)
3	Geografisker Analer (Stockholm)
7	Geographical Association of Rhodesia Proceedings (Salisbury)
3	Geographical Magazine (London)
4	Geographical Review (New York)
4	Geography (Sheffield, U. K.)
5	Geojournal (Wiesbaden)

Periodicals

10	Ghana Journal of Sociology (Accra)
3	Ghana Social Science Journal (Accra)
3	Habitat International (Oxford)
5	Human Organization (Washington, D.C.)
10	Industries et Travaux d'Outremer (Paris)
4	Institute of Development Studies Bulletin (Brighton, U.K.)
7	Inter-African Labour Institute Bulletin (London)
3	International Journal of Comparative Sociology (Leiden)
9	International Labour Review (Geneva)
3	International Migration Review (New York)
5	Journal of Administration Overseas, formerly Journal of African Administration (London)
7	Journal of African History (London)
9	Journal of Asian and African Studies (Leiden)
5	Journal of East(ern) African Research and Development (Nairobi)
4	Journal of Ethiopian Studies (Addis Ababa)
18	Journal of Modern African Studies (London)
4	Journal of the Geographical Association of Tanzania (Dar es Salaam)
8	Journal of Tropical Geography (Singapore)
3	Kyoto University African Studies (Kyoto)
5	Lagos Notes and Records (Lagos)
10	Manpower and Unemployment Research, formerly . . . in Africa (Montreal)
11	Nigeria Magazine (Lagos)
23	Nigerian Geographical Journal (Ibadan)
15	Nigerian Journal of Economic and Social Studies (Ibadan)

Periodicals

4   Nigerian Journal of Public Affairs (Zaria)

3   Odu (Ile-Ife)

14   Pan-African Journal (New York)

16   Planification Habitat Information, formerly Bulletin du SMUH (Paris)

5   Planner, formerly Journal of the Royal Town Planning Institute (London)

3   Population (Paris)

3   Presence Africaine (Paris)

7   Problèmes Sociaux Zairois, formerly Problèmes Sociaux Congolais (Lubumbashi)

5   Quarterly Journal of Administration (Ile-Ife)

3   Review of African Political Economy (London)

10   Revue Française d'Etudes Politiques Africaines (Paris)

3   Rhodes-Livingstone Journal (Manchester)

7   Savanna (Zaria)

5   Sierra Leone Geographical Journal (Freetown)

6   Sierra Leone Studies (Freetown)

4   South African Geographer, formerly Journal for Geography (Stellenbosch)

14   Sudan Notes and Records (Khartoum)

3   Sudan Society (Khartoum)

3   Tanzania Notes and Records (Dar es Salaam)

3   Tiers-Monde (Paris)

7   Tijdschrift voor Economische en Sociale Geografie (Amsterdam)

9   Town Planning Review (Liverpool)

4   Transactions, Institute of British Geographers (London)

Periodicals

3	Transafrican Journal of History (Nairobi)
3	Uganda Journal (Kampala)
3	Urban Affairs Quarterly (Beverly Hills, Calif.)
17	Urban Anthropology (New York)
6	Urban Studies (Glasgow)
7	Urbanisme (Paris)
4	Zaire-Afrique, formerly Congo-Afrique (Kinshasa)
10	Zambezia (Salisbury)

Abbreviations

BRALUP   Bureau of Resource Assessment and Land Use Planning (Dar es Salaam)

CEDAF   Centre d'Etude et de Documentation Africaines (Brussels)

CEDESA   Centre de Documentation Economique et Sociale Africaine (Brussels)

CEGET   Centre d'Etudes de Géographie Tropicale (Bordeaux)

CEMUBAC   Centre Scientifique et Medical de l'Université Libre de Bruxelles en Afrique Centrale (Brussels)

CEPSI   Centre d'Etudes sur les Problèmes Sociaux Indigènes (Lubumbashi)

CNRS   Centre National de la Recherche Scientifique (Paris)

IFAN   Institut Fondamental d'Afrique Noire (Dakar)

ILO   International Labour Office (Geneva)

INADES   Institut Africain pour le Développement Economique et Social (Abidjan)

INCIDI   Institut International des Civilisations Différentes (Brussels)

INSEE   Institut National de la Statistique et des Etudes Economiques (Paris)

OECD   Organization for Economic Cooperation and Development (Paris)

ONAREST   Office National de la Recherche Scientifique et Technique (Yaoundé)

Abbreviations

ORSTOM   Office de la Recherche Scientifique et Technique
          Outre-Mer (Paris)

SEDES   Société d'Etude pour le Développement Economique et
          Social (Paris)

SMUH   Secretariat des Missions d'Urbanisme et d'Habitat (Paris)

UNECA   United Nations Economic Commission for Africa (Addis
          Ababa)

UNESCO   United Nations Educational, Scientific and Cultural
          Organization (Paris)

UNRISD   United Nations Research Institute for Social Development
          (Geneva)

Africa [General]

Bibliographies

0.0.1 AJAEGBU, H.I. African Urbanization: a bibliography.
        International African Institute, London, 1972, 78 pp.
          One of the main predecessors to the present volume,
        listing over 2800 items, arranged geographically, and
        covering the whole continent and the whole period up to
        1971.

0.0.2 BROMLEY, R. Periodic Markets, Daily Markets and Fairs: a
        bibliography supplement to 1979. Center for Development
        Studies, University College of Swansea, 1979, 69 pp.
          Lists historical studies of African markets on pp. 16-17
        and modern studies on pp. 26-34, mostly published since
        completion of the volume listed below.

0.0.3 BROMLEY, R.J.; HODDER, B.W.; and SMITH, R.H.T. Market-Place
        Studies: a world bibliography up to 1972. School of
        Oriental and African Studies, University of London, 1974,
        85 pp.
          Lists historical studies of African markets, rural and
        urban, on pp. 24-28 and modern studies on pp. 42-58.

0.0.4 BRUNN, S.D. Urbanization in Developing Countries: an
        international bibliography. Michigan State University,
        East Lansing, 1971, 693 pp.
          Provides a substantial list of items for Africa and for
        individual countries on pp. 257-420.

0.0.5 BUICK, B. Squatter Settlements in Developing Countries:
        a bibliography. Research School of Pacific Studies,
        Australian National University, Canberra, 1975, 158 pp.
          Provides a list of 280 items for Africa on pp. 19-40.

0.0.6 CENTRE D'ETUDES DE GEOGRAPHIE TROPICALE. La Croissance
        Urbaine en Afrique Noire et à Madagascar. 2 vols. Travaux
        et Documents de Géographie Tropicale: série bibliographies,

no.2. CEGET, Bordeaux-Talence, 1972, 390 pp.
The other main predecessor to the present volume, listing over 4100 items, arranged geographically and covering
the whole period up to 1971, including unpublished theses
at all levels. Excludes North Africa, Sudan, Ethiopia,
Djibouti, Somali Republic, and South Africa. Incorporates
a topic index. Prepared under the direction of P. Vennetier.

0.0.7 DAVIS, L.G. Construction, Building and Planning in Selected
African Cities; Migration to African Cities; Housing
Problems in Selected African Cities. Council of Planning
Librarians Bibliographies 1202, 1204, 1205, Monticello,
1977, 23 pp., 21 pp., 20 pp.
A personal selection of books and articles, interpreting
each topic very widely, and with some overlap among the
three volumes.

0.0.8 DEPARTMENT OF SOCIAL ANTHROPOLOGY, UNIVERSITY OF EDINBURGH.
African Urbanization: a reading list of selected books,
articles and reports. International African Institute,
London, 1965, 27 pp.
A list of 996 items in English and French, covering
demographic, social, and economic aspects, arranged mainly
by country and city. A forerunner of 0.0.1.

0.0.9 GOULD, W.T.S. A Bibliography of Population Mobility in
Tropical Africa. Working Paper 31, African Population
Mobility Project, Department of Geography, University of
Liverpool, 1977, 82 pp.
A comprehensive list of over 800 items concerned with
both internal and international migration and covering
all Africa south of the Sahara. About one-third of the
items relate specifically to urban areas. Incorporates
elaborate classifications of the items for various aspects
of the movements.

0.0.10 GUTKIND, P.C.W. A Bibliography of Unemployment in Africa.
Centre for Developing-Area Studies, McGill University,
Montreal, 1972, 62 pp.
A wide-ranging list of about 700 items, some specifically
urban, including some on Asia and Latin America as well as
Africa.

0.0.11 GUTKIND, P.C.W. Bibliography on Unemployment, with Special
Reference to Africa. Centre for Developing-Area Studies,
McGill University, Montreal, 1977, 76 pp.
A follow-up to the volume noted above, listing a
further 1,100 items relating to the issues of employment
and unemployment.

0.0.12 INADES. La Ville en Afrique. INADES, Abidjan, 1977, 104 pp.

2

A mimeographed document listing by country 764 items
· on African urbanization in the library of INADES-
Documentation, with a topic index. Ivory Coast and
Senegal are particularly well represented.

0.0.13 KAYSER, B. "Bibliographie: urbanisation de l'Afrique."
Tiers Monde, 12, 1971, 229-232.
A brief note on the conference for which the CEGET
bibliography was prepared and a brief listing of major
contributions in the field.

0.0.14 ODIMUKO, C.L. and BOUCHARD, D. Urban Geography of Africa:
bibliography. Centre for Developing-Area Studies, McGill
University, Montreal, 1973, 41 pp.
A list focusing on items published 1966-1972 with a
distinct spatial aspect, arranged by topic.

0.0.15 VERHAEGEN, P. L'Urbanisation de l'Afrique Noire: son cadre,
ses causes et ses consequences économiques, sociales et
culturelles. Enquêtes bibliographiques, CEDESA, Brussels,
1962, 387 pp.
A list of over 2500 items, covering a very large proportion of the published and semipublished material up to
1961 on many aspects of economic and social change in
tropical Africa. Arranged by topic but with a geographical index.

Pre-1960 contributions include:

0.0.16 COMHAIRE, J. Urban Conditions in Africa: select reading
list on urban problems in Africa. Oxford University
Press, London, 1952, 48 pp.

Note also an unpublished thesis:

0.0.17 KEKEKE, D.O. A Bibliographical Review of Geographical
Literature on Urban Geography in Tropical Africa.
Master's thesis, University of Durham, U.K., 1970.

See also 0.2.14, 1.0.3, 1.0.41, 111.0.24, 209.0.10,
304.0.10, 4.0.20.

Methodology/Reviews

0.1.1 BJEREN, G. Some Theoretical and Methodological Aspects of
the Study of African Urbanization. Scandinavian
Institute of African Studies, Uppsala, 1971, 37 pp.
A wide-ranging review of research approaches to, and
the existing literature on, various aspects of African
migration and urbanization.

0.1.2   DE SAINT MOULIN, L. "Les villes d'Afrique (chroniques
        bibliographiques)." Cultures et Développement, 10, 1978,
        445-469.
             Provides brief reviews of twenty books published
        between 1965 and 1976.

0.1.3   EPSTEIN, A.L. "Urban communities in Africa." In Gluckman,
        M. (ed.), Closed Systems and Open Minds: the limits of
        naivety in social anthropology. Aldine, Chicago;
        Oliver & Boyd, Edinburgh, 1964, 83-102.
             Examines how the problem of urban communities being
        part of complex systems emerged during field studies on
        the Zambian Copperbelt, noting both limitations and value
        of orthodox anthropological approaches.

0.1.4   GEROLD-SCHEEPERS, T.J. "The political consciousness of
        African urban workers: a review of recent publications."
        African Perspectives, 1978, No.2, 83-98.
             Surveys a wide range of recent writings on this topic,
        with special reference to proponents and opponents of the
        labor aristocracy thesis, both in theoretical terms and
        in specific African situations.

0.1.5   GUTKIND, P.C.W. "Orientation and research methods in African
        urban studies." In Jongmans, D.G. and Gutkind, P.C.W.
        (eds.), Anthropologists in the Field. Van Gorcum, Assen,
        Netherlands, 1967, 133-169.
             Reviews the work of anthropologists on African urban
        life, argues that they must give more attention to it,
        and suggests that the approach and techniques adopted
        should differ from those used in rural areas.

0.1.6   GUTKIND, P.C.W. "African urban studies: past accomplishments,
        future trends and needs." Canadian Journal of African
        Studies, 2, 1968, 63-80.
             Discusses the strengths and weaknesses of existing
        social science literature, stressing the need for more
        studies of cities in relation to national development and
        more micro-studies of small towns.

0.1.7   KRAPF-ASKARI, E. "African cities." African Affairs, 68,
        1969, 353-357.
             A review article based on books by Bernus, Cohen,
        Mabogunje, Parkin, and Pons.

0.1.8   MERCIER, P. "Quelques remarques sur le développement des
        études urbaines." Cahiers d'Etudes Africaines, 13, 1973,
        397-404.
             A review of some of the main themes evident in African
        urban studies, especially those emerging in the 1960s.

0.1.9 MITCHELL, J.C. "Theoretical orientations in African urban
studies." In Banton, M. (ed.), The Social Anthropology
of Complex Societies. Tavistock, London, 1966, 37-68.
Reviews much of the late-1950s literature, showing
that most comprised social surveys or anthropological
studies contrasting urban and rural life, and indicates
the scope for more studies of urban social relationships
and social systems.

0.1.10 NOLAN, R.W. "Migrants to the city in Africa: the search
for a conceptual framework." African Urban Studies, 5,
1979, 1-10.
Argues that a wide-ranging systems approach is required
for a proper understanding of African rural-urban migration and of migrant behavior in the cities.

0.1.11 PEIL, M. "Urban Africana." Cultures et Développement, 8,
1976, 150-156 and 533-538; 10, 1978, 471-475; 11, 1979,
665-670.
Reviews of a wide range of books on African urbanization and on specific cities.

0.1.12 SAUTTER, G. "Recherches en cours sur les villes d'Afrique
noire: thèmes et problèmes." Cahiers d'Etudes Africaines,
13, 1973, 405-416.
Reviews the major French-language geographical contributions on tropical African cities and points to the priority research needs.

0.1.13 SCHWAB, W.B. "Comparative field techniques in urban
research in Africa." In Freilich, M. (ed.), Marginal
Natives: anthropologists at work. Harper & Row, New
York, 1970, 73-122; and in Freilich, M. (ed.), Marginal
Natives at Work: anthropologists in the field. Schenkman,
Cambridge, Mass., 1977, 39-87.
Compares methods used in 1950s field studies in
Oshogbo (Nigeria) and Gwelo (Zimbabwe), covering both
broad approaches and detailed practicalities.

0.1.14 VINCENT, J. "Urbanisation in Africa: a review article."
Journal of Commonwealth and Comparative Politics, 14,
1976, 286-298.
A review of books by Gutkind, Heisler, Little, Parkin,
Werlin, and Wolpe.

General Studies

0.2.1 CENTRE NATIONAL DE LA RECHERCHE SCIENTIFIQUE. La
Croissance Urbaine en Afrique Noire et à Madagascar.
2 vols. CNRS, Paris, 1972, 1109 pp.

The papers and proceedings of a conference held at the
Centre d'Etudes de Géographie Tropicale in Bordeaux-Talence
in 1970. In addition to fifty-eight papers, mostly listed
elsewhere, these volumes include overviews of individual
themes by A. Benyoussef, R. Blanc, J.I. Clarke, A-M. Cotten,
R.J. Harrison-Church, P. Haeringer, G. Lasserre, P. Le
Bourdiec, A.L. Mabogunje, H. Nicolai, M. Rochefort,
G. Sautter, L.V. Thomas, and P. Vennetier, and transcripts
of discussions on these. Among the topics covered are
demography, employment, urban morphology, and urban-rural
relations. The volumes were edited by P. Vennetier.

0.2.2 CLARKE, J.I. An Advanced Geography of Africa. Hulton,
      Amersham, U.K., 1975, Chap. 8 "Urban Geography," 263-303.
      Discusses the evolution of African towns, present levels
and rates of urbanization, urban primacy, urban functions,
and urban morphology. Includes many maps and photographs.

0.2.3 COMHAIRE, J.L.L. "Les grandes villes de l'Afrique tropicale."
      Afrique Contemporaine, 34, 1967, 6-11.
      A brief survey of the extent of urbanization in various
regions and of the growth and present importance of twelve
major cities.

0.2.4 DENIS, J. "Les villes d'Afrique tropicale." Civilisations,
      16, 1966, 26-44.
      Reviews the pattern of precolonial urbanization, the
immense colonial impact, the diverse demographic structures
and physical forms of the present cities, and early postindependence trends.

0.2.5 DESCLOITRES, R. "Rapport général pour le continent africain
      et conclusions provisoires." In INCIDI, Urban Agglomerations
in the States of the Third World. Brussels, 1971, 436-480.
      Reviews the issues of rapid growth, increasing urban-
rural disparities, and the need for ensuring that the cities
aid national integration; concludes with policy recommendations.

0.2.6 EDINBURGH UNIVERSITY, CENTRE OF AFRICAN STUDIES. Urbanization
      in African Social Change. Edinburgh, 1963, 206 pp.
      A mimeographed report of a symposium, including brief
papers, some on Africa in general, some presenting case
studies, by D. Forde, R.W. Steel, I.G. Stewart, S.H. Ominde,
J. Van Velsen, A.I. Richards, M. Bird, D.P. Gamble,
A.R. Mills, W.H. Chinn, H.W. Ord, P. Mayer, P.E.H. Hair,
G.A. Shepperson, I. Wallerstein, J.F.A. Ajayi, W. Elkan,
A. Hauser, and J. Dawson.

0.2.7 EL-SHAKHS, S. and OBUDHO, R.A. (eds.) Urbanization, National

Development and Regional Planning in Africa. Praeger,
New York, 1974, 230 pp.
     Includes eight papers focused on urbanization and
listed individually elsewhere, in addition to others
focused on national and regional development planning.

0.2.8   FAIR, T.J.D. and DAVIES, R.J. "Constrained urbanization:
        White South Africa and Black Africa compared." In
        Berry, B.J.L. (ed.), Urbanization and Counterurbanization.
        Sage, Beverly Hills, Calif., 1976, 145-168.
             Largely focused on the effects of government policy
        on patterns of urban development in South Africa, but
        with a review of trends in postindependence tropical
        Africa by way of comparison.

0.2.9   GEORGE, P. "L'explosion urbaine en Afrique." Urbanisme,
        159, 1977, 56-65.
             Discusses the diverse origins of African towns, the
        profound colonial impact, accelerated growth since inde-
        pendence, and current physical planning and employment
        problems.

0.2.10 GUTKIND, P.C.W. "The African urban milieu: a force in
        rapid change." Civilisations, 12, 1962, 167-191.
             Distinguishing old and new towns, surveys existing
        knowledge of the latter and reviews the social and eco-
        nomic problems associated with their growth.

0.2.11 HAMDAN, G. "Capitals of the new Africa." Economic Geography,
        40, 1964, 239-253. Reprinted in Breese, G. (ed.), The
        City in Newly Developing Countries. Prentice-Hall,
        Englewood Cliffs, N.J., 1972, 146-161.
             Examines African capital cities in terms of indigenous
        or colonial origins, central or peripheral location, and
        size in relation to other towns in the national urban
        systems.

0.2.12 HANCE, W.A. Population, Migration and Urbanization in
        Africa. Columbia University Press, New York, 1970, 451 pp.
             One chapter, pp. 128-208, examines population movements
        in Africa, including rural-urban flows. Another, pp.
        209-297, focuses on urbanization, with discussions of
        contrasting urban origins, levels of urbanization and
        growth rates, a set of alternative bases for classifying
        African cities, and an analysis of the diverse problems of
        these cities. A third (pp. 298-382) provides "thumbnail
        sketches" of Moroccan cities, Khartoum, Dakar, Abidjan,
        Accra, Kumasi, Lagos, Ibadan, Kano, Luanda, Addis Ababa,
        Nairobi, Kampala, and the Zambian Copperbelt. Other chap-
        ters deal with population growth, distribution, and pres-
        sure at national levels. Numerous maps and photographs are
        included.

0.2.13 HANCE, W.A. "Controlling city size in Africa." In CNRS,
        La Croissance Urbaine en Afrique Noire et à Madagascar.
        Paris, 1972, 653-658.
            Queries the wisdom of either directly limiting city
        growth or promoting new growth poles and argues for easing
        problems of the cities by promoting rural development.

0.2.14 HANNA, W.J. and J.L. Urban Dynamics in Black Africa: an
        interdisciplinary approach. Aldine-Atherton, Chicago,
        1971, 390 pp.
            Brief chapters on urban analysis in Africa and the
        pattern of African urban growth are followed by longer
        chapters discussing rural-urban migration, individual
        adjustment to town life, economic and social conditions
        in town, urban ethnicity, nonethnic associations, and
        political conflict and integration. Examples are widely
        drawn from throughout tropical Africa and much literature
        is synthesized. A 170-page bibliography, not all of its
        items specifically on Africa, occupies almost half the
        book.

0.2.15 HOSSENLOPP, J. "Evolution de l'urbanisation dans 14 états
        d'Afrique Noire et Madagascar avec une esquisse prospective
        à l'horizon 1985." In CNRS, La Croissance Urbaine en
        Afrique Noire et à Madagascar. Paris, 1972, 693-704.
            Provides figures for the urban population of the
        francophone countries from 1920 to 1965 and forecasts
        for 1980, and evaluates the sources for the former and
        reliability of the latter.

0.2.16 INSTITUT INTERNATIONAL DES CIVILISATIONS DIFFERENTES. Urban
        Agglomerations in the States of the Third World. INCIDI,
        Université Libre, Brussels, 1971, 1085 pp.
            The papers and proceedings of a 1967 conference, largely
        arranged continent by continent with the material on Africa
        on pp. 37-435. Most papers review the general urbanization
        trends in individual countries and are thus listed else-
        where.

0.2.17 MABOGUNJE, A.L. "Urbanization and Change." In Paden, J. and
        Soja, E.W. (eds.), The African Experience. Northwestern
        University Press, Evanston, Ill., 1970, Vol. 1, 331-358.
            Discusses precolonial African urbanism, the colonial
        impact, present demographic and socio-economic character-
        istics of African towns, and the political problems raised
        by continued rapid urbanization.

0.2.18 MABOGUNJE, A.L. "Urbanization problems in Africa." In
        El-Shakhs, S. and Obudho, R.A. (eds.), Urbanization,
        National Development and Regional Planning in Africa.
        Praeger, New York, 1974, 13-26.

Argues that rapid urbanization is a traumatic experience
for Africa, with cities consuming rather than producing,
and lacking jobs, housing, social welfare, and effective
administration.

*0.2.19 MABOGUNJE, A.L. Cities and African Development. Oxford
University Press, Ibadan, 1976, 52 pp.

0.2.20 MANSHARD, W. "Some urban developments in tropical Africa."
Geoforum, 4, 1970, 63-74.
Illustrates contracts among African cities in terms
of form, functions, and rate of growth, drawing examples
from West and East Africa.

0.2.21 MARIOTTI, A. and MAGUBANE, B. "Urban ethnology in Africa:
some theoretical issues." In Arens, W. (ed.), A Century
Of Change in Eastern Africa. Mouton, The Hague, 1976,
249-273.
Argues that urbanization in Africa has been an agent
of underdevelopment, increasing dependency and reproduc-
ing the exploitative nature of colonial relationships in
urban-rural relations within Africa.

0.2.22 MINER, H. (ed.) The City in Modern Africa. Pall Mall,
London; Praeger, New York, 1967, 364 pp.
A diverse set of papers on economic, social, and
political aspects of African cities, presented at a 1965
symposium. Most relate to specific cities and are listed
separately. The editor provides an introductory paper on
the city and modernization in Africa.

0.2.23 O'CONNOR, A.M. "The distribution of towns in Subsaharan
Africa." In Gugler, J. (ed.), Urban Growth in Subsaharan
Africa. Makerere University, Kampala, 1970, 5-12.
Examines the distribution of urban centers at both
international and national levels and the factors in-
fluencing the patterns.

0.2.24 O'CONNOR, A.M. The Geography of Tropical African Development.
2d ed., Pergamon, Oxford, 1978. Chap. 8 "Urbanization,"
171-188.
Examines the distribution of urban growth since the
mid-1950s, the evidence for increasing urban primacy, and
changes in the character of the towns.

0.2.25 PALEN, J.J. The Urban World. McGraw-Hill, New York, 1975,
Chap. 15 "African urbanization," 354-381.
Reviews contrasting urban traditions in Africa, social
and economic features of the cities, and housing and planning problems; provides a brief case study of Addis Ababa.

0.2.26 PARKIN, D. (ed.) <u>Town and Country in Central and Eastern
        Africa</u>. Oxford University Press, London, 1975, 362 pp.
             A collection of papers presented at the International
        African Institute seminar in Lusaka in 1972, many of which
        are noted individually elsewhere. Migration is the theme
        of several papers, but others focus on patterns within
        the towns. A lengthy introduction, again largely focus-
        ing on migration, with a French version, is provided by
        the editor.

0.2.27 PEIL, M. <u>Consensus and Conflict in African Societies</u>.
        Longman, London, 1977. Chap. 8 "The cities," 252-303;
        Chap. 9 "Social problems," 304-335.
             In this volume intended mainly as an introduction to
        sociology for African students, chapter 8 provides a
        broad review of rural-urban migration and urban associa-
        tions as well as the nature and extent of African urbani-
        zation, while chapter 9 deals with unemployment, housing
        problems, and crime.

0.2.28 PENOUIL, M. "La ville, centre de transformations économiques
        et sociales: exemple des pays africains." <u>Année
        Africaine</u>, 1970, 161-218.
             Reviews the demographic and economic growth of African
        cities and their role as centers of change and suggests
        that they can benefit surrounding rural areas given appro-
        priate government policies.

0.2.29 SAFIER, M. "Urban growth and urban planning in subsaharan
        Africa." In Gugler, J. (ed.), <u>Urban Growth in Subsaharan
        Africa</u>. Makerere University, Kampala, 1970, 35-44.
             Discusses the relationships between urbanization and
        economic development in Africa and the limited knowledge
        of such matters as the economics of urban size.

0.2.30 SALAU, A.T. "The urban process in Africa: observations on
        the points of divergence from the Western experience."
        <u>African Urban Studies</u>, 4, 1979, 27-34.
             Reviews the historical evolution of African urbaniza-
        tion and notes contrasts between contemporary processes
        in Africa, including rural-urban migration, and the urban
        experience of the "West."

0.2.31 SECRETARIAT DES MISSIONS D'URBANISME ET D'HABITAT. "Urban
        explosion in Africa." <u>Planification Habitat Information</u>.
        79, 1975, 57-86.
             A map and table showing the pattern of urban growth
        and a set of air photographs for each of the capital
        cities of francophone Africa.

0.2.32 SOUTHALL, A. (ed.) <u>Small Towns in African Development</u>.

Special issue of Africa, 49 (3), 1979, 213-328.
Selected papers from a 1978 University of Wisconsin conference, all dealing with towns smaller than any with individual listings in this bibliography. Contributors include A.G.M. Ahmed and M.A. Rahman (Sudan), A.A. Dike (Nigeria), N.S. Hopkins (Mali), T.B. Kabwegyere (Kenya), P.S. Maro and W.F.I. Mlay (Tanzania), J. Middleton (Ghana), O. Otite (Nigeria), and D. Parkin (Kenya).

0.2.33 SPENGLER, J.J. "Africa and the theory of optimum city size." In Miner, H. (ed.), The City in Modern Africa. Praeger, New York; Pall Mall, London, 1970, 55-89.
Suggests that African countries are experiencing excessive rates of urban growth, especially in large cities, and argues for efforts to disperse urbanization to small centers.

0.2.34 STEEL, R.W. "The towns of tropical Africa." In Barbour, K.M. and Prothero, R.M. (eds.), Essays on African Population. Routledge and Kegan Paul, London, 1961, 249-278.
Reviews the origins and distribution of towns, national contrasts in levels of urbanization, and the problems of rapid urban growth.

0.2.35 THOMAS, B.E. "On the growth of African cities." African Studies Review, 13 (1), 1970, 69-74.
Discusses past and present growth rates of African cities and argues that recent rates are exceptional and unlikely to be maintained as the urban pattern matures.

0.2.36 VENNETIER, P. "Le développement urbain en Afrique tropicale." Cahiers d'Outre-Mer, 22, 1969, 5-62.
A wide-ranging geographical review of the origins, distribution, demographic structure, economic characteristics, and physical form and structure of urban centers in tropical Africa, synthesizing much of the material presented more fully in the book listed below.

0.2.37 VENNETIER, P. Les Villes d'Afrique Tropicale. Masson, Paris, 1976, 192 pp.
The only book devoted entirely to a systematic geographical study of urbanization throughout tropical Africa, drawing together the results of much French work on individual cities, but including material on non-francophone countries also. Individual chapters deal with the origins and growth of the towns; in-migration; demographic structures; urban morphology; residential areas; economic activities; and urban-rural relationships.

11

Africa [General]

The main contribution in German is:

0.2.38   MANSHARD, W.   Die Städte des tropischen Afrika.   Gebrüder
         Borntraeger, Berlin, 1977, 258 pp.

Unpublished theses include:

0.2.39   IKEMMA, W.N.   Urbanization in Africa South of the Sahara:
         survey and description of emerging urban trends.   Ph.D.
         thesis, University of Pittsburgh, 1974.

0.2.40   LAGOPOULOS, A.P.   L'Influence des Conceptions Cosmiques sur
         l'Urbanisme Africain Traditionel.   Thèse 3e cycle,
         Université de Paris, 1970.

0.2.41   ONGUENE-OWONA, J.   Urbanisation et Systèmes Urbains de la
         Ville Africaine.   Thèse 3e cycle, Université de Paris,
         1970.

History

0.3.1   CHANDLER, T. and FOX, G.   3000 Years of Urban Growth.
        Academic Press, New York, 1974, 431 pp.
           A vast compilation on world urbanization, which tabu-
        lates city sizes for Africa A.D. 800-1850 (pp. 44-48),
        maps the cities of Africa A.D. 1000-1850 (pp. 49-57), and
        provides a chronology for major African cities (pp. 206-215).

0.3.2   HOWARD, A.   "Pre-colonial centres and regional systems in
        Africa."   Pan-African Journal, 8, 1975, 247-270.
           Shows the variety of nineteenth century urban systems
        in Africa and how these were destroyed by the colonial
        impact in some areas but strengthened in others, pointing
        to the need for more research in this field.

0.3.3   HULL, R.W.   "Urban design and architecture in precolonial
        Africa."   Journal of Urban History, 2, 1975, 387-414.
           Examines the origins, functions, physical form, and
        building styles of precolonial urban centers in various
        parts of Africa, concluding that many combined humane,
        ornamental, and utilitarian qualities very effectively.

0.3.4   HULL, R.W.   African Cities and Towns before the European
        Conquest.   Norton, New York, 1976, 138 pp.
           Reviews the origins of indigenous urban centers through-
        out tropical Africa, examines their physical structure
        and house types and also the relationship of physical form
        to social structure, and discusses aspects of their eco-
        nomic and cultural activities.   Includes numerous sketches,
        photographs, and maps.

0.3.5   SOUTHALL, A. "The impact of imperialism upon urban development
        in Africa." In Turner, V. (ed.), Colonialism in Africa:
        Vol. 3, Profiles of Change. Cambridge University Press,
        1971, 216-255.
           Reviews various indigenous urban traditions, colonial
        destruction of these in some areas, adaptations of and
        additions to these in others, and new urban creations in
        yet others, and the problems left by the colonial urban
        legacies.

0.3.6   TANGA, L. "Note bibliographique sur les villes de l'Afrique
        noire avant 1850." Etudes Congolaises, 10 (3), 1967,
        112-122.
           A broad outline of the present state of knowledge of
        urban development in various parts of tropical Africa
        before the colonial period.

Rural-Urban Migration

0.4.1   ADEPOJU, A. "Migration and rural development in tropical
        Africa." African Urban Studies, 2, 1978, 19-35.
           Analyzes data on rural and urban population increase in
        African countries as indicators of migration, examines the
        implications of this movement for rural development, and
        discusses current strategies for curbing it.

0.4.2   BERRY, S.S. "The marketing of migrant labor services in
        African cities: a relatively unexplored topic." African
        Urban Notes, 5 (3), 1970, 144-153.
           Largely a review of the literature on rural-urban
        migration, but noting also our limited knowledge of the
        operation of labor markets within African cities.

0.4.3   BYERLEE, D. "Rural-urban migration in Africa: theory, policy
        and research implications." International Migration Review,
        8, 1974, 543-566.
           A wide-ranging review of the literature, of some of the
        empirical findings reported within it, and of the attempts
        to formulate theories relevant for policy towards such
        migration.

0.4.4   GOULD, W.T.S. A Bibliography of Population Mobility in
        Tropical Africa. Department of Geography, University of
        Liverpool, 1977, 82 pp.
           Lists about 800 items, alphabetically by author but with
        country and "type of migration" indexes, including many on
        rural-urban movement. (Also listed as 0.0.9.)

0.4.5   GUGLER, J. "On the theory of rural-urban migration: the
        case of subsaharan Africa." In Jackson, J.A. (ed.),

13

Migration. Cambridge University Press, 1969, 134-155.
   Evaluates the economic and noneconomic causes of migration and of continuing urban-rural ties, drawing on evidence from many parts of Africa.

0.4.6   GUGLER, J. "Migrating to urban centres of unemployment in
        tropical Africa." In Richmond, A.H. and Kubat, D. (eds.),
        Internal Migration: the New World and the Third World.
        Sage, London, 1976, 184-204.
           Considers the extent of urban unemployment, discusses
        forces for migration in terms of rural-urban balance of
        economic opportunities but noting other factors also, and
        distinguishes social from individual costs of migrating
        into urban unemployment.

0.4.7   GULLIVER, P.H. "The development of labour migration in
        Africa." Kroniek van Afrika, 6, 1966, 250-265.
           Examines the development of labor migration, largely
        but not entirely rural-urban, in eastern and southern
        Africa, and discusses both the shift to more permanent
        urban residence and the maintenance of strong ties to
        the home areas.

0.4.8   KERRI, J.N. "Applied anthropology, urbanization and
        development in Africa: dream or reality?" Human
        Organization, 36, 1977, 34-42.
           Suggests that anthropologists should be able to assist
        in the formulation of policies to reduce rural-urban
        migration by showing what improvements are needed in
        rural areas.

0.4.9   PROTHERO, R.M. "Socio-economic aspects of rural-urban
        migration in Africa south of the Sahara." Scientia
        (Milan), 59 (Vol. 100), 1965, 278-284.
           Distinguishes movements over different time-scales,
        notes regional contrasts, and discusses the consequences
        of massive rural-urban movements.

0.4.10 PROTHERO, R.M. "Migration in tropical Africa." In Caldwell,
        J.C. and Okonjo, C. (eds.), The Population of Tropical
        Africa. Longmans, London, 1968, 250-263.
           Notes the types of migration occurring in tropical
        Africa and the increasing importance of rural-urban
        movement and reviews the data available on the subject
        in various countries by the mid-1960s.

0.4.11 PROTHERO, R.M. "Population mobility." In Knight, C.G. and
        Newman, J.L. (eds.), Contemporary Africa. Prentice-Hall,
        Englewood Cliffs, N.J., 1976, 356-363.
           Shows how migration patterns in Africa have changed in
        recent years, but still differ greatly from one area to

another, focusing on rural-urban movements more sharply
than in Prothero's numerous other writings on African
migration.

0.4.12   TODARO, M.P.   "Income expectations, rural-urban migration
and employment in Africa."   International Labour Review,
104, 1971, 387-413.
Develops a theoretical framework to show why continued
rural-urban migration in African countries represents a
rational economic decision, despite high levels of urban
unemployment, and suggests policies to reduce it.

0.4.13   WOOD, E.W.   "The implications of migrant labour for urban
social systems in Africa."   Cahiers d'Etudes Africaines,
8, 1968, 5-31.
Draws on a wide range of literature to demonstrate
contrasting patterns of labor migration in various parts
of Africa and consequent contrasts in degree of urban
commitment and in urban social systems.

An unpublished thesis is:

0.4.14   OBBO, C.S.   Town Migration is not for Women.   Ph.D. thesis,
University of Wisconsin, 1977.

Demography

0.5.1   GENDREAU, F.   "Centres urbains."   In Afrique Noire,
Madagascar, Comores: démographie comparée.   INSEE, Paris,
1966, Vol. 2, 1-87.
Examines the growth and 1960 distribution of urban
population in fourteen francophone countries, reviews
censuses and surveys undertaken in their cities and towns
between 1950 and 1963, and compares some of the data
obtained. An appendix estimates the population of each
town for each year from 1916 to 1964.

0.5.2   LAIDLAW, K.A. and STOCKWELL, E.G.   "Trends in the relationship
between urbanisation and development in Africa."   Journal
of Modern African Studies, 17, 1979, 687-694.
Argues that contemporary rapid urbanization in Africa
is not in itself an indication of either modernization
or development, stressing the lack of the fertility decline
associated elsewhere with the "demographic transition."

0.5.3   ROSSER, C.   Urbanization in Tropical Africa: a demographic
introduction.   Ford Foundation, New York, 1972, 74 pp.
A broad review of the development and distribution of
urban centers, current rapid growth rates, patterns of
rural-urban migration, and the political implications of
urbanization.

15

0.5.4 UNITED NATIONS. "Size and growth of urban population in
       Africa." UNECA, Addis Ababa, 1968, 41 pp. Reprinted in
       Breese, G. (ed.), The City in Newly Developing Countries.
       Prentice-Hall, Englewood Cliffs, N.J., 1969, 128-145.
            Assembles and discusses available data on the extent
       of urbanization in tropical Africa and its constituent
       countries and especially the 1950-1960 rate of urban popu-
       lation growth and the extent of concentration in large
       cities.

0.5.5 UNITED NATIONS. Demographic Handbook for Africa 1978. UNECA,
       Addis Ababa, 1979, 122 pp.
            Includes data for each country on the population in
       towns of over 20,000 inhabitants, the rate of increase of
       the urban population, sex ratios, and the projected urban
       population to 1985.

       See also the reviews by R. Blanc and J.I. Clarke in 0.2.1.

Ethnicity

0.6.1 BANTON, M. "Urbanization and the colour line in Africa." In
       Turner, V. (ed.), Colonialism in Africa: Volume 3, Profiles
       of Change. Cambridge University Press, 1971, 256-285.
            Applies a model of group relationships from American
       social anthropology to African cities, revealing the con-
       trasts between the two-strata situation in cities such as
       Salisbury and more blurred patterns elsewhere.

0.6.2 DU TOIT, B.M. "Cultural continuity and African urbanization."
       In Eddy, E.M. (ed.), Urban Anthropology. University of
       Georgia Press, Athens, 1968, 58-74.
            Examines the cultural link with the rural homeland
       maintained by rural-urban migrants in Africa and the con-
       sequent importance of ethnicity in urban social life.

0.6.3 GUGLER, J. "Migration and ethnicity in sub-Saharan Africa:
       affinity, rural interests and urban alignments." In
       Safa, H.I. and Du Toit, B.M. (eds.), Migration and
       Development. Mouton, The Hague, 1975, 295-309.
            Discusses the significance in the social and political
       life of African cities of migrants' ties to their rural
       homelands and of ethnic unions within the cities.

0.6.4 GUGLER, J. "Particularism in sub-Saharan Africa: 'tribalism'
       in town." Canadian Review of Sociology and Anthropology,
       12, 1975, 303-315.
            Shows how migrants in African towns may identify with
       ethnic groups at various scales, some smaller or larger
       than tribes, and that formalized ethnic unions can be of
       great importance.

0.6.5   KUPER, L. "Some aspects of urban plural societies." In
         Lystad, R.A. (ed.), The African World. Pall Mall, London,
         1965, 107-130.
             A general survey of racial, tribal, and class divisions
         in African cities, with some emphasis on southern Africa,
         and a review of research on these.

0.6.6   KUPER, L. "Structural discontinuities in African towns:
         some aspects of racial pluralism." In Miner, H. (ed.),
         The City in Modern Africa. Praeger, New York; Pall Mall,
         London, 1967, 127-150.
             Describes the social cleavages along racial lines in
         the cities of "white settler" countries and discusses the
         likely effects on these of either a transfer of power or
         power-sharing.

0.6.7   LITTLE, K. "Urbanization and regional associations: their
         paradoxical function." In Southall, A. (ed.), Urban
         Anthropology. Oxford University Press, New York, 1973,
         407-423.
             Shows how regional or tribal associations may both
         maintain traditional elements in African cities and also
         assist modernization processes, especially aiding newcomers'
         adaptation to town life.

0.6.8   LITTLE, K. "Countervailing influences in African ethnicity:
         a less apparent factor." In Du Toit, B.M. (ed.), Ethnicity
         in Modern Africa. Westview, Boulder, Colo., 1978,
         175-189.
             Examines the types of organizations joined by women in
         African cities and argues that many of these cut across
         ethnic ties, thus reducing the significance of ethnicity
         in urban life.

0.6.9   RICHARDS, A.I. "Multi-tribalism in African urban areas."
         Civilisations, 16, 1966, 354-361.
             Notes the great strength of ethnic identity in most
         African cities and the problems that this presents to
         governments in such realms as language policy.

0.6.10   SOUTHALL, A. "From segmentary lineage to ethnic association:
         Luo, Luhya, Ibo and others." In Owusu, M. (ed.),
         Colonialism and Change. Mouton, The Hague, 1975,
         203-229.
             With special reference to the groups specified, shows
         how ethnic associations in African cities derive both
         structural features and operating mechanisms from tradi-
         tional social systems.

0.6.11   SOUTHALL, A. "Forms of ethnic linkage between town and
         country." In Arens, W. (ed.), A Century of Change in

17

Eastern Africa. Mouton, The Hague, 1976, 275-285.
Indicates the importance of ethnicity in urban life
and the value of concepts such as "host communities,"
despite many misconceptions about "tribes," but notes
the great variations from country to country.

Social Relationships

0.7.1 BASCOM, W. "The urban African and his world." Cahiers
d'Etudes Africaines, 4, 1963, 163-185.
Discusses the social environment of African urban
dwellers, stressing the contrasts between conditions for
migrants in southern Africa and those in Yoruba traditional
cities in Nigeria.

0.7.2 BINET, J. "Urbanisme et langage dans la ville africaine."
Diogène, 93, 1976, 90-113.
Stresses the cellular structure of most African cities
and investigates people's images of their cities and the
neighborhoods within them, with special reference to the
names used for the latter.

0.7.3 DURAND, J. "Le rôle de la ville dans la vie moderne."
Présence Africaine, 48, 1963, 65-83.
A general discussion of social change associated with
urban development in Africa and of the continuing role of
foreigners in such development.

0.7.4 EPSTEIN, A.L. "Urbanization and social change in Africa."
Current Anthropology, 8, 1967, 275-295. Reprinted in
Breese, G. (ed.), The City in Newly Developing Countries.
Prentice-Hall, Englewood Cliffs, N.J., 1969, 246-284.
Examines the variables that shape the structure of
social relations in African cities and emphasizes the
contrasts from one country to another, while still seeking
to generalize about the nature of the urbanization process.
Includes comments from ten other scholars.

0.7.5 GUGLER, J. "The second sex in town." Canadian Journal of
African Studies, 6, 1972, 289-301.
Draws on a wide range of sources to investigate the
position of women in African cities and to isolate the
forces for change associated with urbanization.

0.7.6 GUTKIND, P.C.W. "African urban family life and the urban
system." Journal of Asian and African Studies, 1, 1966,
35-42. Reprinted in Middleton, J. (ed.), Black Africa.
Macmillan, London, 1970, 181-187.
Shows how African urban life operates within one social
field based on ethnicity and kinship and another based on
economic and political processes.

0.7.7   GUTKIND, P.C.W. "The sociopolitical and economic foundations of social problems in African urban areas." Civilisations, 22, 1972, 18-33.
        Shows how ethnic diversity, hierarchical power structures, class formation, and increasing unemployment all contribute to social unrest in African cities.

0.7.8   GUTKIND, P.C.W. Urban Anthropology: perspectives on Third World urbanization and urbanism. Van Gorcum, Assen, Netherlands, 1974, 262 pp.
        Despite its subtitle, the book is very largely concerned with Africa, combining discussions of conceptual approaches and methodology in studying urban societies with wide-ranging material on the social structures of African cities.

0.7.9   HANNA, W.J. and J.L. "The integrative role of urban Africa's middleplaces and middlemen." Civilisations, 17, 1967, 12-30.
        Examines the contribution to African urban society of those who bridge the gaps between traditional and modern structures and between the city and countryside.

0.7.10   LITTLE, K. African Women in Towns. Cambridge University Press, 1973, 242 pp.
        Discusses with reference to various parts of Africa women as migrants, women's place in economic and political life, women's voluntary associations, and patterns of courtship and marriage.

0.7.11   LITTLE, K. Urbanization as a Social Process: an essay on movement and change in contemporary Africa. Routledge and Kegan Paul, London, 1974, 153 pp.
        A wide-ranging review, with some discussion of migration, attitudes to work, ethnicity, and race relations, but focusing on social organization and on the role of urbanization in accelerating social change.

0.7.12   LITTLE, K. "Some methodological considerations in the study of African women's urban roles." Urban Anthropology, 4 (2), 1975, 107-121.
        Suggests that a realistic approach to the topic must recognize the considerable power held by women in African towns, the extent of their freedom, and the role of their own voluntary associations.

0.7.13   LITTLE, K. "Women in African towns south of the Sahara: the urbanization dilemma." In Tinker, I. and Bramsen, M.B. (eds.), Women and World Development. Overseas Development Council, Washington, D.C., 1976, 78-87.
        Shows how urbanization affects women's role in African

societies, noting rural–urban contrasts, and how urban policies, e.g., towards market trade, may affect that role.

0.7.14   LLOYD, P.C. (ed.) The New Elites of Tropical Africa. Oxford University Press, London, 1966, 390 pp.
The volume is not devoted specifically to urbanization, but the editor's long introduction on the characteristics and social relationships of the new elites is largely concerned with the urban population, as are several other contributions listed individually elsewhere.

0.7.15   MARRIS, P. African City Life. Transition Books, Kampala, 1967, 26 pp.
A discussion of social relationships, social classes, and family ties, drawing heavily on experience in Lagos but seeking wider generalization.

0.7.16   PALUCH, A. "Changement social et urbanisation en Afrique au sud du Sahara." Africana Bulletin, 16, 1972, 9–42.
A broad review of social and cultural changes associated with urbanization in Africa, in the light of general anthropological theories regarding cultural change. Summarizes the thesis noted below.

0.7.17   PLOTNICOV, L. "Social planning for modern urban development in Africa: the power of the people." Pan-African Journal, 8, 1975, 287–295.
Shows how the urban poor in Africa can provide many necessary social institutions for themselves, these often evolving from traditional structures and proving more satisfactory than imported institutions.

0.7.18   SCHWAB, W.B. "Urbanism, corporate groups and culture change in Africa below the Sahara." Anthropological Quarterly, 43, 1970, 187–214.
Examines the role of specific corporate groups within wider urban communities, drawing on work in Nigeria and Zimbabwe as a basis for generalizations applicable to large areas of Africa.

0.7.19   SOUTHALL, A. (ed.) Social Change in Modern Africa. Oxford University Press, London, 1961, 350 pp.
Urbanization as an agent of social change is discussed at length in the editor's introduction and in other papers listed individually elsewhere.

Unpublished theses include:

0.7.20   HOGG, T.C. Urban Immigrants and Associations in Sub-Saharan Africa. Ph.D. thesis, University of Oregon, 1965.

Africa [General]

0.7.21   PALUCH, A.   Changements Sociaux et Culturels en Afrique
             Contemporaine: développement des villes et urbanisation.
             Doctoral thesis, University of Cracow, 1972.

Politics and Administration

0.8.1   BARBADETTE, L.; BUGNICOURT, J.; and CISSE, B.H.   "Action
             training for African towns."   African Environment, 1 (3),
             1975, 17–50.
                Proposes new methods of approach to African urban
             planning, involving more awareness of the inhabitants'
             viewpoints and more public participation, on the basis of
             a 1974 training session in Douala.

0.8.2   BARNES, S.T.   "Political transition in urban Africa."
             Annals of the American Academy of Political and Social
             Science, 432, 1977, 26–41.
                Shows how political stability in African cities depends
             as much on traditional authority figures and spontaneous
             interest-group networks as on formal government
             institutions.

0.8.3   GUTKIND, P.C.W.   "African urban chiefs: agents of stability
             or change in African urban life?"   Anthropologica, 8,
             1966, 249–268.   Reprinted in Meadows, P. and Mizruchi,
             E.H. (eds.), Urbanism, Urbanization and Change.   Addison-
             Wesley, Reading, Mass., 1969, 457–470.
                Draws on studies of a variety of towns to explore the
             contemporary role of traditional chiefs, not only in
             urban administration but also in other aspects of urban
             life.

0.8.4   GUTKIND, P.C.W.   "Tradition, migration, urbanization,
             modernity and unemployment in Africa."   Canadian Journal
             of African Studies, 3, 1969, 343–366.
                Examines the political significance of in-migration
             and rising unemployment in African cities, so far quite
             constrained but potentially very considerable.

0.8.5   GUTKIND, P.C.W.   "The poor in urban Africa."   In Bloomberg,
             G. and Schmandt, H. (eds.), Power, Deprivation and Urban
             Policy.   Sage, Beverly Hills, Calif., 1968, 355–396; and
             in Bloomberg, G. and Schmandt, H. (eds.), Urban Poverty.
             Sage, Beverly Hills, Calif., 1970, 123–164.
                Similar in theme to the above paper, but incorporating
             more case material from studies in Lagos and Nairobi.

0.8.6   GUTKIND, P.C.W.   "From the energy of despair to the anger of
             despair: the transition from social circulation to
             political consciousness among the urban poor in Africa."

Canadian Journal of African Studies, 7, 1973, 179-198.
Extends the discussion of the previous two papers
with more on the general dependency and impoverishment
of Africa and with material on increasing political
consciousness in the "traditional" city of Ibadan.

0.8.7   GUTKIND, P.C.W. "Reformism, populism and proletarianism in
         urban Africa." Ufahamu, 8 (3), 1978, 24-61.
         A discussion in Marxist terms of the development of
         class-consciousness in African cities in the light of
         past colonial experience and the continuing involvement
         in the capitalist world system.

0.8.8   LAMPUE, P. "Le régime municipal dans les états africains
         francophones." Revue Juridique et Politique, 22, 1968,
         463-472.
         Traces the evolution of local administrative structures
         in both the towns and the rural areas of francophone
         Africa and demonstrates their diversity.

0.8.9   ORAM, N. Towns in Africa. Oxford University Press, London,
         1965, 98 pp.
         A very basic introduction to tropical African towns
         and their problems with an emphasis on administration and
         planning and with chapters on such topics as land tenure.

0.8.10   WALSH, A.H. "Urban local government in French-speaking
         Africa." African Urban Notes, 4 (4), 1969, 1-34.
         Examines the nature of urban administration in post-
         colonial francophone Africa, with special reference to
         Casablanca and Dakar, suggesting that this is less dis-
         tinct from national administration than in anglophone
         West Africa.

The Urban Economy and Employment

0.9.1   BUGNICOURT, J. "Which urban alternative for Africa?"
         African Environment, 2 (3), 1976, 3-20.
         Presents a model of the economy of African cities,
         with emphasis on the "modern" and "transitional" subsystems
         and links between them, and considers possible planned
         changes in these structures.

0.9.2   FRANK, C.R. "Urban unemployment and economic growth in
         Africa." Oxford Economic Papers, 20, 1968, 250-274.
         Shows that neither accelerated economic growth nor
         greater labor intensity in urban activities is likely to
         solve the urban unemployment problem so long as income
         prospects for the rural majority are so poor.

0.9.3   FRANK, C.R. "The problem of urban unemployment in Africa."
        In Ridker, R.G. and Lubell, H. (eds.), Employment and
        Unemployment Problems of the Near East and South Asia.
        Vikas, Delhi, 1971, 783-818.
            Similar to the above paper, but with more on migration
        and with a full review of the relevant literature.

0.9.4   GUTKIND, P.C.W. "African responses to urban wage employment."
        International Labour Review, 97, 1968, 135-166.
            A broad review of the movement to urban employment in
        tropical Africa, arguing that workers' commitment to the
        wage economy is determined more by total social change
        and their perception of it than by specific incentives
        for labor stabilization.

0.9.5   GUTKIND, P.C.W. The Emergent African Urban Proletariat.
        Centre for Developing-Area Studies, McGill University,
        Montreal, 1974, 79 pp.
            An essay on African labor history, discussing how urban
        workers saw themselves in the colonial period and how they
        were viewed in Commonwealth Africa by the British
        administrators.

0.9.6   HARVEY, M.E. "Urban economic development." In Knight,
        C.G. and Newman, J.L. (eds.), Contemporary Africa.
        Prentice-Hall, Englewood Cliffs, N.J., 1976, 283-305.
            Traces the evolution of urban economic activities from
        the precolonial base where applicable through the colonial
        and postcolonial phases and analyzes the types of manu-
        facturing recently added in many cities.

0.9.7   HOYLE, B.S. "The port function in the urban development of
        tropical Africa." In CNRS, La Croissance Urbaine en
        Afrique Noire et à Madagascar. Paris, 1972, 705-718.
            Examines for all the port cities of tropical Africa
        the relationship between population size and volume of
        port traffic and discusses physical and political influ-
        ences on cityport growth.

0.9.8   HOYLE, B.S. and HILLING, D. (eds.) Seaports and Development
        in Tropical Africa. Macmillan, London, 1970, 272 pp.
            A set of case studies of the characteristics, function-
        ing, and developmental role of African ports, most noted
        individually elsewhere.

*0.9.9 HUGON, P. et al. La Petite Production Marchande et L'Emploi
        dans la Secteur "Informel": le cas Africain. Institut
        d'Etude du Développement Economique et Social, Université
        de Paris I, 1977, 272 pp.

0.9.10 LUX, A. "Chômage urbain et évolution de la nature de l'offre

23

de travail dans les économies africaines." Canadian
Journal of African Studies, 3, 1969, 395-408.
    Examines the nature of the demand for employment and
the changing patterns of employment opportunity in
African cities.

0.9.11 SALAU, A.T. "The political economy of cities in tropical
       Africa." Civilisations, 28, 1978, 281-292.
    Notes differing attitudes towards rapid urban growth
in Africa and suggests that while cities are not in themselves harmful, they are often the instruments of international capitalism, which is to be resisted.

0.9.12 SETHURAMAN, S.V. "The urban informal sector in Africa."
       International Labour Review, 116, 1977, 343-352.
    Presents a synthesis of the results of ILO studies of
small-scale enterprise in the mid-1970s in Dakar, Freetown,
Kano, Kumasi, Lagos, and Onitsha, and suggests ways in
which it could be assisted throughout Africa.

0.9.13 VENNETIER, P. "L'approvisionnement des villes en Afrique
       noire: un problème à étudier." In Etudes de Géographie
       Tropicale Offertes à Pierre Gourou. Mouton, Paris, 1972,
       477-490.
    Discusses the huge increase in demand for foodstuffs
resulting from the rapid growth of African cities and the
extent of the response from various types of farmers,
stressing the urgent need for more research. A similar
paper forms the introduction to CEGET, Dix Etudes sur
l'Approvisionnement des Villes, Bordeaux, 1972.

0.9.14 WEEKS, J. "An exploration into the nature of urban imbalance
       in Africa." Manpower and Unemployment Research in Africa.
       6 (2), 1973, 9-36.
    Examines the economic problems of African cities,
notably increasing unemployment and the coexistence of
rich, largely alien, and poor, largely indigenous, sectors
in the urban economies.

Urban Morphology and Housing

0.10.1 ASETO, D.O. and COSMINSKY, S. "A model of slum generation
       in Africa." Pan-African Journal, 9, 1976, 17-33.
    Develops a model to explain the generation of slums in
tropical African cities through a combination of economic,
social, and political circumstances.

0.10.2 BRAND, R.R. "The urban housing challenge." In Knight, C.G.
       and Newman, J.L. (eds.), Contemporary Africa. Prentice-
       Hall, Englewood Cliffs, N.J., 1976, 321-335.

Outlines the housing problem presented by rapid growth
of the urban population, with a case study of slum and
shanty development in Accra, and considers the planning
options.

0.10.3 DENYER, S. Traditional African Architecture. Heinemann,
London, 1978, 224 pp.
A volume devoted to traditional styles of building
over tropical Africa as a whole, thus devoted mainly to
rural settlement, but including discussion, plans, and
photographs of urban building styles also.

0.10.4 EL-SHAKHS, S. and SALAU, A. "Modernization and the planning
of cities in Africa: implications for internal structure."
African Urban Studies, 4, 1979, 15-26.
Argues that the dualistic physical structure of most
African cities results both from colonial policies and
from postindependence planning that has failed to tackle
the integration and modernization of the "traditional"
sector.

0.10.5 HAERINGER, P. "L'urbanisation de masse en question: quatre
villes d'Afrique noire." In CNRS, La Croissance Urbaine
en Afrique Noire et à Madagascar. Paris, 1972, 625-651.
Examines the nature of the housing, planned and spontaneous, occupied by the fast-growing population of
Abidjan, Brazzaville, Douala, and San Pedro, and shows
that inadequate attention has been given to the housing
needs of the majority.

0.10.6 LEA, J.P. "Comparative policies towards housing in sub-Saharan
Africa." South African Journal of African Affairs, 6,
1976, 44-51.
A broad outline of the housing problems in African
cities and of the various types of official response to
them.

0.10.7 MAILLARD, A. "Aménagement urbain en Afrique." Bulletin de
Liaison du Centre Universitaire de Recherches de
Développement, 1974, 19-32.
Presents a model of the physical form of the colonial
city in Africa and discusses the problems arising from
the perpetuation of such colonial structures.

0.10.8 NERFIN, M. "Towards a housing policy." Journal of Modern
African Studies, 3, 1965, 543-565.
Examines the housing problem in African cities and
demonstrates the need for more government action in regard
to both physical planning and housing finance.

0.10.9 NORWOOD, H.C. "Squatters compared." African Urban Notes,

B 1 (2), 1975, 119-132.
Compares the squatter areas of Blantyre, Lusaka, and
Nairobi in terms of location, employment patterns, hous-
ing, access to services, and administration.

0.10.10 OLIVER, P. (ed.) Shelter in Africa. Barrie and Jenkins,
London, 1971, 240 pp.
Includes an introduction by the editor and a paper
by T.L. Blair on "Shelter in Urbanising Africa," in
addition to local case studies, some of which are urban
and noted elsewhere.

0.10.11 PEIL, M. "African squatter settlements: a comparative
study." Urban Studies, 13, 1976, 155-166.
Compares the extent and nature of squatter settlements
in cities in various parts of Africa and suggests reasons
for their more limited numbers in West Africa than
elsewhere.

0.10.12 SALAU, A.T. "Housing in Africa: toward a reassessment
of problems, policies and planning strategies."
Civilisations, 29, 1979, 322-337.
Discusses the application of the concepts of housing
standards and housing needs in African cities, notes the
extent of slums and squatter settlements, and briefly
reviews housing policies.

0.10.13 SOMMER, J.W. "The internal structure of African cities."
In Knight, C.G. and Newman, J.L. (eds.), Contemporary
Africa. Prentice-Hall, Englewood Cliffs, N.J., 1976,
306-320.
Describes the typical form of African colonial cities
and the nature of postcolonial physical changes and indicates some of the problems facing urban planners.

0.10.14 STREN, R.E. "Urban policy in Africa: a political analysis."
African Studies Review, 15, 1972, 489-516.
Argues that the provision of housing for the poor is
the greatest problem in African cities and discusses
the diversity, but general inadequacy, of the policies
adopted in various countries.

0.10.15 TURIN, D.A. "Housing in Africa: some problems and major
policy issues." In Nevitt, A.A. (ed.), The Economic
Problems of Housing. Macmillan, London, 1967, 200-214.
A broad review of the growing housing needs in African
cities and of the economic and administrative problems involved in attempting to meet those needs.

0.10.16 UNITED NATIONS. Housing in Africa. New York, 1965, 221 pp.
Reviews the housing situation throughout Africa, with

emphasis on urban housing. Individual chapters deal with
policy, standards, institutions, finance, etc., with examples from a variety of countries.

0.10.17   UNITED NATIONS. Urban Land Policies and Land-Use Control
          Measures. Volume 1: Africa. New York, 1973, 65 pp.
             Drawing examples from many parts of Africa, briefly
          reviews a range of issues, including the scale and nature
          of urban land problems, spontaneous settlement, the urban
          land market, tenure systems, and land-use control measures.

0.10.18   UNITED NATIONS. Economic Housing in Africa. UNECA, Addis
          Ababa, 1976, 274 pp. + appendices.
             A compendium on housing problems and solutions in
          Africa, with a heavy emphasis on urban areas. Includes
          a selection of national policy statements, summaries of
          a wide range of housing studies, and a country by country
          review of housing schemes. Numerous plans and photographs,
          and text in English and French.

0.10.19   UNITED NATIONS. Human Settlements in Africa: the role of
          housing and building. UNECA, Addis Ababa, 1976, 196 pp.
             A review of African housing issues prepared with
          Netherlands government assistance, covering housing
          needs, the frameworks for decision making, and issues of
          house design, building materials, settlement planning,
          and finance. Emphasizes urban situations and includes
          brief case studies of Lusaka and Port Sudan, listed
          individually.

0.10.20   WOOD, S. "Some problems in town and country planning in
          Africa." African Law Studies, 3, 1970, 77-96.
             Reviews the evolution of town planning practice in
          Kenya, Tanzania, Uganda, and Ghana, and examines some of
          the effects of current legislation.

Unpublished theses include:

0.10.21   FADEUILHE, J-J. Eléments pour l'élaboration d'une politique
          de l'habitat des grandes cités africaines. Thèse 3e
          cycle, Université de Bordeaux I, 1972.

0.10.22   MAILLARD, A. Urbanisme et architecture en Afrique
          francophone. Thèse 3e cycle, Université de Paris VIII,
          1974.

Urban Systems

0.11.1   ADALEMO, A. "Towards a model of planned urban development
          in African countries." In Mabogunje, A.L. and Faniran,

A. (eds.), Regional Planning and National Development in Tropical Africa. Ibadan University Press, 1977, 71-85.
Reviews models of urban and regional systems that might be used in planning urban systems that would aid regional development in African countries.

0.11.2 CLARKE, J.I. "The growth of capital cities in Africa."
Afrika Spectrum, 2, 1971, 33-40.
Discusses the location and population growth of African capitals with special reference to their relationship to other urban centers within each country.

0.11.3 CLARKE, J.I. "Urban primacy in tropical Africa." In CNRS, La Croissance Urbaine en Afrique Noire et à Madagascar. Paris, 1972, 447-453.
Investigates the degree of primacy in the urban systems of tropical African countries, using both a two-city index and a four-city index, showing that a totally dominant capital is the most common situation.

0.11.4 HIRST, M.A. "Dimensions of urban systems in tropical Africa." Geographical Analysis, 7, 1975, 441-449.
Compares the results of a principal components analysis of Tanzanian towns with earlier studies of Nigeria by Mabogunje and Ghana by McNulty, revealing a lower degree of functional differentiation.

0.11.5 McNULTY, M.L. "African Urban Systems, transportation networks and regional inequalities." African Urban Notes, 6 (3), 1972, 56-66.
Examines the relationships between the urban systems of African countries and the export-oriented economic systems imposed in the colonial period, including the transport systems then established.

0.11.6 NICOLAI, H. "Les modifications apportées par la croissance urbaine à l'organisation régionale." In CNRS, La Croissance Urbaine en Afrique Noire et à Madagascar. Paris, 1972, 219-227.
Shows the increasing role of African cities as nodes in the organization of the space economy, creating a new set of urban-oriented regions within African countries.

0.11.7 OBUDHO, R.A. "A strategy in periodic market, urbanization and regional development planning in Africa." Pan-African Journal, 8, 1975, 319-345.
Considers the utility of central-place theory in Africa, notes the juxtaposition of indigenous market systems and imposed urban systems, and indicates the need for planners to integrate the two.

0.11.8 OBUDHO, R.A. and EL-SHAKHS, S. (eds.) Development of Urban
         Systems in Africa. Praeger, New York, 1979, 406 pp.
            Includes papers by M.L. McNulty and F.E. Horton on
         "Problems and prospects of planning in an African context"
         (pp. 1-15), and by A.A. Dike on "Misconceptions of African
         urbanism: some Euro-American notions" (pp. 19-30), as
         well as fifteen country case studies from northern, south-
         ern, and tropical Africa, most, but not all, concerned
         with national urban systems.

0.11.9 SOJA, E.W. "Rural-urban interaction." Rural Africana, 6,
         1968, 43-50; and Canadian Journal of African Studies, 3,
         1969, 284-290.
            A review of research on linkages between African cities
         and their rural hinterlands, indicating the great scope
         for more work on spatial systems within African countries.

West Africa

GENERAL

1.0.1 ADAMS, J.G.U. "The measurement and interpretation of change
in West African urban hierarchies." African Urban Notes,
6 (3), 1972, 43-55.
Suggests that the rate of urbanization in West Africa
may be less than often supposed, since figures are inflated
by town populations just crossing minimum thresholds and
since there has been some dispersal from small towns.

1.0.2 ALDOUS, J. "Urbanization, the extended family, and kinship
ties in West Africa." Social Forces, 41, 1962, 6-12.
Reprinted in Van den Berghe, P.L. (ed.), Africa: social
problems of change and conflict. Chandler, San Francisco,
1965, 107-116; and in Fava, S. (ed.), Urbanism in World
Perspective. Crowell, New York, 1968, 297-305.
Draws on earlier literature to show how the extended
family persists in the urban environment and the crucial
functions that it still performs.

1.0.3 ASIEDU, E.S. Public Administration in English-speaking West
Africa: an annotated bibliography. G.K. Hall, Boston,
1977, 365 pp.
A comprehensive listing of works on administration at
national and local levels, including areas such as health
and education, and with a brief section on housing and town
planning, but generally complementary to rather than over-
lapping the present volume for the five countries covered.

1.0.4 BARNES, S.T. and PEIL, M. "Voluntary association membership
in five West African cities." Urban Anthropology, 6 (1),
1977, 65-81.
Shows from surveys of ethnic, religious, financial, and
recreational associations in Lagos, Abeokuta, Aba, Kaduna,
and Tema that voluntary association behavior is more diverse
than often supposed.

31

1.0.5   CONDE, J. "Urbanization and migration in West Africa." In
        <u>Urbanization and Migration in Some Arab and African</u>
        <u>Countries</u>. Cairo Demographic Centre, 1973, 451-471.
           A broad review of the nature and distribution of urban
        development in West Africa and of the pattern of internal
        and international migration, noting the implications of
        both for development.

1.0.6   DENIEL, R. <u>Voix des Jeunes dans la Ville Africaine</u>. INADES,
        Abidjan, 1979, 344 pp.
           A collection of transcripts of discussions by students
        in Bamako, Ouagadougou, and Abidjan on a wide range of
        social and political issues.

1.0.7   ES' ANDAH, B.W. "An archaeological view of the urbanization
        process in the earliest West African states." <u>Journal of</u>
        <u>the Historical Society of Nigeria</u>, 8 (3), 1976, 1-20.
           Reviews evidence on the nature and extent of urban
        life in various parts of West Africa from the eighth to
        the eighteenth century and discusses factors affecting
        this early urbanization.

1.0.8   GELLAR, S. "West African capital cities as motors for
        development." <u>Civilisations</u>, 17, 1967, 254-262.
           Argues that most West African cities have been genera-
        tors of development both before and after independence,
        despite problems of overurbanization and increasing pri-
        macy of the national capitals.

1.0.9   GUGLER, J. and FLANAGAN, W.G. "On the political economy of
        urbanization in the Third World: the case of West Africa."
        <u>International Journal of Urban and Regional Research</u>, 1,
        1977, 272-292.
           Argues that with an excessive share of investment going
        to the capital cities the present pattern of urbanization
        in West Africa wastes scarce resources and intensifies
        inequality.

1.0.10 GUGLER, J. and FLANAGAN, W.G. <u>Urbanization and Social Change</u>
        <u>in West Africa</u>. Cambridge University Press, 1978, 235 pp.
           A wide-ranging study, with chapters on precolonial
        urbanism, the growth of the colonial capitals, rural-urban
        migration, other urban-rural relations, social relation-
        ships in town, the family and the position of women, and
        social stratification and mobility. Reviews and quotes
        extensively from much relevant literature, and includes
        a substantial bibliography. A version of chapter 4, on
        urban-rural ties, appeared in <u>African Perspectives</u>, 1978,
        No.1, 67-78.

1.0.11 HARRISON CHURCH, R.J. "Urban problems and economic development

in West Africa." Journal of Modern African Studies, 5,
1967, 511-520.
　　　Traces the growth of urban centers, notes a wide
variety of contemporary problems in specific cities, and
suggests that decentralization should figure largely in
development plans.

1.0.12　HARRISON CHURCH, R.J.　"The case for industrial and general
　　　　development of the smaller towns of West Africa."　In
　　　　CNRS, La Croissance Urbaine en Afrique Noire et à
　　　　Madagascar.　Paris, 1972, 659-665.
　　　　　Sketches the pattern of urban development in West
　　　　Africa and indicates the need for the development of the
　　　　administrative, commercial, and industrial functions of
　　　　the smaller towns.

1.0.13　HILLING, D.　"The evolution of the major ports of West
　　　　Africa."　Geographical Journal, 135, 1969, 365-378.
　　　　　Traces the development of the present pattern of ports,
　　　　especially within this century, and examines closely post-
　　　　1950 changes, including the opening of several new ports.

0.1.14　KAMIAN, B.　"Les villes dans les nouveaux états d'Afrique
　　　　occidentale."　Tiers-Monde, 4, 1963, 65-80.
　　　　　Outlines the rapid growth of cities in West Africa,
　　　　notes the sharp distinction between European and African
　　　　areas within most of them, but shows also the contrasting
　　　　city types of six subregions.

0.1.15　KUPER, H. (ed.) Urbanization and Migration in West Africa.
　　　　University of California Press, Berkeley, 1965, 227 pp.
　　　　　An interdisciplinary set of seminar papers, including
　　　　papers by Banton on Freetown, Schwab on Oshogbo, and Miner
　　　　on northern Nigeria, all noted elsewhere; and also "The
　　　　Location and Nature of West African cities" by B.E. Thomas;
　　　　"Some thoughts on migration and urban settlement" by
　　　　J.D. Fage; "Urbanism, migration and language" by J.H.
　　　　Greenberg; "Labor migration among the Mossi of the Upper
　　　　Volta" by E.P. Skinner; "Migration in West Africa, the
　　　　political perspective" by I. Wallerstein; and "The
　　　　economics of the migrant labor system" by E.J. Berg.

1.0.16　LE DIVELEC, M-H.　"Les 'nouvelles' classes sociales en
　　　　milieu urbain:　le cas du Sénégal et celui du Nigéria du
　　　　nord."　Civilisations, 17, 1967, 240-253.
　　　　　Discusses the extent to which the elites and the masses
　　　　in the cities of these areas have become distinct social
　　　　classes, in relation to traditional social structures and
　　　　present political activities.

1.0.17　LITTLE, K.L.　"West African urbanization as a social process."

Cahiers d'Etudes Africaines, 1 (3), 1960, 90-102. Reprinted in Hanna, W.J. (ed.), Independent Black Africa:
the politics of freedom. Rand McNally, Chicago, 1964,
137-148.
A broad review of the social changes involved in
contemporary rapid urbanization in West Africa.

*1.0.18   LITTLE, K.L.   "The West African town: its social basis."
Diogène, 29, 1960, 20-37.

1.0.19   LITTLE, K.L.   "Some traditionally based forms of mutual aid
in West African urbanization." Ethnology, 1, 1962,
197-211.
Drawing mainly on examples from Sierra Leone and Ghana,
reviews mutual benefit societies, occupational associations, and recreational associations, all with more specific aims than tribal unions.

1.0.20   LITTLE, K.L.   "The urban role of tribal associations in
West Africa." African Studies, 21, 1962, 1-9.
Discusses the nature and function of tribal unions in
various West African cities, showing how they serve to
adapt traditional institutions to urban conditions of life.

1.0.21   LITTLE, K.L.   West African Urbanization: a study of
voluntary associations in social change. Cambridge
University Press, 1965, 179 pp.
Discusses the ways in which voluntary associations
link old and new social structures and help migrants to
fit into urban communities. Individual chapters show
how the associations relate to the emerging class structures and to the position of women in the towns.

1.0.22   LLOYD, P.C.   Africa in Social Change. Penguin, London, 1967.
Chap. 4 "Urban life," 109-124; Chap. 8 "Urban associations,"
193-213.
Chapter 4 discusses the growth of towns, the position
of migrants, and urban employment, and chapter 8 examines
ethnic associations, trade unions, and elite organizations,
in each case confining the discussion to West Africa.

1.0.23   MABOGUNJE, A.L.   "Urbanization in West Africa." International
Review of Missions, 55, 1966, 298-306.
A very broad review of traditional and modern urbanism
in West Africa, noting the contrasts and discussing the
social problems in the contemporary cities.

1.0.24   MABOGUNJE, A.L.   "Migration and urbanization." In
Caldwell, J.C. (ed.), Population Growth and Socioeconomic
Change in West Africa. Columbia University Press, New
York, 1975, 153-168.

An examination of patterns of colonial labor migration
is followed by a broad review of patterns of urban development and of demographic structures in West African cities.

1.0.25 McNULTY, M.L. "West African Urbanization." In Berry,
B.J.L. (ed.), Urbanization and Counterurbanization. Sage,
Beverly Hills, Calif, 1976, 213-232.
Examines the evolution of the pattern of urban development in West Africa, with special reference to the colonial
legacy, and reviews issues involved in planning future
urbanization.

1.0.26 McNULTY, M.L. and HORTON, F.E. "West African urbanization:
patterns of convergence or divergence?" Pan-African
Journal, 9, 1976, 169-180.
Discusses Berry's thesis of divergent paths of
urbanization in developed and developing countries in
relation to West Africa, arguing that there is evidence
instead of convergence, with universal processes of increasing importance in this region.

1.0.27 MORGAN, W.B. and PUGH, J.C. West Africa. Methuen, London,
1969. Pp. 453-461, "The growth of urbanism."
Discusses the pattern of urban growth during this
century and colonial ideas on appropriate town layouts.
Numerous references to individual towns are found elsewhere in the book.

1.0.28 MORTON-WILLIAMS, P. "Some factors in the location, growth
and survival of towns in West Africa." In Ucko, P. et
al. (ed.), Man, Settlement and Urbanism. Duckworth,
London, 1972, 883-890.
Shows how over a long period trade has been the key
factor in the location and growth of towns in West Africa,
though political structures have also been influential.

1.0.29 OGUNDANA, B. "Seaport development: multi-national
co-operation in West Africa." Journal of Modern African
Studies, 12, 1974, 395-407.
Examines some of the problems of port development in
West Africa and the potential advantages of closer inter-
national co-ordination in this field.

1.0.30 OKEDIJI, F.O. "West African urbanization: a study of
voluntary association in social change." Nigerian Journal
of Economic and Social Studies, 8, 1966, 500-508.
A review article on the book by Little listed above.

1.0.31 OKEDIJI, O.O. "On voluntary associations as adaptive
mechanism in West African urbanization: another perspective."
African Urban Notes, B 1 (2), 1975, 51-74.

Reviews the literature on the role of associations in
African urbanization and suggests on the basis of a study
of domestic servants in Lagos that more attention must be
given to the social contexts in which this mechanism
operates.

1.0.32   PEIL, M. "The expulsion of West African aliens." Journal of
Modern African Studies, 9, 1971, 205–229.
Examines the economic, social, and political position
of African aliens in West African countries, especially
but not exclusively in the towns, and various attempts at
expulsion, notably from Ghana.

1.0.33   PEIL, M. "Social aspects of religion in West African towns."
African Urban Notes, B 1 (2), 1975, 95–104.
Presents and analyzes data on religious affiliation and
practice arising from social surveys in Accra, Aba,
Abeokuta, Kaduna, and Lagos, relating these data to other
social variables.

1.0.34   PEIL, M. "Social life in the burgeoning suburbs." In
Moss, R.P. and Rathbone, R.J.A. (eds.), The Population
Factor in African Studies. University of London Press,
1975, 171–178.
Reflects on demographic and attitude surveys in Madina
near Accra, Ashaiman near Tema, Kukuri and Makera near
Kaduna, and Ajegunle near Lagos, with respect to housing
and social relationships.

1.0.35   PEIL, M. "Female roles in West African towns." In Goody,
J. (ed.), Changing Social Structure in Ghana. International
African Institute, London, 1975, 73–90.
Examines how women in Aba, Abeokuta, Kaduna, Lagos, and
Accra coordinate their economic and other activities,
stressing the implications of their role as traders for
their marriages and social life.

1.0.36   PEIL, M. "Housing the poor in West Africa: public and private
provision." Institute of Development Studies Bulletin,
10 (4), 1979, 28–32.
Compares public and private housing in several West
African towns, with special reference to the physical and
social environment provided, the characteristics of the
residents, and their attitudes to the housing.

1.0.37   PEIL, M. "Urban women in the labor force." Sociology of
Work and Occupations, 6, 1979, 482–501.
Data from surveys in towns in Gambia, Ghana, and Nigeria
are used to show how local values and opportunities and
also factors such as marital status and education affect
women's participation in the labor force.

36

1.0.38 RAYFIELD, J.R. "Theories of urbanization and the colonial
city in West Africa." Africa, 44, 1974, 163-185.
Draws on a wide range of literature to trace phases in
the evolution of urbanism in West Africa and to show how
research on its cities may compel a rethinking of general
theories of urbanization.

1.0.39 REICHMANN, S. "The role of transportation in the urban
development of West Africa." In CNRS, La Croissance
Urbaine en Afrique Noire et à Madagascar. Paris, 1972,
971-983.
Shows how transport patterns have affected the location
of cities, spatial structures within them, and the development of interconnected urban systems.

1.0.40 RIDDELL, J.B. "The migration to the cities of West Africa:
some policy considerations." Journal of Modern African
Studies, 16, 1978, 241-260.
Notes the excessive rural-urban migration flows due
largely to poor income prospects in rural areas and reviews the range of actual and possible government responses.

1.0.41 SIMMS, R.P. Urbanization in West Africa: a review of the
current literature. Northwestern University Press,
Evanston, Ill., 1965, 109 pp.
A wide-ranging review of the 1950-1962 literature on
several aspects of West African urbanization, with a specific discussion of the methodological literature; a
comprehensive bibliography of 234 items from that period,
most briefly annotated; and an appended annotated list of
seventy items mainly from the period 1962-1964.

1.0.42 TABOURET-KELLER, A. "Language use in relation to the growth
of towns in West Africa: a survey." International
Migration Review, 5, 1971, 180-203.
Reviews the state of knowledge on language use in West
African cities, drawing widely on the existing literature,
and examining the diverse migrant groups in the cities of
each country in turn.

1.0.43 VERNIERE, M. "A propos de la marginalité: réflexions
illustrées par quelques enquêtes en milieu urbain et
suburbain africain." Cahiers d'Etudes Africaines, 13,
1973, 587-605.
Reviews the concept of marginality in the light of
studies of planned housing and spontaneous settlement in
Abidjan and Dakar, noting that areas with fewer physical
amenities may show greater social integration.

1.0.44 WHITE, H.P. "The morphological development of West African
seaports." In Hoyle, B.S. and Hilling, D. (eds.), Seaports

and Development in Tropical Africa. Macmillan, London, 1970, 11-25.
 Shows how both the nature of the coastline and the pattern of links with the hinterland have affected the process of port development from numerous small landing places to a few well-equipped modern ports.

1.0.45 WHITE, H.P. and GLEAVE, M.B. An Economic Geography of West Africa. Bell, London, 1971; Chap. 10 "Urbanisation," 258-294.
 A broad discussion of the patterns of urban growth, factors affecting these patterns, functions of selected cities, and the contrasting morphology of traditional and colonial cities.

1.0.46 WINDER, R.B. "The Lebanese in West Africa." Comparative Studies in Society and History, 4, 1962, 296-333. Reprinted in Fallers, L.A. (ed.), Immigrants and Associations. Mouton, The Hague, 1967, 103-153.
 A broad survey of the spread and present (largely urban) distribution of Lebanese in West Africa and of their economic activities, social isolation, and precarious political situation.

Note also the special number of Sociological Review, 7 (1), 1959, which included the following papers:

1.0.47 HARRISON CHURCH, R.J. "West African urbanisation: a geographical view," pp. 15-28.
BASCOM, W. "Urbanism as a traditional African pattern," pp. 29-43.
LLOYD, P.C. "The Yoruba town today," pp. 45-63.
LITTLE, K.L. "Some urban patterns of marriage and domesticity in West Africa," pp. 65-82.
FIAWOO, D.K. "Urbanisation and religion in eastern Ghana," pp. 83-97.
BAKER, T. and BIRD, M. "Urbanisation and the position of women." pp. 99-122.

Another earlier paper still of much use is:

1.0.48 DRESCH, J. "Villes d'Afrique occidentale." Cahiers d'Outre-Mer, 3, 1950, 200-230.

The main contribution in German is:

1.0.49 AVE-LALLEMANT, B. Struktur, Funktion und Genese der zentralen Orte in Nigeria, Ghana und Sierra Leone. Staatsarbeit, Freiburg, 1974.

An unpublished thesis much concerned with urbanization is:

1.0.50   ADAMS, J.G.U.   The Spatial Structure of the Economy of West
Africa.   Ph.D. thesis, University of London, 1970.

Note also:

1.0.51   NETTEY, R.J.T.   Building, Housing and Town Planning in
British West Africa: an annotated bibliography.
Fellowship of the Library Association thesis, London,
1975.

BENIN (formerly DAHOMEY)

General

101.0.1   AHOYO, J-R.   "Les marchés d'Abomey et de Bohicon."
Cahiers d'Outre-Mer, 28, 1975, 162-184.
Examines the contrasting origins of the markets in
the two towns, their present character and organization,
the goods handled, and the customers served.

101.0.2   COSTA, E.   "Back to the land: the campaign against
unemployment in Dahomey."   International Labour Review,
93 (1), 1966, 29-49.
Discusses the extent and nature of urbanization in
Benin, migration into its towns, employment problems
there, and prospects for alternative occupations in the
rural areas.

101.0.3   DAHOMEY.   Enquête Démographique au Dahomey 1961:   résultats
définitifs.   INSEE, Paris, 1964, 309 pp.
A detailed analysis of demographic characteristics,
education, occupations, migration, etc., based on sample
surveys, with data for the urban population distinguished
throughout.

101.0.4   GLELE, M.A.   "Le fait urbain au Dahomey."   In INCIDI, Urban
Agglomerations in the States of the Third World.   Brussels,
1971, 145-167.
A general review of the pattern of urban development,
the role of the towns in the national economy, and the
increasing dominance of Cotonou in the urban system.

101.0.5   MONDJANNAGNI, A.C.   Campagnes et Villes au Sud de la
République Populaire du Bénin.   Mouton, Paris, 1977,
615 pp.
A comprehensive geographical study of town and country

in the southern half of Benin, based on a 1975 University of Paris doctoral thesis. Pages 295-341 trace the evolution of the urban system from the traditional centers, such as Abomey, to the colonial foundations, including Cotonou. Pages 345-470 examine the relationships of each generation of towns with the countryside and present patterns of trade and money flows between urban and rural areas. Pages 529-536 make proposals for the future development of Cotonou and of the whole urban system.

101.0.6 MOREL, A. "Un exemple d'urbanisation en Afrique occidentale: Dassa-Zoumé (Dahomey moyen)." Cahiers d'Etudes Africaines, 14, 1974, 727-748.
A micro-study of a Yoruba community, numbering only 7500 (therefore not listed separately here), which stresses its real urban functions and discusses its relationship to larger urban centers.

Unpublished theses include:

101.0.7 ELEGBE, A. Aménagement et Urbanisation des Petites Villes du Centre-Dahomey: le cas de Save. Thèse 3e cycle, Université de Toulouse II, 1975.

Cotonou (Chief commercial center and port. Population estimate for 1975: 180,000.)

*101.1.1 DAHOMEY. Résultats provisoires du recensement de la ville de Cotonou." Bulletin de Statistique, 1 (1), 1964, 20-30.

*101.1.2 DAHOMEY. "Extraits des résultats définitifs du recensement de la ville de Cotonou." Bulletin de Statistique, 1 (2), 1964, 21-30.

101.1.3 HILLING, D. "Cotonou: Dahomey's new deep-water port." Bulletin of the Ghana Geographical Association, 11 (1), 1966, 64-70.
Discusses the establishment of the new port in the early 1960s, the level and pattern of port traffic, and future prospects.

101.1.4 JANIN, B. "Le nouveau port de Cotonou." Revue de Géographie Alpine, 52, 1964, 701-712.
An account of the origin and activities of the old wharf and the planning and construction of the new port that has replaced it.

101.1.5 MONDJANNAGNI, A. "Cotonou: some problems of port development in Dahomey." In Hoyle, B.S. and Hilling, D. (eds.),

Seaports and Development in Tropical Africa. Macmillan,
London, 1970, 147-166.
Discusses the physical characteristics of the coast,
early port development, the building of the new port in
1960-1965, the growth of traffic up to 1967, and the
prospective economic role of the port.

More was written on Cotonou before 1960, notably:

101.1.6 BRASSEUR-MARION, P. "Cotonou, porte de Dahomey." Cahiers
d'Outre-Mer, 6, 1953, 364-378.

101.1.7 LOMBARD, J. Cotonou, Ville Africaine. Etudes Dahoméennes
(10), Cotonou, 1953, 216 pp.

101.1.8 LOMBARD, J. "Cotonou, ville africaine." Bulletin de
l'IFAN, B 16, 1954, 341-377.

Unpublished theses include:

101.1.9 SACRAMENTO, L. Cotonou, Etude Urbaine, Thèse 3e cycle,
Université de Toulouse II, 1975.

101.1.10 SODOGANDJI, M. Le Développement Urbain en Afrique Noire:
l'exemple de Cotonou. Thèse 3e cycle, Université de
Paris, 1967.

Porto-Novo (Administrative capital and second town. Population
estimate for 1975: 105,000.)

101.2.1 TARDITS, C. "Parenté et classe sociale à Porto-Novo."
In Lloyd, P.C. (ed.), The New Elites of Tropical Africa.
Oxford University Press, London, 1966, 184-198.
Shows that education is the most important factor in
social differentiation today, but that strong kinship
ties hinder the development of a clear-cut class structure separating the educated elite from the mass.

Little else has been written on Porto-Novo since 1960. More substantial earlier works include:

101.2.2 BRASSEUR-MARION, P. and BRASSEUR, G. Porto-Novo et sa
Palmeraie. IFAN, Dakar, 1953, 132 pp.

101.2.3 TARDITS, C. Porto-Novo: les nouvelles générations
africaines entre leurs traditions et l'occident.
Mouton, Paris, 1958, 128 pp.

West Africa

THE GAMBIA

<u>Banjul</u> (The only urban center in the country is Banjul, the capital,
which spills over into adjacent Kombo St. Mary. Population
at the 1973 census: Banjul proper, 39,000; with Kombo St.
Mary, 78,000. Former name: Bathurst.)

102.1.1 CALDWELL, J.C. and THOMPSON, B. "Gambia." In Caldwell,
J.C. (ed.), <u>Population Growth and Socioeconomic Change
in West Africa</u>. Columbia University Press, New York,
1975, 493-526.
A review of the demographic characteristics of the
country as a whole, but with many references to the distinctive features of Banjul-Kombo St. Mary.

102.1.2 GAMBIA. <u>Population Census 1973: statistics for settlements
and enumeration areas</u>. 2 Vols. Central Statistical
Division, Banjul, 1974.
Volume 1 covers demographic characteristics and Volume
2 covers housing, with data for many enumeration areas
within Banjul-Kombo St. Mary.

102.1.3 PEIL, M. "Unemployment in Banjul: the farming/tourist
tradeoff." <u>Manpower and Unemployment Research</u>, 10 (1),
1977, 25-29.
Reports on a 1976 survey of employment and unemployment in the town, noting the large numbers who work for
a season in the tourist industry and for a season on
their farms in the vicinity.

*102.1.4 TYRWHITT, J. <u>Report on Town Planning for Bathurst and
Kombo St. Mary</u>, Gambia. Government Printer, Bathurst,
1963, 112 pp.

Earlier publications include:

102.1.5 JARRETT, H.R. "Bathurst, port of the Gambia River."
<u>Geography</u>, 36, 1951, 98-107.

102.1.6 VAN DER PLAS, C.O. <u>Report of a Socio-Economic Survey of
Bathurst and Kombo St. Mary in the Gambia</u>. United
Nations, New York, 1956.

Further, particularly earlier, references for the town may be
found in:

102.1.6a GAMBLE, D.P. <u>A General Bibliography of The Gambia up to
31 December 1977</u>. G.K. Hall, Boston, 1979, 266 pp.

West Africa

GHANA

General

103.0.1   ABLOH, F.A. Growth of Towns in Ghana. Faculty of
          Architecture, University of Science and Technology,
          Kumasi, 1967, 131 pp.
              A study of the origins, growth and changing physical
          form of selected Ghanaian towns, including Accra, Kumasi,
          Sunyani, and eleven smaller centers. (Mimeographed and
          not widely available.)

*103.0.2 ADDO, N.O. "Demographic aspects of manpower and employment
          in Ghana." Economic Bulletin of Ghana, 10 (3), 1966,
          3-34.

103.0.3   ADDO, N.O. "Spatial distribution and ecological patterns
          among foreign-origin populations in Ghana." Ghana
          Journal of Sociology, 4, 1968, 19-35.
              Analyzes 1960 census data on the regional distribution
          of non-Ghanaians, with some reference to the urban/rural
          distribution for each nationality.

103.0.4   ADDO, N.O. "Some demographic aspects of urbanization in
          Ghana 1931-1960." Ghana Social Science Journal, 1 (1),
          1971, 50-82.
              Reviews problems of urban definition, distribution of
          urban centers, and of urban growth, and also migration
          patterns, demographic structures, and educational levels
          for different size-groups of towns, drawing on the 1960
          and earlier censuses.

103.0.5   ADDO, N.O. "Urbanization, population and employment in
          Ghana." In Ominde, S.H. and Ejiogu, C.N. (eds.),
          Population Growth and Economic Development in Africa.
          Heinemann, London, 1972, 243-251.
              Examines past, present, and prospective rates of urban
          population growth, and also of employment opportunities,
          concluding that the latter are likely to continue to lag
          behind the former.

103.0.6   ANDOH, A.S.Y. "The social, economic and political role of
          urban agglomerations in the new states: Ghana." In
          INCIDI, Urban Agglomerations in the States of the Third
          World. Brussels, 1971, 180-192.
              A very general discussion of the role of Ghanaian
          towns as centers of economic and social change and of
          the problems arising from their failure to provide em-
          ployment for all those attracted to them.

43

103.0.7   BENING, R.B.   "Location of regional and provincial capitals
           in Northern Ghana, 1897-1960." Bulletin of the Ghana
           Geographical Association, 16, 1974, 54-66.
               With much reference to government documents, the
           paper traces the shift of regional headquarters from
           Kintampo through Gambaga to Tamale, various changes in
           provincial headquarters, and the choice of Bolgatanga
           as a new regional headquarters in 1960.

103.0.8   CALDWELL, J.C.   "Family formation and limitation in Ghana:
           a study of the residents of economically superior urban
           areas." In Berelson, B. et al. (eds.), Family Planning
           and Population Programs, University of Chicago Press,
           1966, 595-613.
               Reports on the results of 1962-1964 surveys of
           family planning attitudes and practices among high in-
           come groups in Accra, Kumasi, Takoradi, and Cape Coast.

103.0.9   CALDWELL, J.C.   "Fertility differentials as evidence of
           incipient fertility decline in a developing country:
           the case of Ghana." Population Studies, 21, 1967, 5-21.
               A detailed analysis of fertility patterns in Accra,
           Kumasi, Takoradi, and Cape Coast, based on 1960 census
           data.

103.0.10   CALDWELL, J.C.   "Migration and Urbanisation."   In
           Birmingham, W. et al. (eds.), A Study of Contemporary
           Ghana. Allen and Unwin, London, 1967, Vol. 2, 111-146.
               A broad review of internal and international migra-
           tion, an outline of the distribution and demographic
           structure of the urban population, an estimate of the
           extent of rural-urban movement 1948-1960, and a discus-
           sion of the nature of this migration, based on an ex-
           tensive 1963 survey.

103.0.11   CALDWELL, J.C.   "Determinants of rural-urban migration in
           Ghana." Population Studies, 22, 1968, 361-377.
               On the basis of 1962-1964 questionnaire surveys,
           the paper presents a broad review of rural-urban migra-
           tion in Ghana and identifies demographic, social, and
           economic factors influencing the propensity to move.

103.0.12   CALDWELL, J.C.   Population Growth and Family Change in
           Africa: the new urban elite in Ghana. Australian
           National University Press, Canberra, 1968, 222 pp.
               Presents the results of an extensive 1962-1964
           questionnaire survey of married couples in Accra,
           Kumasi, Takoradi, and Cape Coast. After a general dis-
           cussion of the urban elite, individual chapters examine
           awareness of population issues, changing family struc-
           tures, preferred family size, and family planning

practices. Concludes that in spite of increased pressures, little reduction in family size has yet occurred.

103.0.13 CALDWELL, J.C. African Rural-Urban Migration: the
movement to Ghana's towns. ANU Press, Canberra; Hurst,
London, 1969, 269 pp.
A study examining the type of people migrating to
the towns, the causes and nature of the movement, the
problems facing the migrants in town and their responses
to these, and the continuing links with the rural areas.
It shows the extent to which such migration in Ghana is
of a long-term yet not permanent nature, most migrants
carefully choosing an urban life, yet retaining strong
links with a rural home and anticipating an eventual
return. The study is based on extensive 1962-1964 surveys in Accra and other towns, as well as on census
data.

103.0.14 DARKO, S.A. "The effects of modern mining on settlements
in the mining areas of Ghana." Bulletin of the Ghana
Geographical Association, 8 (1), 1963, 21-31.
Drawing on a London M. A. thesis, the degree to
which mining has formed the basis for urban growth is
examined, with special reference to Bibiani.

103.0.15 DE GRAFT JOHNSON, K.T. "Population growth and rural-urban
migration, with special reference to Ghana."
International Labour Review, 109, 1974, 471-485.
Analyzes migration patterns using 1960 and 1970
census data, investigates rural-urban demographic and
educational differentials, discusses income differences
as a determinant of migration, and concludes that there
is a need to reduce migration through rural development
policies.

103.0.16 DICKSON, K.B. "Evolution of seaports in Ghana, 1800-1928."
Annals of the Association of American Geographers, 55,
1965, 98-111.
Traces the fluctuating fortunes of the many small
ports that were later eclipsed by the artificial deep-
water ports at Takordi and Tema.

103.0.17 DICKSON, K.B. A Historical Geography of Ghana. Cambridge
University Press, 1969, 379 pp.
Chapter 11, "The determinants of urban growth"
(pp. 239-265), discusses the fluctuating fortunes of
towns in selected parts of Ghana in the nineteenth and
early twentieth centuries in the context of political
and economic changes during this period. Chapter 12,
"Population and settlements," includes a section
(pp. 287-301) discussing the increasing number and size

of towns in the 1920s and 1930s and changes in the
physical form of a selection of them.

103.0.18 DICKSON, K.B. The Ghanaian Town: its nature and functions.
Ghana Universities Press, Accra, 1971, 17 pp.
Reviews political and commercial precolonial urban
origins, the colonial impetus for urban growth, and the
present economic role of the towns, taking Tarkwa,
Winneba, Tamale, and Accra as case studies.

103.0.19 DICKSON, K.B. "Generation and transmission of regional
growth impulses: Ghana." In Helleiner, F. and Stohr,
W.(eds.), Spatial Aspects of the Development Process.
Allister, Toronto for International Geographical Union,
1974, 259-287.
Explores the relationships between urban development
and Ghana's regional economies, concluding that most
towns have had very limited regional economic impact.

103.0.20 DICKSON, K.B. and BENNEH, G. A New Geography of Ghana.
Longman, London, 1970, 173 pp.
Includes a very brief general review of urban settlements (pp. 61-65), but also descriptions, and often maps,
of numerous individual towns within the "regional" chapters.

103.0.21 ENGMANN, E.V.T. "Some consequences of population movements
(Ghana)." In Ominde, S.H. and Ejiogu, C. (eds.),
Population Growth and Economic Development in Tropical
Africa. Heinemann, London, 1972, 173-187.
Wide-ranging discussion of migration in Ghana,
including, but not primarily focused on, rural-urban
migration.

103.0.22 EWUSI, K. "The growth rate of urban centres in Ghana,
and its implications for rural-urban migration."
Nigerian Journal of Economic and Social Studies, 16,
1974, 479-491.
Drawing on 1960 and 1970 census results, the paper
argues that rural-urban migration in Ghana is smaller
than often supposed and that there is no correlation
between town size and rate of growth.

103.0.23 EWUSI, K. "The towns of Ghana and their level of
development." Universitas, 6 (1), 1977, 156-169.
Discusses the value of population size, occupational
structure, and social amenities as alternative criteria
of urbanization in Ghana and suggests that there are
many "rural towns" to which development efforts might
be directed.

103.0.24 GARLICK, P.C. African Traders and Economic Development in

46

Ghana. Oxford University Press, London, 1971, 172 pp.
An intensive study of both the economic activities
and organization and the social background of traders
in Accra and Kumasi, with discussions of their problems
and of government policies affecting them. Based in
part on a 1962 London doctoral thesis.

103.0.25 GHANA. 1960 Population Census of Ghana. Special Report A:
Statistics of Towns. Accra, 1964, 267 pp.
Includes data on demographic characteristics, education, occupations, and birthplace for the population of
each town, and some data on each of these for enumeration areas within the larger towns.

103.0.26 GHANA. 1970 Population Census of Ghana. Vol. 2,
Statistics of localities and enumeration areas. Accra,
1972.
Includes data on age, birthplace, education, and
employment for the population of towns and also some
data for areas within towns. (Special Report A:
Statistics of large towns is still awaited.)

103.0.27 GHANA. 1970 Population Census of Ghana. Vol. 3,
Demographic Characteristics. Accra, 1975, 345 pp.
Provides detailed demographic data for the urban
population as a whole and for each town.

103.0.28 GHANA. 1970 Population Census of Ghana. Special Report
D. Accra. 7 vols. 1971.
Provides data on the population in 1948, 1960, and
1970, and the number of houses in 1970, for small
localities within each town (e.g., about 700 within
Greater Accra).

103.0.29 GROVE, D. and HUSZAR, L. The Towns of Ghana: the role
of service centres in regional planning. Ghana
Universities Press, Accra, 1964, 98 pp.
After a general discussion of central place theory,
the study assembles much information on the hierarchy
of towns in Ghana in terms of the functions performed
by each of 258 centers. In the light of the analysis,
proposals for investment in new or upgraded centers are
made. Many maps and diagrams supplement the text.

103.0.30 GROVE, D. and HUSZAR, L. "Towards a regional plan for
service centres in Ghana." Economic Bulletin of Ghana,
9 (2), 1965, 14-26.
Summarizes the study noted above, proposing a carefully planned comprehensive hierarchy of service centers
throughout the country.

103.0.31 HART, J.K. "Migration and the opportunity structure: a
          Ghanaian case study." In Amin, S. (ed.), <u>Modern
          Migration in Western Africa</u>. Oxford University Press,
          London, 1974, 321-339.
              Considers the economic alternatives open to the
          Frafra of NE Ghana, within their homelands, in the
          local town of Bolgatanga, and in the cities of the
          south, and discusses the changing pattern of migration
          in response to these opportunities.

*103.0.32 HILL, P. <u>The Occupations of Migrants in Ghana</u>. Museum
          of Anthropology, University of Michigan, Ann Arbor,
          1970, 82 pp.

103.0.33 HILLING, D. "Port development and economic growth: the
          case of Ghana." In Hoyle, B.S. and Hilling, D. (eds.),
          <u>Seaports and Development in Tropical Africa</u>. Macmillan,
          London, 1970, 127-145.
              Describes the ports of Takoradi and Tema, examines
          their traffic patterns, and discusses their role in
          assisting economic growth since the 1940s.

103.0.34 HUNTER, J.M. "An exercise in applied geography.
          Geographical planning in urban areas for the 1960
          census of Ghana." <u>Geography</u>, 46, 1961, 1-8.
              Describes some of the processes involved in the
          delimitation of enumeration areas that provided the
          framework for data collection in the census.

103.0.35 KNIGHT, J.B. "Rural-urban income comparisons and migration
          in Ghana." <u>Bulletin of the Oxford University Institute
          of Economics and Statistics</u>, 34, 1972, 199-228.
              Analyzes factors influencing migration rates, follow-
          ing up the Caldwell study noted above. Stresses the
          problems of measurement.

103.0.36 KUDIABOR, C.D.K. "Urbanization and growth pole strategy
          for regional development in Ghana." In Mabogunje, A.L.
          and Faniran, A. (eds.), <u>Regional Planning and National
          Development in Tropical Africa</u>. Ibadan University
          Press, 1977, 86-92.
              Describes the official designation of a hierarchy of
          growth poles, growth centers, and growth points to
          assist in regional development in Ghana, stressing the
          planned role of the thirty-nine growth points as ser-
          vice centers.

103.0.37 McNULTY, M.L. "Urban structure and development: the urban
          system of Ghana." <u>Journal of Developing Areas</u>, 3, 1969,
          159-176.
              Uses a multivariate analysis of urban attributes to

show patterns of similarity and diversity among Ghanaian towns. Draws especially on 1960 census data on birth-place and occupations. Shows towns to be diverse without falling into clear groups.

103.0.38 PEIL, M. The Ghanaian Factory Worker. Cambridge University Press, 1972, 254 pp.
A wide-ranging sociological study of workers in factories in Accra, Kumasi, and Takoradi. After an introduction on the extent of urbanization and industrial development in Ghana, individual chapters consider occupations, including occupational mobility and unemployment, job satisfaction, migration to the towns, urban living conditions and attitudes to these, and household structures and continuing ties with rural homes.

103.0.39 POLEMAN, T.T. "The food economies of urban middle Africa: the case of Ghana." Food Research Institute Studies, 2 (2), 1961, 121-174.
A detailed analysis of food consumption patterns in Accra, Kumasi, and Takoradi, based on household budget surveys. Reviews the resulting diets and discusses the flows of foodstuffs from rural areas.

103.0.40 PRUSSIN, I. Architecture in Northern Ghana. University of California Press, Berkeley, 1970, 120 pp.
Includes examples of indigenous building styles within the towns of the north.

103.0.41 REMY, M. Ghana Today. Jeune Afrique, Paris, 1977, 255 pp.
Includes lavishly illustrated descriptions of twenty-eight towns (pp. 104-206), stressing features of tourist interest.

103.0.42 SIMMS, R. and DUMOR, E. "Women in the urban economy of Ghana: associational activity and the enclave economy." African Urban Notes, B 2 (3), 1976, 43-64.
Discusses the dependency that characterizes the urban economy in Ghana, assesses women's role in this economy, and examines their participation in mutual aid societies in this context.

103.0.43 SONGSORE, J. "Towards building a model of urban growth dynamics: the case of the 'large' Northern Ghanaian towns." Universitas, 6 (1), 1977, 114-127.
Discusses briefly the growth and 1960 occupation structure of Bawku, Bolgatanga, Tamale, Wa, and Yendi, but is mainly concerned to formulate a model of administrative and commercial linkages to assist regional planning.

103.0.44 WUNSCH, J.S. "Voluntary associations and structural
          development in West African urbanization." Journal of
          African Studies, 5, 1978, 79-102.
              Reports on a quantitative analysis of relationships
          between voluntary associations and development, based
          on data from Obuasi and Techiman in central Ghana.

103.0.45 WUNSCH, J.S. "Political development and planning in Ghana:
          a comparative study of two medium cities." In Obudho,
          R.A. and El-Shakhs, S. (eds.), Development of Urban
          Systems in Africa. Praeger, New York, 1979, 137-156.
              Examines the relationship between urbanization and
          the development of political institutions in Ghana, with
          special reference to Obuasi and Techiman.

103.0.46 YANNOULIS, U. and BOSTOCK, M. "Urban household income and
          expenditure patterns in Ghana." Economic Bulletin of
          Ghana, 7 (3), 1963, 12-18.
              Drawing on household budget surveys in Accra, Kumasi,
          and Takoradi, the paper relates food expenditure pat-
          terns to total household incomes.

Notable items published before 1960 include:

103.0.47 ABRAMS, C. Housing in Ghana. United Nations, New York,
          1954, 220 pp.

Works in German include:

103.0.48 LUHRING, J. Urbanisierung und Entwicklungsplanung in
          Ghana. Institut für Afrika-Kunde, Hamburg, 1976,
          212 pp.

Unpublished theses include:

103.0.49 ADDO, N.O. Dymanics of Urban Growth in South-eastern
          Ghana. Ph.D. thesis, University of London, 1969.

103.0.50 AMOAH, F.E.K. The Growth and Decline of Seaports in Ghana,
          1800-1962. Ph.D. thesis, University of California, Los
          Angeles, 1969.

103.0.51 BOAMAH-WIAFE, D. The Pattern and Correlates of Urbanbound
          Migration in Ghana. Ph.D. thesis, University of
          Wisconsin, 1978.

103.0.52 GARLICK, P.C. The Ghanaian Entrepreneur: studies of
          trading in Ghana. Ph.D. thesis, University of London,
          1962.

103.0.53 HILLING, D. The Development of the Ghanaian Port System.
          Ph.D. thesis, University of London, 1974.

103.0.54 McNULTY, M.L. Urban Centers and the Spatial Pattern of
          Development in Ghana. Ph.D. thesis, Northwestern
          University, Evanston, Ill., 1966.

103.0.55 MATTHEWSON, M.A. Southern Ghanian Women: urban residence
          and migrational cycles. Ph.D. thesis, University of
          Rochester, New York, 1973.

103.0.56 SANJEK, R. Ghanaian Networks: an analysis of inter-ethnic
          relations in urban situations. Ph.D. thesis, Columbia
          University, New York, 1972.

103.0.57 TACKIE, E.A. Spatial Aspects of Urban Development in
          Selected Regions of Ghana. Ph.D. thesis, Cambridge
          University, 1975.

103.0.58 WUNSCH, J.S. Voluntary Associations: determinants of
          associational structure and activity in two Ghanaian
          cities. Ph.D. thesis, Indiana University, 1974.

Many shorter theses on urban topics have been prepared for M.Sc.
degrees in architecture, urban planning, and regional planning at
the University of Science and Technology, Kumasi.

Accra (Capital city. Population at 1970 census: 850,000 including
        634,000 in city proper and 103,000 in the port and industrial
        satellite of Tema.)

103.1.1 ADDO, N.O. "Demographic and socio-economic aspects of
          Madina, an Accra suburb." Ghana Journal of Sociology,
          2 (2), 1966, 1-7.
              Presents the results of a 1966 survey of this new
          peripheral settlement, providing information on demo-
          graphic structure, duration of stay and areas of origin,
          and economic activities.

103.1.2 ADDO, N.O., QUARCOO, A.K. and PEIL, M. The Madina Survey.
          Institute of African Studies, University of Ghana,
          Accra, 1967, 124 pp.
              Presents the history of the settlement and a fuller
          report of the survey mentioned above.

103.1.3 AMARTEIFIO, G.W.; BUTCHER, D.A.P.; and WHITHAM, D. Tema
          Manhean: a Study of Resettlement. Ghana Universities
          Press, Accra, 1966, 97 pp.
              Presents the results of a detailed architectural and
          sociological survey of the community established for the
          people moved from the old Tema fishing village and now a
          suburb of new Tema.

103.1.4 AZU, D.G. The Ga Family and Social Change.

Afrika-Studiecentrum, Leiden, Netherlands, 1974, 137 pp.
A detailed examination of social organization, family
structures, and residential patterns among the Ga in
Labadi, an old settlement now incorporated within Accra,
with a focus on contrasts between two localities that
have experienced different degrees of European influence.

103.1.5 BANNERMAN, J.Y. The Cry for Justice in Tema (Ghana). Tema
Industrial Mission, Accra, 1973, 75 pp.
A brief outline of social conditions in Tema, noting
the role of the churches, the development of civic
consciousness, and the activities of the Tema Welfare
Association.

103.1.6 BERKOH, D.K. "Perception, migration and urban primacy in
Ghana." Bulletin of the Ghana Geographical Association,
17, 1975, 80-95.
A discussion of how the rate of migration to Accra
is affected by people's perception of it, especially
in relation to other centers.

103.1.7 BOBO, B.F. "Population density, housing demand and land
values: Accra." Journal of African Studies, 4, 1977,
140-160.
Shows how land values fall outwards from the center,
but faster in some directions, (e.g., into the high-
density inner residential areas of James Town and Ussher
Town) than in others (e.g., the low-density fashionable
suburbs).

103.1.8 BOBO, B.F. "Some observations on orderly development in
an emerging city." Annals of Regional Science, 11,
1977, 86-97.
Shows that there is more order in migration and
settlement processes and also more upward social and
economic mobility in Accra than is often presumed to
be the case in cities of less developed countries.

103.1.9 BRAND, R.R. A Selected Bibliography on Accra 1877-1960.
Council of Planning Librarians, Monticello, Illinois,
Exchange Bibliography 242, 1971, 27 pp.
A wide-ranging bibliography, including many items
not specific to Accra or even Ghana, but complementary
to the present list in its coverage of pre-1960 items
on the city.

103.1.10 BRAND, R.R. "The role of cocoa in the growth and spatial
organization of Accra prior to 1921." African Studies
Review, 15, 1972, 271-282.
Shows how the cocoa trade boosted the prosperity of
Accra in the early twentieth century and discusses its
impact on the physical growth of the city during that
period.

103.1.11 BRAND, R.R. "The spatial organization of residential areas
in Accra." Economic Geography, 48, 1972, 284-296.
Shows the city's diversity in terms of residential
density, ethnic and demographic structures, and various
components of modernization and suggests that no single
model of urban social morphology fits Accra at all
closely.

103.1.12 CLIGNET, R. and SWEEN, J. "Accra and Abidjan: a
comparative examination of the notion of increase in
scale." Urban Affairs Quarterly, 4, 1969, 297-324.
Examines the extent and nature of social differentiation in the two cities and compares the patterns with
those in Rome and San Francisco to test the Shevky and
Bell theory of increase in scale.

103.1.13 DINAN, C. "Socialization in an Accra suburb: the Zongo
and its distinct sub-culture." In Oppong, C. (ed.),
Changing Family Studies. Institute of African Studies,
University of Ghana, Accra, 1975, 45-62.
Examines the ways in which the children of the Zongo
area are trained in the values and behavior patterns of
their community.

103.1.14 DINAN, C. "Pragmatists or feminists? The professional
'single' women of Accra, Ghana." Cahiers d'Etudes
Africaines, 17, 1977, 155-176.
Considers whether modernization and movement to town
have improved or worsened women's status. Concludes
that the women of Accra are very independent of men and
very confident in their major economic roles.

103.1.15 DOXIADIS ASSOCIATES. "The town of Tema, Ghana: plans for
two communities." Ekistics, 77, 1962, 159-171.
Outlines the master plan for the expansion of Tema
prepared by Doxiadis Associates in 1961-1962, with
detailed proposals for two neighborhoods.

103.1.16 GRINDAL, B.T. "Islamic affiliations and urban adaptation:
the Sisala migrant in Accra." Africa, 43, 1973, 333-346.
Suggests that for Sisala migrants in the Mamobi
area of Accra, Islam assists in the process of adjustment to urban life.

103.1.17 HART, K. "Informal income opportunities and urban
employment in Ghana." Journal of Modern African
Studies, 11, 1973, 61-89.
Investigates the nature of informal sector activities,
with special reference to the Nima district of Accra,
and suggests that they can offer an attractive alternative to formal sector employment.

103.1.18 HARVEY, M.E. and BRAND, R.R. "The spatial allocation of
          migrants in Accra." Geographical Review, 64, 1974, 1-30.
          Investigates the complex distributions of recent and
          less recent migrants, observing contrasts between some
          central areas that can accommodate few new migrants and
          some peripheral areas where such people predominate.

103.1.19 HILLING, D. "Tema: the geography of a new port."
          Geography, 51, 1966, 111-125.
          Examines the location, construction, and emerging
          traffic patterns of the new port and also the industrial
          development associated with it.

103.1.20 JOPP, K. Ghana's New Town and Harbour: Tema. Ministry
          of Information, Accra, 1961, 52 pp.
          A profusely illustrated account of the planning,
          design, and early phases of construction of the new
          town and port.

103.1.21 KILSON, M.D. "The Ga and non-Ga populations of central
          Accra." Ghana Journal of Sociology, 2 (2), 1966, 23-28.
          Draws on 1960 census data to show differences in
          demographic structure, education, and occupations be-
          tween Ga and other residents in the city center.

103.1.22 KILSON, M.D. "Continuity and change in the Ga residential
          system." Ghana Journal of Sociology, 3, 1967, 81-97.
          Analyzes the results of surveys in central Accra
          investigating which family members live together as
          households in more traditional and more modern Ga
          communities.

103.1.23 KILSON, M.D. "Variations in Ga culture in central Accra."
          Ghana Journal of Sociology, 3, 1967, 33-54.
          Discusses variations in adherence to traditional Ga
          culture, with a statistical analysis of surveys relat-
          ing knowledge of traditional ritual to age, education,
          etc.

103.1.24 KILSON, M. African Urban Kinsmen: the Ga of Central
          Accra. Hurst, London, 1974, 122 pp.
          A study of the continuing relevance of traditional
          kinship conceptions and institutions for the long-
          settled Ga community around whom the city has grown.
          Individual chapters provide the historical background,
          examine these conceptions, and discuss their relation-
          ship to residential patterns and the ceremonies of the
          lifecycle.

103.1.25 KIRCHHERR, E.C. "Tema 1951-1962: the evolution of a
          planned city in West Africa." Urban Studies, 5, 1968,

207-217. Reprinted in Ekistics 27, 1969, 228-239.
Traces the growth of Tema from a fishing settlement
to a major port and industrial area, with special reference to planning procedures and problems.

103.1.26 KONINGS, P. "Political consciousness and political action
of industrial workers in Ghana: a case study of Valco
workers at Tema." African Perspectives, 1978, No. 2,
69-82.
Reports on a 1975 survey among workers at the Tema
aluminium smelter, providing data both on their socio-
economic characteristics and on their political attitudes.

103.1.27 KUMEKPOR, T.K. "Mothers and wage labour employment: some
aspects of problems of the working mother in Accra."
Ghana Journal of Sociology, 7 (2), 1974, 68-91.
Analyzes the results of 1969-70 questionnaire
surveys covering reasons for seeking employment, the
incomes obtained, and methods of arranging for the care
of children.

103.1.28 LAWSON, R.M. "The supply response of retail trading
services to urban population growth in Ghana." In
Meillasoux, C. (ed.), The Development of Indigenous
Trade and Markets in West Africa. Oxford University
Press, London, 1971, 377-398.
Examines the theory that retail services lag when
population increases quickly and shows that these services have kept up with demand better in Accra than in
the rural Lower Volta area.

103.1.29 McELRATH, D.C. "Societal scale and social differentiation."
In Greer, S. et al. (eds.), The New Urbanization. St.
Martin's Press, New York, 1968, 33-52.
Analyzes the covariation of many attributes of the
population for the 314 subareas of Accra distinguished
in the 1960 census and compares the resulting patterns
of social differentiation with those in Kingston
(Jamaica), Rome, and some cities in the United States.

103.1.30 NYAPAN, A. Market Trade: a sample survey of market
traders in Accra. University College of Ghana, Accra,
1960, 78 pp.
Presents the results of a survey investigating who
is involved in the market trade and what are the levels
of capital and annual turnover involved.

103.1.31 NYAPAN, A. "Market trade in Accra." The Economic Bulletin
(Ghana), 4, 1960, 7-16.
A summary of the report noted above.

103.1.32   OPPONG, C. "A note on matriliny and marriage in Accra."
           Journal of Asian and African Studies, 7, 1972, 211-218.
             Examines aspects of the economic rights and obliga-
           tions between Akan senior civil servants and their wives
           and kin, showing the persistence of traditional behavior
           patterns.

103.1.33   OPPONG, C. "Attitudes to family size among unmarried
           junior civil servants in Accra." Journal of Asian and
           African Studies, 9, 1974, 76-82.
             Examines the extent of the reduction in the preferred
           family size among one sector of the urban population.

103.1.34   OPPONG, C. Marriage Among a Matrilineal Elite: a family
           study of Ghanaian senior civil servants. Cambridge
           University Press, 1974, 187 pp.
             The published version of a Cambridge thesis based on
           1967-1968 fieldwork in Accra, which studied the relative
           strength of marriage compared with other kinship ties
           and the extent of joint or separate decision-making,
           financial affairs, etc. The emphasis throughout is on
           the extent of shift away from traditional patterns in
           the urban environment.

103.1.35   OPPONG, C. "A study of domestic continuity and change:
           Akan senior service families in Accra." In Goody, J.
           (ed.), Changing Social Structures in Ghana. International
           African Institute, London, 1975, 181-200.
             Examines the degree to which the contrasting tradi-
           tional behavior of different ethnic groups persists in
           town, especially with regard to family relationships.

103.1.36   OPPONG, C. "An explanatory note on financial constraint
           and desired family size: analysis of data from a pilot
           study of male clerical officers in Accra." Canadian
           Journal of African Studies, 10, 1976, 403-408.
             Reports on a survey of desired family size among
           this group, distinguishing subgroups according to ethnic
           origin, migration status, and financial situation.

103.1.37   PEIL, M. "Factory management and workers in the Accra
           capital district." Economic Bulletin of Ghana, 10,
           1966, 23-35.
             Reports on a 1965 survey on the characteristics of
           management and workers in seventy-three manufacturing
           firms, revealing features such as low labor turnover.

103.1.38   PEIL, M. "Reactions to estate housing: a survey of Tema."
           Ghana Journal of Sociology, 4, 1968, 1-18.
             Presents the results of a 1963 questionnaire provid-
           ing information on density of occupation, household

composition, etc., but especially on attitudes to the housing provided on the early Tema estates.

103.1.39 PEIL, M. "Unemployment in Tema: the plight of the skilled worker." Canadian Journal of African Studies, 3, 1969, 409-419.
Presents the results of a survey of the extent and nature of unemployment among the residents of two sections of Tema and those of the neighboring settlement of Ashaiman.

103.1.40 PEIL, M. "The apprenticeship system in Accra." Africa, 40, 1970, 137-150.
Investigates patterns of recruitment, training, earnings, etc., contrasting traditional industries with those newly established.

103.1.41 PEIL, M. "Ghana's aliens." International Migration Review, 8, 1974, 367-381.
Indicates the large number of aliens in Ghana, especially in the towns, in the 1960s, discusses the pressures for the 1969 expulsions, and reports on a 1970 survey of attitudes to aliens in the suburb of Ashaiman.

103.1.42 PEIL, M. "Men's Lib? The effects of marriage on the social life of men in Ashaiman." In Oppong, C. (ed.), Changing Family Studies. Institute of African Studies, University of Ghana, Accra, 1975, 22-28.
Discusses the results of an enquiry in the suburb of Ashaiman that indicated the ways in which marriage constrains men's social life.

103.1.43 PEIL, M. "Demographic changes in a Ghanaian suburb." Ghana Social Science Journal, 3 (1), 1976, 63-78.
Discusses the results of two sample censuses in Ashaiman, covering origins, education, and occupations, as well as demography, and compares the results with 1960 official census data on Nima.

103.1.44 PEIL, M. "Host reactions: aliens in Ghana." In Shack, W.A. and Skinner, E.P. (eds.), Strangers in African Societies. University of California Press, Berkeley, 1979, 123-140.
Examines relations between aliens and their host communities in Ghana and factors reducing tolerance and leading to the 1969 expulsions, incorporating findings from an enquiry in Tema and Ashaiman, and expanding on the 1974 paper.

103.1.45 PELLOW, D. Women in Accra: options for autonomy.

Reference Publications, Algonac, Michigan, 1977, 272 pp.
An intensive study of the lives of women in the
Adabraka neighborhood of Accra, making use of extensive
quotations from interviewees. Includes a background
discussion of Adabraka and its people, but mainly
sharply focused on women's social relationships and the
extent of their autonomy or subservience to men.

103.1.46 PELLOW, D. "Work and autonomy: women in Accra."
American Ethnologist, 5, 1978, 770-785.
Examines the factors influencing the work options
of nonelite Accra women and limiting the extent of their
autonomy.

103.1.47 PFISTER, F. "Historical development of Tema (Ghana)."
Planification Habitat Information, 89, 1977, 63-72.
A brief account of the planning and physical develop-
ment of Tema. In French and English.

103.1.48 QUARCOO, A.K. "Social control in Madina." Ghana Journal
of Sociology, 2 (2), 1966, 8-14.
Discusses how law and order is maintained in a new
peripheral settlement, with special reference to the
role of a village chief installed in 1964.

103.1.49 REUSSE, E. and LAWSON, R.M. "The effect of economic
development on metropolitan food marketing: a case
study of food retail trade in Accra." East African
Journal of Rural Development, 2 (1), 1969, 35-55.
Describes the structure of retail trade in local
and imported foodstuffs, based on an extensive survey
of shops, market stalls, and hawkers, and shows how new
channels of trade have developed.

103.1.50 ROBERTSON, C. "Economic woman in Africa: profit-making
techniques of Accra market women." Journal of Modern
African Studies, 12, 1974, 657-664.
Explores factors contributing to the commercial
success of many Ga market women, including the apprenticeship system and specific techniques of marketing.

103.1.51 ROBERTSON, C. "Ga women and change in marketing conditions
in the Accra area." Rural Africana, 29, 1975/6, 157-171.
Discusses how twentieth century changes in supply
conditions of imports and in transport have affected
Accra market women and considers implications for the
whole rural-urban market network.

103.1.52 ROBERTSON, C. "Change in the organization of the fish
trade in twentieth-century Accra." African Urban Notes,
B 2 (2), 1976, 43-58.

       Shows how the fish trade in Ussher Town, central
Accra, has changed as a result of technological and
social factors, drawing on 1971-1972 interviews with
Ga women traders.

103.1.53 ROBERTSON, C. "Ga women and socioeconomic change in
       Accra, Ghana." In Hafkin, N.J. and Bay, E.G. (eds.),
       Women in Africa. Stanford University Press, 1976,
       111-133.
       Examines twentieth century changes in the socio-
economic status of Ga women in Ussher Town, long-settled
and largely engaged in trade, drawing on an intensive
questionnaire survey.

103.1.54 SANDBROOK, R. and ARN, J. The Labouring Poor and Urban
       Class Formation: the case of Greater Accra. Centre
       for Developing-Area Studies, McGill University, Montreal,
       1977, 86 pp.
       A study of the origins of the laboring poor, their
place in the urban economy, their social relationships,
and especially their political orientation, based on
surveys in Nima and Ashaiman.

103.1.55 SANJEK, R, and L.M. "Notes on women and work in Adabraka."
       African Urban Notes, B 2 (2), 1976, 1-26.
       Reports on studies of wage-employed and self-employed
women in this district of Accra, relating occupations
to age and education; considers seven specific cases of
women who have moved between wage- and self-employment.

103.1.56 STEEL, W.F. "Development of the urban artisanal sector in
       Ghana and Cameroun." Journal of Modern African Studies,
       17, 1979, 271-284.
       A comparative study of the structure and composition
of small-scale industry and services in Accra and
Yaoundé, based on 1973 and 1976 surveys, stressing the
similarities between the two cities.

103.1.57 TUCEY, M.L. "Ga concepts of neighbourhood in central
       Accra: a cognitive-behavioural approach." Journal of
       the Geographical Association of Tanzania, 14, 1976,
       37-78.
       Reports on a study of how Ga people in the long-
settled Ussher Town area identify with local neighborhoods and what factors affect their perceptions and their
spatial activity patterns.

103.1.58 WEINBERG, S.K. "Urbanization and male delinquency in
       Ghana." Journal of Research in Crime and Delinquency,
       2 (2), 1965, 85-94. Reprinted in Meadows, P. and
       Mizruchi, E.H. (eds.), Urbanism, Urbanization and Change.

Addison-Wesley, Reading, Mass., 1969, 368-379.
    Examines the effects of urbanization on the extent
and nature of delinquency on the basis of studies of
boys in an Accra remand school.

Notable items published before 1960 include:

103.1.59 ACQUAH, I. Accra Survey: a social survey of the capital
    of Ghana. University of London Press, 1958, 176 pp.

103.1.60 BOATENG, E.A. "The growth and functions of Accra."
    Bulletin of the Ghana Geographical Association, 4 (2),
    1959, 4-15.

103.1.61 GHANA. "Ministry of Housing." Accra: a plan for the
    town. Government Printer, Accra, 1958, 137 pp.

Unpublished theses include:

103.1.62 AUWERTER, J.P. The Role of Migrant Attributes in Successful
    Relocation in Accra, Ghana. Ph.D. thesis, Clark
    University, Worcester, Mass., 1976.

103.1.63 BERKOH, D.K. Urban Primacy in a Developing Country, Ghana:
    a case study of Accra-Tema metropolitan area. Ph.D.
    thesis, Columbia University, New York, 1974.

103.1.64 BOBO, B.F. Economic Factors Influencing Migration, and
    Urban Growth and Structure: Accra, Ghana. Ph.D. thesis,
    University of California, Los Angeles, 1974.

103.1.65 BRAND, R.R. A Geographical Interpretation of the European
    Influence on Accra since 1877. Ed.D. thesis, Columbia
    University, New York, 1971.

103.1.66 ERLICH, H. Accra, Ghana: politics in an African city as
    illustrated by a comparison of two neighborhoods.
    Ph.D. thesis, Northwestern University, Evanston, Ill.,
    1973.

103.1.67 GEZANN, G.A. Place Utility and the Spatial Dynamics of
    Migration in the Low-Income Communities of Accra, Ghana.
    Ph.D. thesis, Kent State University, Ohio, 1976.

103.1.68 HAMILTON, R.S. Urban Social Differentiation and Membership
    Recruitment among Selected Voluntary Associations in
    Accra, Ghana. Ph.D. thesis, Northwestern University,
    Evanston, Ill., 1966.

103.1.69 HART, K. Frafra Entrepreneurs in Accra. Ph.D. thesis,
    Cambridge University, 1970.

<u>Bawku</u> (Town in the extreme northeast. Population in 1970: 21,000.)

103.2.1 BENNEH, G. "Bawku, une ville marché du Ghana du Nord."
         <u>Cahiers d'Outre-Mer</u>, 27, 1974, 168-182.
             Examines the origins and growth of the town, its
         physical structure, and especially its role as a market
         center for the surrounding area.

<u>Cape Coast</u> (Fifth town of Ghana and headquarters of Central Region.
             Population in 1970: 52,000 [Municipality 71,000] .)

103.3.1 HINDERINK, J. and STERKENBURG, J. <u>Anatomy of an African</u>
         <u>Town: a socio-economic study of Cape Coast, Ghana</u>.
         Geographical Institute, University of Utrecht, Netherlands,
         1975, 344 pp.
             Sets Cape Coast in its context of the Ghanaian urban
         system and the Ghanaian economy, then provides a compre-
         hensive survey of the town's economy, sector by sector;
         discusses the population in terms of employment and in-
         come; and ends with an analysis of the patterns of land
         use and housing.

103.3.2 HINDERINK, J. and STERKENBURG, J. "Income inequality under
         changing urban conditions in tropical Africa: a case
         study of Cape Coast, Ghana." <u>Tijdschrift voor Economische</u>
         <u>en Sociale Geografie</u>, 69, 1978, 46-57.
             Reviews the evolution of the urban economy of Cape
         Coast from the seventeenth century and considers the
         consequences of changes for the distribution of incomes
         among the population.

103.3.3 MANSVELT-BECK, J. and STERKENBURG, J. <u>The Fishing Industry</u>
         <u>in Cape Coast, Ghana</u>. Geographical Institute, University
         of Utrecht, Netherlands, 1976, 60 pp.
             Examines the fishing industry as a sector of the urban
         economy, providing a detailed account of the production,
         marketing, and distribution of fish, and discussing the
         social and economic characteristics of the fishermen
         and fish traders.

103.3.4 PACHAI, B. "An outline of the history of municipal
         government at Cape Coast." <u>Transactions of the Historical</u>
         <u>Society of Ghana</u>, 8, 1965, 130-160.
             An account of the structure and activity of the
         municipal council from its orgin in 1858 up to 1965.

Unpublished theses include:

103.3.5 BART, F. Cape Coast, Ghana: étude de géographie urbaine.
         Thèse 3e cycle, Université de Bordeaux III, 1976.

West Africa

103.3.6 CAWSON, A. Local Politics and Indirect Rule in Cape Coast, Ghana, 1928–1957. D.Phil. thesis, Oxford University, 1975.

103.3.7 NINSIN, K.A. Politics, Local Administration and Community Development in Ghana, 1951–1966: a case study of community power and its impact on socioeconomic development at Cape Coast. Ph.D. thesis, Boston University, 1977.

Ho (Headquarters of Volta Region: Population in 1970: 24,000.)

103.4.1 CALLAWAY, B. "Local politics in Ho and Aba." Canadian Journal of African Studies, 4, 1970, 121–144.
Compares local councils and local political activity in Ho and Aba (Nigeria) in the 1950s and early 1960s, showing how different sets of values and goals were reflected.

Koforidua (Headquarters of Eastern Region. Population in 1970: 46,000.)

103.5.1 LOWY, M.J. "Me ko court: the impact of urbanization on conflict resolution in a Ghanaian town." In Foster, G. and Kemper, R. (eds.), Anthropologists in Cities. Little, Brown, Boston, 1974, 153–177.
Discusses a research project investigating methods of settling disputes, through legal channels and otherwise, in Koforidua; primarily concerned with approach rather than results.

103.5.2 McCALL, D. "Trade and the role of wife in a modern West African town." In Southall, A. (ed.), Social Change in Modern Africa. Oxford University Press, London, 1961, 286–299.
Discusses the dominance of women in urban retail trade and presents the results of a 1952 survey of the marital status, labor inputs, and financial situation of the market women of the town.

103.5.3 McCALL, D.F. "The Koforidua Market." In Bohannan, P. and Dalton, G. (eds.), Markets in Africa. Northwestern University Press, Evanston, Ill., 1962, 667–697.
Provides an account of the organization of the market and the economic activities of the traders operating there and examines its relationship to the surrounding rural markets.

Unpublished theses include:

103.5.4 LOWY, M.J. The Ethnography of Law in a Changing Ghanaian
         Town. Ph.D. thesis, University of California, Berkeley,
         1971.

Kumasi (Second city and headquarters of Ashanti Region. Population
         in 1970: 340,000.)

103.6.1 AFRE, S.A. Ashanti Region of Ghana: an annotated
         bibliography. G.K. Hall, Boston, 1975, 494 pp.
            Numerous, largely historical, items on Kumasi
         scattered through the bibliography are accessible through
         the index.

103.6.2 ARYEE, G.A. "Education and training and informal sector
         employment in Kumasi, Ghana." In Damachi, U.G. and
         Diejomaoh, V.P. (eds.), Human Resources and African
         Development. Praeger, New York, 1978, 288–319.
            Reports on a 1975-1976 study of small-scale manufac-
         turing in Kumasi, analyzing the performance of entre-
         preneurs with various levels and types of education and
         training.

103.6.3 BERRY, B.J.L. "Urban growth and the economic development
         of Ashanti." In Pitts, F.R. (ed.), Urban Systems and
         Economic Development. University of Oregon, Eugene,
         1962, 53–64.
            Stresses the dominance of Kumasi within the system
         of urban centers in Ashanti both before and during the
         colonial period, despite a shift from a mainly political
         to a mainly economic role within the region.

103.6.4 BRAND, R.R. "Migration and residential site selection
         in Kumasi." African Urban Notes, 7 (1), 1972, 73–94.
            Presents the results of a survey in four areas of the
         city and also some peripheral villages, testing various
         hypotheses on residential attitudes and processes.

103.6.5 BROWN, J.W. "Kumasi 1896–1923: urban Africa during the
         early colonial period." African Urban Studies, 1, 1978,
         57–66.
            An abstract of a 1972 Wisconsin doctoral thesis and
         a nine-page bibliography.

103.6.6 FEWINGS, B.T. and POLONYI, C.K. (eds.) Kumasi Study.
         Faculty of Architecture, University of Kumasi, Occasional
         Report 7, 1966.
            A mimeographed report including papers on social,
         economic, and morphological aspects of the city by

students of urban planning, with numerous maps and plans
of the city and individual localities.

103.6.7   GARLICK, P.C. African Traders in Kumasi. University
College of Ghana, Accra, 1960, 115 pp.
A mimeographed report of a survey of traders later
incorporated in a thesis and monograph covering Kumasi
and Accra and listed under "Ghana: General."

103.6.8   SCHILDKROUT, E. "Government and chiefs in Kumasi Zongo."
In Crowder, M. and Ikime, O. (eds.), West African
Chiefs. Africana Publishing Corp., New York, 1970,
370-392.
An account of the political and administrative history of the Zongo area, which houses Muslim immigrants
from northern Ghana and beyond, with special reference
to colonial policy and local reaction to this.

103.6.9   SCHILDKROUT, E. "Strangers and local government in Kumasi."
Journal of Modern African Studies, 8, 1970, 251-269.
Examines the relationships of immigrant groups from
the north to the city's administrative structures and
political processes, focusing largely on the contemporary scene.

103.6.10 SCHILDKROUT, E. "The fostering of children in urban Ghana:
problems of ethnographic analysis in a multi-cultural
context." Urban Anthropology, 2, 1973, 48-73.
Examines patterns of child fostering in Kumasi in
relation to traditional practice, changing kinship relationships, and the changing role of women, with special references to differences among ethnic groups.

103.6.11 SCHILDKROUT, E. "Ethnicity and generational differences
among urban immigrants in Ghana." In Cohen, A. (ed.),
Urban Ethnicity. Tavistock, London, 1974, 187-222.
Deals with the changing significance of ethnic identity among the Mossi population of Kumasi, both migrant
and local-born.

103.6.12 SCHILDKROUT, E. "Islam and politics in Kumasi: an analysis
of disputes over the Kumasi Central Mosque."
Anthropological Papers of the American Museum of Natural
History, 52, 1974, 111-137.
Shows how a long-standing controversy over leadership
in the Mosque reflects the changing position of Muslims
in the city and also the changing political significance
of ethnicity.

103.6.13 SCHILDKROUT, E. "Economics and kinship in multi-ethnic
dwellings." In Goody, J. (ed.), Changing Social

Structure in Ghana. International African Institute, London, 1975, 167-179.
Examines some factors contributing to a sense of community among immigrants of different ethnic backgrounds in the Zongo area, where they reside together in large multicelled dwellings.

103.6.14 SCHILDKROUT, E. People of the Zongo: the transformation of ethnic identities in Ghana. Cambridge University Press, 1978, 384 pp.
An intensive study of ethnic identity and social relationships in the Zongo area of Kumasi. Particular attention is given to Mossi migrants from Upper Volta and the whole process of Mossi settlement in Ghana is reviewed. Specific chapters trace the growth of the Zongo community and its political history over seventy years. Ethnicity, cultural integration, and social stratification are brought together in the concluding chapters.

103.6.15 SUDARKASA, N. "Commercial migration in West Africa, with special reference to the Yoruba in Ghana." African Urban Notes, B, 1, 1975, 61-103.
After a broad introduction on migration of traders in West Africa and on the Yoruba migrants in Ghana, the results of research on the internal organization and external relationships of the Yoruba in Kumasi in 1968-1969 are analyzed.

103.6.16 SUDARKASA, N. "From stranger to alien: the socio-political history of the Nigerian Yoruba in Ghana 1900-1970." In Shack, W.A. and Skinner, E.P. (eds.), Strangers in African Societies. University of California Press, Berkeley, 1979, 141-167.
Traces the changing relationships of Yoruba in Kumasi to both the Ashanti host community and other stranger groups and also the political developments leading to the 1969 expulsions.

103.6.17 TETTEH, A. "Social background of the Kumasi plan." Ghana Journal of Sociology, 1 (1), 1962, 14-23.
Reports on a 1959 social survey and discusses Kumasi's growth and housing, educational and health problems.

103.6.18 WILKS, I. "The position of Muslims in metropolitan Ashanti in the early nineteenth Century." In Lewis, I.M. (ed.), Islam in Tropical Africa. Oxford University Press, London, 1966, 318-339.
Draws on the 1816-1820 reports of five European company agents to reconstruct the nature of the Muslim cummunity in Kumasi, the stresses to which it was

subject, and the influence that it exerted elsewhere in Ashanti.

Earlier publications include:

103.6.19   NYARKO, K.A.J.   "The development of Kumasi."   Bulletin of the Ghana Geographical Association, 4 (1), 1959, 3-8.

Publications in German include:

103.6.20   MANSHARD, W.   "Die Stadt Kumasi."   Erdkunde, 15, 1961, 161-180.

Unpublished theses include:

103.6.21   BROWN, J.W.   Kumasi 1896-1923:   urban Africa during the early colonial period.   Ph.D. thesis, University of Wisconsin, 1972.

103.6.22   WINCHESTER, N.B.   Strangers and Politics in Urban Africa: a study of the Hausa in Kumasi, Ghana.   Ph.D. thesis, Indiana University, 1976.

Obuasi   (Mining town in southern Ashanti.   Population at 1970 census: 31,000.)

103.7.1   AMPENE, E.   "Obuasi and its miners."   Ghana Journal of Sociology, 3, 1967, 73-80.
          Presents the results of a social survey largely concerned with areas of origin, contacts with these areas, and membership of tribal associations.

       See also 103.0.44, 45, 58.

Sekondi-Takoradi   (Two settlements that have coalesced to form the the third urban agglomeration of Ghana.   Population at 1970 census: 161,000.)

103.8.1   JEFFRIES, R.D.   "Populist tendencies in the Ghanaian trade union movement."   In Sandbrook, R. and Cohen, R. (eds.), The Development of an African Working Class.   Longman, London, 1975, 261-280.
          Examines the causes and significance of the 1961 strike by the town's railway and harbor workers, noting how its economy and labor force differ from those of other Ghana towns.

103.8.2   JEFFRIES, R.D.   Class, Power and Ideology in Ghana: the railwaymen of Sekondi.   Cambridge University Press,

1978, 244 pp.
  The book begins with a social profile of the town's railway and harbor workers, although it is primarily a study of trade union affairs, class formation, and political culture, rather than specifically of urbanization.

103.8.3 MEREDITH, D. "The construction of Takoradi harbour in the Gold Coast, 1919 to 1930: a case study in colonial development and administration." Transafrican Journal of History, 5 (1), 1976, 134-149.
  Examines why Takoradi was developed as a major port in the 1920s and the problems that the enterprise presented to the colonial authorities.

A notable earlier publication is:

103.8.4 BUSIA, K.A. Report on a Social Survey of Sekondi-Takoradi. Crown Agents, London, 1950, 164 pp.

Tamale (Fourth town of Ghana and headquarters of Northern Region. Population at 1970 census: 84,000.)

103.9.1 EADES, J.S. "The growth of a migrant community: the Yoruba in northern Ghana." In Goody, J. (ed.), Changing Social Structure in Ghana. International African Institute, London, 1975, 37-57.
  Examines the nature of Yoruba migration to Tamale, the economic role of this group before the 1969 expulsions, and the isolated yet segmented community that they formed.

103.9.2 EADES, J.S. "Church fission in a migrant community: Yoruba Baptists in northern Ghana." Savanna, 6, 1977, 167-177.
  Analyzes the main factors producing conflict and fission within this group in Tamale, stressing relationships between church organization and the total social structure of the community.

103.9.3 EADES, J.S. "Kinship and entrepreneurship among Yoruba in northern Ghana." In Shack, W.A. and Skinner, E.P. (eds.), Strangers in African Societies. University of California Press, Berkeley, 1979, 169-182.
  Discusses the success of Yoruba migrants as traders in Tamale in the 1960s and ways in which membership of the wider Yoruba migrant community in Ghana assisted this.

103.9.4 GAVEH, D. "Tamale: a geographical study." Bulletin of the Ghana Geographical Association, 6, 1961, 12-29.
  Examines the physical form, economic activities, and land-use pattern of the town.

Unpublished theses include:

103.9.5 EADES, J.S. Enterprise in a Migrant Community: a study of
Yoruba immigrants in northern Ghana, with special reference to Tamale. Ph.D. thesis, Cambridge University,
1975.

GUINEA

General

104.0.1 RIVIERE, C. Classes et Stratifications Sociales en Afrique:
le cas guinéen. Presses Universitaires de France, Paris,
1978, 296 pp.
A study of the country as a whole, not concerned
specifically with urbanization, but one with much material relating to the topic scattered through its pages.

104.0.2 SURET-CANALE, J. La République de Guinée. Editions
Sociales, Paris, 1970. Pp. 384-396, "La poussée urbaine."
Discusses the scale and nature of recent urban development, in Conakry, in provincial towns, and in emerging
small towns of which Kouroussa provides a case study.
There are numerous brief references to Conakry and other
towns elsewhere in the book.

Conakry (Capital city. Population variously estimated between
200,000 and 300,000.)

*104.1.1 INSTITUT D'URBANISME DE ZAGREB. Conakry: plan directeur
d'urbanisme. Zagreb, 1963, 79 pp.

104.1.2 RIVIERE, C. "La toponymie de Conakry et du Kaloum."
Bulletin de l'IFAN, B 28, 1966, 1009-1018.
Investigates the origins of the name Conakry and of
numerous place-names within its suburbs and surroundings.

104.1.3 RIVIERE, C. "Dixinn-Port: enquête sur un quartier de
Conakry." Bulletin de l'IFAN, B 29, 1967, 425-452.
Examines the demographic structure and some social
and economic characteristics of the population of this
suburb and reviews its evolution with special reference
to the arrival of distinct groups.

104.1.4 RIVIERE, C. "Les travailleurs de Wassa-Wassa." Canadian
Journal of African Studies, 2, 1968, 81-96.

Presents the results of a 1965 survey of the demographic characteristics, education, income, and housing
conditions of workers in a cigarette factory on the outskirts of Conakry.

A Notable earlier study is:

104.1.5 DOLLFUSS, O. "Conakry en 1951-1952: étude humaine et
économique." Etudes Guinéennes, 10/11, 1952, 3-111.

Fria (Bauxite mining settlement. Population estmate for 1970:
20,000.)

104.2.1 SPIRE, B. "L'élimination du bidonville de Fria/Clearance
of the shanty area of Fria." Bulletin du SMUH, 60/61,
1970, 15-107.
A detailed examination of the shanty town that grew
up beside the planned town in the early 1960s and of the
provision of alternative housing in the Katourou estates.
In French and English and with many illustrations.

Kankan (Main inland provincial town. Population estimate for 1970:
60,000.)

104.3   No publications found.

West Africa

GUINEA-BISSAU

Bissau (Capital city and the only major urban center. Population at
1970 census: 71,000.)

The only specific publication traced is in Portuguese:

105.1.1 VARANDA, F. "Um estudo de habitação para indígenas em
Bissau." Geographica (Lisbon), 4 (15), 1968, 22-43.

There are, of course, some references to the city in various works
on the country as a whole, e.g.:

105.1.2 ANDREINI, J-C. and LAMBERT, M-L. La Guinée-Bissau.
Harmattan, Paris, 1978, 215 pp.

For other references that make some allusions to Bissau, see:

105.1.3 McCARTHY, J.M. Guinea-Bissau and the Cape Verde Islands:
a comprehensive bibliography. Garland, New York, 1977,
196 pp.

IVORY COAST

General

106.0.1 CAMIER, L. "Aspects économiques de la constitution du
réseau urbain de la Côte d'Ivoire." Mondes en
Développement, 9, 1975, 89-105.
Examines the growth of the urban system from 1921 to
1970, relating this to economic growth, and examines the
distribution of urban centers in relation to agricultural
population and production.

106.0.2 CHEVASSU, J. Etude de Quelques Centres Semi-Urbains.
ORSTOM, Abidjan, 1968, 225 pp.
A mimeographed report on socioeconomic studies of the
small towns of Béoumi, Brobo, Ferkessedougou, Katiola,
M'Bakiakro, Sakassou, and Tiébissou.

106.0.3 CHEVASSU, J. "Essai de définition de quelques indicateurs
de structure et de fonctionnement de l'économie des
petites villes de Côte d'Ivoire." In CNRS, La Croissance
Urbaine en Afrique Noire et à Madagascar, Paris, 1972,
415-432.
Shows how a range of indicators can be used to compare

seven small towns in regard to their economic activities and hinterland relationships.

106.0.4   CHEVASSU, J. "Essai d'appréciation de l'évolution récente de quelques petites villes de Côte d'Ivoire." In CNRS, La Croissance Urbaine en Afrique Noire et à Madagascar, Paris, 1972, 433-455.
Discusses the factors contributing to the recent growth at different rates of seven small towns and investigates the extent of the hinterland of each.

*106.0.5   CHRISTOPHER, G. "Les causes de la migration de la campagne à la ville: le cas de la Côte d'Ivoire." Cahiers Ivoiriens de Recherche Economique et Sociale, 10, 1976, 43-71.

106.0.6   CHRISTOPHER, G. "Urbanization, rural to urban migration, and development policies in the Ivory Coast." In Obudho, R.A. and El-Shakhs, S. (eds.), Development of Urban Systems in Africa. Praeger, New York, 1979, 157-176.
Examines the causes and consequences of rural-urban migration in Ivory Coast and various postindependence plans and projects for regional development to deflect the flow away from Abidjan and Bouaké.

106.0.7   CLIGNET, R. "Environmental change, types of descent, and child rearing practices." In Miner, H. (ed.), The City in Modern Africa. Praeger, New York; Pall Mall, London, 1967, 257-296.
Shows how urbanization modifies the traditional contrasts in child-rearing practices between the Abure and the Bete, drawing on surveys in Abidjan, Gagnoa, and Grand Bassam.

106.0.8   COHEN, M.A. Urban Policy and Political Conflict in Africa: a study of the Ivory Coast. University of Chicago Press, 1974, 262 pp.
A study of the consequences of public policy for social, economic, and political life, especially for social stratification and political conflict, showing how insistence on high standards of housing and infrastructure for a minority of urban dwellers heightens intra- and interurban disparities.

106.0.9   COTE D'IVOIRE. Recensement des Centres Urbains d'Abengourou, Agboville, Dimbokro et Man, 1956-1957: résultats définitifs. INSEE, Paris, 1960, 113 pp.
Presents and analyzes data on age, sex, ethnic group, occupations, household size, and housing for each town.

*106.0.10   COTE D'IVOIRE. Villes de Côte d'Ivoire--Man, Daloa, Gagnoa:

enquête socio-economique. 2 vols. SEDES, Paris, 1962, 62, 176 pp.

106.0.11 COTTEN, A-M. "Les villes de Côte d'Ivoire: une méthode d'approche par l'étude des équipements tertiaires." Bulletin de l'Association des Géographes Français, 45, 1968, 223-238.
Classifies the country's provincial towns on the basis of their infrastructure and the administrative and commercial services that they provide.

106.0.12 COTTEN, A-M. "Introduction à une étude des petites villes de Côte d'Ivoire." Cahiers ORSTOM, Série Sciences Humaines, 6 (1), 1969, 61-70.
Examines the distribution of small towns within Ivory Coast, discusses their functions, and considers appropriate definitions of "urban" in this context.

106.0.13 COTTEN, A-M. "Le développement urbain et la polarisation de l'espace: l'exemple de la Côte d'Ivoire." Tiers-Monde, 12, 1971, 161-174.
Briefly discusses the growth of urban centers since 1955 and their role in the emerging patterns of spatial organization of the national economy.

106.0.14 COTTEN, A-M. "Les villes: le secteur tertiaire." In Atlas de la Côte d'Ivoire, ORSTOM, Abidjan, 1971.
Four maps and text show the growth and distribution of urban centers and the range and scale of tertiary activities within each.

106.0.15 COTTEN, A-M. "Les villes de Côte d'Ivoire: essai de typologie fonctionelle." In CNRS, La Croissance Urbaine en Afrique Noire et à Madagascar, Paris, 1972, 455-474.
Reviews the functions performed by the provincial towns, examines the employment structure of sixteen, and produces a functional classification for these and many more.

106.0.16 COTTEN, A-M. "Le rôle des villes moyennes en Côte d'Ivoire." Bulletin de l'Association des Géographes Français, 50, 1973, 619-625.
Brief discussion of the vital economic role played by provincial towns as a link between the capital city and the rural population.

106.0.17 COTTEN, A-M. "Un aspect de l'urbanisation en Côte d'Ivoire." Cahiers d'Outre-Mer, 27, 1974, 183-193.
Examines the course of urban population growth over fifty years, the spatial distribution of recent growth, and the consequent regional contrasts in levels of urbanization.

106.0.18 COTTEN, A-M. and MARGUERAT, Y. "Deux réseaux urbains
          africains: Cameroun et Côte d'Ivoire." Cahiers d'Outre-
          Mer, 29, 1976, 348-385; 30, 1977, 348-382.
          The two countries are compared first in terms of
          the origins and evolution of their urban systems and
          then in terms of the functioning of the systems with
          reference to administration, commerce, and industry.

106.0.19 DUCHEMIN, J-P. and TROUCHARD, J-P. "Données démographiques
          sur la croissance des villes en Côte d'Ivoire." Cahiers
          ORSTOM, Série Sciences Humaines, 6 (1), 1969, 71-82.
          Examines the growth of the urban population from
          1921 to 1965, evaluating the data sources, and distin-
          guishing centers of slow, moderate, and rapid growth.

106.0.20 ESPARRE, P-L. "Le travailleur de Côte d'Ivoire: une
          intégration à la société industrielle difficile."
          Genève-Afrique, 6, 1967, 181-192.
          Examines problems of adjustment to conditions of
          urban industrial employment, such as absenteeism, ex-
          plicable in terms of cultural background.

106.0.21 ETIENNE, P. and M. "L'émigration baoulé actuelle."
          Cahiers d'Outre-Mer, 21, 1968, 155-195.
          Examines the patterns of out-migration of Baoulé
          people from rural central Ivory Coast, discussing in
          turn those on plantations and those in the towns.

106.0.22 GIBBAL, J-M. "Relations ville-campagne et interprétation
          de la malchance en milieu urbain de Côte d'Ivoire."
          In CNRS, La Croissance Urbaine en Afrique Noire et à
          Madagascar. Paris, 1972, 617-624.
          On the basis of studies in Abidjan and smaller towns
          shows how urban-rural visits and other contacts perpe-
          tuate belief in witchcraft as an explanation of misfor-
          tune even in town.

106.0.23 JANVIER, G. Bibliographie de la Côte d'Ivoire: sciences
          de l'homme. Université d'Abidjan, 1973.
          Lists numerous items relating to the towns, notably
          106 under "villes" (pp. 222-232) and 140 under "urbanisme,
          habitat, architecture" (pp. 255-264).

106.0.24 KIPRE, P. "La place des centres urbains dans l'économie
          de la Côte d'Ivoire de 1920 à 1930." Annales de
          l'Université d'Abidjan: Histoire, 3, 1975, 93-120.
          Reviews the nature of the Ivory Coast economy in the
          1920s, discusses the role of provincial towns in the
          emerging space economy, and examines the functions per-
          formed by them.

106.0.25 KIPRE, P. "La crise économique dans les centres urbains en Côte d'Ivoire, 1930-1935." Cahiers d'Etudes Africaines, 16, 1976, 119-146.
Discusses the impact of the 1930s Depression on the economic life of the towns, creating bankruptcies and unemployment, and how the crisis was handled.

106.0.26 KOFFI N'ZIAN. "Les villes." In Vennetier, P. (ed.), Atlas de la Côte d'Ivoire. Jeune Afrique, Paris, 1978, 34-37.
Provides colored maps of Abidjan, Bouaké, Gagnoa, and San Pedro, with a brief text.

106.0.27 ORSTOM. "Les petites villes de Côte d'Ivoire. Cahiers ORSTOM, Série Sciences Humaines, 6 (1), 1969, 61-111; 6 (2), 1969, 3-92.
Includes studies of the small towns of Anyama (M. Vernière), Bouna (J-L. Boutillier), Odienné (A-M. Cotten), Toulepleu (A. Schwarz), and Toumodi (J. De Bettignies), as well as introductory papers by Cotten and by Duchemin and Trouchard noted above. Also produced as a 250-page mimeographed volume by ORSTOM, Abidjan in 1968.

106.0.28 REMY, M. The Ivory Coast Today. Jeune Afrique, Paris, 1976, 255 pp.
Includes lavishly illustrated descriptions of thirty-six towns (pp. 80-205), emphasizing aspects of tourist interest.

106.0.29 ANON. "Côte d'Ivoire: l'effort d'urbanisation." Urbansime, 111/112, 1969, 105-110.
Brief illustrated descriptions of, and outlines of plans for, Abengourou, Bingerville, Bouaké, Dabou, Gagnoa, and Grand Bassam. (Most of the issue is devoted to Abidjan, as noted below.)

106.0.30 ANON. "Croissance urbaine en Côte d'Ivoire, les réalisations." Urbanisme, 130, 1972, 67-81.
Largely photographs and plans of recent construction works in Abidjan and other towns.

Unpublished theses include:

106.0.31 TOURE, M. Etude Socio-démographique des Populations Actives des Centres Urbains de Côte d'Ivoire. Thèse 3e cycle, Université de Strasbourg, 1971.

Abidjan (Capital city. Population at 1975 census: 920,000.)

106.1.1 BERNUS, E. "Abidjan: note sur l'agglomération d'Abidjan

et sa population." Bulletin de l'IFAN, B 24, 1962, 54–85.
Draws on the 1955 municipal census and subsequent surveys for an analysis of demographic structure, length of
urban residence, employment and housing conditions, and
notes contrasting residential areas.

106.1.2 BERRON, H. "Ivoiriens et étrangers dans l'approvisionnement
d'Abidjan en poisson." In CEGET, Nouvelles Recherches
sur l'Approvisionnement des Villes. Bordeaux, 1977,
103–137.
Reviews the diverse sources of fish supplied to the
city, describes the production of smoked fish, and examines patterns of distribution through the city markets,
noting the many nationalities involved.

*106.1.3 BLOCH-LEMOINE, M. "Abidjan, ville dont tous les habitants
ne sont pas citadins." Terre Entière, 34, 1969, 39–79.

106.1.4 BOUTHIER, M. "Le port d'Abidjan." Cahiers d'Outre-Mer, 22,
1969, 288–312.
Examines the development of the port, the economic
consequences of its great improvement in the 1950s, and
the pattern of port traffic.

106.1.5 BOUTHIER, M. "The development of the port of Abidjan and
the economic growth of Ivory Coast." In Hoyle, B.S. and
Hilling, D. (eds.), Seaports and Development in Tropical
Africa. Macmillan, London, 1970, 103–126.
An English version of the above paper.

106.1.6 CLIGNET, R. "Urbanization and family structure in the
Ivory Coast." Comparative Studies in Society and History,
8, 1966, 385–401.
Examines ways in which urbanization among Abure and
Bete migrants has eroded certain differences in family
structure and behavior, with a partial shift to patterns
found in Western societies.

106.1.7 CLIGNET, R. and SWEEN, J. "Accra and Abidjan: a comparative
examination of the notion of increase in scale." Urban
Affairs Quarterly, 4, 1969, 297–324.
Examines the extent and nature of social differentiation in the two cities and compares the patterns with
those in Rome and San Francisco to test the Shevky and
Bell theory of increase in scale.

106.1.8 COTE D'IVOIRE. "Budgets familiaux des salariés africains
en Abidjan." Bulletin of the Inter-African Labour
Institute, 7 (2), 1960, 55–76.
A report prepared by the Ministry of Planning (in an
earlier version by E. Bernus) outlining the methods and

results of a 1956 survey of household budgets. Includes
a four-page English summary.

106.1.9   COTE D'IVOIRE. Recensement d'Abidjan, 1955: résultats
           définitifs. INSEE, Paris, 1960, 106 pp.
               Presents and analyzes data on age, sex, ethnic group,
           religion, marital status, birthplace, and occupation, in
           each case for the city as a whole.

*106.1.10 COTE D'IVOIRE. Etude Socio-économique de la Zone Urbaine
           d'Abidjan, 1963. 8 vols. Abidjan, 1964-66.

106.1.11   COTE D'IVOIRE. Recensement Général de la Population, 1975.
           Vol. 1, Agglomération de Grand Abidjan. Abidjan, 1978,
           280 pp.
               Provides detailed data on age and sex, marital status,
           ethnic groups and nationality, religion, education, occu-
           pations, and birthplace, in many cases for fifteen zones
           within the city.

106.1.12   CRAPUCHET, S. "Femmes Agni en milieu urbain." Cahiers
           d'Etudes Africaines, 11, 1971, 298-307.
               Discusses how the role of Agni women as mothers dif-
           fers in Abidjan from that in the rural home area.

106.1.13   CROUZET, E. "Abidjan ou un pôle de développement prédestiné."
           Industries et Travaux d'Outremer, 24, 1976, 689-695.
               Examines the past growth and future prospects of
           Abidjan port in relation to ports and hinterlands through-
           out West Africa and refers more briefly to the physical
           growth of the city.

106.1.14   DELFIEU, L. "Le rôle des transports dans le développement
           d'Abidjan." In CEGET, Transports et Croissance Urbaine
           dans les Pays Tropicaux. Bordeaux, 1976, 33-41.
               Outlines the role of successively the railway, the
           deep-water port, and the spread of road transport in
           the city's development.

106.1.15   DEMUR, C. "Les transports urbains à Abidjan." In CNRS,
           La Croissance Urbaine en Afrique Noire et à Madagascar.
           Paris, 1972, 501-523.
               Describes the main forms of transport used within
           the city, the organization of each, and the spatial
           patterns of movement, with an emphasis on the extensive
           bus network.

106.1.16   DENIEL, R. De la Savane à la Ville: essai sur la
           migration des Mossi vers Abidjan et sa région. Aubier-
           Montaigne, Paris, 1968, 223 pp.
               An intensive study of Mossi labor migration from

Upper Volta to Abidjan. Individual chapters deal with
the motives for migration, the processes of establishment in the city, contrasts between image and reality,
and the social changes resulting from the migration.

106.1.17 DENIEL, R. Réligions dans la Ville: croyances et
changements sociaux à Abidjan. INADES, Abidjan, 1975,
208 pp.
    Examines the ways in which religious belief affects
processes of modernization and development in the city.
Individual chapters consider attitudes to family life,
to work and money, and to the notion of personal success
and achievement.

*106.1.18 DEPRET, R. Etudes d'Urbanisme d'Abidjan, 1968-1969-1970.
SMUH, Paris, 1967, 72 pp.

106.1.19 DESCLOITRES, R. "Evolution des structures familiales et
migrations à Abidjan." In CNRS, La Croissance Urbaine
en Afrique Noire et à Madagascar. Paris, 1972, 525-534.
    Examines the household structures of migrants in the
city, drawing on a 1964-1965 survey, revealing complex
patterns and processes of fission and fusion within kin
groups.

106.1.20 DIAMBRA-HAUHOUOT, A. "Le commerce de détail dans
l'agglomération d'Abidjan." Annales de l'Université
d'Abidjan, series G, 4, 1972, 39-90.
    A detailed study of European, Lebanese, and African
retail trade, especially of the spatial pattern of each
and the goods involved, noting also a government program to aid increasing Ivorian participation.

106.1.21 DIAMBRA-HAUHOUOT, A. "Etude géographique des migrations
quotidiennes de travailleurs à Abidjan." Annales de
l'Université d'Abidjan, series G, 5, 1973, 147-266.
    Presents, analyzes, and discusses the results of an
intensive study of daily travel patterns within the
city and of the transport systems used for this movement.
Includes numerous maps and photographs.

106.1.22 DIAMBRA-HAUHOUOT, A. "Le ravitaillement d'Abidjan en
produits vivriers de base non importés." Annales de
l'Université d'Abidjan, series G, 6, 1974, 7-45.
    Examines the structure of the trade in fresh foods
within the city, the source areas for these foods, and
their relationships with the city.

106.1.23 DUCHARME, M. "L'habitat, outil d'urbanisation."
Bulletin du SMUH, 54, 1968, 1-17.
    Discusses in the context of Abidjan the city as a

social melting pot, the significance of appropriate
housing for an urban life-style, and the elements of an
effective housing policy. Also produced in an English
version.

106.1.24 DUCHEMIN, A. "Commerce--Abidjan." In <u>Atlas de la Côte</u>
<u>d'Ivoire</u>. ORSTOM, Abidjan, 1971.
    Maps the distribution of commercial establishments
in the city and discusses each of the elements represented.

106.1.25 GENNET, P. "Le plan directeur d'urbanisme d'Abidjan."
<u>Industries et Travaux d'Outremer</u>, 10, 1962, 165-174.
    Summarizes the plans for the physical development of
the city.

106.1.26 GIBBAL, J-M. "Sociétés urbaines de l'ouest africain:
l'exemple d'Abidjan." <u>Revue Française d'Etudes</u>
<u>Politiques Africaines</u>, 29, 1968, 61-83.
    A broad review of urban origins and urban social
problems in West Africa is followed by an examination
of ethnic diversity and socioeconomic differentiation
in Abidjan.

106.1.27 GIBBAL, J-M. <u>Citadins et Villageois dans la Ville Africaine:</u>
<u>l'exemple d'Abidjan</u>. Presses Universitaires de Grenoble;
Maspero, Paris, 1974, 403 pp.
    A sociological study based on a 1969 Paris 3e cycle
thesis. Part 1 examines contrasts in demographic sturc-
ture, ethnic origins, economic status, and housing between the Marcory and Nouveau Koumassi areas. Part 2
discusses family relationships, social networks, and
voluntary associations. Part 3 investigates rural-urban
relationships, including periodic visits and the prospects of eventual return to the rural homeland.

*106.1.28 HAERINGER, P. <u>Organisation Spatiale du Grand Abidjan</u>.
ORSTOM, Abidjan, 1968.

106.1.29 HAERINGER, P. "Structures foncières et création urbaine
à Abidjan." <u>Cahiers d'Etudes Africaines</u>, 9, 1969,
219-270.
    Shows the significance of land legislation and land-
tenure patterns for the physical form of the city, distinguishing areas of large holdings, small surveyed
plots, spontaneous occupance, etc.

106.1.30 JOSHI, H.; LUBELL, H.; and MOULY, J. "Urban development
and employment in Abidjan." <u>International Labour</u>
<u>Review</u>, 111, 1975, 289-306.
    Summarizes the results and especially the policy
recommendations of the study noted below.

106.1.31 JOSHI, H.; LUBELL, H.; and MOULY, J. Abidjan: urban
development and employment in the Ivory Coast. ILO,
Geneva, 1976, 115 pp.
A review of the urban population, labor force and
pattern of large-scale employment is followed by chapters on in-migration, the urban informal sector, and
housing and social problems. A final chapter examines
policy options with regard to increasing employment
opportunities.

106.1.32 KASH-WEISKEL, K. "Urban planning in Africa: Abidjan, a
case study." Bulletin de Liaison du Centre Universitaire
de Recherches de Développement, Université d'Abidjan,
1/2, 1974, 33-40.
Outlines the physical growth of the city, stressing
the extent of spatial segregation both of economic
functions and of social classes under colonial planning.

106.1.33 LEWIS, B.C. "The limitations of group action among
entrepreneurs: the market women of Abidjan, Ivory
Coast." In Hafkin, N.J. and Bay, E.G. (eds.), Women in
Africa. Stanford University Press, 1976, 135-156.
Examines the organization of the women traders in
the central Treichville market, emphasizing divisive
factors such as ethnic differentiation.

106.1.34 LEWIS, B.C. "Urban stratification and extraurban ties."
Pan-African Journal, 9, 1976, 135-151.
Assesses the effects of urban social stratification
on the pattern of rural contacts maintained by rural-
urban migrants, on the basis of a survey of 603 residents of Abidjan.

*106.1.35 LIET-VEAUX, G. "Commentaire du reglement d'urbanisme de
l'agglomération d'Abidjan." Revue Ivoirienne du Droit,
1977, 4-20.

106.1.36 MONNIER, Y. "L'approvisionnement d'Abidjan en bois et
charbon de bois." In CEGET, Dix Etudes sur
l'Approvisionnement des Villes, Bordeaux, 1972, 143-161.
Examines the production of fuelwood and charcoal in
the forests around Abidjan and the organization of supplies to the city, suggesting ecological and economic
reasons for more official control.

106.1.37 MONNIER, Y. "Problèmes de l'approvisionnement d'Abidjan
en vin de palme." In CEGET, Nouvelles Recherches sur
l'Approvisionnement des Villes, Bordeaux, 1977, 139-179.
Examines traditional patterns of palm wine production
and consumption and changing patterns of supply to
Abidjan as wild palm groves are replaced by plantations.

106.1.38 PARIS, ., and BOISADAM, . Abidjan. Revue Française
d'Etudes Politiques Africaines, 69, 1971, 26-42.
Describes Abidjan's origins and growth, population,
infrastructure, and economic functions, and also attitudes towards the city.

106.1.39 ROUSSEL, L.; TURLOT, F.; and VAURS, R. "La mobilité de la
population urbaine en Afrique Noire: deux essais de
mesure, Abidjan et Yaoundé." Population, 23, 1968,
333-352.
Compares the results of 1963-1965 surveys in the two
cities, which provided much information on population
movements into, out of, and within each of them.

106.1.40 SOCIETE D'ECONOMIE ET DE MATHEMATIQUES APPLIQUEES. Etude
Socio-économique de la Zone Urbaine d'Abidjan. 17 vols.
Paris, 1962-67.
Individual volumes cover methodology, population,
housing, employment, land ownership, daily movements,
social relationships, household budgets, perception of
space, etc.

*106.1.41 VENARD, J.L. and DUMOULIN, J.C. "Le développement
d'Abidjan." Métra, 7, 1968, 259-273.

106.1.42 VERNARD, J.L. and DUMOULIN, J.C. "Le développement
d'Abidjan dans le cadre du plan de la Côte d'Ivoire."
Industries et Travaux d'Outremer, 16, 1968, 753-760.
Discusses the rapid growth of the city's population,
the consequent physical spread, and planning proposals
to deal with this.

106.1.43 VIDAL, C. "Guerre des sexes à Abidjan: masculin, féminin,
CFA." Cahiers d'Etudes Africaines, 17, 1977, 121-153.
Argues that in Abidjan the relationship between the
sexes in all social strata is openly antagonistic,
partly as a result of the booming capitalist economy.

106.1.44 ANON. "Abidjan." Urbanisme, 111/112, 1969, 12-104.
An account of the history of planning in Abidjan,
its present infrastructure and housing, and the present
character of and plans for each quarter, lavishly illustrated with photographs and maps.

A major item in German is:

106.1.45 GOTTLICH, G. Der Raum Abidjan als Industriestandort.
J.W. Goethe Universität, Frankfurt, 1973, 277 pp.

Unpublished theses include:

106.1.46 BASSITCHE, A. Relations et Représentations Sociales dans
          les Quartiers d'Abidjan: le camp des fonctionnaires et
          la caserne des douaniers de Treichville. Thèse, 3e
          cycle, Université de Paris V, 1972.

106.1.47 HAUHOUOT, A. Abidjan, des Résidences aux Zones Actives:
          étude des migrations quotidiennes des travailleurs.
          Thèse 3e cycle, Université de Caen, 1971.

106.1.48 KOUAKOU N'GUESSAN. Etude de Cocody et sa Population dans
          le Développement Urbain d'Abidjan. Thèse 3e cycle,
          Université de Paris V, 1972.

106.1.49 LACHAUD, J-P. Contribution à l'Etude du Secteur Informel
          en Côte d'Ivoire: le cas du secteur de l'habillement à
          Abidjan. Thèse 3e cycle, Université de Bordeaux I, 1976.

Agboville (Small town just north of Abidjan. Population at 1975
           census: 27,000.)

106.2.1   LE STRAT, J. "Agboville et le pays Abbey: influence du
          chemin de fer sur une ville et sa région." In CEGET,
          Transports et Croissance Urbaine dans les Pays Tropicaux.
          Bordeaux, 1976, 137-193.
             Shows how the railway assisted the early growth of
          the town as a commercial center and how the shift to
          roads which bypass it has brought a relative decline.

*106.2.2 ORSTOM. Recensement d'Agboville. ORSTOM, Abidjan, 1968,
          65 pp.

An earlier study is:

106.2.3   GRIVOT, R. "Agboville, esquisse d'une cité d'Afrique noire."
          Etudes Eburnéennes, 4, 1955, 84-107.

An unpublished thesis is:

106.2.4   LE STRAT, J. Agboville, une Ville Soudanaise dans la
          Forêt. Thèse 3e cycle, Université de Paris X, 1974.

Bouaké (Second city, in the center of the country. Population at
        1975 census: 156,000.)

106.3.1   ANCEY, G. Relations de Voisinage Ville-Campagne. Une
          analyse appliquée à Bouaké: sa couronne et sa région.
          ORSTOM, Paris, 1974, 258 pp.

The published version of a 1971 doctoral thesis of the Université de Montpellier, examining first patterns of rural settlement and economy and then rural relationships with Bouaké, including daily movements of people, patterns of trade, and the general extent of economic integration.

*106.3.2   CASTELLA, P. and BAILLON, D.   Note de Synthèse sur l'Economie de la Ville de Bouaké.   ORSTOM, Abidjan, 1970, 94 pp.

*106.3.3   CASTELLA, P. and BAILLON, D.   Etude Démographique de Bouaké. ORSTOM, Abidjan, 1971.

106.3.4   COTE D'IVOIRE.   Recensement Démographique de Bouaké, 1958: résultats définitifs.   INSEE, Paris, 1961, 58 pp.
Presents and analyzes data on age and sex, ethnic groups, birthplace, marital status, religion, education, and occupations, in each case for the town as a whole.

*106.3.5   COTE D'IVOIRE.   Etude Socio-Economique de la Ville de Bouaké. 2 vols.   SEDES, Paris, 1963.

*106.3.6   LE CHAU, C.   "Le commerce dans la région de Bouaké; une étude économique du commerce régional et interrégional dans l'Ouest africain."   Cahiers ORSTOM, Série Sciences Humaines, 3 (3), 1966, 3-104.

106.3.7   SIRVEN, P.   L'Evolution des Villages Suburbains de Bouaké: contribution a l'étude gëographique du phenomène de croissance d'une ville africaine.   CEGET, Bordeaux, 1972, 141 pp.
The published version of a 1969 Université de Bordeaux thesis, outlining the geography and settlement history of the Bouaké area, discussing traditional society and economy and the growth of the town, and examining in detail its impact on surrounding villages, distinguishing those little affected, those being largely transformed, and those being occupied by migrants to the town.

106.3.8   SIRVEN, P.   "Les villages suburbains de Bouaké en voie d'urbanisation."   In CNRS, La Croissance Urbaine en Afrique Noire et à Madagascar.   Paris, 1972, 989-1014.
Presents the main conclusions of the study noted above, stressing the contrasts among the villages.

Unpublished theses include:

106.3.9   BOISRAME, R.   Bouaké et sa Région: essai de géographie urbaine.   Thèse 3e cycle, Université de Strasbourg, 1965.

<u>Daloa</u>   (Provincial town in the West. Population at 1975 census:
       60,000.)

106.4 No references found other than 106.0.10.

<u>Gagnoa</u> (Provincial town in the West. Population at 1975 census:
       42,000.)

106.5.1 SAINT-VIL, J. "L'immigration scolaire et ses conséquences
          sur la démographie urbaine en Afrique noire: l'exemple
          de Gagnoa (Côte d'Ivoire)." <u>Cahiers d'Outre-Mer</u>, 28,
          1975, 376-387.
            Examines Gagnoa's function as an educational center,
          shows that schoolchildren form a large proportion of
          the town's in-migrants, and suggests that this is a
          largely neglected element in African urban studies.

106.5.2 SAINT-VIL, J. "La riziculture intra-urbaine à Gagnoa
          (Côte d'Ivoire)." In CEGET, <u>Nouvelles Recherches sur</u>
          <u>l'Approvisionnement des Villes</u>. Bordeaux, 1977, 231-257.
            Examines a scheme for using swampy valley floors
          within the town for rice production, its early success,
          and its later problems as imported rice flooded the
          market.

An unpublished thesis is:

106.5.3 SAINT-VIL, J. Gagnoa: étude de géographie urbaine. Thèse
          3e cycle, Université de Bordeaux, 1972.

<u>Korhogo</u> (Provincial town in the North. Population at 1975 census:
       39,000.)

106.6.1 BERNUS, E. "Notes sur l'histoire de Korhogo." <u>Bulletin de</u>
          l'IFAN, B 23, 1961, 284-290.
            Brief notes on nineteenth-century politics and per-
          sonalities, with some discussion of the founding of the
          town.

<u>Man</u> (Provincial town in the West. Population at 1975 census:
       49,000.)

106.7 No references found other than 106.0.9 and 10.

<u>San Pedro</u> (New port-town in the southwest. Population at 1975
            census: 32,000.)

*106.8.1 BUREAU NATIONAL D'ETUDES TECHNIQUES DE DEVELOPPEMENT. San Pedro, Ville Nouvelle: approche d'urbanisation. Abidjan, 1966, 65 pp.

*106.8.2 CHEVASSU, J. San Pedro: recensement démographique, 1969. ORSTOM, Abidjan, 1970.

106.8.3 HAERINGER, P. "San Pedro 1969--la première vague d'immigrants." Cahiers ORSTOM, Série Sciences Humaines, 10, 1973, 245-267.
   Reports on a survey of the first 4000 immigrants to the new town, analyzing in detail their occupations and the emerging patterns of urban settlement. (Produced in mimeographed form by ORSTOM in 1969.)

106.8.4 HAERINGER, P. "San Pedro 1973--quatre années d'évolution." Cahiers ORSTOM, Série Sciences Humaines, 10, 1973, 269-287.
   Reports on a second survey, tracing changes in demographic structure, occupations, and housing patterns over four years of rapid growth.

106.8.5 HARTER, G. "San Pedro: urban development studies for 100,000 and 300,000 inhabitants." Planification Habitat Information, 89, 1977, 73-98.
   Describes and summarizes studies of the physical site, the projected urban economy, and alternatives open with respect to physical planning and housing provision.

106.8.6 LADUGUIE, P. "Un nouveau pôle côtier de développement: San Pedro." Coopération et Développement, 22, 1968, 17-25.
   A brief outline of plans for development of the new port and town and of the economic prospects of the surrounding area.

*106.8.7 PARRIAUD, . et al. "Les études d'urbanisme de San Pedro." Industries et Travaux d'Outremer, 15, 1967, 370-377.

106.8.8 TATE, M. "San Pedro: travaux d'infrastructure de base pour le développement du Sud-Ouest de la Côte d'Ivoire." Industries et Travaux d'Outremer, 19, 1971, 813-817.
   An illustrated account of the planning and construction of the port and some elements of the urban infrastructure.

*106.8.9 ANON. "Naissance de San Pedro." Industries et Travaux d'Outremer, 17, 1969, 570-576.

Unpublished theses include:

106.8.10   HOOPENGARDNER, T.A.   Labor Migration to San Pedro, Ivory
           Coast. Ph.D. thesis, University of Michigan, 1974.

                              LIBERIA

General

107.0.1   HASSELMANN, K-H. "Migrancy and its effect on the economy
           in Liberia." Liberian Economic and Management Review,
           2 (1), 1973, 3-34.
           See item below.

107.0.2   HASSELMANN, K-H. Migrancy and its Effect on the Economy
           in Liberia. Department of Geography, University of
           Liberia, 1973, 31 pp.
           A broad review of the economic motivations for migra-
           tion, its social consequences, and general urban-rural
           relationships.

107.0.3   HASSELMANN, K-H. Urban Mobility and Economic Stability.
           Department of Geography, University of Liberia, 1973,
           23 pp.
           Considers whether migration is aiding economic advance
           on a sound basis, using the results of interviews in five
           towns.

107.0.4   HASSELMANN, K-H. Preliminary Reflections on the Development
           of the Urban System in Liberia. Department of Geography,
           University of Liberia, 1975, 53 pp.
           Examines the extent and distribution of urban devel-
           opment according to the 1962 and 1974 censuses. Reviews
           factors influencing the growth of Monrovia and the
           emergence of many new small centers.

107.0.5   HASSELMANN, K-H. Chain Migration in Liberia. Department
           of Geography, University of Liberia, 1975, 43 pp.
           With reference to Monrovia and five small centers,
           evidence of chain or step migration is produced, and
           the motives for such movement are discussed.

107.0.6   JURGENS, H.W.; TRACEY, K.A.; and MITCHELL, P.K. "Internal
           migration in Liberia." The Bulletin, Journal of the
           Sierra Leone Geographical Association, 10, 1966, 39-59.
           Discusses the country's demographic and ethnic struc-
           ture, uses the results of a survey of birthplace of
           school pupils in Monrovia and seven small towns to show
           the extent of migration, and considers some of its causes.

                                85

107.0.7   LIBERIA. 1962 Census of Population. Office of National
           Planning, Monrovia, 1965.
                A substantial volume with detailed tables for each
           locality, e.g., giving the population of Monrovia by
           age and sex, household structure, birthplace, education,
           and occupations on pp. 5:36 to 5:51.

107.0.8   LIBERIA. 1974 Census of Population and Housing. Population
           Bulletin No. 2. Ministry of Planning and Economic
           Affairs, Monrovia, 1976, 217 pp.
                Provides data on population numbers, citizenship,
           school attendance, literacy, etc., for each locality.

107.0.9   LIBERIA. National Socio-Economic Development Plan July
           1976 - June 1980. National Planning Council, Monrovia,
           1976, 82 pp.
                Chap. 17 (pp. 73-76), "Housing and Urban Development,"
           is largely concerned with the past, present, and future
           role of the National Housing Authority.

107.0.10   SCHULZE, W. "The ports of Liberia." In Hoyle, B.S. and
           Hilling, D. (eds.), Seaports and Development in Tropical
           Africa, Macmillan, London, 1970, 75-101.
                Examines the characteristics of each port and its
           hinterland; assesses the economic significance of each
           on the basis of traffic handled; and reviews the develop-
           ment problems and prospects of the ports.

107.0.11   SCHULZE, W. A New Geography of Liberia. Longmans, London,
           1973. Chap. 17 "Settlements: urban and functional
           settlements," 75-84.
                Discusses the distribution and nature of Liberian
           towns, with plans of Harper, Robertsport, and Zorzor.
           Distinguishes towns from plantations and mining camps.

107.0.12   VON GNIELINSKI, S. "Internal migration, an indicator of
           the development of Liberia." University of Liberia
           Journal, 9, 1970, 22-28.
                A brief outline of traditional migration and of
           contemporary migration to towns, plantations, and mines.

107.0.13   VON GNIELINSKI, S. Liberia in Maps. University of London
           Press, 1972, 111 pp.
                Includes maps (pp. 48-55), each with accompanying
           text, of town size and sites, of land-use patterns in
           small towns, and of Monrovia. Maps and text on manu-
           facturing industries, local trade, ports, etc., also
           relate to the urban centers.

Other works on Liberia that relate in part to urban areas include:

107.0.14   AMERICAN UNIVERSITY. Area Handbook for Liberia. United
           States Government, Washington, 1964, 419 pp.

107.0.15   CLOWER, R.W.; DALTON, G.; and HARWITZ, M. Growth without
           Development: an economic survey of Liberia. Northwestern
           University Press, Evanston, Ill., 1966, 385 pp.

107.0.16   HLOPHE, S.S. Class, Ethnicity and Politics in Liberia.
           University Press of America, Washington, D.C., 1979,
           317 pp.

107.0.17   LOWENKOPF, M. Politics in Liberia: the conservative road
           to development. Hoover Institution Press, Stanford,
           1976, 237 pp.

Publications in German include:

107.0.18   JURGENS, H.W. Beiträge zur Binnenwanderung und
           Bevölkerungsentwicklung in Liberia. Springer Verlag,
           Heidelberg, 1965, 92 pp.

Monrovia   (Capital city. Population at 1978 census: 209,000.)

107.1.1   BATTELLE INSTITUTE. City and Regional Planning, Monrovia,
           Liberia. 8 vols. Frankfurt, 1964.
              A set of volumes providing a very thorough survey of
           the city and its surroundings and presenting detailed
           plans for future development.

107.1.2   CARTER, J.E. "The rural Loma and Monrovia: ties with an
           urban center." Liberian Studies Journal, 2, 1970,
           143-152.
              Reports a survey showing that most people in the
           city from one sample rural area make visits home and
           intend to return there and that rural dwellers are in-
           creasingly visiting the city.

107.1.3   FRAENKEL, M. Tribe and Class in Monrovia. Oxford
           University Press, London, 1964, 244 pp.
              A comprehensive sociological survey, based on field-
           work in 1958-1959. Provides a full account of the city's
           origins, growth, and present form, as background to in-
           tensive studies of its tribal communities and their in-
           ternal government, kinship and household structures,
           churches and other organizations, and the issues of
           social stratification and social mobility.

107.1.4   HANDWERKER, W.P. "Kinship, friendship and business failure
           among market sellers in Monrovia, Liberia, 1970."
           Africa, 43, 1973, 288-301.

Examines patterns of kinship and friendship among
market sellers and relates these to patterns of business
success and failure, stressing that the relationship is
more complex than often thought.

107.1.5   HANDWERKER, W.P. "Entrepreneurship in Liberia." Liberian
          Studies Journal, 5, 1972/4, 113-147.
          A broad survey of the Liberian market system and of
          entrepreneurship within it, but with a focus on market
          sellers in Monrovia whose activities were surveyed in
          detail.

107.1.6   HANDWERKER, W.P. "Daily markets and economic development."
          Human Organization, 38, 1979, 366-376.
          Examines the emergence, function and differentiation
          of markets in Monrovia and patterns of consumer travel
          to them, stressing their effective adaptation to the
          townspeople's needs.

107.1.7   ROBINSON, B.W. "The African art trade in Monrovia."
          Liberian Studies Journal, 6, 1975, 73-79.
          Describes the structure of the Monrovia trade in
          African art, the characteristics of the traders, and
          some issues of policy towards art exports.

107.1.8   SCHULZE, W. A New Geography of Liberia. Longmans, London,
          1973. Chap. 18 "Settlements: Monrovia," 85-89.
          A brief outline of the city's growth, form, and
          functions, with a map.

107.1.9   SEIBEL, H.D. and MASSING, A. Traditional Organizations
          and Economic Development: studies of indigenous
          cooperatives in Liberia. Praeger, New York, 1974,
          264 pp.
          Part 4 (pp. 141-231) examines urban voluntary organi-
          zations, largely in Monrovia, discussing their origin,
          structure, functions, and relationship to economic
          development.

Publications in German include:

107.1.10 VON GNIELINSKI, S. "Luftbild, Monrovia." Die Erde, 101,
          1970, 238-242.

Unpublished theses include:

107.1.11 HANDWERKER, W.P. The Liberian Internal Market System.
          Ph.D. thesis, University of Oregon, 1971.

107.1.12 HENNELLY, J.J. The Free Port of Monrovia and its Impact
          on the Republic of Liberia, 1943-1971. Ph.D. thesis,
          St. John's University, New York, 1973.

West Africa

MALI

General

108.0.1 BRASSEUR, G. Les Etablissements Humains au Mali. IFAN, Dakar, 1968. Pp. 403-434, "Les citadins."
Within the context of a detailed survey of forms of traditional settlement in Mali, this chapter discusses the precolonial importance and character of Sikasso, Ségou, Djenné, and Tombouctou. The last two are shown to have both a longer history and a greater persistence of traditional forms up to the present.

108.0.2 CALLAIS, J. Le Delta Intérieur du Niger. IFAN, Dakar, 1967. Pt. 5, "La vie commerciale et urbaine," pp. 469-600.
Three chapters examine (a) the history of trade in the delta, notably the relative decline of Djenné in favor of Mopti over the past century, (b) the nature of Mopti's present trade both in fish and farm produce and in imported goods, (c) the population, economic structure, and physical form of Dia, Djenné, and especially Mopti.

108.0.3 MALI. Enquête Démographique au Mali, 1960-1961. INSEE, Paris, 1968, 349 pp.
Presents and analyzes the results of a sample survey, with data for urban and rural population given separately, covering age and sex, ethnic groups, marital status, fertility, mortality, migration, religion, and occupation.

108.0.4 SILLA, O. "Historic African cities of the Soudanaise Sahara." Africa Quarterly, 8, 1968, 146-157; and (in French) Revue Française d'Etudes Politiques Africaines, 29, 1968, 25-38.
A general discussion of the past importance of cities on the desert margin and brief specific studies of Djenné, Gao, and Tombouctou.

Unpublished theses include:

108.0.5 COULIBALY, T. Le Mali: le pays, le développement économique et la croissance urbaine de 1960 à 1968. Thèse 3e cycle, Université de Paris I, 1972.

108.0.6 WINTERS, C. Cities of the Pondo: the geography of urbanism in the interior Niger delta of Mali. Ph.D. thesis, University of California, Berkeley, 1973.

Bamako (Capital city. Population at 1976 census: 404,000.)

108.1.1 AMSELLE, J-L. "Les réseaux marchands kooroko." African
Urban Notes, 5 (2), 1970, 143-158.
Examines the patterns of trade controlled by the
Kooroko merchant community of Bamako, especially the
trade in kola nuts originating in Ivory Coast and Guinea.

108.1.2 AMSELLE, J-L. Les Négociants de la Savane. Editions
Anthropos, Paris, 1977, 292 pp.
A study of Kooroko traders in the past and present,
with a section specifically on this community in Bamako
(pp. 151-187) and various subsequent references to the
city in discussions of their trading activities and modes
of thought.

108.1.3 BAZIN-TARDIEU, D. Femmes du Mali: statut-image-réactions
au changement. Leméac, Ottawa, 1975, 259 pp.
A study of the evolution of the legal and social
status and the economic role of women in Mali since independence and of attitudes to their status and role,
with special reference to Bamako, where extensive questionnaire surveys were conducted.

108.1.4 BLENEAU, D. "Démographie bamakoise." Etudes Maliennes,
19, 1976, 1-36.
Analyzes demographic structures and processes in
Bamako, drawing on a 1974 municipal census and on birth
and death registration figures.

108.1.5 BLENEAU, D. and LA COGNATA, G. "L'évolution de la
population de Bamako." Etudes Maliennes, 3, 1972, 26-46.
Examines the growth of the Bamako population between
1945 and 1966 drawing on the 1965-1966 census and earlier
counts and noting changes in demographic structures and
ethnic composition.

108.1.6 DIALLO, I. "Economie urbaine et formes de participation
traditionelle." Etudes Maliennes, 1, 1970, 21-28.
A brief discussion of the importance of the self-
employed, including both traders and farmers, in the
economy of Bamako.

108.1.7 GIBBAL, J.M. "Début d'une enquête de sociologie urbaine:
problème de méthode." Etudes Maliennes, 9, 1974, 77-84.
Outlines a proposed research project on urban social
stratification and urban-rural relations to follow up
similar studies in Abidjan.

108.1.8 LA COGNATA, G. "Agriculture citadine et controle de la
croissance urbaine: l'expérience malienne et ses

enseignements." In Ceget, Recherches sur l'Approvisionnement des Villes, CNRS, Paris, 1976, 259-295.
   Shows how efforts to curtail Bamako's growth by moving
people to new cooperative farming villages have largely
failed, for while a few townsmen have set up individual
farms, the rural-urban flow and rising urban unemployment continue.

108.1.9   MALI. Bamako: Recensement 1958, Enquête Démographique
          1960-61, résultats définitifs. INSEE, Paris, 1969,
          104 pp.
             Presents and analyzes data on age and sex, ethnic
          groups, marital status, occupations, education, and
          religion, and additional data on households, in all
          cases for the city as a whole.

108.1.10 MALI. Recensement de la Ville de Bamako: rapport
          provisoire. Bamako, 1967, 48 pp.
             Provides the results of the 1965-1966 census of the
          city, covering age and sex, ethnic groups, and occupa-
          tions for thirty-nine distinct zones.

108.1.11 MEILLASSOUX, C. "Histoire et institutions du kafo de
          Bamako, d'après la tradition des Niaré." Cahiers
          d'Etudes Africaines, 4, 1963, 186-227.
             A reconstruction of the small precolonial town of
          Bamako, including its functions, social and political
          institutions, and physical form, follows an account of
          the wider community (kafo) of which it was the focus.

108.1.12 MEILLASSOUX, C. "The social structure of modern Bamako."
          Africa, 35, 1965, 125-142.
             A brief account of the town's origins, growth, demo-
          graphy, and functions is followed by an analysis of
          socio-economic groups, i.e., civil servants, other wage
          earners, big merchants, other self-employed, and season-
          al workers.

108.1.13 MEILLASSOUX, C. Urbanization of an African Community:
          voluntary associations in Bamako. University of
          Washington Press, Seattle, 1968, 165 pp.
             Begins with an outline of the origins and growth of
          the city and a discussion of its main economic and ethnic
          groups. Then examines in detail a wide range of volun-
          tary associations and their role in the life of the city
          in the early 1960s, with special reference to immediate
          postcolonial changes.

108.1.14 TAMIATTO, M. "The restructuring of Banconi-Sikoroni."
          Planification Habitat Information, 92, 1978, 73-78.
             Reports on a study of the population, occupations,

housing, infrastructure, and land problems in an area
on the northern periphery of Bamako and makes various
planning proposals. (English and French.)

*108.1.15 TRAORE, A-B. <u>Réinsertion d'un Quartier Spontané de Bamako</u>
<u>au Mali: Banconi-Sikoroni</u>. SMUH, Paris, 1979, 145 pp.
Published version of a Master's thesis on urban
renewal.

108.1.16 VILLIEN-ROSSI, M-L. "Bamako, capitale du Mali." <u>Cahiers</u>
<u>d'Outre-Mer</u>, 16, 1963, 379-393.
A brief account of the city's site and history and
a fuller discussion of its physical form, especially in
terms of European and African quarters.

108.1.17 VILLIEN-ROSSI, M-L. "Bamako, capitale du Mali." <u>Bulletin</u>
<u>de l'IFAN</u>, 28 B, 1966, 249-380.
A comprehensive survey covering origins and growth,
economic functions, demographic structure, and the social
conditions of both indigenous and alien inhabitants.
Includes many illustrations.

108.1.18 VILLIEN-ROSSI, M-L. "Les "kinda" de Bamako." <u>Cahiers</u>
<u>d'Outre-Mer</u>, 19, 1966, 364-381.
Analyzes the demographic structure, occupations, and
income levels in the various residential quarters (kinda
in Bambara), based on 1957 and 1962 sample surveys.

Unpublished theses include:

108.1.19 DEKOYO, A. Habitat et Urbanisme à Bamako. Thèse 3e cycle,
Université de Paris I, 1976.

108.1.20 KEITA, M. Croissance Urbaine au Mali et Appropriation de
l'Espace d'Habitation. Thèse 3e cycle, Université de
Paris X, 1978.

108.1.21 THIAM, B. La Population de Bamako dans l'Ensemble de Mali.
Thèse 3e cycle, Université de Paris I, 1974.

108.1.22 VILLIEN-ROSSI, M-L. Bamako, Capitale du Mali. Thèse 3e
cycle, Université de Bordeaux, 1964.

<u>Kayes</u> (Provincial town in the far west. Population estimated in
1970: 30,000.)

108.2.1 KEITA, R.N'D. <u>Kayes et le Haut Sénégal: les étapes de la</u>
<u>croissance urbaine</u>. Vol. 1. Editions Populaires,
Bamako, 1972, 235 pp.
A detailed account of the origins and growth of the

town as a colonial administrative and commercial center, with a comprehensive analysis of its trade up to the 1950s and its relations with its hinterland. It was due to be followed by a second volume on the town's economic role in independent Mali.

The thesis from which the above study was drawn is:

108.2.2 KEITA, R.N'D. Kayes et sa Région: étude de géographie urbaine au Mali. Thèse doctorat, Université de Strasbourg, 1971.

Mopti (Second town east of Bamako. Population estimate in 1970: 35,000.)

108.3 The main piece of writing on Mopti is GALLAIS, see 108.0.2.

Tombouctou (One of the most famous historic cities of Africa, but now a relic with under 10,000 inhabitants.)

108.4.1 HARRISON CHRUCH, R.J. "Timbuktu: small town in the Sahara Desert." Geographical Magazine, 42, 1970, 683-689.
         A brief illustrated account of the former importance of the town and its present very different character.

A classic study is:

108.4.2 MINER, H. The Primitive City of Timbuctoo. Princeton University Press, 1953, 317 pp.

An unpublished thesis is:

108.4.3 IBRAHIMA, M.A. Tombouctou: étude de géographie humaine, économique et sociale. Thèse 3e cycle, Université de Paris I, 1970.

MAURITANIA

General

109.0.1 ARNAUD, J. "Profils démographiques des villes de Mauritanie,
d'après l'enquête urbaine de 1975." Bulletin de l'IFAN,
B 38, 1976, 619-635.
    Examines the distribution of urban centers, the evo-
lution of the pattern, and the demographic structure of
the urban population.

*109.0.2 GOSSELIN, M. Mauritanie: urbanisme et habitat, étude de
programmation. SMUH, Paris, 1966, 2 vols.

109.0.3 MAURITANIE. Seconds Résultats Provisoires du Recensement
Général de la Population, 1977. Nouakchott, 1977, 54 pp.
    Reports on various aspects of the population, with
some data separated for the urban centers and especially
Nouakchott.

109.0.4 PITTE, J.R. "Villes et tourisme." In Toupet, C. and
Laclavère, G. (eds.), Atlas de la République Islamique
de Mauritanie. Jeune Afrique, Paris, 1979, 53-55.
    Colored maps of Nouakchott, Nouadhibou, and Tidjkja,
with a brief text.

109.0.5 SOCIETE DE CONSTRUCTION ET DE GESTION IMMOBILIERE DE LA
MAURITANIE. Le Logement en Mauritanie: besoins et
ressources. Nouakchott, 1976, 213 pp.
    Part 1 presents and analyzes the results of a socio-
economic survey of eight towns, focusing on housing conditions and preferences. Part 2 reviews likely population
growth, housing needs, housing costs, and personal and
government financial resources.

Nouadhibou (Second town and leading port. Population at 1977
census: 22,000. Former name: Port Etienne.)

109.1.1 HARRISON CHURCH, R.J. "Port Etienne: a Mauritanian pioneer
town." Geographical Journal, 127, 1962, 498-504.
    Examines the town's origins and growth largely as a
fisheries base and notes the plans for its new function
as an iron-exporting port.

109.1.2 TOUPET, C. "Les activités maritimes de Port-Etienne."
Cahiers d'Outre-Mer, 21, 1968, 381-394.
    Discusses the developing role of the town as an iron-
ore port as well as a fisheries base.

109.1.3 TOUPET, C. "Nouadhibou (Port Etienne) and the economic
         development of Mauritania." In Hoyle, B.S. and Hilling,
         D. (eds.), Seaports and Development in Tropical Africa.
         Macmillan, London, 1970, 27-40.
              An English version of the above paper.

Nouakchott (Capital city. Population at 1977 census: 135,000.)

109.2.1 NIHAN, G. and JOURDAIN, R. "The modern informal sector in
         Nouakchott." International Labour Review, 117, 1978,
         709-720.
              Summarizes the findings of a census of informal sector
         activities and analyzes the results of a sample survey
         covering training, employment, incomes, and problems of
         those occupied in them.

109.2.2 PITTE, J-R. Nouakchott: Capitale de la Mauritanie.
         Département de Géographie de l'Université de Paris-
         Sorbonne, Paris, 1977, 198 pp.
              A brief account of the decision to build a new capital
         for Mauritania at Nouakchott is followed by a comprehen-
         sive account of its physical environment, the plans for
         the city, its growth with in-migration much accelerated
         by the Sahel drought, the composition of the population,
         the problems of employment and infrastructure provision,
         and the functions of the city at both national and local
         levels.

West Africa

NIGER

General

*110.0.1 ARNAUD, M. and SPIRE, B. Urbanisme et Habitat: République du Niger. Paris, 1960, 87 pp.

110.0.2 POITOU, D. La Délinquence Juvenile au Niger. Institut de Recherche en Sciences Humaines, Niamey, 1978 (Etudes Nigériennes, 41), 219 pp.
    Presents the results of an extensive survey of juvenile delinquency, largely confined to the towns, but including Agadez, Maradi, Tahoua, and Zinder, as well as Niamey.

*110.0.3 SMUH. Niger: Urbanisme et Habitat, 1961-1965. SMUH, Paris, 1966, 109 pp.

110.0.4 TRIBILLON, J-F. Des Principales Conditions Institutionelles et Juridiques d'une Politique Nigérienne de l'Urbanisme et de l'Aménagement Foncier. SMUH, Paris, 1971, 202 pp.
    Examines the laws of both the traditional authorities and the modern state that affect urban land tenure, housing, and planning in Niger.

110.0.5 VAN HOEY, L. "The coercive process of urbanization: the case of Niger." In Greer, S. et al. (eds.), The New Urbanization. St. Martin's Press, New York, 1968, 15-32.
    Reviews historically the process of urbanization in Niger, notably the slow growth of Zinder and the more rapid growth of Niamey and Maradi, in terms of changing social and political organization.

Unpublished theses include:

110.0.6 KING, M.H.W. Rural-urban Migration in Niger: the fate of the migrant in an urban setting. Ph.D. thesis, University of Michigan, 1977.

110.0.7 SPIRE, B. Villes du Niger. 2 vols. Mémoire Fin d'Etudes, Institut d'Urbanisme de l'Université de Paris, 1964.

110.0.8 VAN HOEY, L. Emergent Urbanization: implications of the theory of social scale verified in Niger, West Africa. Ph.D. thesis, Northwestern University, Evanston, Ill., 1966.

Maradi (Third town of Niger. Population at 1977 census: 46,000.)

*110.1.1 DAVID, P. Maradi: l'Ancien Etat et l'Ancienne Ville.

IFAN, Niamey; CNRS, Paris, 1964, 176 pp. (Etudes Nigériennes, 18.)

110.1.2 DAVID, P. "Maradi précoloniale: l'état et la ville." Bulletin de l'IFAN, B 31, 1969, 638-688.
A detailed history of settlement processes and political relationships in the eighteenth and nineteenth centuries, without a strong focus on the town.

110.1.3 NICOLAS, G. "Processus d'approvisionnement vivrier d'une ville de savane: Maradi (Niger)." In CEGET, Dix Etudes sur l'Approvisionnement des Villes. Bordeaux, 1972, 163-189.
Shows that while many Maradi residents have farms, most people depend heavily on the markets for basic foods and that trade in food is a major element in the town's economic activity.

110.1.4 THOM, D.J. "The city of Maradi: French influence on a Hausa center." Journal of Geography, 70, 1971, 472-482.
Examines the functions of Maradi both before and during the colonial period and its physical form both before and after its relocation following a flood in 1945, noting the interplay of traditional and colonial influences.

110.1.5 THOM, D.J. "The morphology of Maradi, Niger." African Urban Notes, 7 (1), 1972, 26-35.
Similar to the above paper.

Niamey (Capital city. Population at 1977 census: 225,000.)

110.2.1 BERNUS, S. Niamey: Population et Habitat. IFAN, Niamey; CNRS, Paris, 1962, 68 pp. (Etudes Nigériennes, 11.)
Provides a brief account of the development of the city and draws on official household surveys to provide an analysis of its demographic structure, of household budgets, and of housing conditions.

110.2.2 BERNUS, S. Particularismes Ethniques en Milieu Urbain: l'Exemple de Niamey. Musée de l'Homme, Paris, 1969, 268 pp.
Published version of a 1966 thesis, examining the situation, origins, and physical form of the city, its economic activities and demographic and social structures, and especially the significance of ethnic and religious differentiation.

*110.2.3 GREGORY, J.W. "Les migrations des hommes de Niamey." Population et Famille, 35, 1975, 127-137.

*110.2.4   JAKOB, J.   <u>Etude de Quelques Types de Quartiers à Niamey</u>.
           CNRS-IFAN, Niamey, 1970, 176 pp.

110.2.5   NIGER. <u>Les Budgets Familiaux Africains à Niamey, 1961-1962</u>.
          INSEE, Paris, 1964.
              Presents and analyzes the results of a survey of
          household expenditure, with a full discussion of food
          consumption patterns revealed.

110.2.6   NIGER. <u>Ville de Niamey: schéma directeur d'urbanisme</u>.
          3 vols. and 6 appendices. Niamey, 1973.
              A comprehensive survey of the site, population, func-
          tions, urban-rural relations, housing, and infrastructure,
          and a set of plans for future physical development.

110.2.7   SIDIKOU, A.H.   "Niamey." <u>Cahiers d'Outre-Mer</u>, 28, 1975,
          201-217.
              An account of the city's origins and growth, physical
          form, demographic structure, and economic functions,
          suggesting that it is quite typical of former French
          colonial cities.

*110.2.8   SOIROT, C.   <u>L'Habitat à Niamey</u>. Ministère des Travaux
           Publics, des Mines, de l'Urbanisme, Niamey, 1969, 89 pp.

West Africa

NIGERIA

General

111.0.1 ABIODUN, J.O. "Urban hierarchy in a developing country."
        Economic Geography, 43, 1967, 347-367.
            For Ijebu Province in the southwest, a hierarchy is
        identified, with five levels of urban centers distinguish-
        ed on the basis of services provided.

111.0.2 ABIODUN, J.O. "Central place study in Abeokuta Province."
        Journal of Regional Science, 8, 1968, 57-76.
            Tests the validity of the concept of a hierarchy of
        central places for Abeokuta Province in the southwest
        using a principal components analysis of the central
        place functions of eighty-one settlements.

111.0.3 ABIODUN, J.O. "Service centres and consumer behavior within
        the Nigerian cocoa area." Geografisker Analer, B 53,
        1971, 78-93.
            Analyzes patterns of movement to urban shops, banks,
        and hospitals in the Ife-Ilesha area of southwest Nigeria,
        in the context of central place theory.

111.0.4 ABIODUN, J.O. "Housing problems in Nigerian cities."
        Town Planning Review, 47, 1976, 339-347.
            Outlines the widespread housing shortage and the in-
        adequacy of government efforts in this field, arguing
        for the allocation of more funds to low-cost housing.

111.0.5 ADEDEJI, A. and ROWLAND, L. (eds.) Management Problems of
        Rapid Urbanisation in Nigeria. University of Ife Press,
        Ile-Ife, 1973, 368 pp.
            A report of the 1972 national conference on local
        government, focusing on urban administration and planning,
        but providing much information also on patterns of recent
        urban development in Nigeria and the problems arising.
        In addition to a summary of the conference proceedings
        and background papers from nine states outlining their
        patterns of urbanization and their urban planning proce-
        dures, the volume includes papers on administrative
        agencies by S.O. Fadahunsi, C.J. Greenhill, and S.A.
        Oladosu, on urban trends and problems by P.O. Sada, and
        on urbanization and development by U.I. Ukwu.

111.0.6 ADENIYI, E.O. "National development, urban and regional
        planning in Nigeria." ITCC Review, 4 (2), 1975, 61-71.
            Argues for stronger urban and regional planning poli-
        cies, since rural-urban migration is depressing rural
        economies and overloading the housing stock and public
        services of the cities.

111.0.7   ADENIYI, E.O.   "The management of urban and regional planning
          in Nigeria."   Quarterly Journal of Administration, 10,
          1976, 399-408.
                Approves Third National Development Plan proposals to
          strengthen urban administrations and to tackle the urban
          and rural problems created by rapid urban growth.

111.0.8   ADEPOJU, A.   "Migration and socio-economic links between
          urban migrants and their home communities in Nigeria."
          Africa, 44, 1974, 383-395.
                Reports on a survey of relationships between migrants
          in Ife and Oshogbo and their families at their place of
          origin, covering visits, remittances, and the use to
          which these are put.

111.0.9   ADEPOJU, A.   "Urban migration differentials and selectivity:
          the example of western Nigeria."   African Urban Notes,
          B 2 (1), 1975, 1-24.
                Examines the characteristics and intentions of the
          migrants in Ife and Oshogbo, making comparisons with
          local-born people, and also comparing migrants of rural
          and other urban origin, noting that the latter are the
          more numerous.

111.0.10 ADEPOJU, A.   "Urban migration in south-west Nigeria: origin
          and contemporary patterns."   In Adepoju, A. (ed.),
          Internal Migration in Nigeria.   University of Ife, 1976,
          71-87.
                Reviews migration from the precolonial period to the
          present, noting the increasing urban focus, and reports
          on the survey of migrants in Ife and Oshogbo, showing
          economic motives dominant but education as an additional
          attraction.

111.0.11 AJAEGBU, H.I.   Urban and Rural Development in Nigeria.
          Heinemann, London, 1976, 112 pp.
                Considers the increasing proportion of the population
          living in towns and the need for integrated regional
          planning for rural and urban areas, while two chapters
          are devoted specifically to the emerging urban system
          and to the growth and planning problems of individual
          towns.

111.0.12 AKINOLA, R.A.   "Urban tradition in Yorubaland."   Nigeria
          Magazine, 95, 1967, 344-350.
                Brief review of the character, past and present dis-
          tribution, and physical form of the Yoruba towns of the
          southwest.

111.0.13 ALAO, N. and ADEGBOLA, O.   "Public policy and the dynamics
          of urban settlement system in Nigeria."   Nigerian

Geographical Journal, 21, 1978, 161-178.
Considers the implications for the urban system of
the distribution of federal government expenditure planned
for 1975-1980, discusses aspects of planning for Lagos,
and proposes a new federal urban planning agency.

111.0.14 ALLEN, H.J.B. "Aspects of urban administration in the
northern States of Nigeria." Savanna, 1, 1972, 15-27.
Reviews the forms of urban administration in precolonial and colonial periods and examines problems facing postcolonial municipal authorities, especially those
of Kano and Kaduna, for which elaborate physical plans
were prepared in the 1960s.

111.0.15 AWOTONA, A.A. "Financing appropriate housing in Nigeria."
Ekistics, 44, 1977, 100-105.
Reviews alternative sources of finance for urban
housing in Nigeria and examines possible ways of lower-
ing the cost of producing houses.

111.0.16 AYENI, B. "Mathematical modelling of urban systems in
Nigeria." Geojournal, 2, 1978, 393-402.
Describes the mathematical models that have been
applied to Nigerian cities and exemplifies their use
with reference to the impact on Lagos of removing its
function as federal capital.

111.0.17 AYENI, B. Concepts and Techniques in Urban Analysis.
Croom Helm, London, 1979, 372 pp.
Presented as an advanced text in urban geography,
with chapters on spatial patterns of urban economic
activity, of residential areas and of daily interaction,
and expositions of various modelling techniques; but
draws on studies of Lagos or Jos at considerable length
in most of the chapters.

111.0.18 AYENI, M.A.O. "Patterns, processes and problems of urban
development." In Oguntoyinbo, J.S. et al. (eds.), A
Geography of Nigerian Development. Heinemann, Ibadan,
1978, 156-174.
Reviews the spatial patterns of precolonial and
colonial urban development, changes since independence,
the role of cities in development, and problems of urban
management.

111.0.19 BASCOM, W.R. "Some aspects of Yoruba urbanism." American
Anthropologist, 64, 1962, 699-709. Reprinted in Van den
Berghe, P.L. (ed.), Africa: social problems of change
and conflict. Chandler, San Francisco, 1965, 369-380.
Investigates the extent of urbanism in southwest
Nigeria in terms of population density, demographic

structures, ethnic diversity, occupations, etc., drawing
on 1952 census data.

111.0.20 BASCOM, W.R. "The Urban African and his world." In
Fava, S.F. (ed.), Urbanism in World Perspective.
Crowell, New York, 1968, 81-97.
  Reprint of the portion of a paper in Cahiers d'Etudes
Africaines, 1963, which examines the origins and nature
of Yoruba urbanism, especially in the light of the ideas
of Wirth.

111.0.21 BASCOM, W.R. "The early historical evidence of Yoruba
urbanism." In Damachi, U.G. and Sebel, H.D. (eds.),
Social Change and Economic Development in Nigeria.
Praeger, New York, 1973, 11-39.
  Brings together what is known of Yoruba urbanism
before the nineteenth century both from Yoruba tradition
and from the writings of travellers from outside.

111.0.22 COHEN, A. "Politics of the kola trade: some processes of
tribal community formation among migrants in West African
towns." Africa, 36, 1966, 18-36.
  Examines the social organization of Hausa kola traders
in Yoruba towns, with some focus on Ibadan but less than
in the monograph listed under that city.

111.0.23 EL-SHAKHS, S. "Planning for systems of settlements in
emerging nations with special reference to Northwest
Nigeria." Town Planning Review, 47, 1976, 127-138.
  Examines the pattern of urban settlement in the former
Northwestern State and suggests the ideal future sizes
of eleven towns based on a theoretical rank-size relationship.

111.0.24 EMEZI, H.O. Nigerian Population and Urbanization, 1911-1974:
a bibliography. African Studies Center, University of
California, Los Angeles, 1975, 145 pp.
  Lists 1627 items, about half on urbanization, including undergraduate dissertations, etc., arranged by topic
with an author index.

111.0.25 ENDSJO, P.C. "Urbanisation in Nigeria." Norsk Geografisk
Tidsskrift, 27, 1973, 207-219.
  Reviews the current rate and distribution of urban
development, notes increasing unemployment, and suggests
that urban growth is proceeding too fast.

111.0.26 EZE, J.O.N. "The urban concept in relation to inter-
tropical Africa: a re-appraisal." In Osborne, R.H. et
al. (eds.), Geographical Essays in Honour of K.C.
Edwards. Department of Geography, University of

Nottingham, 1970, 161-169.
　　Reviews alternative definitions of "urban," and criteria for distinguishing urban from rural population,
with special reference to Nigeria rather than to tropical Africa in general.

111.0.27　FAMORIYO, S.　"Aspects of rural and urban land-tenure
　　　　　structures in Nigeria."　African Urban Notes, B 1 (2),
　　　　　1975, 37-49.
　　　　　　Examines prevailing structures in rural and urban
　　　　　areas, exemplifies anomalies in recent land transactions,
　　　　　and stresses that while more study and clearer policies
　　　　　are needed in both rural and urban areas, their problems
　　　　　are interrelated.

111.0.28　GREEN, H.A.　Urban Conditions in Nigeria:　a preliminary
　　　　　bibliography.　Institute of Administration, Ahmadu Bello
　　　　　University, Zaria, 1973, 31 pp.
　　　　　　A highly selective listing, but including many news-
　　　　　paper items, semipublications, etc., on urban administra-
　　　　　tion not included in this bibliography.

111.0.29　GREEN, H.A.　"Urban management in Nigeria:　a systems and
　　　　　organizational approach."　Quarterly Journal of
　　　　　Administration, 10, 1976, 381-397.
　　　　　　Notes the weakness of urban local governments in
　　　　　Nigeria and the fragmented responsibility for planning,
　　　　　and argues for coordinated planning organizations both
　　　　　for individual cities and for the national urban system.

111.0.30　GREEN, H.A.　"The spatial pattern of Nigerian urban
　　　　　development:　some policy implications."　Nigerian
　　　　　Geographical Journal, 20, 1977, 105-121.
　　　　　　Examines patterns of urban development since inde-
　　　　　pendence, especially in terms of the spatial distribu-
　　　　　tion of public investment and the issue of concentration
　　　　　or deconcentration within the Nigerian urban system.

111.0.31　GREEN, H.A.　"Urban management and federalism:　an overview
　　　　　of the Nigerian situation."　Nigerian Journal of Public
　　　　　Affairs, 7, 1977, 7-24.
　　　　　　Examines the role of the federal government, and
　　　　　especially the Ministry of Housing, Urban Development,
　　　　　and Environment, and proposes a polyarchic system with
　　　　　distinct roles for federal, state, and local authorities.

111.0.32　GREEN, H.A.　"Urban planning in Nigeria."　Journal of
　　　　　Administration Overseas, 18, 1979, 22-33.
　　　　　　Discusses broad issues affecting Nigerian urban plan-
　　　　　ning, reviewing relevant parts of the Third National
　　　　　Development Plan and official guidelines for local

government reform, and suggesting less comprehensive but
more coordinated policies.

111.0.33 GREEN, L. "Migration, urbanization, and national development
in Nigeria." In Amin, S. (ed.), Modern Migrations in
Western Africa. Oxford University Press, London, 1974,
281-301.
    Argues that the 1950s and 1960s brought a massive
surge of urbanization to Nigeria for the first time,
rural-to-rural movement becoming overshadowed by movement to cities, and especially to the core areas of
Lagos, Onitsha-Enugu-Port Harcourt, and Kaduna-Zaria-
Kano.

111.0.34 GREEN, L. and MILONE, V.M. Urbanization in Nigeria: a
planning commentary. Ford Foundation, New York, 1972,
44 pp.
    A broad outline of the rates and patterns of rural-
urban migration and urban growth, the consequent need
for urban and regional planning, and government responses
in the 1960s at both federal and regional levels.

111.0.35 HARRIS, J.R. "Nigerian entrepreneurship in industry." In
Eicher, C. and Liedholm, C. (eds.), Growth and Development
of the Nigerian Economy. Michigan State University Press,
East Lansing, 1970, 299-324. Reprinted in Kilby, P. (ed.),
Entrepreneurship and Economic Development. Free Press,
New York, 1971, 331-355.
    Identifies the main determinants of indigenous entre-
preneurship in manufacturing in Nigeria on the basis of
a 1965 survey of 168 firms in greater Lagos and 101 in
other towns.

111.0.36 HAY, A.M. and SMITH, R.H.T. Inter-Regional Trade and Money
Flows in Nigeria. Oxford University Press, Ibadan, 1970.
Pp. 113-147, "The role of major towns."
    Notes the extent to which interregional trade,
especially that moving by rail, is channelled through
twenty-three major towns and examines the resulting
pattern of intertown movements.

111.0.37 HINCHCLIFFE, K. "Labour aristocracy: a Northern Nigerian
case study." Journal of Modern African Studies, 12,
1974, 57-67.
    Shows from studies in Kaduna and Kano that rural-urban
differences in real renumeration for effort are less than
often supposed and stresses major distinctions among different urban groups.

111.0.38 HODDER, B.W. "Periodic markets and daily markets in West
Africa." In Meillassoux, C. (ed.), The Development of

104

Indigenous Trade and Markets in West Africa. Oxford
University Press, London, 1971, 347-356.
Examines contrasts in southwest Nigeria between the
mainly rural periodic markets and the mainly urban daily
markets and notes the gradual shift towards shops and
specialized wholesale markets.

111.0.39 HODDER, B.W. and UKWU, U.I. Markets in West Africa. Ibadan
University Press, 1969, 254 pp.
Part 1 examines Yoruba markets, before and after
European impact, largely in rural areas but with a special study of Ibadan: part 2 examines the development
of trade and the present market systems of the Ibo area
with rural and urban case studies.

111.0.40 HOME, R.K. "Urban growth and urban government; contradictions in the colonial political economy." In Williams,
G. (ed.), Nigeria: economy and society. Rex Collings,
London, 1976, 55-75.
Reviews colonial policies towards urban development
in Nigeria and argues that present overrapid urbanization and inadequate urban government are due to past
colonial policies of export orientation and indirect
rule.

111.0.41 HUNT, C.L. "Study of the political, social and economic
role of urban agglomerations in the states of the Third
World: Nigeria." In INCIDI, Urban Agglomerations in
the States of the Third World. Brussels, 1971, 264-279.
Notes the diversity of urban traditions in Nigeria,
examines social and economic relations between town and
country, and offers some conclusions about some of the
increasing problems of the cities.

111.0.42 ILORI, F.A. "Determinants of urban growth in Western
Nigeria, 1952-1963." Odu, 13, 1976, 60-79.
Delineates the provincial pattern of urban growth,
with 1952 and 1963 census data for the five provinces
of the former Western Region, and discusses factors
influencing it.

111.0.43 IMOAGENE, O. "The impact of industrialisation and urbanisation on the people of Nigeria." Présence Africaine,
96, 1975, 563-591.
Argues that industrial and urban growth has eroded
traditional culture, bringing congestion and overcrowd-
ing, and recommends more efforts to decentralize industry and urban growth even beyond the state capitals.

111.0.44 IMOAGENE, O. "Migrating into unemployment and poverty:
some consequences of the urban revolution in Nigeria."

In Adepoju, A. (ed.), <u>Internal Migration in Nigeria</u>.
University of Ife, 1976, 175-186. Reprinted in <u>Africa
Development</u>, 3 (1), 1978, 53-64.
Notes the rapid urban growth of the 1950s and 1960s,
suggests that it largely reflects rural disorganization
rather than urban opportunities, and reviews the planning
implications.

*111.0.45 IMOAGENE, O. "Urban ecology and urban renewal: the case
of Ibadan and Sapele." In Aschenbrenner, J. and Collins,
L.R. (eds.), <u>The Process of Urbanism</u>. Mouton, The Hague,
1978.

111.0.46 KARMON, Y. <u>Geography of Settlement in Eastern Nigeria</u>.
Hebrew University, Jerusalem, 1966. Pp. 67-77,
"Urbanisation."
Discusses processes contributing to urban growth in
the former Eastern Region and provides brief descrip-
tions of Aba, Calabar, Enugu, Onitsha, and Port Harcourt.

111.0.47 KRAPF-ASKARI, E. <u>Yoruba Towns and Cities: an enquiry into
the nature of urban social phenomena</u>. Oxford University
Press, London, 1969, 195 pp.
Surveys the pattern of Yoruba settlements, ancient
and more recent; considers how far various types are
truly urban; examines their physical structure; and
studies in depth social relationships and stratification.
Incorporates much discussion of previous work on Yoruba
urbanism, but adds considerably to this.

111.0.48 LAW, R. "Towards a history of urbanization in pre-colonial
Yorubaland." In <u>African Historical Demography: proceedings of a seminar</u>. Centre of African Studies, University
of Edinburgh, 1977, 260-271.
Argues that historical reconstruction can provide an
explanation of Yoruba urbanism and that much of the evidence needed for such a reconstruction exists.

111.0.49 LLOYD, P.C. <u>Yoruba Land Law</u>. Oxford University Press,
London, 1962, 378 pp.
A study of land-tenure and land law in southwest
Nigeria, with special emphasis on the towns, originally
prepared for the former Western Region government.
Chap. 3 provides an outline of the social, political,
and physical structure of Yoruba towns. Chaps. 5-8
provide for Ondo, Ijebu Ode, Ado Ekiti, and Abeokuta
an outline of each town's history, social and political
structure, and land-tenure situation, illustrating the
latter by reference to court cases.

111.0.50 LLOYD, P.C. "The Yoruba: an urban people?" In Southall,

A.W. (ed.), <u>Urban Anthropology</u>. Oxford University Press, New York, 1973, 107-123.
Examines Yoruba towns with respect to features commonly ascribed to urban areas, noting that many of these are absent, although some are now becoming increasingly apparent.

111.0.51 LLOYD, P.C. <u>Power and Independence: urban Africans' perception of social inequality</u>. Routledge and Kegan Paul, London, 1974, 248 pp.
A sociological study of the Yoruba, focusing upon those in urban areas including Lagos, but drawing most material from Ibadan. Individual chapters deal with social rank in traditional society, social mobility, patterns of interaction, and attitudes to social inequality.

111.0.52 LOCKWOOD, S.C. "Plan for Nigeria's new capital city: unique symbol or urban prototype." In <u>Urban and Regional Planning in Developing Countries: proceedings of a seminar</u>. Planning and Transport Research and Computation Ltd., London, 1979, 23-48.
Provides a summary of the master plan for the new capital city prepared by International Planning Associates, discussing some of the issues involved in preparing it and some issues of implementation.

111.0.53 MABOGUNJE, A.L. <u>Yoruba Towns</u>. Ibadan University Press, 1962, 22 pp. Part also in Dwyer, D.J. (ed.), <u>The City in the Third World</u>. Macmillan, London, 1974, 26-33.
Discusses the urban attributes of large Yoruba settlements, traces their evolution, describes their morphology, and examines their problems.

111.0.54 MABOGUNJE, A.L. "The economic implications of the pattern of urbanisation in Nigeria." <u>Nigerian Journal of Economic and Social Studies</u>, 7, 1965, 9-30.
Advances four hypotheses relating to the economic implications of urbanization, tests these for 329 Nigerian towns by factor analysis of 1952 census data, discusses the regional contrasts in results, and considers the implications for government investment decisions.

111.0.55 MABOGUNJE, A.L. "Urbanization in Nigeria: a constraint on economic development." <u>Economic Development and Cultural Change</u>, 13, 1965, 413-438.
Uses the factor analysis noted above to show how variable and complex is the relationship between urbanization and economic development in Nigeria, with some indigenous towns adjusting to new economic conditions, but others forming a constraint on development.

111.0.56 MABOGUNJE, A.L. "Research in urban geography in Nigeria."
 Nigerian Geographical Journal, 11, 1968, 101-114.
   Distinguishes five areas of study--definitional problems, the central place system, city structures, urban-
 rural relationships, and urban growth dynamics--and reviews work done on each of these.

111.0.57 MABOGUNJE, A.L. "Urban land-use problems in Nigeria." In
 Institute of British Geographers Special Publication,
 1, 1968, 203-218.
   Relates problems of central decay, shantytown formation, and traffic congestion to dual urban orgins, land
 ownership patterns, and lack of planning, stressing the
 need for improved urban management.

111.0.58 MABOGUNJE, A.L. Urbanization in Nigeria. University of
 London Press, 1968, 353 pp.
   A very comprehensive study, which includes reviews
 of precolonial urbanization in both northern and western
 Nigeria, an examination of new forms of urban development brought by the British, and an analysis of the
 pattern of urbanization revealed by the 1952-1953 census,
 using factor analysis for thirty-two demographic, social,
 and economic variables. These are followed by detailed
 studies of Ibadan and Lagos, listed separately, and a
 conclusion on problems and prospects. Includes numerous
 maps, photographs, and a statistical appendix.

111.0.59 MABOGUNJE, A.L. "Industrialization within an existing
 system of cities in Nigeria." Nigerian Geographical
 Journal, 12, 1969, 3-16.
   Examines the dynamics of the Nigerian urban system,
 produces an index of urban employment for fifty-one
 towns, notes key elements of the industrialization process, and offers guidelines for industrial location
 policy.

111.0.60 MABOGUNJE, A.L. Growth Poles and Growth Centres in the
 Regional Development of Nigeria. UNRISD, Geneva, 1971,
 81 pp. Reprinted in Kuklinski, A. (ed.), Regional
 policies in Nigeria, India and Brazil. Mouton, The
 Hague, 1978, 1-93.
   Reviews the growth pole hypothesis and examines regional patterns and structural change in the Nigerian
 economy; outlines the pattern of urban development and
 the emergence of distinct growth centers; and considers
 the prospects for building a growth pole strategy into
 the country's regional planning activities.

111.0.61 MABOGUNJE, A.L. "Industrialization and metropolitan
 development in Nigeria." In CNRS, La Croissance Urbaine

en Afrique Noire et à Madagascar. Paris, 1972, 827-840.
  Examines the growth of manufacturing and its high
degree of concentration in Lagos and fifteen other centers, which are therefore so attractive to migrants that
they have employment as well as physical planning problems.

111.0.62 MABOGUNJE, A.L. "Urban land policy and population growth
  in Nigeria." In Ominde, S.H. and Ejiogu, C.N. (eds.),
  Population Growth and Economic Development in Africa.
  Heinemann, London, 1972, 235-242.
    Undertakes a correlation analysis of several variables
  in forty-nine towns, focusing on the child-woman ratio,
  concludes that in Nigeria urbanization may not reduce
  fertility since many preindustrial urbanites retain
  traditional values, and suggests that new urban land
  policies might force change in these.

*111.0.63 MABOGUNJE, A.L. Cities and Social Order. Ibadan University
  Press, 1974.
    The text of an inaugural lecture at the University
  of Ibadan.

111.0.64 MABOGUNJE, A.L. "Towards an urban policy in Nigeria."
  Nigerian Journal of Economic and Social Studies, 16,
  1974, 85-98.
    A broad review of the nature of Nigeria's urban prob-
  lems, of the need for a national urbanization policy,
  and of appropriate elements in that policy.

111.0.65 MABOGUNJE, A.L. "The urban situation in Nigeria." In
  Goldstein, S. and Sly, D.F. (eds.), Patterns of
  Urbanization: comparative country studies. Ordina,
  Dolhain, 1977, vol. 2, 569-641.
    A wide-ranging review of the distribution, nature,
  and problems of urban centers in Nigeria. Special attention is given to definitional and data issues, to
  patterns of migration, to government policies, and to
  contrasts among Nigeria's diverse urban centers.

111.0.66 MITCHEL, N.C. "Yoruba towns." In Barbour, K.M. and
  Prothero, R.M. (eds.), Essays on African Population.
  Routledge and Kegan Paul, London, 1961, 279-301.
    Discusses the evolution and character of Yoruba towns
  and their relationships with surrounding areas and examines more closely the morphology of Ibadan.

111.0.67 MITCHELL, R.C. and ARONSON, D. "Urban research in Nigeria:
  an inventory of recent and current research projects."
  African Urban Notes, 2 (2), 1967, 26-36.
    Lists research projects undertaken since 1960 but
  that had not yet given rise to publications.

111.0.68 MORTIMORE, M.J. "Peri-urban pressures." In Moss, R.P. and
          Rathbone, R.J.A. (eds.), The Population Factor in African
          Studies. University of London Press, 1975, 188-197.
              Examines briefly the relationships of Kano and Kaduna
          with their rural hinterlands, stressing contrasts due to
          difference in population density.

111.0.69 MOUGHTIN, J.C. "The traditional settlements of the Hausa
          people." Town Planning Review, 35, 1964, 21-34.
              Describes the design and layout of houses in the Hausa
          towns of northern Nigeria, with plans and photographs.

111.0.70 MUENCH, L.H. and C.Z. "Planning and antiplanning in
          Nigeria: Lagos and Ibadan." Journal of the American
          Institute of Planners, 34, 1968, 374-381; and Ekistics,
          27, 1969, 238-242.
              Contrasts Ibadan as a preindustrial city with a re-
          laxed atmosphere and little effort at planning, with
          more industrialized and faster growing Lagos, which has
          much greater problems despite some (poorly coordinated)
          planning efforts.

111.0.71 NIGERIA. Population Census of Nigeria, 1963. 8 vols.
          Lagos, n.d.
              Mimeographed reports with two volumes each for Lagos,
          Eastern Region, Northern Region, and Western Region. In
          each case vol. 1 gives the total population for wards
          and subwards, while vol. 2 gives figures on age and sex,
          nationality and ethnic groups, occupations, etc., for
          the total urban and rural population of each division.

111.0.72 NIGERIA. Third National Development Plan 1975-80. Lagos,
          1975, vol. 1, 405 pp.
              Various chapters, e.g., those on manufacturing,
          transport, education, and health, relate in part to
          urban areas; but note especially chap. 24, pp. 307-312,
          "Housing," which shows that government spending on hous-
          ing will be largely in urban areas and indicates the
          distribution of such spending, and chap. 25, pp. 313-318,
          "Town and Country Planning," which stresses the need for
          more town planning effort and shows the distribution
          among towns of planned spending on urban infrastructure.

111.0.73 NIGERIA. Report of the Committee on the Location of the
          Federal Capital of Nigeria. Lagos, 1975, 72 pp.
              Summarizes the committee's findings on tours of
          Nigeria's state capitals and of new capital cities else-
          where, discusses the present role and problems of Lagos,
          outlines the criteria for selecting a new capital, and
          considers how the proposed site meets these criteria.

111.0.74 NWAKA, G.I. "Urban development in eastern Nigeria: some
         problems of concepts and method in African urban history."
         African Urban Notes, B 1 (2), 1975, 19-35.
              Assesses the value of existing literature on urban
         history, in Africa and elsewhere, with respect to formu-
         lating a concept of "urban" and a method of approach
         suited to eastern Nigerian circumstances.

111.0.75 NWAKA, G.I. "Urban culture and the problems of urban
         development in Imo State, Nigeria: a historian's view."
         Civilisations, 28, 1978, 307-318.
              Discusses traditional Igbo settlement and alien urban
         origins in Imo State, but argues that urban life need
         not conflict with Igbo culture and that urbanization
         should be accepted rather than resisted.

111.0.76 NZIMIRO, I. "A study of mobility among the Ibos of southern
         Nigeria." International Journal of Comparative Sociology,
         6, 1965, 117-130; and in Piddington, R. (ed.), Kinship
         and Geographical Mobility. Brill, Leiden, 1965, 117-130.
              Discusses various aspects of both traditional mobility
         and the new pattern of migration to the towns, focusing
         on the role of unions and associations.

111.0.77 OGUNDANA, B. "Patterns and problems of seaport evolution
         in Nigeria." In Hoyle, B.S. and Hilling, D. (eds.),
         Seaports and Development in Tropical Africa. Macmillan,
         London, 1970, 167-182.
              Examines the evolution of the system of ports, the
         factors favoring diffusion or concentration, and the
         implications for port development policy.

111.0.78 OGUNDANA, B. "The location factor in changing seaport
         significance in Nigeria." Nigerian Geographical Journal,
         14, 1971, 71-88.
              Examines the physical characteristics of site and
         the landward connections of nine sea and delta ports.

111.0.79 OGUNDANA, B. "Oscillating seaport location in Nigeria."
         Annals of the Association of American Geographers, 62,
         1972, 110-121.
              Shows how technological development and political
         and economic change in the hinterland have together
         brought shifts in the fortunes of various Nigerian
         ports, from Lagos to Calabar.

111.0.80 OJO, G.J.A. Yoruba Culture: a geographical analysis.
         University of London Press, 1966. Chap. 5, "Yoruba
         settlements," (104-130); Chap. 6, "The layout and
         morphology of Yoruba towns," (131-157).
              Chapter 5 examines the evolution of Yoruba urbanism

and the political, cultural, and economic factors influencing it; chapter 6 considers both the broad morphological features common to many Yoruba towns and the detailed form of the palaces and various house-types.

111.0.81 OJO, G.J.A. Yoruba Palaces. University of London Press,
1966, 110 pp.
Examines the "Afins" or royal palaces in Yoruba
towns, not only in terms of their architecture and functions, but also in terms of their influence on the whole
layout of the towns. Many illustrations are included.

111.0.82 OJO, G.J.A. "Development of Yoruba towns in Nigeria."
Ekistics, 27, 1969, 243-247.
Examines briefly the physical and social structures
of traditional Yoruba towns, the varying degree of alien
impact, and some current changes.

111.0.83 OKIN, T.A. The Urbanised Nigerian: an examination of the
African and his new environment. Exposition Press, New
York, 1968, 72 pp.
A very general discussion of the urbanization process
in Nigeria, noting aspects of social change requiring
particular attention from urban planners.

111.0.84 OKONJO, C. "Some demographic characteristics of urbanisation
in Nigeria." Ikenga, 1 (1), 1972, 73-100.
A brief discussion of urban definition, the size
distribution of Nigerian towns, and the growth of the
urban population, with twenty pages of tables analyzing
for four regions town sizes in 1952-1953 and changes by
1963.

111.0.85 OKOYE, Y.O. "Urban planning in Nigeria and the problem of
slums." Third World Planning Review, 1, 1979, 71-85.
Identifies the factors producing residential slums in
Nigerian cities, with some emphasis on Enugu as an example, and discusses possible ways of dealing with the
problem.

111.0.86 OKPALA, D.C.I. "The urban housing situation and the issue
of rent control in Nigeria." Nigerian Journal of Public
Affairs, 7, 1977, 54-72.
Reviews the nature of the housing industry and the
housing market in Nigerian cities and indicates the
need for new government policies.

111.0.87 OKPALA, D.C.I. "A critique of the application of new town
concepts in Nigeria: the case of Ajoda New Town."
Third World Planning Review, 1, 1979, 57-70.
Discusses the relevance and appropriateness of new

satellite towns in Nigeria, with special reference to
that planned for Ajoda near Ibadan, concluding that they
are costly luxuries.

111.0.88 OKPALA, D.C.I. "Municipal governments and city planning
and management in Nigeria." African Studies Review, 22
(3), 1979, 15-31.
Examines the weaknesses of municipal authorities in
Nigeria in historical perspective, the fragmentation of
urban planning responsibility, and the need for city
governments with greater powers.

111.0.89 OLANREWAJU, S.A. "Combatting urban traffic congestion in
Nigeria." Nigerian Journal of Public Affairs, 7, 1977,
40-53.
Examines the causes and cost implications of traffic
congestion in Nigerian cities and suggests new strategies for handling the problem.

111.0.90 OLUSANYA, G.O. "The Sabon-Gari system in northern Nigeria."
Nigeria Magazine, 94, 1967, 242-248.
Discusses the origins of the distinct Sabon Gari
quarters established for southerners in the towns of
northern Nigeria during the colonial period.

111.0.91 OLUSANYA, P.O. Socio-economic Aspects of Rural-urban
Migration in Western Nigeria. Nigerian Institute of
Social and Economic Research, University of Ibadan,
1969, 164 pp.
Reports on a survey in five villages, focusing on
migration to town and on attitudes to urban and rural
life.

111.0.92 ONAH, J.O. and IWUSI, E.C. "Urban poverty in Nigeria."
Genève-Afrique, 14 (2), 1975, 74-82.
A very general discussion of the causes of poverty
and possible remedies, not sharply urban focused.

111.0.93 ONOKERHORAYE, A.G. "Sociocultural factors in the development of residential districts in traditional Nigerian
cities." African Urban Notes, B 2 (1), 1975, 29-37.
Discusses theoretical work on residential land-use
patterns in Western cities and presents a model adapted
to fit traditional Nigerian cities, stressing social
structure as the key to spatial structure.

111.0.94 ONOKERHORAYE, A.G. "The planning implications of the
present pattern of urban economies in traditional
Nigerian cities." Planning Outlook, 18, 1976, 19-34.
Reviews the present economic structure in Nigerian
cities of indigenous origin, incorporating the results

of a survey of small businesses in Benin, and shows how an understanding of this can aid planning.

111.0.95 ONOKERHORAYE, A.G. "The spatial aspects of urban growth in Nigeria: some planning implications." Cultures et Développement, 8, 1976, 287-303.
A broad review of the distribution of urban centers and of their differing growth rates, suggesting a dearth of medium-sized towns and a need for planning a system with more regional and local growth centers.

111.0.96 ONOKERHORAYE, A. "Urban land use in Nigeria: problems and implications for policy." Town Planning Review, 48, 1977, 59-72.
Argues for comprehensive urban land planning, with designation of areas for occupation by new migrants, a parcel of land being provided for each family and services provided for the new communities.

111.0.97 ONOKERHORAYE, A.G. "The urban system and national integration in Nigeria." Journal of Black Studies, 9 (2), 1978, 169-180.
Examines the towns of Nigeria as a spatial system, discussing the structure and problems of the system and appropriate planning strategies to ensure that it contributes to the spatial integration of the country.

111.0.98 OSUNTOGUN, A. "Some causes and implications for socio-economic development of city-ward migration of rural youths: a Western Nigeria case study." In Adepoju, A. (ed.), Internal Migration in Nigeria. University of Ife, 1976, 240-249.
Reports on a survey in four villages to discover the nature and causes of migration to town, which showed that of respondents' grown-up children most had moved--for employment, education, or marriage.

111.0.99 OYEBANDE, L. "Urban water supply planning and management in Nigeria." Geojournal, 2, 1978, 403-412.
Examines past efforts to provide urban water supplies, notes remaining deficiencies, and argues that higher charges for water would provide funds to develop more of the potential supply.

111.0.100 PEIL, M. "Interethnic contacts in Nigerian cities." Africa, 45, 1975, 107-121.
Reports on a study in Aba, Abeokuta, Kaduna, and Lagos, assessing the extent and nature of interaction among ethnic groups, e.g., in housing, friendships, and marriage, and the implications of this for national life.

111.0.101 PEIL, M. "Migration and labour force participation: a
study of four towns." In Adepoju, A. (ed.), Internal
Migration in Nigeria. University of Ife, 1976, 206-222.
Examines the relationships between employment experience and local/migrant origins, age, and education
indicated by a survey of Aba, Abeokuta, and suburban
areas of Kaduna and Lagos, noting major differences
among these towns.

111.0.102 SADA, P.O. "Urban growth and development in Nigeria."
Journal of Tropical Geography, 38, 1974, 45-54.
Reviews the broad pattern of urban development in
Nigeria and analyzes the sometimes misleading data on
urban growth provided by the 1952-1953 and 1963 censuses.

111.0.103 SADA, P.O. "Environmental sanitation in urban areas of
Nigeria." Nigerian Geographical Journal, 20, 1977,
13-25.
Shows the paucity of sanitary infrastructure in
Nigerian cities, exemplified with data on water supplies, toilet facilities, and refuse disposal in wards
of Benin city, stressing the urgency of government
action.

111.0.104 SALAU, A.T. "A new capital for Nigeria." Africa Today,
24 (4), 1977, 11-22.
Outlines the rationale for relocating the capital,
the selection of the new site, and prospects in the
light of experience with new capitals elsewhere.

111.0.105 SALAU, A.T. "Land policies for urban and national
development in Nigeria." Journal of Administration
Overseas, 17, 1978, 177-184.
Suggests that Nigerian urban planning problems lie
partly in lack of urban land development control and
the highly confused pattern of ownership, and stresses
the need for comprehensive land policies.

111.0.106 SALAU, A.T. "Urbanization, planning, and public policies
in Nigeria." In Obudho, R.A. and El-Shakhs, S. (eds.),
Development of Urban Systems in Africa. Praeger, New
York, 1979, 196-209.
Outlines the evolution of the urban system of
Nigeria and reviews both government policies towards
urbanization in general and specific aspects of urban
planning.

111.0.107 SEYMOUR, T. Housing Conditions in Towns of Northern
Nigeria: a review of existing data. Centre for Social
and Economic Research, Ahmadu Bello University, Zaria,
1978, 28 pp.
Reviews and summarizes data available on housing

types, household sizes, household facilities, and rents
in various towns, from sources such as the Federal
Office of Statistics 1971-1972 Housing Enquiries.

111.0.108 SMYTHE, H.H. "Urbanization in Nigeria." Anthropological
Quarterly, 33, 1960, 143-148.
A very broad review of the extent and distribution
of urban development in Nigeria and of factors encouraging cohesion among different urban communities.

111.0.109 SULE, O.R.A. "An assessment of the Nigerian housing
allocation policy: the case of the ballot system."
African Urban Studies, 1, 1978, 67-85.
Discusses the increasing housing shortage in Nigerian
cities and evaluates the federal government policy for
allocating public housing, using Calabar as a case
study.

111.0.110 TAMUNO, T. "The capital city in modern Nigeria."
Nigerian Journal of Economic and Social Studies, 14,
1972, 93-108.
A review of the various short-lived nineteenth century capitals, of the choice and role of Kaduna as the
former northern capital, and of the increasing dominance
in the 1950s of Lagos as federal capital.

111.0.111 UDO, R.K. "Migration and Urbanization in Nigeria." In
Caldwell, J.C. (ed.), Population Growth and Socioeconomic
Change in West Africa. Columbia University Press, New
York, 1975, 298-307.
Includes broad reviews of patterns of interregional
migration and of urban development, a comparison of
the characteristics of rural-rural and rural-urban
migrants, and a discussion of the role of urbanization
in development.

111.0.112 UDO, R.K. and OGUNDANA, B. "Factors influencing the
fortunes of ports in the Niger delta." Scottish
Geographical Magazine, 82, 1966, 169-183.
Examines the changing fortunes over 100 years of
ports such as Sapele, Burutu, and Port Harcourt, in
relation to their sites and facilities and change in
the hinterland.

111.0.113 UMO, J.U. "Some aspects of urbanization and implications
for development in Nigeria." African Urban Notes, B
1 (3), 1975, 61-75.
A broad review of increasing urbanization in Nigeria,
the urban-rural income gap, the problem of the increasing primacy of Lagos, and appropriate development
policies.

111.0.114 URQUHART, A.W. Planned Urban Landscapes of Northern Nigeria. Ahmadu Bello University Press, Zaria, 1977, 94 pp.
   Reviews both Hausa/Fulani and colonial urban traditions, examines the evolution of the present pattern of towns, provides plans of nine of these, and focuses on Zaria for a case study of the urban landscape resulting from diverse influences.

111.0.115 USMAN, Y.B. (ed.) Cities of the Savanna. Nigeria Magazine, Lagos, 1977, 125 pp.
   A set of brief essays on the history of Kano, Kaduna, Katsina, Bauchi, Ilorin, Jos, Zaria, and other cities of northern and central Nigeria. Includes numerous maps and photographs.

111.0.116 UYANGA, J. "Empirical and policy perspectives on Nigerian postwar urban-regional development problems." Journal of Tropical Geography, 47, 1978, 75-87.
   Compares the distribution of urban settlement and recent urban growth within Nigeria with that of economic development and reviews national urban development strategies.

111.0.117 UYANGA, J. "Urban planning strategy in Nigeria: the institutional policy perspective." African Urban Studies, 4, 1979, 49-58.
   Reviews precolonial, colonial, and postcolonial urban planning in Nigeria and evaluates current planning efforts, seeing the basic problems in the institutional framework rather than in the policies adopted.

111.0.118 WHEATLEY, P. "The significance of traditional Yoruba urbanism." Comparative Studies in Society and History, 12, 1970, 393-423.
   Examines the origins and evolution of urbanism among the Yoruba, considers their cities as cult centers, and concludes that they represent not an anomaly but a typical early phase of city evolution.

111.0.119 WRAITH, R.E. "Local government." In Mackintosh, J.P. (ed.), Nigerian Government and Politics. Allen and Unwin, London, 1966, 200-267.
   Describes the colonial Native Authority system and the establishment of new forms of local government in the 1950s and 1960s, examining each region in turn and ending with Lagos. Concerned largely, though not exclusively, with the towns.

111.0.120 YUSUF, A.B. "A reconsideration of urban conceptions: Hausa urbanization and the Hausa rural-urban continuum." Urban Anthropology, 3, 1974, 200-221.

117

Reviews definitions of urbanism in Africa and elsewhere and examines the distinctive features of Hausa
towns with reference to the Hausa terms for various
forms of settlements.

Unpublished theses include:

111.0.121 ADEKANYE, A.S. Model for a National Urban Development
Policy: a case study of Nigeria. Ph.D. thesis,
University of Pittsburgh, 1975.

111.0.122 ADEPOJU, J.A. Internal Migration in South West Nigeria:
a demographic and socio-economic study of recent in-
migrants into the towns of Ife and Oshogbo. Ph.D.
thesis, University of London, 1974.

111.0.123 ADEYEMI, E.A. Kaduna Capital Territory and Metropolitan
Lagos Case Studies: an analysis of the institutional
and administrative framework for urban land planning
and development. Ph.D. thesis, New York University,
1974.

111.0.124 ANAWANA, B.O. The Towns of Northern Nigeria: geographical
analysis of their characteristics, function and problems.
Ph.D. thesis, University of London, 1972.

111.0.125 EZE, J.O.N. The Towns of Biafra: a study of the changes
in an urban system in response to changes in politico-
economic organization. Ph.D. thesis, University of
Nottingham, U.K., 1969.

111.0.126 FAMORIYO, S. Changing Land Tenure in Nigeria. Ph.D.
thesis, University of London, 1971.

111.0.127 HOME, R.K. The Influence of Colonial Government upon
Urbanisation in Nigeria. Ph.D. thesis, University of
London, 1975.

111.0.128 KUMUYI, J.O. The Interaction of Central Places in Kano
State, Northern Nigeria. Ph.D. thesis, University of
Ibadan, 1973.

111.0.129 McDEVITT, T.M. On the Economic Determinants of Rural-
urban Migration in Southwestern Nigeria. Ph.D. thesis,
University of Michigan, 1977.

111.0.130 OGUNDANA, T.T.B. Seaport Development in Nigeria. Ph.D.
thesis, University of London, 1971.

111.0.131 OHAJI, G.C. Rural-urban Migration in the Anambra and Imo
States: basic economic implications. Ph.D. thesis,
Saint Louis University, Missouri, 1976.

111.0.132   OLUSANYA, P.O.   Urban Fertility Patterns in Western
            Nigeria.   Ph.D. thesis, University of London, 1968.

111.0.133   PETTISS, S.T.   Social Consequences of Rural-urban Youth
            Migration in Two African Countries: Nigeria and Kenya.
            Ph.D. thesis, Brandeis University, Waltham, Mass., 1971.

111.0.134   SULE, R.A.   Urban Housing Development in South-western
            Nigeria: policy and administration.   Ph.D. thesis,
            Claremont Graduate School, Calif., 1976.

Aba   (Town in Imo State in the southeast.   Population in 1975:
      about 180,000.)

111.1.1   CALLAWAY, B.   "Local politics in Ho and Aba."   Canadian
            Journal of African Studies, 4, 1970, 121-144.
                Compares local councils and local political activity
            in Aba and Ho (Ghana) in the 1950s and early 1960s,
            showing how different sets of values and goals were
            reflected.

Unpublished theses include:

111.1.2   CALLAWAY, B.   Confusion and Diffusion in Local Government
            (A case study from Eastern Nigeria).   Ph.D. thesis,
            Boston University, 1970.

111.1.3   OSAKWE, B.   Local Government in Aba.   Ph.D. thesis,
            University of California, Los Angeles, 1969.

Abeokuta   (Capital of Ogun State, in the southwest.   Population in
           1975:   about 250,000.)

111.2.1   CAMARA, C.   "L'organisation de l'espace géographique par
            les villes Yoruba: l'exemple d'Abeokuta."   Annales de
            Géographie, 80, 1971, 257-287.
                Sets Abeokuta in its context as one of the large
            group of indigenous Yoruba towns, discusses its origin
            and growth, and examines its present physical structure.

111.2.2   CAMARA, C.   "Les relations ville-campagne autour d'Abeokuta."
            In CNRS, La Croissance Urbaine en Afrique Noire et à
            Madagascar.   Paris, 1972, 375-400.
                Notes the indigenous origin and character of the
            town, analyzes its present functions, and identifies
            its sphere of influence in various respects vis-à-vis
            neighboring Lagos and Ibadan.

111.2.3   JOHNSON, A.W.   "Abeokuta."   Nigerian Geographical Journal,

6, 1963, 89-95.
Briefly describes the town's physical setting, origins,
growth, and present functions.

111.2.4 PHILLIPS, E. "The Egba at Abeokuta: acculturation and
political change, 1830-1870." Journal of African History,
10, 1969, 117-131.
Discusses the first forty years of the town's history,
showing how economic and political changes brought problems for its original system of town government.

See also 111.0.49.

Ado-Ekiti (Yoruba town in Ondo State. Population in 1975: about
150,000.)

111.3   No references found other than one chapter in Lloyd, P.C.
Yoruba Land Law (111.0.49).

Benin (Capital of Bendel State, in the south. Population in 1975:
about 150,000.)

111.4.1 LEGUM, C. "Great Benin; the elusive city." In Nigeria
1960, Nigeria Magazine, Lagos, 1960, 157-166.
An illustrated account of the city's long history,
with special reference to its contributions to traditional
Nigerian arts and crafts.

111.4.2 ONOKERHORAYE, A.G. "Urbanism as an organ of traditional
African civilization: the example of Benin, Nigeria."
Civilisations, 25, 1975, 294-305.
Examines the historical development of Benin over many
centuries as an indigenous city and its role in the evo-
lution of precolonial Bini civilization.

111.4.3 ONOKERHORAYE, A.G. "The influence of different cultures on
the patterns of change in traditional African cities."
Cultures et Développement, 8, 1976, 623-645.
Examines the relative contributions of indigenous and
alien elements in African cities of precolonial origin,
with special reference to Benin.

111.4.4 ONOKERHORAYE, A.G. "The pattern of housing, Benin, Nigeria."
Ekistics, 41, 1976, 55-59.
Drawing on a sample survey of 890 dwellings, examines
the nature and spatial variations of housing in the city,
with various measures of housing quality and certain related variables subjected to statistical analysis.

111.4.5   ONOKERHORAYE, A.G. "Evolution and spatial structure of
           house types in the traditional Nigerian city: a Benin
           example." Journal of Tropical Geography, 45, 1977,
           34-42.
              Similar to the above paper, but with less emphasis
           on housing quality and more on the evolution of the spa-
           tial patterns of house types.

111.4.6   ONOKERHORAYE, A.G. "The spatial pattern of residential
           districts in Benin, Nigeria." Urban Studies, 14, 1977,
           291-302.
              Analyzes the social characteristics of the various
           residential districts, using principal components analy-
           sis of household survey data to identify factors responsi-
           ble for the differentiation of these districts.

111.4.7   ONOKERHORAYE, A.G. "The changing patterns of retail outlets
           in West African urban areas: the case of Benin, Nigeria."
           Geografisker Analer, B 59, 1977, 28-42.
              Discusses the relative roles of traditional market
           places and other retail outlets in the city's economy,
           analyzing types of business in the markets, along the
           central streets, and in neighborhood centers.

111.4.8   ONOKERHORAYE, A.G. "Occupational specialization by ethnic
           groups in the informal sector of the urban economies of
           traditional Nigerian cities: the case of Benin."
           African Studies Review, 20 (1), 1977, 53-70.
              Examines the extent to which particular ethnic groups
           dominate particular components of small-scale market
           trade.

111.4.9   SADA, P.O. "Urban housing and the spatial pattern of
           modernization in Benin City." Nigerian Geographical
           Journal, 18, 1975, 39-55.
              Reports the results of a survey of age and condition
           of housing for sixteen zones of the city, shedding light
           on spatial patterns of modernization, and outlines gov-
           ernment policies for housing and central-area land use.

Unpublished theses include:

111.4.10   BEN-AMOS, P.D. Social Change in the Organization of Wood
           Carving in Benin City, Nigeria. Ph.D. thesis, Indiana
           University, 1971.

111.4.11   ONOKERHORAYE, A.G. Patterns of Change in a Traditional
           Nigerian City: an urban geography of Benin. Ph.D.
           thesis, University of London, 1974.

       See also 111.0.103.

Calabar (Capital of Cross River State, in the extreme southeast. Population in 1975: about 150,000.)

111.5.1 MORRILL, W.T. "Socio-cultural adaptation in a West African Lebanese community." Anthropological Quarterly, 35, 1962, 143-157.
Briefly describes the town, then examines the growth and decline of the Lebanese community and the social problems for those remaining.

111.5.2 MORRILL, W.T. "Immigrants and associations: the Ibo in twentieth-century Calabar." Comparative Studies in Society and History, 5, 1963, 424-448; and in Fallers, L.A. (ed.), Immigrants and Associations. Mouton, The Hague, 1967, 154-187.
Brief outlines of Efik and Ibo culture and of the history of Calabar are followed by a discussion of the local Efik and immigrant Ibo within the town, stressing contrasts in occupations and associations.

111.5.3 UDO, R.K. "The growth and decline of Calabar." Nigerian Geographical Journal, 10, 1967, 91-106.
Traces the town's growth from around 1650 to around 1900 and its subsequent decline, stressing the effects of its location, and considers implications for the present townscape.

111.5.4 UYANGA, J. "Fertility behaviour in crowded urban living." African Urban Studies, 2, 1978, 49-59.
Reports on a statistical analysis of the relationship between housing density and levels of fertility in Calabar, showing higher fertility to be associated with higher density.

111.5.5 UYANGA, J. "The Lowry model and the population of Calabar." Nigerian Geographical Journal, 21, 1978, 73-84.
Uses a simulation model to investigate the likely effects of a new industrial complex on activity and travel patterns and on land-use in different parts of the town.

Unpublished theses include:

111.5.6 EBONG, M.O. Policy Implications of Rural-urban Migration in Calabar, Nigeria: the relative effects on housing. Ph.D. thesis, Michigan State University, 1978.

111.5.7 MORRILL, W.T. Two Urban Cultures of Calabar. Ph.D. thesis, University of Chicago, 1961.

N.B. Several works on the history of Old Calabar deal with the ancient town as well as the surrounding area.

West Africa

See also 111.0.109, 111.22.1.

Enugu (Former Eastern Region capital, and now capital of Anambra
       State. Population in 1975: about 200,000.)

111.6.1 GUGLER, J. "Life in a dual system: Eastern Nigerians in
         town, 1961." In Gugler, J. (ed.), Urban Growth in
         Subsaharan Africa. Makerere University, Kampala, 1970,
         24-34; and Cahiers d'Etudes Africaines, 11, 1971, 400-421.
         Shows that ties with rural homes are even stronger
         among migrants to Enugu than among those in most African
         towns and suggests some reasons for this.

111.6.2 OGBUAGU, B. "Enugu: coal town." Nigerian Magazine, 70,
         1961, 241-251.
         A brief illustrated account of the town's history and
         its physical, cultural, and economic characteristics in
         1960.

111.6.3 OKONJO, U. The Impact of Urbanization on the Ibo Family
         Structure. Udo Breger, Göttingen, 1970, 307 pp.
         Examines the economic organization of households in
         rural and urban areas and its effects on family struc-
         tures and relationships, drawing on a questionnaire sur-
         vey of households in Enugu, in semiurban Udi, and in a
         rural locality.

111.6.4 SMOCK, D.R. "Urban-rural contrasts in political values in
         Eastern Nigeria." Journal of Asian and African Studies,
         6, 1971, 81-90.
         Assesses the impact of urban living on attitudes toward
         power and decision-making among migrants to Enugu, on the
         basis of a 1963 survey of coal miners.

111.6.5 WHITNEY, A. "Consumer shopping habits in Ogbete market,
         Enugu, Nigeria." African Urban Notes, 5 (3), 1970,
         134-143.
         Reports on a survey among shoppers in the main food
         market of Enugu, investigating various aspects of their
         food shopping patterns.

An earlier paper was:

111.6.6 JENNINGS, J.H. "Enugu: a geographical outline." Nigerian
         Geographical Journal, 3 (1), 1959, 28-38.

See also 111.0.85.

Ibadan (The largest of the indigenous urban centers of the southwest. Former Western Region capital, now capital of Oyo State. Population in 1975 about one million, second only to Lagos.)

111.7.1 ADEBISI, B. "The politics of development control in a Nigerian city: Ibadan." Nigerian Journal of Economic and Social Studies, 16, 1974, 311-324.
    Shows how Ibadan Planning Authority has few real powers and how political opposition prevents action to enforce official planning controls.

111.7.2 ADEDEJI, A. "Ibadan." In Laquian, A.A (ed.), Rural-Urban Migrants and Metropolitan Development. Intermet, Toronto, 1971, 55-69.
    Outlines the origins and growth of the city, its local government, the extent of in-migration, its slum development, and slum clearance efforts.

111.7.3 AKINOLA, R.A. "The Ibadan region." Nigerian Geographical Journal, 6, 1963, 102-115.
    Examines factors influencing the growth of the city, and the nature of its functions as a regional center.

111.7.4 AKINOLA, R.A. "The industrial structure of Ibadan." Nigerian Geographical Journal, 7, 1964, 115-130.
    Analyzes the patterns of both small-scale and large-scale industry in the city, noting the decline of the former and the factors contributing to the growth of the latter.

111.7.5 AKINOLA, R.A. "The growth and development of Ibadan." Bulletin of the Ghana Geographical Association, 11 (1), 1966, 48-63.
    An account of the physical growth of the city through the nineteenth and twentieth centuries, in relation to changing economic circumstances.

111.7.6 AKINOLA, R.A. "Problems of urban development in Nigeria: the example of Ibadan." Bulletin of the Ghana Geographical Association, 12, 1967, 7-22.
    Indicates some of the city's deficiencies with regard to housing, health, roads, etc., and suggests some palliatives.

111.7.7 AKINOLA, R.A. "The retail structure of Ibadan." Sierra Leone Geographical Journal, 12, 1968, 45-55.
    Describes and maps the various types of market and of retail shopping areas in Ibadan, stressing the complementarity of the two parts of this dual retail structure.

111.7.8 ARONSON, D.R. "Ijebu Yoruba urban-rural relationships and class formation." <u>Canadian Journal of African Studies</u>, 5, 1971, 263-279.

Study in Ijebu rural communities and in Ibadan shows that social inequality among the Ijebu Yoruba is only partly related to wealth and that the sociopolitical implications of increased wealth are not what much literature would imply, partly due to intense urban-rural interaction.

111.7.9 ARONSON, D.R. "Residential growth in Ibadan, 1966-1972." <u>Journal of Tropical Geography</u>, 40, 1975, 8-17.

Follows up Mabogunje and Oyelese studies for a later period and directs attention to the builders and owners of the new houses.

111.7.10 ARONSON, D.R. "Capitalism and culture in Ibadan urban development." <u>Urban Anthropology</u>, 7, 1978, 253-270.

Examination of a single land transaction shows how distinctly Yoruba social processes persist even though traditional structures are giving way to individual land tenure on a Western model.

111.7.11 ARONSON, D.R. <u>The City is our Farm: seven migrant Ijebu Yoruba families</u>. Schenkman, Cambridge, Mass., 1978, 208 pp.

After brief accounts of the Ijebu people and the Ijebu community within Ibadan, the lives of seven families from this community are examined in great depth as a contribution to the study of social change among the Yoruba. The book is based on intensive 1966-1967 field-work and the resulting University of Chicago doctoral thesis.

111.7.12 AROWOLO. O.U. "Fertility of urban Yoruba working women: a case study of Ibadan city." <u>Nigerian Journal of Economic and Social Studies</u>, 19, 1977, 37-66.

Presents and analyzes the results of a 1974 survey of working women in Ibadan investigating how education, occupations, and levels of fertility are interrelated.

111.7.13 BAMISAIYE, A. "Begging in Ibadan, southern Nigeria." <u>Human Organization</u>, 33, 1974, 197-202.

Examines the social organization of migrant Hausa beggars in the city and contrasts their position in a predominantly Yoruba society with their role in traditional Hausa society.

111.7.14 BOGDAN, R. "Youth clubs in a West African city." In Meadows, P. and Mizruchi, E.H. (eds.), <u>Urbanism, Urbanization and Change</u>. Addison-Wesley, Reading, Mass., 1969, 223-241.

Describes government-sponsored youth clubs in Ibadan, discussing their members' characteristics, the activities pursued, the organization behind them, and their role as socializing agents.

111.7.15   CALDWELL, J.C. and WARE, H. "The evolution of family planning in an African city: Ibadan, Nigeria." Population Studies, 31, 1977, 487-507.
Reports on a 1973 survey of over 6,600 Ibadan residents with respect to changing birth control practice.

111.7.16   CALLAWAY, A. "From traditional crafts to modern industries." Odu, 2 (1), 1965, 28-51. Reprinted in Lloyd, P.C. et al. (See 111.7.26).
Examines the nature of craft industry in Ibadan, with special reference to entrepreneurship and apprenticeship, and the obstacles to expansion of small businesses into larger industrial firms.

111.7.17   COHEN, A. "The social organization of credit in a West African cattle market." Africa, 35, 1965, 8-20. Reprinted in Melson, R. and Wolpe, H. (eds.), Nigeria: modernization and the politics of communalism. Michigan State University Press, East Lansing, 1971, 93-112.
Discusses the organization and operation of credit in the Ibadan cattle market, stressing the vital importance of social relationships that are built into the system.

111.7.18   COHEN, A. Custom and Politics in Urban Africa: a study of Hausa migrants in Yoruba towns. Routledge and Kegan Paul, London, 1969, 252 pp.
Largely focused on the Sabo Quarter of Ibadan, which houses nearly all the city's Hausa, showing how the community has developed, how it has remained very distinct, and how it has adapted traditional Muslim beliefs into a powerful religious brotherhood of considerable political significance. Provides much information on the nature of the Hausa community and its trading links with the north.

111.7.19   FILANI, M.O. and OSAYIMWESE, I. "Intra-city traffic flow problems in Nigeria: the case of Ibadan metropolitan area." Nigerian Journal of Economic and Social Studies, 22, 1979, 17-31.
Discusses the nature of road traffic in Ibadan, recent increase in traffic flows, and possible policies to improve the efficiency of such flows.

111.7.20   GREEN, L.P. "Ibadan." In Robson, W.A. and Regan, D.E. (eds.), Great Cities of the World; their government, politics and planning. 3rd ed. Allen and Unwin, London,

1972, 439-481.

Discusses the city council, the administration of education, health, water, transport and planning, and local government finance, noting the range of current problems and making proposals for change.

111.7.21   GUTKIND, P.C.W. "The view from below: political conscious- ness of the urban poor in Ibadan." Cahiers d'Etudes Africaines, 15, 1975, 5-35.

Contends that the Nigerian bourgeoisie prevent the poor from altering their inferior status, but shows how class consciousness is developing among the poor in Ibadan and reports on a survey of their attitudes and their hopes for improvement.

111.7.22   HODDER, B.W. "The markets of Ibadan." In Hodder, B.W. and Ukwu, U.I., Markets in West Africa. Ibadan University Press, 1969, 94-109.

A modified version of a chapter in Lloyd, et al. (See 111.7.26.), analyzing the form and functioning of the city's daily and periodic markets.

111.7.23   JENKINS, G. "An informal political economy." In Butler, J. and Castagno, A.A. (eds.), Transition in African Politics. Praeger, New York, 1967, 166-194.

Presents evidence and speculation on the largely illegal transactions linking the city council and the city's commerce and industry and examines the conse- quences of the bribery, etc., for the city's political and economic systems.

111.7.24   KOLL, M. (ed.) African Urban Development: four political approaches. Bertelsmann Universitätsverlag, Düsseldorf, 1972, 215 pp.

Includes papers by L.H. Muench on the evolution of the physical form of Ibadan and the politics of the city's development (pp. 26-94) and by M. Koll on the past and present finances of Ibadan City Council (pp. 95-127), along with two papers not specifically on Africa at all.

111.7.25   LEVINE, R.A.; KLEIN, N.H.; and OWEN, C.R. "Father-child relationships and changing life-styles in Ibadan, Nigeria." In Miner, H. (ed.), The City in Modern Africa. Praeger, New York; Pall Mall, London, 1967, 215-255.

Surveys father-child relationships among both tradi- tional and elite groups as a case study of sociopsycho- logical change among the Yoruba during the modernization process.

111.7.26 LLOYD, P.C.; MABOGUNJE, A.L.; and AWE, B. (eds.) The City
of Ibadan, Cambridge University Press, 1967, 280 pp.
A wide-ranging collection of papers, including an
introduction by P.C Lloyd; "Early beginnings" by B. Awe;
"The agricultural environment" by H.A. Oluwasanmi; "The
morphology of Ibadan" by A.L. Mabogunje; "Indigenous
Ibadan" by B.B. Lloyd; "The Ijebu" by A.L. Mabogunje;
"The Western Ibo" by C. Okonjo; "The Hausa" by A. Cohen;
"The elite" by P.C. Lloyd; "Traditional crafts to modern
industry" by A. Callaway; 'Markets of Ibadan' by B.W.
Hodder; 'Education and youth unemployment' by A. Callaway;
'Government and politics' by G. Jenkins; 'Traditional
religion and Christianity' by E.B. Idowu; 'Islam' by
F.H. El-Masri; and 'The problems of a metropolis' by
A.L. Mabogunje.

111.7.27 MABOGUNJE, A.L. "Ibadan: Black metropolis." Nigeria
Magazine, 68, 1961, 12-26.
An illustrated account of the city's history and
present physical, cultural, and economic characteristics.

111.7.28 MABOGUNJE, A.L. "The growth of residential districts in
Ibadan." Geographical Review, 52, 1962, 56-77.
Shows how the city has grown, both by fission within
old compounds and by peripheral spread, and distinguishes
seven types of residential area.

111.7.29 MABOGUNJE, A.L. Urbanization in Nigeria. University of
London Press, 1968. Chap. 8 "Ibadan, a traditional
metropolis," 186-204; Chap. 9 "The internal structure
of Ibadan," 205-237.
Chapter 8 reviews the growth of the city chronologi-
cally through the nineteenth and twentieth centuries;
Chapter 9 examines the spatial structure of its commercial
and residential areas.

111.7.30 MACLEAN, C.M.U. "Hospitals or healers? An attitude survey
in Ibadan." Human Organization, 25, 1966, 131-139.
Reports on a survey of attitudes to, and use of,
traditional medicine and modern hospitals, both in a
poor part of the city and among the families of secondary
school children.

111.7.31 MACLEAN, U. Magical Medicine: a Nigerian case study.
Allen Lane, Penguin Books, London, 1971, 167 pp.
Discusses the alternative forms of medical treatment
available in Ibadan and, after a review of "sickness
behavior" in both poor and elite homes, offers conclusions about the tenacity of traditional medicine in
Ibadan and beyond.

111.7.32   OKEDIJI, F.O.   "Socioeconomic status and differential
           fertility in an African city." Journal of Developing
           Areas, 3, 1969, 339-353; and Human Organization, 28,
           1969, 42-49.
                Reports on a survey of married women in Ibadan, show-
           ing that those of highest socioeconomic status living in
           the most modern areas have fewest children and lowest
           preferred family size.

111.7.33   OKEDIJI, F.O.   "Socioeconomic status and attitudes to public
           health problems in the Western State: a case study of
           Ibadan." In Caldwell, J.C. (ed.), Population Growth and
           Socioeconomic Change in West Africa. Columbia University
           Press, New York, 1975, 275-297.
                Examines public health conditions, levels of morbidi-
           ty and mortality, and attitudes to health, medical facil-
           ities, and child care in selected areas, and relates
           variations in these factors to socioeconomic character-
           istics in each area.

111.7.34   OKEDIJI, O.O. and F.O.   "Marital stability and social
           structure in an African city." Nigerian Journal of
           Economic and Social Studies, 8, 1966, 151-163.
                Reports on a study of patterns of divorce in the
           oldest section of Ibadan, testing various hypothses re-
           lated to changes in traditional extended family relation-
           ships.

111.7.35   OLAYEMI, O.A.   "Movements of population from urban to rural
           areas of Yoruba towns, Nigeria: case study of Ibadan."
           Genève-Afrique, 17 (2), 1979, 65-81.
                Examines the extent and nature of migration from
           Ibadan to the surrounding rural areas, the factors re-
           sponsible, and the social and economic implications,
           concluding that it greatly benefits both the city and
           the rural areas.

111.7.36   ONIBOKUN, G.A.   "Socio-cultural constraints on urban
           renewal policies in emerging nations: the Ibadan case."
           Nigerian Journal of Economic and Social Studies, 11,
           1969, 343-354; and Human Organization, 29, 1970, 133-139.
                Presents the conclusions of an M.A. thesis on the
           relevance of both sociocultural factors and the local
           leadership structure for the success of redevelopment
           programs in areas such as the traditional core of Ibadan.

111.7.37   ONIBOKUN, G.A.   "Nigerian cities: their rehabilitation and
           redevelopment." African Studies Review, 13, 1970, 291-310.
                Reviews alternative strategies for overcoming the
           immense physical planning problems of central Ibadan,
           stressing the need for cooperation among technical ex-
           perts, social workers, and neighborhood leaders.

111.7.38   ONIBOKUN, G.A.   "Nigeria: strategies for urban redevelopment."   Journal of the Royal Town Planning Institute, 58,
1972, 51-56.
Reviews possible policies for improving housing conditions and infrastructure in Ibadan, especially mobiliz-
ing people for self-help and providing funds for individual house-building.

111.7.39   ONIBOKUN, G.A.   "Forces shaping the physical environment
of cities in developing countries; the Ibadan case."
Land Economics, 49, 1973, 424-431.
Examines housing and environmental conditions in
central Ibadan and the factors causing continuing deterioration, and calls for more government action.

111.7.40   ONOKERHORAYE, A.G.   "Public involvement in urban development
planning: the case of environmental sanitation in Ibadan."
Journal of Administration Overseas, 16, 1977, 171-177.
Shows that government urban development programs re-
quire campaigns of public enlightenment and structures
designed to assist the involvement of local community
leaders in the planning process.

111.7.41   ONYEMELUKWE, J.O.C.   "Structural and spatial dynamics of
industrial activity in a traditional city: Ibadan,
Nigeria."   Nigerian Geographical Journal, 21, 1978,
119-132.
Examines the development of the city's industrial
activity from traditional crafts to modern factories
and analyzes the structure and spatial pattern of factory industry in 1972.

111.7.42   OYELESE, J.O.   "The growth of Ibadan city and its impact
on land use patterns 1961 to 1965."   Journal of Tropical
Geography, 32, 1971, 49-55.
Examines a phase in the physical growth of the city,
using air photographs, and investigates the processes
behind the land-use changes.

*111.7.43   SPLANSKY, J.B.   "The concentric zone theory of city
structure as applied to an African city: Ibadan."
Yearbook of the Association of Pacific Coast Geographers,
28, 1966, 135-146.

111.7.44   STEIGENGA, W.   "Ibadan: city in transition."   Tijdschrift
van het Koninklijk Nederlandsch Aardijksundig Genootschap,
88, 1965, 169-195.
Examines the effects of economic, social, and political changes on the physical form of the city and notes
some of its physical planning problems.

111.7.45 VAGALE, L.R. and ADEKOYA, O.C. Industrial Environment of
          a Nigerian City: Case study of Ibadan. Town Planning
          Department, The Polytechnic, Ibadan, 1974, 96 pp.
             Analyzes existing industrial development in Ibadan
          in terms of type of enterprise, employment structure,
          etc., as well as location, physical sites, buildings,
          and infrastructure; and makes proposals for future in-
          dustrial estate development.

111.7.46 WILLIAMS, G. "Political consciousness among the Ibadan
          poor." In De Kadt, E. and Williams, G. (eds.), Sociology
          and Development. Tavistock, London, 1974, 109-139.
             Discusses the values and aspirations of both town-
          dwelling traders and craftsmen and farmers in surround-
          ing areas and shows how each group seeks, largely un-
          successfully, to improve its economic and political
          situation.

Unpublished theses include:

111.7.47 AKINOLA, R.A. Ibadan: a study in urban geography. Ph.D.
          thesis, University of London, 1963.

111.7.48 AMINU, F.A. The social, cultural and economic bases for
          housing preference in Ibadan, Nigeria. Ph.D. thesis,
          University of Michigan, 1977.

111.7.49 JENKINS, G. Politics in Ibadan. Ph.D. thesis, Northwestern
          University, Evanston, Ill., 1965.

111.7.50 OTUDEKO, A.O. Adjustment of Migrants in an African City.
          Ph.D. thesis, Stanford University, California, 1977.

111.7.51 SCHWERDTFEGER, F.W. Comparative Study of Conventional
          Urban Houses in Three Regions of Africa. Ph.D. thesis,
          University of London, 1975.

          See also 111.0.22, 111.0.39, 111.0.45, 111.0.51, 110.0.65,
          110.0.70, 111.0.87.

Ijebu-Ode (Yoruba town southeast of Ibadan. Population in 1975:
           about 100,000.)

111.8.1 MASOOD, M. "The traditional organization of a Yoruba town:
         a study of Ijebu-Ode." Oriental Geographer, 18, 1974,
         125-139; and Ekistics, 45, 1978, 307-312.
            Examines the origins and growth of the town, its
         traditional social organization and residential units,
         and the extent to which its spatial structure is charac-
         teristic of Yoruba towns.

See also 111.0.49.

Ile-Ife   (Ancient Yoruba town, east of Ibadan. Population in 1975:
           about 180,000.)

111.9.1   LEWIS, A.O. "The small-scale industrial scene of Ile-Ife."
           Quarterly Journal of Administration, 6, 1972, 427-440.
                Reports the main findings of a comprehensive survey
           of the town's small-scale industries undertaken in 1969
           by the Industrial Research Unit of the University of Ife.

111.9.2   OJO, G.J.A. "Hausa quarters of Yoruba towns, with special
           reference to Ile-Ife." Journal of Tropical Geography,
           27, 1968, 40-49.
                Reports on a survey of housing and occupations in the
           Hausa quarter (Sabo) of Ile-Ife, stressing its highly
           distinctive character there as in other Yoruba towns.

111.9.3   OLAYEMI, A.O. "Problems of the planning administration,
           Ile-Ife, Nigeria." Ekistics, 44, 1977, 140-144.
                Notes the recent burst of growth of the town and
           discusses the inadequacy of the existing administrative
           machinery for planning its physical growth.

Numerous items have been published on the archaeology and traditional
art of Ife, including:

111.9.4   FAGG, W. and WILLETT, F. "Ancient Ife." Odu, 8, 1960,
           21-35.

111.9.5   OZANNE, P. "A new archaeological survey of Ife." Odu, NS 1,
           1969, 28-45.

111.9.6   WILLETT, F. "Ife and its archaeology." Journal of African
           History, 1, 1960, 231-248. Reprinted in Oliver, R. and
           Fage, J.D. (eds.), Papers in African Prehistory.
           Cambridge University Press, 1970, 303-326.

Unpublished theses include:

111.9.7   McDOWELL, D.W. Educational, Occupational and Residential
           Mobility in an Urban Nigerian Community. Ph.D. thesis,
           Columbia University, New York, 1971.

See also 111.0.8-10, 111.0.122, 111.0.132.

<u>Ilesa</u> (Yoruba town in the far east of Oyo State. Population in
          1975: about 200,000.)

111.10.1 TRAGER, L. "Market women in the urban economy: the role
          of Yoruba intermediaries in a medium-sized city."
          <u>African Urban Notes</u>, B 2 (3), 1976, 1-9.
             Demonstrates the vital role played by Ilesa market
          women in the distribution of goods in and around the
          town, notes their relatively small earnings, and con-
          siders how they live on these earnings.

Unpublished theses include:

111.10.2 TRAGER, L. Yoruba Markets and Trade: analysis of spatial
          structure and social organization in the Ijesaland
          marketing system. Ph.D. thesis, University of Washington,
          1976.

<u>Ilorin</u> (The most northerly of the Yoruba cities and capital of Kwara
          State. Population in 1975: about 280,000.)

111.11.1 AKOREDE, V.E.A. "The impact of sociocultural changes on
          the pattern of urban land use: the case of Ilorin."
          <u>African Urban Studies</u>, 5, 1979, 71-84.
             Examines the growth of the city over the past 200
          years and the physical structure that has resulted from
          the diverse influences on this growth.

Nothing else of substance appears to have been published since:

111.11.2 MACROW, D.W. "Ilorin." <u>Nigeria Magazine</u>, 49, 1956, 148-167.

<u>Iseyin</u> (Yoruba town northwest of Ibadan. Population in 1975: about
          120,000.)

111.12.1 BRAY, J.M. "The organization of traditional weaving in
          Iseyin, Nigeria." <u>Africa</u>, 38, 1968, 270-280.
             One of three papers drawn from an Ibadan M.A. thesis,
          emphasizing the social structure of the town and the
          activities involved in its traditional weaving industry.

111.12.2 BRAY, J.M. "The craft structure of a traditional Yoruba
          town." <u>Transactions, Institute of British Geographers</u>,
          46, 1969, 179-193.
             Examines the nature, and especially the distribution
          patterns within the town, of its craft industries, in-
          cluding dyeing, etc., as well as weaving.

111.12.3 BRAY, J.M. "The economics of traditional cloth production
          in Iseyin, Nigeria." <u>Economic Development and Cultural</u>

Change, 17, 1969, 540-551.
Examines the expenditure and income of those engaged
in weaving, especially in relation to the changing economic environment of the mid-twentieth century.

Iwo   (Yoruba town 25 km northeast of Ibadan. Population in 1975:
about 150,000.)

111.13.1 WESTERN NIGERIA. Structure of a Yoruba Town: outline
development proposals for Iwo, 1969-1989. Ministry of
Lands and Housing, Ibadan, 1969, 67 pp.
Provides a thorough survey of the existing demographic
and economic characteristics of the population and the
physical structure of the town, and presents plans for
its development.

Jos (Capital of Plateau State. Population in 1975: about 150,000.)

*111.14.1 AYENI, M.A.O. "A model of the metropolis: the development
of an activity allocation model for Jos, Benue-Plateau
State of Nigeria." Socio-Economic Planning Sciences,
9, 1975, 273-283.

111.14.2 AYENI, M.A.O. "Some determinants of the propensity to
interact in an urban system: a case study of Jos,
Nigeria." Nigerian Geographical Journal, 18, 1975,
111-120.
Reports on a household survey concerned with intra-
city movements, e.g., to work or market, and with factors influencing the frequency of such movements.

111.14.3 AYENI, M.A.O. "A predictive model of urban stock and
activity. 2) Empirical." Environment and Planning,
8, 1976, 59-77.
A spatial interaction model applied to eighteen
zones within Jos suggests likely future employment
trends in each of these and consequent journey-to-work
patterns.

111.14.4 AYENI, M.A.O. "The city system and the use of entropy in
urban analysis." Urban Ecology, 2, 1976, 33-53.
A study of patterns of journey to work in Jos is
used to exemplify the value of the entropy concept in
studies of urban spatial structure.

111.14.5 AYENI, M.A.O. "The empirical development of a disaggregated
residential model in Nigeria." Annals of Regional
Science, 10 (3), 1976, 31-54.
Applies to Jos, with the aid of sample survey data

for eighteen zones, a model in which residential location is determined by quantifiable factors such as prox-
imity to employment, transport costs, and rents.

111.14.6   PLOTNICOV, L. Strangers to the City: urban man in Jos,
           Nigeria. University of Pittsburgh Press, 1967, 320 pp.
               Published version of a 1964 Ph.D. thesis examining
           individuals' responses to the problems of migrants in a
           rapidly-growing town. Provides a full discussion of the
           town's growth and its social and economic structure, but
           much space is also devoted to the life history of four
           representative individuals.

111.14.7   PLOTNICOV, L. "The modern African elite of Jos, Nigeria."
           In Tuden, A. and Plotnicov, L. (eds.), Social Stratifi-
           cation in Africa. Free Press, New York, 1970, 269-302.
               Shows how a modern elite has emerged even in a pro-
           vicial town, discusses the social relations and politi-
           cal behavior of this group, and also identifies an
           incipient middle class.

111.14.8   PLOTNICOV, L. "Rural-urban communications in contemporary
           Nigeria." Journal of Asian and African Studies, 5,
           1970, 66-82. Reprinted in Gutkind, P. (ed.), The
           Passing of Tribal Man. Brill, Leiden, Netherlands, 1970.
               Reviews the range of contacts between townspeople
           and rural kinsfolk and ways in which town dwellers re-
           main in touch with traditional social institutions,
           drawing largely on Jos for examples.

111.14.9   PLOTNICOV, L. "Who owns Jos? Ethnic ideology in Nigerian
           urban politics." Urban Anthropology, 1, 1972.
               Shows that Jos is ethnically more heterogeneous than
           most Nigerian cities, and discusses the rival claims of
           the Birom and the Tiv to be the real owners of Jos
           despite their small numbers.

The unpublished thesis from which five papers noted above were drawn
is:

111.14.10 AYENI, M.A.O. Predictive Modelling of Urban Spatial
           Structure: the example of Jos, Benue-Plateau State,
           Nigeria. Ph.D. thesis, University Of Ibadan, 1974.

           See also 111.0.17.

Kaduna (Capital of Kaduna State and formerly Northern Region capital.
         Population in 1975: about 200,000.)

111.15.1   HINCHLIFFE, K. "The Kaduna textile workers: characteristics
           of an African labour force." Savanna, 2, 1973, 27-37.

Examines the social, educational, and economic
characteristics of the workers in the Kaduna textile
industry on the basis of a sample survey of 3,900 employees in five firms.

111.15.2 LOCK, M. et al. Kaduna 1917, 1967, 2017. Faber, London,
1967, 245 pp.
A survey and plan of the capital territory for the
government of northern Nigeria. A detailed report on
existing conditions and comprehensive future plans in
regard to land use, infrastructure, social services,
employment, housing, and traffic. Considers the central
area in particular detail, but also covers the city as a
whole and considers its regional relationships. Lavishly illustrated with photographs and maps.

111.15.3 OWOYELE, D. "Kaduna: administrative town." Nigeria
Magazine, 71, 1961, 306-320.
Brief illustrated account of the history and the
physical, cultural, and economic characteristics of
the city.

111.15.4 SEYMOUR, T. "Housing policy and income distribution in
Kaduna." Nigerian Journal of Public Affairs, 7, 1977,
73-98.
Examines the failure of Federal housing efforts in
the 1970s to effect a redistribution of urban incomes
by providing for the very poor and discusses possible
policies for the 1980s.

Unpublished theses include:

111.15.5 MEDUGBON, A.K. Kaduna, Nigeria: the vicissitudes of a
capital city, 1917-1975. Ph.D. thesis, University of
California, Los Angeles, 1976.

See also 111.0.123.

Kano (Ancient northern city. Capital of Kano State. Population in
1975: about 500,000.)

111.16.1 ARMSTRONG, R. "The nightwatchmen of Kano." Middle
Eastern Studies, 3, 1967, 269-282.
A general description of the Buzu community who have
migrated from Niger and of the way in which so many have
become nightwatchmen.

111.16.2 DOUTRE, N.H. "Kano: ancient and modern." Geographical
Magazine, 36, 1964, 594-602.
A brief description of the city and its economic
life, with several photographs.

111.16.3　FRISHMAN, A.　"The population growth of Kano, Nigeria."
In African Historical Demography: proceedings of a
seminar, Centre of African Studies, University of
Edinburgh, 1977, 212-250.
Examines the growth of the city's population from
its distant origins up to the 1970s, discussing prevailing influences in each period and noting also the developing physical form of the city.

111.16.4　GREEN, H.A.　"Managing a metropolis: the case of Kano."
Quarterly Journal of Administration, 9, 1975, 261-277.
An account of the city's complex administrative
framework, with division of authority even for basic
service provision; makes proposals for a new administrative polyarchy.

111.16.5　HALLAM, W.R.K.　"The great emporium." Nigeria Magazine,
81, 1964, 84-97.
An account of the history of the city, supplemented
by numerous photographs of contemporary Kano.

111.16.6　HILL, P.　Population, Prosperity and Poverty: rural Kano
1900 and 1970.　Cambridge University Press, 1977, 240 pp.
The study is focused on a small rural area very
close to the city and includes a chapter on the economic
ties between city and countryside in 1900 and a chapter
on the lack of recent rural-urban migration.

111.16.7　JAGGAR, P.J.　"Kano City blacksmiths: precolonial
distribution, structure and organisation." Savanna, 2,
1973, 11-25.
Reconstructs the distribution and organization of
this craft industry in nineteenth-century Kano, traces
subsequent changes, and makes comparisons with the situation in Bida described by Nadel.

111.16.8　LOVEJOY, P.E.　"The wholesale kola trade of Kano."
African Urban Notes, 5 (2), 1970, 129-142.
Examines the expansion of kola wholesaling in Kano
over the last seventy years, its importance to the
city, and the way in which the Hausa traders have
successfully responded to new economic opportunities.

111.16.9　LUBECK, P.　"Unions, workers and consciousness in Kano,
Nigeria: a view from below." In Sandbrook, R. and
Cohen, R. (eds.), The Development of an African Working
Class. Longman, London, 1975, 139-160.
Discusses why factory workers have given little
support to formal trade unions in Kano and shows how
they are able to organize and take action in particular
circumstances.

111.16.10   LUBECK, P.   "Contrasts and continuity in a dependent city:
            Kano, Nigeria."   In Abu Lughod, J. and Hay, R. (eds.),
            Third World Urbanization.   Maaroufa Press, Chicago,
            1977, 281-292.
                Examines the establishment of a wage labor force,
            but notes the resilience of precolonial institutions,
            with some discussion of urban-rural relations and of
            spatial patterns within the city.

111.16.11   McDONNELL, G.   "The dynamics of geographic change: the
            case of Kano."   Annals of the Association of American
            Geographers, 54, 1964, 355-371.
                Explores the changing relationships of Kano city
            and its hinterland, both with each other and with areas
            beyond, over several centuries, suggesting that recent
            urban growth has strangled the surrounding rural areas.

111.16.12   MORTIMORE, M.J.   Land Use in Kano City and Township.
            Department of Geography, Ahmadu Bello University, Zaria,
            1966, 10 pp.
                A land-use map at a scale of 1: 12,500 based on
            1962 air photographs, with a brief commentary.

111.16.13   MORTIMORE, M.J.   "Some comments on pre-industrial urbanism
            and the emergence of growth poles, with reference to
            Kano."   Ghana Social Science Journal, 2 (2), 1972,
            117-128.
                Analyzes the past and present settlement hierarchy
            of Kano Emirate and the nature of relationships between
            the city and its hinterland.

111.16.14   MORTIMORE, M.J.   "Some aspects of rural-urban relations
            in Kano, Nigeria."   In CNRS, La Croissance Urbaine en
            Afrique Noire et à Madagascar.   Paris, 1972, 872-888.
                Examines past and present symbiosis between Kano
            and its immediate surroundings, with an analysis of
            1965 and 1969 surveys of donkey movements carrying
            firewood and foodstuffs in and manure out.

111.16.15   PADEN, J.N.   "Urban pluralism, integration and adaptation
            of communal identity in Kano, Nigeria."   In Cohen,
            R. and Middleton, J. (eds.), From Tribe to Nation in
            Africa.   Chandler, Scranton, Pa., 1970, 242-270.
                Surveys the in-migration of diverse groups of Muslim
            northerners and resulting patterns of ethnic integra-
            tion and separation, noting the integrative role of
            Islamic brotherhoods.

111.16.16   PADEN, J.N.   "Communal competition, conflict and violence
            in Kano."   In Melson, R. and Wolpe, H. (eds.), Nigeria:
            modernization and the politics of communalism.

Michigan State University Press, East Lansing, 1971,
113-144.
Discusses the evolution of the city's dual social
and economic structure and shows that violence between
Hausa and Ibo in the 1960s stemmed more from economic
competition than from differences in cultural values.

111.16.17 PADEN, J.N. Religion and Political Culture in Kano.
University of California Press, Berkeley, 1973, 461 pp.
A study of the past and present relationships between
religion and politics in Kano Emirate as a whole, but
much discussion is concerned with the city in view of
the focusing of both religious and political authority
there and many aspects of its life receive some
attention.

111.16.18 TREVALLION, B.A.W. Metropolitan Kano: report on the 20
year development plan 1963-1983. Newman Neame, London,
1966, 160 pp.
Provides a comprehensive survey of the existing
situation and also detailed projections and proposals
in regard to the city's physical form, housing provision, social services, commerce and industry, transport
systems, and relations with its hinterland. Includes
numerous maps and charts, while detailed maps of planned
land-use form a supplementary volume.

111.16.19 YUSUF, A.B. "Capital formation and management among the
Muslim Hausa traders of Kano, Nigeria." Africa, 45,
1975, 167-182.
Examines the techniques by which Kano Hausa traders
raise capital and invest it for diverse economic and
social purposes, stressing the significance of both
religion and kinship.

A much older paper still of some value is:

111.16.20 WHITTLESEY, D. "Kano: a Sudanese metropolis."
Geographical Review, 27, 1937, 177-199.

A comprehensive geographical study in German is:

111.16.21 BECKER, C. Kano: eine afrikanische Grosstadt. Deutsches
Institut für Afrika-Forschung, Hamburg, 1969, 184 pp.

Unpublished theses include:

111.16.22 BISHOP, V.F. Multilingualism and National Orientations
in Kano, Nigeria. Ph.D. thesis, Northwestern
University, Evanston, Ill., 1974.

111.16.23 FRISHMAN, A.I. The Spatial Growth and Residential
           Location Pattern of Kano, Nigeria. Ph.D. thesis,
           Northwestern University, Evanston, Ill., 1977.

111.16.24 GILBERT, E.H. Marketing of Staple Foods in Northern
           Nigeria: a study of the staple food marketing systems
           serving Kano city. Ph.D. thesis, Stanford University,
           Calif., 1969.

111.16.25 LUBECK, P.M. Early Industrialization and Social Class
           Formation among Factory Workers in Kano, Nigeria.
           Ph.D. thesis, Northwestern University, Evanston, Ill.,
           1975.

111.16.26 THOMSON, R.J. Voluntary Association Participation in
           Kano, Nigeria: a longitudinal analysis. Ph.D. thesis,
           Indiana University, 1978.

Katsina (Ancient Hausa town in the extreme north. Population in
         1975: about 110,000.)

111.17.1 DIHOFF, G. Katsina, Profile of a Nigerian City. Praeger,
          New York, 1970, 176 pp.
             A study dealing with the origin and relatively slow
          growth of the town, its social and economic structure,
          and especially its layout and physical appearance.
          Numerous photographs are included.

Lagos (Capital city of the federation, but due to be replaced as
       capital by a new interior city in the 1980s. Population in
       1975: about 2 million.)

111.18.1 ABIODUN, J.O. "Urban growth and problems in metropolitan
          Lagos." Urban Studies, 11, 1974, 341-347.
             Notes the city's rapid growth since 1950, the high
          proportion of migrants, especially in suburbs such as
          Mushin and Ajeromi, and the problems resulting.

111.18.2 ADEFOLALU, A.A. "Traffic congestion in the city of Lagos."
          Nigerian Geographical Journal, 20, 1977, 123-144.
             Examines the city's traffic congestion in relation
          to the physical environment, the road network, planning
          policies, and public behavior, reviews its consequences,
          and considers policy implications.

111.18.3 ADEGBOLA, O. "Urban sex ratios in Lagos, Nigeria."
          Nigerian Geographical Journal, 18, 1975, 27-38.
             Notes that the ratio of males to females in Lagos
          rose in the early twentieth century, but has recently

fallen again with more education for girls and more
female employment opportunities as key factors.

111.18.4   ADEJUYIGBE, O. "Evolution of the boundaries of Lagos."
            Nigeria Magazine, 101, 1969, 480-484.
                Brief account of the original delimitation of the
            city, later modifications, and the boundary problems
            created by urban growth in the 1960s.

111.18.5   ADEJUYIGBE, O. "The case for a new federal capital in
            Nigeria." Journal of Modern African Studies, 8, 1970,
            301-306.
                Discusses the establishment of Lagos as capital,
            the limitations on its present effectiveness, and the
            need for a shift to a more suitable location.

111.18.6   ADENIYI, P.O. "Applications of aerial photography to the
            estimation of the characteristics of residential
            buildings." Nigerian Geographical Journal, 19, 1976,
            189-200.
                Shows how information on housing and population can
            be obtained from air photographs of urban areas to sup-
            plement inadequate census data, on the basis of a sur-
            vey in five areas of Lagos.

111.18.7   ADEOLU, O. "Influence of swamp land on the growth of
            Lagos." African Environment, 3 (2), 1978, 31-47.
                Shows how a site among swamps and lagoons has influ-
            enced the physical form of the city and examines pro-
            gress over ninety years in swamp reclamation.

111.18.8   ADERIBIGBE, A.B. (ed.) Lagos: the development of an
            African city. Longman Nigeria, Lagos, 1975, 276 pp.
                Starts with accounts of the city's early history by
            the editor and late nineteenth-century history by P.D.
            Cole. B.A. Williams examines changing relationships
            between the federal, Lagos State, and city governments.
            P.O. Sada and A.A. Adefolalu discuss population growth,
            physical expansion, and planning problems. R.A. Akinola
            and N.O. Alao examine industrial structure, problems,
            and policies. S. Adesina reviews the development of
            Western education, and S.O. Daniel considers health
            conditions and social welfare services. G.O. Gbadamosi
            traces the city's religious history, and F. Aig-Imoukhuede
            examines contemporary culture, especially art and music.
            A fifty-page bibliography by A.O. Banjo concludes the
            volume.

111.18.9   AJAEGBU, H.I. "Population and local resource development
            in the Lagos State of Nigeria." Nigerian Geographical
            Journal, 12, 1969, 37-52.

An examination of the sparse population and limited
development of the rural areas of the state reveals the
limited local impact of the city, discussed further in
the author's doctoral thesis.

111.18.10   AKINOLA, R.A. "Factors in the geographical concentration
of manufacturing in Greater Lagos." Lagos Notes and
Records, 1 (1), 1967, 30-47.
Examines the extent of industrial growth in Lagos
and reviews relevant factors such as land, labor, raw
materials, transport, and markets.

111.18.11   ARIBIAH, O. "Social aspects of urban rehousing in Lagos."
Lagos Notes and Records, 3 (2), 1972, 40-49.
Outlines the housing situation in Lagos and offers
a positive view of the Surulere rehousing project in
terms of residents' satisfaction with it.

111.18.12   ARIBIAH, O. "The politics of rehousing." Lagos Notes
and Records, 5, 1974, 5-13.
Discusses the political problems arising from the
decision of Lagos Executive Development Board to under-
take a major slum clearance scheme in the 1950s.

111.18.13   ARIBIAH, O. "Community creation in a rehousing estate."
African Urban Notes, B 2 (1), 1975, 39-54.
Examines the processes by which the Surulere rehousing estate evolved into a social community over
its first fifteen years of existence.

111.18.14   AYENI, B. "A model-based approach to structure planning:
the example of Lagos." Nigerian Journal of Economic
and Social Studies, 18, 1976, 79-102.
Uses urban systems modelling techniques to show
that current development strategies for Lagos will not
resolve the city's planning problems as its population
expands.

111.18.15   AYENI, M.A.O. "Living conditions of the poor in Lagos."
Ekistics, 43, 1977, 77-80.
Reports on a study of house ownership and occupation
and of household amenities in both central and peripheral
low-income residential areas of Lagos.

111.18.16   BAKER, P.H. Urbanization and Political Change: the
politics of Lagos 1917-1967. University of California
Press, Berkeley, 1974, 384 pp.
A doctoral thesis examining the impact of urbanization on political life in the city, giving special
attention to the political role of the urban poor, the
formation of community power structures, and the

dynamics of modernization, by which the influence of the chiefs has given way to that of people with wealth as well as new government structures.

111.18.17 BARNES, S.T. "Voluntary associations in a metropolis: the case of Lagos, Nigeria." African Studies Review, 18 (2), 1975, 75-87.
Examines voluntary association behavior among the residents of the suburb of Mushin, focusing on what type of people join what type of association.

111.18.18 BARNES, S.T. "Social involvement of migrants in Lagos." In Adepoju, A. (ed.), Internal Migration in Nigeria. University of Ife, 1976, 224-239.
Shows that the strength of residential social involvement among migrants in the Mushin area is influenced more by socioeconomic status than by area of origin.

111.18.19 BARNES, S.T. "Political transition in Urban Africa." Annals of the American Academy of Political and Social Science, 432, 1977, 26-41.
Examines emerging political structures in the suburban area of Mushin as a case study of the failure of formal administrative systems to handle rapid urban growth and the development of spontaneous systems partly traditional in character.

111.18.20 BARNES, S.T. "Migration and land acquisition: the new landowners of Lagos." African Urban Studies, 4, 1979, 59-70.
Examines the nature of the private land and housing market in Lagos and shows how the evolving pattern of land ownership has affected both migration patterns and social organization.

111.18.21 COLE, P. Modern and Traditional Elites in the Politics of Lagos. Cambridge University Press, 1975, 297 pp.
A historical study of Lagos politics from the 1880s to the 1930s, focusing on local response to colonial rule and on relations between the traditional authorities and the new elite that emerged under the British.

111.18.22 COMHAIRE, J.L.L. "Leopoldville and Lagos: comparative study of conditions in 1960." U.N. Economic Bulletin for Africa, 1 (2), 1961, 50-65. Reprinted in Breese, G. (ed.), The City in Newly Developing Countries. Prentice-Hall, Englewood Cliffs, N.J., 1969, 436-460.
Compares the two cities with respect to a wide range of issues, from age and size to patterns of in-migration, ethnicity, foreign influence, economic activities, public services, housing, and administration.

111.18.23 EBONG, B.J. "Urban growth and housing problems in Nigeria:
a case study of Lagos." African Urban Studies, 4, 1979,
71-81.
Outlines the city's physical growth, with special
reference to the extensive yet still inadequate new
housing developments of recent years, and the need both
for further investment in Lagos and for decentralization.

111.18.24 ECHUERO, M.J.C. "The Lagos scene in the nineteenth century."
Presence Africaine, 82, 1972, 77-93.
Draws on contemporary sources to provide a description of economic and social life in Lagos towards the
end of the century.

111.18.25 ECHUERO, M.J.C. Victorian Lagos: aspects of nineteenth-
century Lagos life. Macmillan, London, 1977, 124 pp.
Draws on the local press of the period to present a
picture of cultural and intellectual life in late nineteenth-century Lagos. Individual chapters deal with
education, music, religion, and politics, all set in
the context of contact between two cultures.

111.18.26 EJIOGU, C.N. "African rural-urban migrants in the main
migrant areas of the Lagos Federal Territory." In
Caldwell, J.C. and Okonjo, C. (eds.), The Population of
Tropical Africa. Longmans, London, 1968, 320-330.
Reports on a 1964 demographic survey of households
mainly in Ebute Metta, Yaba, and Suru Lere, covering
age and sex, marital status, household composition,
education, and occupation.

111.18.27 EJIOGU, C.N. "Metropolitanization: the growth of Lagos."
In Caldwell, J.C. (ed.), Population Growth and Socio-
economic Change in West Africa. Columbia University
Press, New York, 1975, 308-320.
Traces the growth of the city's population over 100
years, examines the contributions of natural increase
and in-migration, and notes changes in its demography
and ethnic structure.

*111.18.28 FAPOHUNDA, E.R. "Characteristics of women workers in
Lagos." Labour and Society, 3 (2), 1978, 158-171.

111.18.29 FAPOHUNDA, O.J. and LUBELL, H. Lagos: urban development
and employment. ILO, Geneva, 1978, 109 pp.
One of a series of city studies undertaken within
the ILO World Employment Programme. Examines the city's
role in the Nigerian economy, patterns of in-migration
and employment, journeys to work, and the urban infrastructure. Concludes with policy recommendations on
both employment and decongestion.

111.18.30 GALE, T.S. "Lagos: the history of British colonial
           neglect of traditional African cities." African Urban
           Studies, 5, 1979, 11-24.
                Examines colonial policies towards the physical de-
           velopment of Lagos, especially from the 1870s to the
           1920s, with special reference to the failure to deal
           with problems of health and sanitation.

111.18.31 GEORGE, M.V. and EIGBEFOH, A.A. "Population growth and
           migration in Lagos, 1911-1963." In Urbanization and
           Migration in some Arab and African Countries. Cairo
           Demographic Centre, 1973, 403-429.
                Reviews the census data available for Lagos, traces
           the growth and changing character of the population,
           and reviews the pattern of in-migration indicated by
           the censuses and the 1967 University of Lagos Population
           Dynamics Survey.

111.18.32 GRENZEBACH, K. "The structure and development of Greater
           Lagos: a documentation in aerial photographs."
           Geojournal, 2, 1978, 295-309.
                Uses a series of air photographs to demonstrate the
           physical growth of the city and to highlight some fea-
           tures of its present morphology.

111.18.33 GRIFFIN, D.W. "Urban development in Africa: the case of
           Lagos." California Geographer, 8, 1967, 37-46.
                Evaluates the slum clearance project for the central
           area in the light of the general African experience of
           rapid urban population growth.

111.18.34 GUTKIND, P.C.W. "The energy of despair: social organiza-
           tion of the unemployed in two African cities--Lagos
           and Nairobi." Civilisations, 17, 1967, 186-214,
           380-405.
                A comparative study showing how in both cases family
           and kinship ties enable the unemployed to survive in
           town and prevent their becoming a force for revolution.

111.18.35 HAUGHTON, J.P. "The government reservation as a town
           planning factor in tropical Africa." International
           Geographical Union, 21st Congress, Selected Papers.
           Calcutta, 1971, vol. 3, 121-126.
                Describes the residential areas established for
           expatriates in the colonial period in Lagos, noting
           how they have been preserved as low-density areas
           since Independence.

111.18.36 HUGHES, A. and COHEN, R. "An emerging Nigerian working
           class: the Lagos experience, 1897-1939." In Gutkind,
           P.C.W. et al. (eds.), African Labor History. Sage,

Beverly Hills, Calif., 1979, 31-55.
Outlines the character of the early twentieth-century Lagos economy and examines more closely the emergence of a wage labor force and its developing political orgainzation.

111.18.37 IZZETT, A. "Family life among the Yoruba in Lagos, Nigeria." In Southall, A. (ed.), <u>Social Change in Modern Africa</u>. Oxford University Press, 1961, 305-315.
A description of the changing patterns of marriage and of particular husband/wife relationships among the Yoruba who are settled in Lagos.

111.18.38 KOENIGSBERGER, O. et al. <u>Metropolitan Lagos</u>. United Nations, New York, 1964, 306 pp.
A study prepared for the Nigerian Government, examining in depth competition for land, journeys to work, traffic problems, housing shortage, growth of slums, health hazards, lack of community services, and lack of effective city government. Opens with a summary of the problems identified and recommendations made.

111.18.39 LAW, R.C.C. "The dynastic chronology of Lagos." <u>Lagos Notes and Records</u>, 2 (2), 1968, 46-54.
Reconstructs the sequence of rulers based in Lagos from the seventeenth century to the British arrival in 1851.

111.18.40 MABOGUNJE, A.L. "The evolution and analysis of the retail structure of Lagos." <u>Economic Geography</u>, 40, 1964, 304-323.
Examines the evolution, structure, organization, and spatial patterns of retailing in the city, including both the formal sector and market trade.

111.18.41 MABOGUNJE, A.L. <u>Urbanization in Nigeria</u>. University of London Press, 1968. Chap. 10, "Lagos, the rise of a modern metropolis," 238-273; Chap. 11 "The internal structure of Lagos," pp. 274-311.
Chapter 10 examines the city's historical development from the eighteenth century, reviewing its population growth and its changing economic functions. Chapter 11 examines the city's site, the structure of its commercial, industrial, and port zones, its contrasting residential areas, and patterns of internal circulation.

111.18.42 McCLUSKY, J. "The city as a force: three novels by Cyprian Ekwensi." <u>Journal of Black Studies</u>, 7, 1976, 211-224.

Shows that the city of Lagos is more than just the
setting for People of the City, Jagua Nana, and Beauti-
ful Feathers, but is also revealed as a destructive
force in people's lives.

111.18.43   MARRIS, P.   "Slum clearance and family life in Lagos."
            Human Organization, 19, 1960, 123-128.
            Examines the nature of family and community life in
            central Lagos and the largely disruptive consequences
            of a major slum clearance scheme.

111.18.44   MARRIS, P.   Family and Social Change in an African City:
            a study of rehousing in Lagos.   Routledge and Kegan
            Paul, London, 1961, 180 pp.
            A study of the late-1950s scheme to shift people
            from a central slum area to new housing at Surulere,
            showing how such resettlement can disrupt family, com-
            munity, and economic life.   Individual chapters deal
            with family relationships and economic activities in
            the central area, as well as the clearance scheme and
            the development of the new estate.

111.18.45   MARRIS, P.   "Motives and methods: reflections on a study
            in Lagos."   In Miner, H. (ed.), The City in Modern
            Africa.   Praeger, New York; Pall Mall, London, 1967,
            39-54.
            The author examines his own motives and methods in
            undertaking the study noted above as a comparison with
            similar experience in London and suggests new lines of
            approach to African urban studies.

111.18.46   MARRIS, P.   Loss and Change.   Routledge and Kegan Paul,
            London, 1974.   Chap. 3 "Slum clearance," 43-58.
            Largely concerned with the social consequences of
            the 1950s slum clearance scheme in central Lagos,
            especially for marriage patterns, as a case study of
            universal social issues.

111.18.47   MILLER, N.S.   "Aspects of the development of Lagos."
            Nigerian Field, 28 (4), 1963, 149-172.
            An illustrated account of the city's growth over
            400 years, with maps showing change in land-use.

111.18.48   MORGAN, R.W. and KANNISTO, V.   "A population dynamics
            survey of Lagos, Nigeria."   Social Science and Medicine,
            7, 1973, 1-30.
            Discusses the methodology and results of an intensive
            1967-1968 survey in thirty areas of the city to produce
            information on demographic processes.

111.18.49   NZEKWU, O. (ed.) "Lagos 1861-1961:   a special centenary

supplement." Nigeria Magazine, 69, 1961, 95-181.
Includes discussions of the British occupation of
Lagos by J.F.A. Ajayi; of later historical development
by N.S. Miller; of the city's physical growth by A.L.
Mabogunje; of Brazilian influences by A.B. Laotan; and
of the independence celebrations by C. Ekwensi. Incorporates numerous photographs.

111.18.50 OGUNDANA, B. "Lagos: Nigeria's premier port." Nigerian
Geographical Journal, 4 (2), 1961, 26-40.
Examines the growth and present pattern of port
traffic at Lagos, the extent of its hinterland for various commodities, and its future prospects.

111.18.51 OHADIKE, P.O. "A demographic note on marriage, family
and family growth in Lagos, Nigeria." In Caldwell,
J.C. and Okonjo, C. (eds.), The Population of Tropical
Africa. Longmans, London, 1968, 379-392.
Summarizes data on marriage, preferred family size
and actual fertility, and related socioeconomic characteristics, from a 1964 survey on women in Lagos.

111.18.52 OHADIKE, P.O. "Urbanization: growth, transitions, and
problems of a premier West African city (Lagos, Nigeria)."
Urban Affairs Quarterly, 3 (4), 1968, 69-90.
Discusses the growth of the urban population and a
variety of demographic and social characteristics on
the basis of a 1964 survey, analyzed more fully in a
Canberra doctoral thesis.

111.18.53 OHADIKE, P.O. "The possibility of fertility change in
modern Africa: a West African case." African Social
Research, 8, 1969, 602-614.
Reports further on the 1964 survey of women in Lagos,
which revealed some relationship between increased
socioeconomic status and reduced fertility and preferred
family size.

111.18.54 OKPALA, D.C.I. "Urban ecology and urban residential
theories: application in Nigeria's socio-cultural
milieu." Socio-Economic Planning Sciences, 12 (4),
1978, 177-183.
Shows how Western theories have limited application
in Lagos, where ecological patterns are often different,
and where even apparently similar patterns may have
different causes.

111.18.55 OKPALA, D.C.I. "Accessibility distribution aspects of
public urban land management: a Nigerian case."
African Urban Studies, 5, 1979, 25-44.
Examines the public management of urban land in

Lagos, with special reference to the access that different groups of people have to land, and the implications for the city's housing problems.

111.18.56 OKUNROTIFA, P.O. "Manufacturing industries in Lagos, Nigeria." Professional Geographer, 22, 1970, 62–66.
A summary of the industries represented in Lagos and the factors favoring their concentration there.

111.18.57 OLAFIOYE, A.O. Lagos Past and Present: an historical bibliography. National Library of Nigeria, Lagos, 1968, 1970, 102 pp.
A mimeographed list, largely of local material, and largely complementary to the list given here.

111.18.58 OLAYEMI, O.A. "Intra-city personal travel in metropolitan Lagos." Geoforum, 8, 1977, 19–27.
Shows how the sharp separation of workplace and residence involves much daily travel, especially by bus, and notes the frequency of long journeys to school also.

111.18.59 OLORUNTIMEHIN, O. "The role of family structure in the development of delinquent behaviour among juveniles in Lagos." Nigerian Journal of Economic and Social Studies, 12, 1970, 185–203.
Shows how family structures and relationships influence the propensity to delinquency among the youth of Lagos, drawing on interviews in Approved Schools and in ordinary schools.

111.18.60 OLORUNTIMEHIN, O. "A study of juvenile delinquency in a Nigerian city." British Journal of Criminology, 13, 1973, 157–169.
Very similar to the paper noted above, but with more reference to other studies elsewhere.

111.18.61 OLUSANYA, G.O. "The origin of the Lagos City Council." Lagos Notes and Records, 2 (1), 1968, 51–58.
Discusses the steps taken between 1908 and 1920 to set up the authority that later became the City Council.

111.18.62 PEACE, A. "The Lagos proletariat: labour aristocrats or populist militants?" In Sandbrook, R. and Cohen, R. (eds.), The Development of an African Working Class. Longman, London, 1975, 291–302.
Examines the circumstances and the actions of factory workers in Lagos, largely rejecting the thesis that they are a privileged group and noting their deeply-felt sense of exploitation.

111.18.63 PEACE, A.J. Choice, Class and Conflict: a study of

southern Nigerian factory workers. Harvester Press, Brighton, U.K., 1979, 204 pp.
  The published version of a 1973 Sussex doctoral thesis concerned with the social organization of people living and working in an urban environment for the first time, based on 1970-1971 fieldwork among people living in the suburb of Agege and working on the Ikeja industrial estate. Individual chapters deal with the social setting facing the migrants, friendship networks, employment and self-employment, status and class, and trade union activity.

111.18.64 PEACE, A.J. "Prestige, power and legitimacy in a modern Nigerian town." Canadian Journal of African Studies, 13, 1979, 25-51.
  Examines social processes in the suburb of Agege that hinder economic change and especially improvement for the poorest, as a case study of processes found throughout West Africa and beyond.

111.18.65 PEIL, M. "Male unemployment in Lagos, 1971." Manpower and Unemployment Research in Africa, 5 (2), 1972, 18-24.
  Reports on a small house-to-house survey, providing information on the extent and nature of unemployment within the city.

111.18.66 PULLEN, G. "Some problems of rapid urbanization in Lagos." Journal of Tropical Geography, 23, 1966, 55-61; and Ekistics, 24, 1967, 196-200.
  A brief discussion of social structure, housing conditions, and planning problems in the rapidly growing dormitory suburbs of Lagos.

111.18.67 SADA, P.O. "Political policies and the development of transportation in metropolitan Lagos." Nigerian Geographical Journal, 13, 1970, 185-199.
  Examines the city's internal transport patterns and problems against the background of the changing political structures in the area.

111.18.68 SADA, P.O. "The rural urban fringe of Lagos: growth and planning problems." Nigeria Magazine, 104, 1970, 40-45.
  Describes the recent growth of several peripheral settlements and reviews planning problems posed by local government structures, land-tenure systems, and the lack of planning control.

111.18.69 SADA, P.O. "The rural-urban fringe of Lagos: population and land use." Nigerian Journal of Economic and Social Studies, 12, 1970, 225-241.
  Reports on surveys of residential, commercial, and

industrial land-use, and of housing, household structures, and occupations, in fringe areas such as Mushin,
Shomolu, and Ajeromi.

111.18.70   SADA, P.O.   "Residential land use in Lagos: the relevance
of traditional models."   African Urban Notes, 7 (1),
1972, 3-25.
Examines spatial patterns of land values and of
various grades of residential area and shows the limited
value of urban land-use models formulated in developed
countries for explaining these patterns.

111.18.71   SADA, P.O. and ADEGBOLA, O.   "Migration and urban development: the case of Lagos."   In Adepoju, A. (ed.),
Internal Migration in Nigeria.   University of Ife,
1976, 187-205.
Examines the origins of migrants to Lagos, their
motives for moving and length of stay, their residential distribution, and the housing problems that they
present.

111.18.72   SADA, P.O. and McNULTY, M.L.   "Traditional markets in
Lagos: a study of the changing administrative processes and marketing transactions."   Quarterly Journal
of Administration, 8, 1974, 149-165.
Examines both traditional and modern systems of
regulating markets in Lagos, suggesting that market
trade has suffered from the coexistence of two parallel
administrative systems with little integration.

111.18.73   SADA, P.O. and McNULTY, M.L.   "Traditional markets in
Lagos: a note on consumer behaviour."   Nigerian
Geographical Journal, 17, 1974, 9-21.
Presents the results of a survey of over 2500 people
in all parts of the city, investigating their use of
traditional markets, and examines the resulting travel
patterns.

111.18.74   SADA, P.O.; McNULTY, M.L.; and ADALEMO, I.A.   "Periodic
markets in a metropolitan environment: the example
of Lagos, Nigeria."   In Smith, R.H.T. (ed.), Market-
Place Trade: periodic markets, hawkers and traders in
Africa, Asian and Latin America.   Centre for Transportation Studies, University of British Columbia, Vancouver,
1978, 155-166.
Reports on a survey of traders and commodities in
thirty Lagos markets, relating the findings to theoretical ideas on periodic markets.

111.18.75   SINCLAIR, S.W.   "Ease of entry into small-scale trading
in African cities: some case studies from Lagos."

Manpower and Unemployment Research, 10 (1), 1977, 79-90.
Examines the characteristics of people in various trades, with special reference to their age and their experience of city life before entering the trade.

111.18.76 SULE, O.R.A. "The deterioration of the Nigerian environment: problems of solid wastes disposal in the metropolitan Lagos." Geojournal, 3, 1979, 571-577.
Examines the city's refuse disposal problems on the basis of a survey of facilities, needs, and attitudes in the Surulere area, showing the total inadequacy of existing provisions.

111.18.77 WILLIAMS, B.A. and WALSH, A.H. Urban Government for
Metropolitan Lagos. Praeger, New York, 1968, 183 pp.
One of twelve case studies in urban government undertaken for the American Institute of Public Administration.
A brief review of the city's population and economy is followed by an analysis of its administrative structure in the mid-1960s, with special reference to federal-
metropolitan relations, to administration of its physi-
cal planning, and to administration of water supply, transport, housing, and education.

Unpublished theses include:

111.18.78 ACHUNINE, O.B. Dynamics and Strategies for Urban Housing
and Infrastructure in Developing Countries: a case
study of Lagos metropolitan area. Ph.D. thesis,
Michigan State University, 1977.

111.18.79 AFOLAYAN, A.A. Behavioural Approach to the Study of
Migration into and Mobility within Metropolitan Lagos.
Ph.D. thesis, University of Ibadan, 1975.

111.18.80 AJAEGBU, H.I. The Impact of Lagos on the Changing Rural
Economy of the Creeks and Lagoon Area of Epe and Ikeja
Divisions, Western Nigeria. Ph.D. thesis, University
of Ibadan, 1968.

111.18.81 AKEREDOLU-ALE, E.O. Nigerian Entrepreneurs in the Lagos
State: a study in the origins and performance of
indigenous business leadership in a young economy.
Ph.D. thesis, University of London, 1971.

111.18.82 AMOS, A. Land Use and Industrialization in Lagos, Nigeria.
Ph.D. thesis, University of Leicester, U.K., 1975.

111.18.83 BARNES, S.T. Becoming a Lagosian. Ph.D. thesis, University
of Wisconsin, 1974.

111.18.84 BROWN, S.H. A History of the People of Lagos, 1852–1886.
Ph.D. thesis, Northwestern University, Evanston, Ill.,
1964.

111.18.85 DOSUNMU, W.O. An Area-wide Planning Methodology for
Metropolitan Lagos. Ph.D. thesis, New York University,
1972.

111.18.86 GEIGER, R.P. Youth and Social Change in Lagos. Ph.D.
thesis, University of Southern Illinois, 1976.

111.18.87 HOPKINS, A.G. An Economic History of Lagos, 1880–1914.
Ph.D. thesis, University of London, 1964.

111.18.88 LUCAS, D.W. The Participation of Women in the Nigerian
Labour Force since the 1950s, with special reference
to Lagos. Ph.D. thesis, University of London, 1975.

111.18.89 MABOGUNJE, A.L. Lagos: a study in urban geography.
Ph.D. thesis, University of London, 1962.

111.18.90 OHADIKE, P.O. Patterns and Variations in Fertility and
Family Formation: a study of urban Africans in Lagos,
Nigeria. Ph.D. thesis, Australian National University,
Canberra, 1965.

111.18.91 OKPALA, D.C.I. The Potentials and Perils of Public Urban
Land Ownership and Management: a case study of the
Lagos Executive Development Board (Nigeria) 1928–1972.
Ph.D. thesis, Massachusetts Institute of Technology,
1977.

111.18.92 OLAYEMI, O.A. Workplace and Residence: an analysis of
commuting in metropolitan Lagos and its implications
for regional planning. Ph.D. thesis, University of
London, 1975.

111.18.93 ROWE, M.P. Indigenous Industrial Entrepreneurship in
Lagos, Nigeria. Ph.D. thesis, Columbia University,
New York, 1971.

111.18.94 SADA, P.O. The Metropolitan Region of Lagos: a study of
the political factor in urban geography. Ph.D. thesis,
Indiana University, 1968.

See also 1.0.31, 111.0.16, 111.0.17, 111.0.70, 111.0.73,
111.0.97, 111.0.104, 111.0.110, 111.0.123.

<u>Maiduguri</u> (Capital of Borno State in the extreme northeast.
Population in 1975: about 180,000.)

111.19 No substantial publications have been found.

<u>Ogbomoso</u> (Yoruba town in the north of Oyo State. The 1963 census
placed it third in population among all Nigerian urban
centers. Probable 1975 population: between 250,000 and
350,000.)

Despite its size, the only reference found is:

111.20.1 AGIRI, B.A. "When was Ogbomoso founded?" <u>Transafrican
Journal of History</u>, 5, 1976, 32-51.
Examines the traditions regarding the town's origin,
probably in the seventeenth century, with special reference to problems of chronology when only oral tradition
exists.

<u>Ondo</u> (Yoruba town in Ondo State in the southwest. Population in
1975: about 150,000.)

111.21.1 BENDER, D.R. "De facto families and de jure households in
Ondo." <u>American Anthropologist</u>, 73, 1971, 223-241.
Shows how people in Ondo live as members of large
households, which often have houses in surrounding villages as well as in town, and which are the basic social
units in Yoruba society.

111.21.2 CAMARA, C. "Une ville precoloniale au Nigeria: Ondo."
<u>Cahiers d'Etudes Africaines</u>, 13, 1973, 417-441.
Examines the site and growth of the town, its economic
and political institutions and relations with the surrounding area, and its physical structure.

See also 111.0.49.

<u>Onitsha</u> (Provincial town in Anambra State. Population in 1975:
about 200,000.)

111.22.1 HENDERSON, R.N. "Generalized cultures and evolutionary
adaptability: a comparison of urban Efik and Ibo in
Nigeria." <u>Ethnology</u>, 5, 1966, 365-391. Reprinted in
Melson, R. and Wolpe, H. (eds.), <u>Nigeria: modernization
and the politics of communalism</u>. Michigan State
University Press, East Lansing, 1971, 215-253.
Begins with a critique of Morrill's model of Ibo and
Efik adaptation to Calabar urban life and broadens the

perspective through an analysis of the evolution of social and political structures in Onitsha.

111.22.2 ONYEMELUKWE, J.O.C. "Aspects of staple foods trade in Onitsha market." Nigerian Geographical Journal, 13, 1970, 121-139.
Examines ways of entering the trade and methods by which it is financed, stressing "informal" sources of credit.

111.22.3 ONYEMELUKWE, J.O.C. "Foodstuff price variation in the service area of Onitsha market." Nigerian Geographical Journal, 15, 1972, 13-23.
Examines the system of food supply to Onitsha market and the factors causing fluctuations in prices.

111.22.4 ONYEMELUKWE, J.O.C. "Some factors in the growth of West African market towns: the example of pre-civil war Onitsha." Urban Studies, 11, 1974, 47-59.
Examines the town's growth as a market center and factors influencing its prosperity, with special reference to the cumulative effects of scale economies.

111.22.5 UKWU, U.I. "Onitsha: a metropolitan centre." In Hodder, B.W. and Ukwu, U.I. Markets in West Africa. Ibadan University Press, 1969, 232-243.
Discusses the town's evolution, its trading function, and its physical structure with special reference to its retail trade areas and markets.

Unpublished theses include:

111.22.6 ONYEMELUKWE, J.O.C. Staple Foods Trade in Onitsha Market. Ph.D. thesis, University of Ibadan, 1970.

Oshogbo (Provincial town in Oyo State in the southwest. Population in 1975: about 280,000.)

111.23.1 ADEPOJU, A. "Rural-urban socio-economic links: the example of migrants in South-West Nigeria." In Amin, S. (ed.), Modern Migrations in Western Africa. Oxford University Press, London, 1974, 127-136.
Reports on a survey of migrant household heads in Oshogbo, focusing on place of residence on arrival, visits home and remittances, and suggesting that migration brings a large urban-rural flow of resources.

111.23.2 BEIER, U. "Oshogbo: portrait of a Yoruba town." Nigeria Magazine, 66, 1960, 94-102.
A brief account of the town's growth and its social and cultural life.

111.23.3 SCHWAB, W.B. "Oshogbo: an urban community?" In Kuper,
          H. (ed.), Urbanization and Migration in West Africa.
          University of California Press, Berkeley, 1965, 85-109.
              Examines briefly Oshogbo's physical form and, more
          fully, its social structures, concluding that the per-
          sistence of traditional Yoruba elements differentiates
          it sharply from new urban centers elsewhere in Africa.

111.23.4 SCHWAB, W.B. "Urbanism, corporate groups and cultural
          change in Africa." Anthropological Quarterly, 43, 1970,
          187-214.
              After a general discussion of African urbanization,
          the relationships between corporate groups and social
          communities are examined for Oshogbo and for Gwelo in
          Zimbabwe, towns of sharply contrasting character.

          See also 110.0.8-10, 110.0.122.

Owerri (Town in the southeast, recently chosen as capital of Imo
        State. Population in 1975: about 100,000.)

111.24.1 GALANTAY, E.Y. "The planning of Owerri: a new capital
          for Imo State, Nigeria." Town Planning Review, 49,
          1978, 371-386.
              Examines the process of planning substantial physical
          growth for Owerri, following its selection as a state
          capital in 1976, and outlines the master plan prepared
          for the state government.

Note also a German publication:

111.24.2 GRENZEBACH, K. "Luftbild Owerri." Die Erde, 99, 1968,
          1-4.
              Analysis of an air photograph.

Oyo (Yoruba town in Oyo State in the southwest. Population in
     1975: about 150,000.)

111.25.1 BRAY, J.M. "The tim-tim makers of Oyo." Savanna, 5,
          1976, 127-137.
              Shows how socioeconomic factors have influenced the
          location and functioning of traditional leather-working
          in Oyo, discussing the organization of both production
          and marketing.

111.25.2 GODDARD, S. "Town-farm relations in Yoruba land: a case
          study from Oyo." Africa, 35, 1965, 21-29.
              Examines the close links between the town and the
          surrounding farms, noting the many people who live

outside during the week but stay in town at weekends
and for special occasions.

There are also many references to the town of Oyo in:

111.25.3 ATANDA, J.A. The New Oyo Empire: indirect rule and change
in Western Nigeria, 1894-1934. Longman, London, 1973,
334 pp.

See also 110.0.132.

Port Harcourt (Capital of Rivers State, in the southeast. Population in 1975: about 250,000.)

111.26.1 SMOCK, A. Ibo Politics: the role of ethnic unions in
Eastern Nigeria. Harvard University Press, Cambridge,
Mass., 1971, 274 pp.
A detailed examination of the evolution, character,
and role of ethnic unions, both in rural areas and in
Port Harcourt, and of the impact of these unions on
political development in the 1960s.

111.26.2 WOLPE, H.E. "Port Harcourt: Ibo politics in microcosm."
Journal of Modern African Studies, 7, 1969, 469-493.
Reprinted in Melson, R. and Wolpe, H. (eds.), Nigeria:
modernization and the politics of communalism. Michigan
State University Press, East Lansing, 1971, 483-513.
Analyzes changing patterns of power in the city
while it was dominated by Ibo and their relation to
Ibo politics in general.

111.26.3 WOLPE, H.E. Urban Politics in Nigeria: a study of Port
Harcourt. University of California Press, Berkeley,
1974, 314 pp.
A brief background on the city and its physical and
cultural setting is followed by a full account of its
political history. Several chapters then examine community power structures in the decade 1955-1965, especially relations between the local Ijaw and the dominant Ibo,
and the book concludes with a more general discussion of
the issues of communalism and communal conflict. Based
on a 1967 Massachusetts Institute of Technology Ph.D.
thesis.

Unpublished theses include:

111.26.4 ANYANWU, C. Port Harcourt: the rise and development of a
Nigerian municipality, 1913-1955. Ph.D. thesis,
University of Ibadan, 1971.

Sapele (Town and minor port in Bendel State in the south. Population
        in 1975: about 100,000.)

111.27.1 GORDON, J.U. "West African city-state: a study of Sapele
          town council and development." Umoja, 1, 1977, 71-82.
               Examines the development of local government in mid-
          western Nigeria and the functioning of the Sapele Town
          Council as a case study in African political development.

111.27.2 IMOAGENE, S.O. "Mechanisms of immigrant adjustment in a
          West African urban community." Nigerian Journal of
          Economic and Social Studies, 9, 1967, 51-66.
               Investigates the mechanisms enabling people of rural
          origin to settle in the town of Sapele, especially the
          clan and village unions.

111.27.3 IMOAGENE, S.O. "Psycho-social factors in rural-urban
          migration." Nigerian Journal of Economic and Social
          Studies, 9, 1967, 375-386.
               Emphasizes the significance of attitudes and perceived
          needs rather than economic opportunities as factors that
          have encouraged migration into Sapele.

111.27.4 IMOAGENE, S.O. "Urban involvement and rural detachment."
          Nigerian Journal of Economic and Social Studies, 10,
          1968, 397-411.
               Investigates the degree of involvement of immigrants
          in urban social structures and institutions, both in
          general terms and for Sapele.

111.27.5 IMOAGENE, S.O. "Sapele: an emergent city in depression."
          Ibadan, 28, 1970, 49-53.
               Discusses the town's rapid growth, its demographic
          and social structure, and the effects of falling rubber
          and timber prices and political upheaval in the 1960s.

111.27.6 SALUBI, A. "The origins of Sapele township." Journal of
          the Historical Society of Nigeria, 2 (1), 1960, 115-131.
               Examines the original locating factors for the town
          and its subsequent population and economic growth.

     See also 111.0.45.

Sokoto (Capital of Sokoto State in the northwest. Population in
        1975: about 120,000.)

111.28.1 TREVOR, J. "Family change in Sokoto: a traditional
          Moslem Fulani/Hausa city." In Caldwell, J.C. (ed.),
          Population Growth and Socioeconomic Change in West
          Africa. Columbia University Press, New York, 1975.
          236-253.

Discusses recent changes in patterns of marriage and
family life and reports on a survey of women's attitudes
to family size and contraception, stressing the significance of continued high infant mortality.

Umuahia (Town in Imo State, in the southeast. Population in 1975:
about 100,000.)

111.29.1 HANNA, W.J. and HANNA, J.L. "The political structure of
urban-centered African communities." In Miner, H. (ed.),
The City in Modern Africa. Praeger, New York; Pall Mall,
London, 1965, 151-184.
Describes the political structures of Mbale and of
Umuahia in Nigeria, emphasizing ethnic differentiation,
ineffectiveness of local administrative authorities,
and the importance instead of influential individuals.

111.29.2 HANNA, W.J. and HANNA, J.L. "Influence and influentials in
two urban-centered African communities." Comparative
Politics, 2, 1969, 17-39.
Develops the third theme from the paper noted above.

111.29.3 HANNA, W.J. and HANNA, J.L. "Polyethnicity and political
integration in Umuahia and Mbale." In Daland, R.T. (ed.),
Comparative Urban Research. Sage, Beverly Hills, Calif.,
1969, 163-202.
On the basis of surveys of relationships among ethnic
groups, the extent and nature of social and political
integration in the two towns is examined.

Warri (Town in Bendel State and a major center for the oil industry.
Population in 1975: about 100,000.)

111.30.1 LLOYD, P.C. "Ethnicity and the structure of inequality in
a Nigerian town in the mid-1950s." In Cohen, A. (ed.),
Urban Ethnicity. Tavistock, London, 1974, 223-250.
Examines the relationships between the Itsekiri,
Urhobo, and Ibo in Warri against the background of the
town's origins and growth, economic structure, and local
government system.

Zaria (Ancient northern city in Kaduna State. Population in 1975:
about 230,000.)

111.31.1 BEDAWI, H.Y. "Variation in residential space standards in
Zaria." Savanna, 5, 1976, 75-79.
Presents the results of a survey of housing conditions
and their influence on household structure in four zones
of the city.

111.31.2 DAVIES, H.R.J. "Aspects of urban development in northern
          Nigeria." In CNRS, La Croissance Urbaine en Afrique
          Noire et à Madagascar. Paris, 1972, 493-499.
          Outlines the economic basis of Zaria's twentieth
          century growth, its limited impact on the surrounding
          area, and its position and prospects vis-à-vis Kano and
          Kaduna.

111.31.3 GIHRING, T.A. "Urban imagery in Zaria: a study of
          environmental perception." Savanna, 4, 1975, 125-137.
          Reports on a sample survey in Zaria's four main resi-
          dential quarters to discover people's images of the city,
          emphasizing their much stronger responses on social than
          on physical aspects.

111.31.4 MORTIMORE, M.J. (ed.) Zaria and its Region. Occasional
          Paper 4, Department of Geography, Ahmadu Bello University,
          Zaria, 1970, 191 pp.
          The majority of papers are on the broad region around
          Zaria, but four concerned essentially with the city are
          those by A.W. Urquhart on its morphology, by A.D. Goddard
          on industry, by J.G.T. Van Raay on education, and by
          H.R.J. Davies on relations with the hinterland.

111.31.5 REMY, D. "Economic security and industrial unionism: a
          Nigerian case study." In Sandbrook, R. and Cohen, R.
          (eds.), The Development of an African Working Class.
          Longman, London, 1975, 161-177.
          A study of workers in the Zaria tobacco factory,
          showing that working class solidarity and effective
          trade union action cannot develop where economic security
          is tied either to education or to ethnically-based
          patronage.

111.31.6 REMY, D. "Underdevelopment and the experience of women: a
          Nigerian case study." In Reiter, R.R. (ed.), Towards
          an Anthropology of Women. Monthly Review Press, New
          York, 1976, 358-371; and in Williams, G. (ed.), Nigeria:
          economy and society. Rex Collings, London, 1976,
          123-134.
          Shows how economic options in Zaria have widened dur-
          ing this century far more for men than for women and
          shows that women's economic autonomy has been partly
          undermined.

111.31.7 REMY, D. and WEEKS, J. "Employment and inequality in a
          non-industrial city." In Wohlmuth, K (ed.), Employment
          Creation in Developing Societies. Praeger, New York,
          1973, 293-309.
          Examines the city's economy, including the formal and
          informal sectors and the links between these, and

160

highlights mechanisms that generate and perpetuate
economic inequality.

111.31.8   SCHWERDTFEGER, F. "Housing in Zaria." In Oliver, P. (ed.),
            Shelter in Africa. Barrie and Jenkins, London, 1971,
            58-79.
               Outlines the historical evolution of the city and
            examines in detail a selection of traditional house
            types, with some notes on household structure and ac-
            tivities also. Includes many plans and photographs.

111.31.9   SCHWERDTFEGER, F.W. "Urban settlement patterns in
            Northern Nigeria." In Ucko, P.J., et al. (eds.), Man,
            Settlement and Urbanism. Duckworth, London, 1972,
            547-556.
               Shows how dual structures have evolved in northern
            Nigerian cities and illustrates typical building styles
            in different parts of Zaria.

111.31.10   URQUHART, A.W. Planned Urban Landscapes of Northern
            Nigeria: a case study of Zaria. Ahmadu Bello University
            Press, Zaria, 1977, 94 pp.
               Three chapters of this book, already noted at
            111.0.114, are concerned specifically with Zaria, deal-
            ing respectively with Birnin Zaria (the old city), the
            colonial Zaria Township, and Tudun Wada and Samaru.
            They include details of past plans and legislation and
            reproductions of both old and recent maps.

A notable earlier study is:

111.31.11   SMITH, M.G. The Economy of Hausa Communities of Zaria.
            H.M.S.O., London, 1955, 271 pp.

Unpublished theses include:

111.31.12   REMY-WEEKS, D. Adaptive Strategies of Men and Women in
            Zaria, Nigeria: industrial workers and their wives.
            Ph.D. thesis, University of Michigan, 1973.

111.31.13   SCHWERDTFEGER, F.W. Comparative Study of Conventional
            Urban Houses in Three Regions of Africa. Ph.D. thesis,
            University of London, 1975.

SENEGAL

General

112.0.1   BAYLET, R., et al.   "Recherches sur la morbidité et la
          mortalité différentielles urbaines-rurales au Sénégal."
          In CNRS, La Criossance Urbaine en Afrique Noire et à
          Madagascar.   Paris, 1972, 317-337.
             Shows that some diseases are more prevalent in towns
          and others in rural areas, but that in general total and
          infant mortality is lower in town.

112.0.2   BOUQUILLON-VAUGELADE, C. and VIGNAC-BOTTIN, B.   "Les unités
          collectives et l'urbanisation au Sénégal: étude de la
          famille Wolof."   In CNRS, La Croissance Urbaine en
          Afrique Noire et à Madagascar.   Paris, 1972, 357-370.
             Compares the Pikine suburb of Dakar and the small town
          of Nioro du Rip with rural areas, to show the breakup of
          large families, the increased number of lodgers, and the
          increase in female household heads with progressive
          urbanization.

112.0.3   BRIGAUD, F.   Histoire Moderne et Contemporaine du Sénégal.
          CRDS, Saint Louis, 1966, 148 pp.
             Pages 64-79 examine the growth of the towns and social
          and economic structures within them.

112.0.4   COLLOMB, H. and AYATS, H.   "Les migrations au Sénégal:
          étude psychopathologique."   Cahiers d'Etudes Africaines,
          2, 1962, 570-597.
             Includes a broad review of rural-urban migration in
          Senegal, but focuses on the relationship between such
          migration and the incidence of mental disorder, drug-
          taking, etc.

112.0.5   FOUGEYROLLAS, P.   Modernisation des Hommes: l'exemple du
          Sénégal.   Flammarion, Paris, 1967, 237 pp.
             Includes a lengthy report on a questionnaire survey
          of workers in Dakar and Thiès regarding clothing, food,
          recreation, and attitudes to African and European ways
          of life.

112.0.6   JOHNSON, G.W.   The Emergence of Black Politics in Senegal:
          the struggle for power in four communes, 1900-1920.
          Stanford University Press, Calif., 1971, 260 pp.
             Examines the development of local government in Dakar,
          Gorée, Rufisque, and Saint-Louis, the gradual movement of
          Africans into positions of authority, and the significance
          of this development for the twentieth-century political
          history of Africa in general.

112.0.7   JOHNSON, G.W. "The Senegalese urban elite, 1900–1945."
          In Curtin, P.D. (ed.), Africa and the West. University
          of Wisconsin Press, Madison, 1972, 139–187.
          Discusses the social structure of Dakar, Gorée,
          Rufisque, and Saint-Louis during the colonial period
          and especially the attitude of the African elite to the
          French colonial presence.

112.0.8   LEGIER, H.J. "Institutions municipales et politique
          coloniale: les communes du Sénégal." Revue Française
          d'Histoire d'Outre-Mer, 55, 1968, 414–464.
          Examines the conflicts between administrative and
          legal structures and social reality during the colonial
          period in Dakar, Gorée, Rufisque, and Saint-Louis.

112.0.9   LOMBARD, J. Géographie Humaine du Sénégal. CRDS,
          Saint-Louis, 1963, 183 pp.
          Pages 133–159 examine the towns and the economic
          activities undertaken within them.

112.0.10 MARTIN, V. "Structure de la famille chez les Serer et les
          Wolof du Sénégal." Population, 4, 1970, 771–796.
          Includes a report on a 1960 demographic sample survey
          of Djourbel, Kaolack, and Thiès.

112.0.11 MERCIER, P. "L'urbanisation au Sénégal." In Frohlich,
          W. (ed.), Afrika im Wandel seiner Gesellschaftsformen.
          Brill, Leiden, Netherlands, 1964, 48–70.
          A general essay on the extent, evolution, and nature
          of urbanization in Senegal, with some emphasis on the
          roles of different groups in the social and political
          life of the towns.

*112.0.12 METGE, J. "La formation et le développement de l'urban-
          isation sans industrialisation au Sénégal." In Petit-
          Pont, M. (ed.), Structures Traditionelles et Développe-
          ment. Eyrolles, Paris, 1968.

112.0.13 PASQUIER, R. "Villes du Sénégal au XIXe siècle." Revue
          Française d'Histoire d'Outre-Mer, 47, 1960, 387–426.
          An account of the growth and development of the
          towns, especially Dakar and Saint-Louis, during the
          second half of the nineteenth century.

112.0.14 PORGES, L. Bibliographie des Régions du Sénégal. Ministère
          du Plan et du Développement, Dakar, 1967, 705 pp.
          Index includes references on individual towns scat-
          tered through the volume, in addition to those on Dakar
          in chapter 1.

112.0.15 PORGES, L. Bibliographie des Régions du Sénégal:

complément pour la période des origines à 1965 et mise
à jour 1966-1973. Mouton, Paris, 1977, 637 pp.
   A supplement to the volume listed above, with more
items than the original volume.

112.0.16 REMY, M. Senegal Today. Jeune Afrique, Paris, 1976, 239 pp.
   Includes lavishly illustrated descriptions of twenty-
eight towns (pp. 78-173), stressing aspects of tourist
interest.

112.0.17 SAMSON, A. "L'urbanisme face aux problèmes du développement:
l'exemple des villes secondaires au Sénégal." Industries
et Travaux d'Outremer, 22, 1974, 977-985.
   Examines the present role and form of small towns in
Senegal and considers how they might be developed in
physical planning terms.

112.0.18 TRIBILLON, J-F. Urbanisation, Colonisation et Développement
au Sénégal. 3 vols. SMUH, Paris, 1969, 536 pp.
   Semipublication of a thesis for the Faculty of Law in
the University of Paris, reviewing the history of urbanization in Senegal and its relationships with French colonial policies and the pattern of economic development.
Special attention is given to the administrative and
legislative aspects of urban development and urban
planning.

112.0.19 TRIBILLON, J-F. "In search of a town-planning doctrine
and policy." Bulletin du SMUH, 67, 1971, 27-58.
   Reviews the objectives of the Senegal government in
regard to urban development and specific policies adopted
towards urbanization and towards particular town-planning
issues. In English and French.

112.0.20 TRIBILLON, J-F. "Sénégal: pour une politique urbaine,
urbanisation et développement." Penant, 84, 1974,
333-362, 498-536.
   Extracts from the thesis noted above, discussing the
economic basis and social implications of urbanization
in Senegal, the potential contribution to development
of further urbanization, and appropriate urban planning
procedures.

112.0.21 VERNIERE, M. "Villes de l'intérieur." In Van-Chi-
Bonnardel, R. (ed.), Atlas National du Sénégal. Institut
Géographique National, Paris, 1977, 118-123.
   Detailed maps of thirteen towns and a discussion of
the evolution of the urban system, with brief case
studies of four of the smaller towns.

Another work largely concerned with activities in urban areas is:

112.0.22   PFEFFERMAN, G.   Industrial Labor in the Republic of Senegal.
             Praeger, New York, 1968, 325 pp.

Unpublished theses include:

112.0.23   MERCIER, P.   Contribution à la Sociologie des Villes du
             Sénégal Occidental à la Fin de la Période Coloniale.
             Thèse Doctorat d'Etat, Université de Paris, 1968.

Dakar   (Capital city.   Population at 1976 census: 800,000.   Cap-Vert
         Region, including neighboring Rufisque: 950,000.)

112.1.1   ARNAUD, J-C.   "Le ravitaillement de Dakar en Produits
             maraîchers."   Annales de l'Université d'Abidjan, series
             G, 4, 1972, 91-146.
                Examines the demand for fresh vegetables in the city,
             the local sources of supply, and the marketing channels
             involved.

112.1.2   ARNAUD-LUTZWILLER, S.   "Yoff, village de pêcheurs
             cultivateurs lébou dans la grande banlieue de Dakar."
             Annales de l'Université d'Abidjan, series G, 3, 1971,
             123-155.
                Summary of a Dakar "maîtrise" thesis, examining
             physical, social, and economic changes amongst this
             community as it has become engulfed by the growing city.

112.1.3   BARTHEL, D.L.   "The rise of a female professional elite:
             the case of Senegal."   African Studies Review, 18 (3),
             1975, 1-17.
                Presents the results of a 1974 questionnaire survey
             of professional women in Dakar, concerned with family
             background, education, attitudes, and aspirations.

112.1.4   BETTS, R.F.   "The problem of the Medina in the urban
             planning of Dakar."   African Urban Notes, 4 (3), 1969,
             5-15.
                Describes the establishment of this African quarter
             in 1914 and discusses subsequent ambivalent official
             attitudes towards it.   Also provides insights on French
             planning for Dakar as a whole and is supplemented by a
             bibliography on the history of Dakar.

112.1.5   BETTS, R.F.   "The establishment of the Medina in Dakar,
             Senegal, 1914."   Africa, 41, 1971, 143-152.
                A detailed account of the factors leading to, and
             the consequences of, the hasty government decision to
             relocate the city's African population in the area later
             known as the Medina.

112.1.6   BOUQUILLON-VAUGELADE, C. "Typologie de l'emploi urbain
          (formel et informel) à Pikine-Dakar." Manpower and
          Unemployment Research, 11 (1), 1978, 31-54.
              Reports on a survey of employment and unemployment
          among the men of this suburb, discussing the nature of
          their employment and different categories of umemployment.

112.1.7   COMHAIRE-SYLVAIN, S. "Vieillir à Dakar." Ethnographie,
          65, 1971, 12-37.
              Examines the life style of the elderly in the city,
          their attitudes to life, and the attitudes of other
          people towards them.

112.1.8   DAVID, P. Paysages Dakarois de l'Epoque Coloniale. ENDA,
          Dakar, 1978, 42 pp.
              Discusses the physical growth of the city from 1857
          to 1922, with several maps and old photographs and many
          extracts from contemporary documents.

112.1.9   DIAITE, I. "Le statut administratif des capitales:
          l'exemple de Dakar." Annales Africaines, 1976, 25-51.
              Examines the nature and problems of the municipal
          administration of Dakar in the postindependence period.

112.1.10 DIENG, I.M. "The "redevelopment" of Nimzatt-Anglemouss
          and its consequences." Manpower and Unemployment
          Research, 9 (2), 1976, 3-16.
              Discusses the clearance of this shantytown outside
          Dakar in 1975 and the resettlement of nearly 20,000
          inhabitants at Guediawaye, where housing and infrastruc-
          ture are better, but the unemployment problem is even
          greater.

*112.1.11 DIENG, I.M. "Déguerpissement de bidonvilles: le cas de
          Nimzatt et Angle-Mousse à Dakar." Environnement Africain,
          supplementary paper 17, 1977.

112.1.12 DIOP, A.B. "Enquête sur la migration toucouleur à Dakar."
          Bulletin de l'IFAN, B 22, 1960, 393-418.
              A study of the social and economic characteristics
          of this group of migrants, including housing and employ-
          ment patterns, with special reference to the degree of
          permanence of movement.

112.1.13 DIOP, A.B. Société Toucouleur et Migration: enquête sur
          l'immigration toucouleur à Dakar. IFAN, Dakar, 1965,
          232 pp.
              Examines society and economy in the area of origin;
          the scale, character and causes of migration to the
          city; working and living conditions within Dakar; and
          the migrants' patterns of social organization.

166

112.1.14 DREYFUS, J. "An experiment in self-help housing at Dakar."
In Self-help Practices in Housing: selected case
studies, United Nations, New York, 1973, 97-109.
An evaluation of a project undertaken by a housing
cooperative in 1955-1958.

112.1.15 FALADE, S. "Women of Dakar and the surrounding urban
areas." In Paulme, D. (ed.), Women of Tropical Africa.
Routledge and Kegan Paul, London, 1963, 217-229.
Surveys patterns of upbringing, marriage, motherhood,
divorce, and widowhood, and also examines women's economic status, drawing on 145 interviews.

112.1.16 GERRY, C. "The wrong side of the factory gate: casual
workers and capitalist industry in Dakar, Senegal."
Manpower and Unemployment Research, 9 (2), 1976, 17-27.
Shows that casual workers, with very intermittent
employment, are mainly not young in-migrants but a basic
element of the city's population.

112.1.17 GERRY, C. "The crisis of the self-employed: petty
production and capitalist production in Dakar." World
Development, 8, 1978, 1147-1160; and in O'Brien, R.C.
(ed.), The Political Economy of Underdevelopment:
Dependence in Senegal. Sage, Beverly Hills, Calif.,
1979, 126-155.
Examines the relationships between petty producers
and large-scale enterprise in Dakar, investigates the
extent of economic differentiation among the petty producers, and concludes that the prospects for most are
bleak while capitalist structures remain.

112.1.18 GERRY, C. "Small-scale manufacturing and repairs in Dakar:
a survey of market relations within the urban economy."
In Bromley, R. and Gerry, C. (eds.), Casual Work and
Poverty in Third World Cities. Wiley, Chichester, U.K.,
1979, 229-250.
Reports on a study of small-scale furniture makers,
leather workers, metal workers, and tailors in Dakar,
with special reference to their backward and forward
linkages with large-scale formal sector enterprise,
arguing that they suffer exploitation.

112.1.19 GIROULT, E. "Le nouveau plan directeur d'urbanisme de
Dakar." Industries et Travaux d'Outremer, 177, 1968,
668-679.
An outline of the 1968 plan for the physical development of the city.

112.1.20 GOSSELIN, M., et al. "Housing typology monograph: Dakar."
Planification Habitat Information, 78, 1974, 45-100.

A set of plans and photographs of housing types in various parts of the city, prepared in the architecture department of the National Institute of the Arts, Dakar.

112.1.21 HAUSER, A. Les Ouvriers de Dakar; étude psychosociologique. ORSTOM, Paris, 1968, 172 pp.
Briefly reviews employment, unemployment, and work conditions in Dakar; then reports in detail on a 1959 survey of workers in eight factories, covering socio-economic characteristics, mobility and absenteeism, and attitudes to industrial employment.

112.1.22 JACOLIN, P.; SECK, F.; and NDIAYE, A. "Actors and social forces: dynamics of change in an urban ward of Dakar." African Environment, 2 (1-2), 1976, 20-36.
Examines the rapid growth of the peripheral settlement of Arafat in 1973-75 and a government attempt to destroy it, with special reference to the various decision-makers involved and the possible alternative policies.

*112.1.23 JODOIN, M. Les Industries Manufacturières de la Région Dakaroise. Département de Géographie, Université de Montréal, 1963, 120 pp.

112.1.24 KANE, F. "Femmes prolétaires du Sénégal." Cahiers d'Etudes Africaines, 17, 1977, 77-94.
A comparison of women employed on plantations and in the Dakar food canning industry, showing much similarity but better wages and conditions in the city as a result of trade union activity.

*112.1.25 LACOMBE, B. "Note descriptive sur les groupes de migrants relevés au Sénégal dans les enquêtes rurales de Ngayorhème et Ndéméne de 1968 à 1970 et dans l'enquête urbaine de Pikine en 1969." Cahiers ORSTOM, Série sciences humaines, 9, 1972, 413-424.

112.1.26 LACOMBE, B. "The migrant group as a description of the demographic characteristics of migration: an application to the migrations recorded in 1969 in a suburban commune of Dakar: Pikine." In Cantrelle, P. (ed.), Population in African Development. Ordina, Dolhain, Belgium, 1974, 119-127.
Drawing on a 1969 sample survey, shows the value of considering rural-migrants not only as individuals but also as family and other groups who move together.

112.1.27 LACOMBE, B., et al. Exode Rural et Urbanisation au Sénégal: sociologie de la migration des Sérèr de Niakhar vers Dakar en 1970. ORSTOM, Paris, 1977, 206 pp.

Describes a survey undertaken both in this rural area
150 km inland and in Dakar and presents the results,
which provide much information on the social conditions
and relationships of the Serer in both environments.

112.1.28 LAURENT, O. "Une banlieue ouvrière: l'agglomération
suburbaine de Grand Yoff." Bulletin de l'IFAN, B 32,
1970, 518-557.
Brief outline of the origin, growth, and physical
form of this suburb and a fuller account of its demographic structure, economic activities, housing conditions, social infrastructure, and planning problems.

112.1.29 LAURENT, O. "Dakar et ses banlieues." In CNRS, La
Croissance Urbaine en Afrique Noire et à Madagascar.
Paris, 1972, 763-784.
Discusses the causes and consequences of the growth
of the city, examines more closely the recent development
of different types of suburb, and considers the problems
of two of these, Grand Yoff and Dagoudane Pikine.

112.1.30 LEBRUN, O. and GERRY, C. "Petty producers and capitalism."
Review of African Political Economy, 3, 1975, 20-32.
Provides a theoretical framework for an analysis of
labor in Dakar, examining the relationship between the
dominant capitalist mode of production and certain subordinate forms.

112.1.31 LECOUR GRANDMAISON, C. "Activités économiques des femmes
dakaroises." Africa, 39, 1969, 138-152.
Examines the levels, sources, and uses of women's
incomes, and the extent to which women have moved from
traditional occupations to new ones as urbanization has
proceeded.

112.1.32 LECOUR GRANDMAISON, C. "Stratégies matrimoniales des
femmes dakaroises." Cahiers ORSTOM, Série Sciences
Humaines, 8, 1971, 201-220.
Examines the transition from traditional Lebou marriage customs to modern urban marriage laws, and considers the implications for women's status in the city.

112.1.33 LECOUR GRANDMAISON, C. "Femmes Dakaroises. Rôles
traditionels féminins et urbanisation: Lebou et Wolof
de Dakar." Annales de l'Université d'Abidjan, Série F,
vol. 4, 1972, 254 pp.
Presents the results of a study of the social life
and economic activities of Dakar women, with special
reference to the Lebou, the indigenous people of the
area. Individual chapters cover marriage, social relationships, occupations, and incomes.

112.1.34 LERICOLLAIS, A. and VERNIERE, M. "L'émigration toucouleur
du fleuve Sénégal à Dakar." Cahiers ORSTOM, Série
sciences humaines, 12, 1975, 161-175.
Traces the movement of people from one Senegal valley
village to Dakar, their movements within the city to
find homes, and their relationships with the local Lebou
landowners.

112.1.35 MAACK, S.C. "Public taps: the human dynamics of urban
improvement." African Environment, 1 (4), 1975, 93-110.
Shows how the provision of public water supply in the
Pikine suburb has been influenced by, and had repercus-
sions on, lifestyles, social interaction, and local
political activity.

112.1.36 MARTIN, V. Etude Socio-démographique de la Ville de Dakar:
Recensement démographique de Dakar 1955. INSEE, Paris,
1962, 215 pp.
Discusses the growth of the city and its distinct
quarters, its demographic and ethnic structure, migration patterns, occupations, and housing, with sixty-nine
pages of detailed tables.

112.1.37 MARTIN, V. La Chrétienté Africaine de Dakar. 3 vols.
Fraternité St. Dominique, Dakar, 1964.
A study of the adherents of the Roman Catholic Church
in terms of different ethnic groups and of different
areas within the city.

112.1.38 MARTIN, V. "Mariage et famille dans les groupes
christianisés ou en voie de christianisation de Dakar."
In Baeta, C.G. (ed.), Christianity in Tropical Africa.
Oxford University Press, London, 1968, 362-395.
Presents the results of a survey of patterns of
marriage among the Christian minority of the population
of Dakar. In French with a four-page English summary.

112.1.39 MERSADIER, Y. "Dakar entre hier et aujourd'hui." Revue
Française d'Etudes Politiques Africaines, 29, 1968
39-50.
Brief review of the development of Dakar, of its
present social and economic structure, and of its
prospects.

112.1.40 NIZURUGERO, J. "Budget temps des sénégalais de Dakar."
Bulletin de l'IFAN, B 34, 1972, 558-606.
Examines how the wage-employed, the self-employed,
and the unemployed in the city allocate their time from
day to day.

112.1.41 ODINET, B. Aspects de la Politique du Logement à Dakar.

Ministère du Plan, Dakar, 1962, 74 pp.
A study of the housing shortage, the resulting problems for the majority of the population, and the political implications of these factors.

112.1.42 OSMONT, A. "La formation d'une communauté locale à Dakar."
Cahiers d'Etudes Africaines, 13, 1973, 497-510.
Shows how the residents of a cooperative housing
estate have become a cohesive community, with the experience of communal organization giving the group considerable political power.

112.1.43 OSMONT. A. Une Communauté en Ville Africaine: les Castors
de Dakar. Presses Universitaires de Grenoble, 1978,
193 pp.
Examines the development of the Castor self-help
community in Dakar in the 1950s and 1960s, the ethnic
and socioeconomic characteristics of its members, the
residential area that it has established, and especially
how it has gained and now exercises political power at
the local level. The published version of a 1973
University of Paris thesis.

112.1.44 OSMONT-DOTTELONDE, A. "Un cas réussi d'intégration urbaine:
la cité des Castors de Dekhuele à Dakar." Revue
Française d'Etudes Politiques Africaines, 29, 1968,
51-60.
The first publication from the above study, examining
the growth of the community and the nature of social relationships within it.

112.1.45 PETEREC, R.J. Dakar and West African Economic Development.
Columbia University Press, New York, 1967, 206 pp.
Essentially a study of Dakar as a port, covering its
physical site, its history, the present port facilities
and traffic patterns, and its relations with its hinterland. Concludes with comments on its prospects and its
relationship to other Senegalese ports.

112.1.46 PINSON, J.C. Rufisque: étude de géographie urbaine.
L'Information Géographique, Paris, 1964, 241 pp.
The published version of a thesis for the University
of Paris, examining the site, origins, growth, population, functions, and morphology of Rufisque.

112.1.47 PORGES, L. Bibliographie des Régions du Sénégal. Ministère
du Plan et du Développement, Dakar, 1967. Chap. 1
"Region du Cap-Vert," 33-143.
A comprehensive list of 715 items on Dakar and its
vicinity, mostly prior to 1960 or brief, anonymous, or
unpublished items from 1960-1965 not listed here.

112.1.48 PORGES, L. Bibliographie des Régions du Sénégal: complément
pour la période des origines à 1965 et mise à jour
1966-1973. Mouton, Paris, 1977, 1-78.
Adds a further 862 items on Dakar and its vicinity.

112.1.49 SANKALE, M. and BA, H. "Introduction aux problèmes
d'urbanisation: l'agglomération dakaroise." Afrique
Documents, 66, 1963, 3-23.
Discusses the causes and consequences of rapid urban
growth at Dakar and the planning measures that might be
taken to check the rate of rural-urban migration.

112.1.50 SANKALE, M.; THOMAS, L.V.; and FOUGEYROLLAS, P. (eds.)
Dakar en Devenir. Présence Africaine, Paris, 1968,
517 pp.
A wide-ranging collection of essays, comprising
"Dakar, ville champignon" by A. Seck; "l'urbanisme et
l'aspect de la ville" by G. Jost; "la situation
démographique" by S.L. Diop; "fonctions politiques et
administratives" by L. Couvreur and M. Diaw; "fonctions
économiques" by A. Bouc; "fonctions sociales et
culturelles" by L.V. Thomas; "l'islam" by V. Monteil;
"le christianisme" by V. Martin; "les langues parlées"
by F. Wioland; "les niveaux de vie" by Y. Mersadier;
"urbanisation et santé" by M. Sankalé; "l'organisation
de la famille africaine" by A.B. Diop; "le problème des
jeunes" by P. Satgé; "les problèmes du travail" by
A. Hauser; "femmes commerçantes" by D. Aguessy; "les
classes sociales" by B. Delbard; "valeurs et attitudes"
by P. Fougeyrollas; and "perspectives" by J. Bugnicourt
and M. Sar.

112.1.51 SAR, M. "Problèmes d'urbanisme et d'aménagement de
l'agglomération dakaroise." Urbanisme, 159, 1977,
66-73.
Notes the dominance of Dakar within Senegal and the
need for regional planning, discusses successive plans
for the city, and outlines present problems of housing
and land ownership.

112.1.52 SECK, A. "Dakar." Cahiers d'Outre-Mer, 14, 1961, 372-392.
An outline of the city's origins, growth, and func-
tions as the political and economic capital of former
French West Africa, and of its physical form.

112.1.53 SECK, A. "Les grandes villes d'Afrique et de Madagascar:
Dakar." Notes et Etudes Documentaires, 2505/6, 1968,
112 pp.
A detailed account of the city's site and physical
form, and examination of the demographic and economic
characteristics of its population, and a comprehensive

analysis of its administrative, commercial, industrial, and port functions.

112.1.54 SECK, A. Dakar, Metropole Ouest-africaine. IFAN, Dakar, 1970, 516 pp.
A comprehensive geographical study, presented as a doctoral thesis in the University of Dakar. The first part surveys the city's economic activities, its morphology, and its population; the second part examines its physical environment and its historical evolution; and the third part discusses its functions as a port and as a nodal center and its relations with other towns and with the rural surroundings.

112.1.55 SECK, A. "The changing role of the port of Dakar." In Hoyle, B.S. and Hilling, D. (eds.), Seaports and Development in Tropical Africa. Macmillan, London, 1970, 41-56.
Examines the facilities and bunkering role of the port and shows how its commercial importance remains despite the partial loss of Mauritania and Mali hinterlands.

112.1.56 SECK, A. "Dakar: 'paysages urbains'." Planification Habitation Information, 78, 1974, 4-18.
An excerpt from the IFAN monograph, examining the city's morphology. In French and English.

112.1.57 SENEGAL. Le Recensement Démographique de Dakar, 1955: résultats définitifs. INSEE, Paris, 1962, 212 pp.
Presents and analyzes a mass of data on the demographic and social characteristics of the 1955 population.

112.1.58 SMUH. "Excerpt of the urban study of the three southwestern neighbourhoods of Rufisque." Planification Habitat Information, 86, 1977, 45-73.
An illustrated report on a survey of population and occupations, roads, water and drainage, social infrastructure, and housing. In English and French.

112.1.59 SOMMER, J.W. "Illicit shops in an African suburb: Sicap, Dakar." African Urban Notes, 7 (1), 1972, 62-72.
Compares the planned Sicap suburb with an adjacent unplanned residential area, Grand Dakar, noting the inadequacy of the shops in Sicap and the need for the spontaneous small stores that are officially illicit.

112.1.60 THOMAS, L.V. "La croissance urbaine au Sénégal: pour une analyse sociologique de Dakar." In CNRS, La Croissance Urbaine en Afrique Noire et à Madagascar. Paris, 1972, 1015-1028.

Examines the role of Dakar as the focus of economic, political, and cultural life in Senegal, suggesting that the polarization is excessive, that the flow of migrants exceeds the city's absorptive capacity, and that this exacerbates the already extreme social and economic disparities.

112.1.61   THORE, L. "Dagoudane-Pikine: étude démographique et sociologique." Bulletin de l'IFAN, B 24, 1962, 155-198.
A full account of the demographic and ethnic structure of this suburban community and of patterns of education, religion, housing, and employment there.

112.1.62   THORE, L. "Mariage et divorce dans la banlieue de Dakar." Cahiers d'Etudes Africaines, 4, 1964, 479-551.
Analyzes marriage and divorce in terms of both attitudes and practice, with special reference to Wolof and Toucouleur customary law.

112.1.63   VAN DER VAEREN-AGUESSY, D. "Les femmes commerçantes en détail sur les marchés dakarois." In Lloyd, P.D. (ed.), The New Elites of Tropical Africa. Oxford University Press, London, 1966, 244-255.
Discusses the social and economic characteristics of the women market traders of Dakar, noting the associations they have formed to protect their interests and their position as a distinct social group within the city.

112.1.64   VERNIERE, M. Etapes et Modalités de la Croissance de Dagoudane-Pikine, Banlieue de Dakar. ORSTOM, Dakar, 1971, 103 pp.
The preliminary version of a study of this suburban zone, published in amplified and final form in 1977 and listed below.

112.1.65   VERNIERE, M. "Campagne, ville, bidonville, banlieue: migrations intra-urbaines vers Dagoudane-Pikine, ville nouvelle de Dakar." Cahiers ORSTOM, Série sciences humaines, 10, 1973, 217-243.
Examines in detail the migration history of a large sample of the inhabitants, noting that the majority migrated first to central Dakar, but had to move out in their search for a permanent home.

112.1.66   VERNIERE, M. "Pikine, ville nouvelle de Dakar: un cas de pseudo-urbanisation." L'Espace Géographique, 2, 1973, 121-140.
Traces the rapid growth of this suburb with the aid of many maps and air photographs, discusses its planned and spontaneous housing areas, and notes the problems of scarce jobs and low incomes.

112.1.67 VERNIERE, M. <u>Dakar et son Double: Dagoudane Pikine</u>.
Bibliothèque Nationale, Paris, 1977, 278 pp.
The published version of a 1973 Paris doctoral thesis
in geography, examining in depth the large suburban area
of Pikine. Shows how the physical growth of Dakar has
engulfed former villages and how air photographs can
aid the analysis of the new settlements. The processes
of migration and of occupation of the land are discussed,
as is the "marginal" nature of much of the population in
economic terms.

112.1.68 VERNIERE, M. "Dakar." In Van-Chi-Bonnardel, R. (ed.),
<u>Atlas National du Sénégal</u>. Institut Géographique
National, Paris, 1977, 125-132.
Maps and text on the structure of the city, the port,
and the suburb of Pikine.

112.1.69 VERNIERE, M. "Les oubliés de l'haussmannisation dakaroise."
<u>L'Espace Géographique</u>, 6, 1977, 5-23.
Shows how policies to eradicate the central slums of
Dakar by moving people to the outskirts have led to the
creation of new slums as private landlords house those
unwilling to move, notably in Fass-Delorme; and also
notes the increasing exodus to France.

112.1.70 WADE, M.T. "L'habitat du grande nombre et son étude dans
la région du Cap-Vert (Sénégal)." <u>Bulletin de l'IFAN</u>,
39B, 1977, 133-170.
A detailed study of the nature and costs of contrasting types of housing in various parts of the Dakar
agglomeration.

112.1.71 WADE, M.T.; GALLE, M.; and SNELDER, R. "Adapted traditional
housing: a self-planned urban environment?" <u>African
Environment</u>, 2 (1-2), 1976, 65-73.
Compares the effectiveness of the housing layouts in
the rapidly changing traditional settlement of Sam-
Diamegueune in the Pikine suburb.

Unpublished theses include:

112.1.72 BOUQUILLON-VAUGELADE, C. Chômage, Emploi et Niveau de Vie
des Travailleurs de Pikine, Banlieue de Dakar. Thèse
de Doctorat, Université de Paris I, 1977.

112.1.73 CHAPPEX, J.C. Le Port de Dakar. Thèse de Doctorat,
Université de Dakar, 1967.

112.1.74 DIALLA, I.P. La Migration des Guinéens à Dakar. Thèse 3e
cycle, Université de Lille, 1975.

112.1.75   DIALLO, I.   Les Circuits Economiques Traditionels dans une
           Agglomération Africaine Moderne: Dakar, les conflits
           entre les structures anciennes et les modèles actuels.
           Thèse 3e cycle, Université de Dakar, 1968.

112.1.76   DIALLO, J.   L'Etude d'une Minorité Nationale: le groupe
           émigré des Guinéens à Dakar.   Thèse 3e cycle, Université
           de Lille, 1969.

112.1.77   DUBRESSON, A.   La Croissance Urbaine et Industrielle sur
           l'Axe Dakar-Rufisque.   Thèse 3e cycle, Université de
           Paris X, 1976.

112.1.78   MAACK, S.C.   Urban Change and Quarter Routinization in
           Pikine, Senegal.   Ph.D. thesis, Columbia University,
           New York, 1978.

112.1.79   THORE, L.   Pikine: evolution des groupes familiaux en
           milieu urbain.   Thèse 3e cycle, Université de Paris,
           1964.

Kaolack   (Headquarters of Sine-Saloum Region and third town of
          Senegal.   Population in 1976:   107,000.)

112.2.1   DESSERTINE, A.   Kaolack, un Port Secondaire de la Côte
           Occidentale d'Afrique.   Chambre de Commerce, Kaolack,
           1967, 192 pp.
              The published version of a history of the port pre-
           sented as a thesis at the University of Dakar.

*112.2.2   GARDERET, A.   Les Fonctions de Capitale Régionale de
           Kaolack.   Institut de Géographie, Université de Bordeaux,
           1968, 129 pp.

Louga   (Provincial town that has recently become a regional head-
        quarters.   Population in 1976:   33,000.)

112.3.1   SAR, M.   Louga et sa Region (Sénégal):   essai d'intégration
           des rapports ville-campagne dans la problématique de
           développement.   IFAN, Dakar, 1973, 308 pp.
              The published version of a 1970 University of Dakar
           thesis, examining the town in relation to the past eco-
           nomic development and recent economic stagnation of the
           surrounding region.   Includes discussions of the town's
           origins, the impact upon it of the spread of groundnut
           cultivation in the area around, and recent changes in
           its economic structure.

Saint-Louis   (Former capital, but now the fourth town of the country.
              Population in 1976: 88,000.)

112.4.1   CAMARA, C. Saint-Louis du Sénégal: évolution d'une ville
          en milieu africain. IFAN, Dakar, 1968, 292 pp.
              A detailed geographical study of the town, with chap-
          ters on its origin and growth, its population, the port,
          fisheries, commerce, administration, the physical struc-
          ture of the town, and the distribution of distinct ethnic
          groups among its residential quarters.

112.4.2   CAMARA, C. "St. Louis, Senegal." Nigerian Geographical
          Journal, 12, 1969, 17-36.
              Briefly describes the town's growth, port functions,
          trading and fishing activities, ethnic groups, and urban
          landscape, summarizing the study noted above.

112.4.3   DEROURE, F. "La vie quotidienne à Saint-Louis par ses
          archives (1779-1809)." Bulletin de l'IFAN, B 26, 1964,
          397-439.
              A detailed reconstruction of social and economic con-
          ditions in the town during this period.

*112.4.4 GINESTE, M. "Les grands traits de développement de la ville
          de Saint-Louis." Coopération Pédagogique, 8, 1964, 51-64.

112.4.5   LOTTIN, J.J. "La croissance urbaine de Saint-Louis du
          Sénégal." In CNRS, La Croissance Urbaine en Afrique
          Noire et à Madagascar. Paris, 1972, 803-815.
              An attempt to estimate the rate of population growth
          in Saint-Louis during the 1960s, showing that rapid
          growth continues despite a contraction in functions since
          independence.

Unpublished theses include:

112.4.6   LOTTIN, J-J. Saint-Louis du Sénégal: décadence d'une ville
          coloniale. Thèse 3e cycle, Université de Lille, 1975.

Tambacounda   (The smallest of the regional headquarters. Population
              in 1976: 25,000.)

112.5.1   DUPON, J-F. "Tambacounda, capitale du Sénégal oriental."
          Cahiers d'Outre-Mer, 17, 1964, 175-214.
              A discussion of the town as the economic focus of
          eastern Senegal, of its distinctive quarters, of its
          demographic and ethnic structure, and of the components
          of the urban economy.

<u>Thiès</u>   (Second town of Senegal. Population in 1976: 117,000.)

There have been no major studies of Thiès since:

112.6.1   SAVONNET, G. <u>La Ville de Thiès</u>. IFAN, Saint-Louis, 1955,
        180 pp.

which was summarized in:

112.6.2   SAVONNET, G. "Une ville neuve du Sénégal: Thiès." <u>Cahiers</u>
        <u>d'Outre-Mer</u>, 9, 1956, 70-93.

<u>Ziguinchor</u>   (Regional headquarters in the extreme south. Population
        in 1976: 73,000.)

*112.7.1   BRUNEAU, J-C. <u>Ziguinchor en Casamance: une ville moyenne</u>
        <u>du Sénégal</u>. CEGET, Bordeaux, 1979, 163 pp.
          The published version of a 1975 Bordeaux 3e cycle
        thesis.

112.7.2   ROCHE, C. "Ziguinchor et son passé (1645-1920)." <u>Boletim</u>
        <u>Cultural da Guiné Portugesa</u>, 28, 1973, 35-59.
          An account of the origins and history of the town,
        with special reference to both early Portuguese and later
        French colonial activities.

SIERRA LEONE

General

113.0.1 BYERLEE, D.; TOMMY, J.L.; and FATOO, H. Rural-urban
Migration in Sierra Leone: determinants and policy
implications. Department of Agricultural Economics,
Michigan State University, East Lansing, 1976, 113 pp.
Reports on a survey conducted in numerous urban and
rural areas, providing information on migration rates,
demographic and socioeconomic characteristics of migrants,
the migration process, urban employment and earnings,
and unemployment. Concludes with various policy
recommendations.

113.0.2 FORDE, E.R.A. "Urbanism: medium for diffusion of
modernization in Sierra Leone." Sierra Leone Geographical
Journal, 15, 1971, 12-41.
Analyzes data from the 1963 census and 1966-1969
household surveys to show urban-rural and interurban
differences in ways of living, using twenty social and
economic indicators.

113.0.3 GWYNNE-JONES, D.R.G., et al. A New Geography of Sierra
Leone. Longman, London, 1978. Chap. 15 "The towns of
Sierra Leone," 152-163; Chap. 16, "Freetown," 164-173.
This school text provides brief descriptions of Bo,
Kenema, Makeni, and Koidu, and a discussion of the site,
growth, and functions of Freetown.

113.0.4 HARVEY, M.E. "Town size; town sites; urban land use." In
Clarke, J.I. (ed.), Sierra Leone in Maps. University of
London Press, 1966, 48-57.
Maps and supplementary text show the distribution of
urban settlement in 1963, illustrate the diversity of
town sites, and present the land-use pattern of twelve
towns.

113.0.5 HARVEY, M.E. "The changing urban network in Sierra Leone."
In International Geographical Union, 21st Congress,
Selected Papers, vol. 3. Calcutta, 1971, 104-120.
A broad outline of the evolving spatial pattern of
urban centers, with a discussion of the relationship be-
tween the capital city and the provincial towns.

113.0.6 HARVEY, M.E. "The study of the social, economic and political
role of urban agglomerations in developing Sierra Leone."
In INCIDI, Urban Agglomerations in the States of the
Third World. Brussels, 1971, 293-315.
Examines the nature of urbanization in Sierra Leone

179

and the demographic, social, and political schisms between town and country.

113.0.7   KING, D. "Population characteristics of diamond boom towns
in Kono." Africana Research Bulletin (Freetown), 5 (4),
1975, 61-80.
Examines the population structure of four small towns
as recorded in the 1963 census and discusses the extent
and nature of their subsequent population growth.

113.0.8   LEVI, J.F.S. "Migration from the land and urban unemployment
in Sierra Leone." Bulletin of the Oxford University
Institute of Economics and Statistics, 35, 1973, 309-326.
Examines factors affecting spatial variations in
rates of out-migration from rural areas and variations
over time in rates of urban unemployment.

113.0.9   MANLY-SPAIN, P.F.V. "Urbanization and regional development
in Sierra Leone." In Mabogunje, A.L. and Faniran, A.
(eds.), Regional Planning and National Development in
Tropical Africa. Ibadan University Press, 1977, 93-99.
A brief outline of the pattern of urban development
up to the 1963 census, with a suggestion that more
medium-sized regional centers are needed.

113.0.10   MINIKIN, V. and MITCHELL, P.K. "Demography and politics in
Kenema and Makeni, Sierra Leone." Pan-African Journal,
4, 1971, 22-34.
A rejoinder to the 1969 paper by Simpson, noted
below (with a reply by Simpson on pp. 267-271).

113.0.11   MITCHELL, P.K. "Settlement hierarchy and urban definition
in Sierra Leone." In CNRS, La Croissance urbaine en
Afrique Noire et à Madagascar. Paris, 1972, 847-869.
Uses 1963 census data to identify social and economic
characteristics of all settlements of over 2000 people
and proposes a functional basis for defining those that
are truly urban.

113.0.12   RIDDELL, J.B. "Population migration and urbanization in
tropical Africa." Pan-African Journal, 8, 1975, 271-285.
Briefly reviews migration models in general and migration research in Africa, but then examines patterns of
rural-urban movement in Sierra Leone, mapping the migration fields of ten towns and seeking explanatory factors
by statistical analysis.

113.0.13   RIDDELL, J.B. and HARVEY, M.E. "The urban system in the
migration process: an evaluation of stepwise migration
in Sierra Leone." Economic Geography, 48, 1972, 270-283.
Finds some evidence from the 1963 census for the

occurrence of stepwise migration and suggests that aiding
the growth of provincial towns may thus accelerate the
already excessive migration to the capital city.

113.0.14 SIERRA LEONE. Census of Sierra Leone, 1963. 3 vols.
      Central Statistical Office, Freetown, 1965.
         Provides much data on the demographic, social, and
economic characteristics of the population of each urban
center.

113.0.15 SIERRA LEONE. Household Survey of the Western Province
      1966-68 (also of Eastern, Northern, and Southern Province
urban areas, all 1968-1969). Central Statistics Office,
Freetown, 1970.
         Four reports, which provide data on household size
and structure, income, tenure, and house age and condition for each town.

113.0.16 SIMPSON, D. "The generation gap in two provincial Sierra
      Leonean towns." Pan-African Journal, 2, 1969, 15-25.
         Discusses the growth of political factions in Kenema
and Makeni and notes that the generation gap largely
coincided with support for opposing parties in the 1960s.

113.0.17 SWINDELL, K. "Sierra Leonean mining migrants, their
      composition and origins." Transactions, Institute of
      British Geographers, 61, 1974, 47-63.
         Focuses on migrants at mines rather than in urban
centers, but relates findings to the urban system,
especially with regard to migration histories.

113.0.18 VAN DER LAAN, H.L. The Lebanese Traders in Sierra Leone.
      Mouton, The Hague, 1975, 385 pp.
         Examines the role of the Lebanese in mining, trade
and transport, and certain social aspects of the community,
and their significance in political life. Not explicitly
on urbanization, but relevant due to the concentration of
the Lebanese in urban centers.

Unpublished theses include:

113.0.19 HARVEY, M.E. A Geographical Study of the Pattern, Processes
      and Consequences of Urban Growth in Sierra Leone in the
Twentieth Century. Ph.D. thesis, University of Durham,
U.K., 1966.

113.0.20 SIMPSON, D.W. The Political Evolution of Two African Towns.
      Ph.D. thesis, Indiana University, 1968.

113.0.21 TOMMY, J.L. Socioeconomic Determinants and Policy
      Implications of the Decision to Migrate: an empirical

evidence of the Sierra Leone migration study. Ph.D.
thesis, Ohio State University, 1977.

Bo (Headquarters of Southern Province. Population at 1974 census:
40,000.)

113.1.1 HARVEY, M.E. "Sierra Leone's largest provincial town."
Sierra Leone Studies, 18, 1966, 29-42.
   Describes the situation, growth, functions, and land-
use pattern of the town.

Freetown (Capital city. Population at 1974 census: 274,000.)

113.2.1 BANTON, M.P. "Social alignment and identity in a West
African city." In Kuper, H. (ed.), Urbanization and
Migration in West Africa. University of California
Press, Berkeley, 1965, 131-147.
   A sociological study of relationships among the towns-
people, with special reference to the effects of ethnic
diversity on social organization.

113.2.2 BERRY, R. and SOMMER, J. "Freetown: images of the urban
environment." Pan-African Journal, 9, 1976, 93-102.
   Reports on a 1974 survey of 150 Freetown residents,
seeking their views of and attitudes towards the city
and its various parts.

113.2.3 FORDE, E.R.A. and HARVEY, M.E. "Graphical analysis of
migration to Freetown." Sierra Leone Geographical Journal,
13, 1969, 13-27.
   Uses birthplace data from the 1963 census to identify
rates of in-migration from 147 source areas and seeks to
explain the great differences among them.

113.2.4 FYFE, C. and JONES, E. (eds.) Freetown: a symposium.
Oxford University Press, London, 1968, 232 pp.
   A wide-ranging set of papers presented at a 1966 meet-
ing, with contributions on the founding of Freetown by
C. Fyfe; the Enlightenment and the founding of the city
by J. Peterson; the physical growth of Freetown by R.J.
Olu-Wright; the city's role in national commercial life
by A. Howard; commerce within the city by J. McKay;
Freetown as a port by S.M. Sesay and P.K. Mitchell; the
Creole community by J. Peterson; the city's architecture
by E.H. Davies; religion by E.W. Fashole-Luke; education
by G. Harding; city government by S. Pratt; the law by
C.O.E. Cole; planning problems by M. Harvey and J. Dewdney;
social problems by S.R. Dixon-Fyle; and the contemporary
cultural scene by E. Jones.

113.2.5   HARBACH, H. "Occupational stratification in Freetown."
           Africana Research Bulletin, 4 (1), 1973, 3-55.
                Summarizes the results of research for a German doc-
           toral thesis, examining occupational stratification in
           relation to the prestige and income of each occupation,
           and to education and to social background.

*113.2.6   HARRELL-BOND, B.E. "The fear of poisoning and the
           management of urban social relations among the profes-
           sional group in Freetown, Sierra Leone." Urban
           Anthropology, 7, 1978, 229-251.

113.2.7   HARRELL-BOND, B.E.; HOWARD, A.M.; and SKINNER, D.E.
           Community Leadership and the Transformation of Freetown
           (1801-1976). Mouton, The Hague, 1978, 416 pp.
                An interdisciplinary historical/sociological study
           of tribal headmen in Freetown. Examines early patterns
           of in-migration and the formation of ethnic communities;
           the development of the institution of headman to assist
           such migrants in a city dominated by Europeans and
           Creoles; its incorporation into the colonial administra-
           tion; and changes during the twentieth century.

113.2.8   HARVEY, M.E. "Implications of migration to Freetown."
           Civilisations, 18, 1968, 247-267.
                A discussion of socioeconomic cleavages among the
           ethnic groups in the city, focusing on demographic struc-
           tures, housing patterns, education levels, and occupations.

113.2.9   LITTLE, K.L. "Voluntary associations in urban life: a
           case study of differential adaptation." In Freedman,
           M. (ed.), Social Organization. Cass, London, 1967,
           153-165.
                With special reference to dancing compins, originally
           formed for entertainment but now of economic and poli-
           tical significance also, shows how Temne migrants value
           such associations more than do the Mende and considers
           reasons for this.

113.2.10   McKAY, J. "Freetown." In Clarke, J.I. (ed.), Sierra Leone
           in Maps. University of London Press, 1966, 58-59.
                Maps and brief text portray the physical growth of
           the city and the present pattern of land-use.

113.2.11   McKAY, J. "Physical potential and economic reality: the
           underdevelopment of the port of Freetown." In Hoyle,
           B.S. and Hilling, D. (eds.), Seaports and Development
           in Tropical Africa. Macmillan, London, 1970, 57-74.
                Examines the emergence of Freetown as the main port
           of Sierra Leone, the nature of its traffic, and its po-
           tential for serving a wider hinterland if political
           circumstances allowed.

113.2.12 PORTER, A.T. Creoledom: a study of the development of
          Freetown Society. Oxford University Press, London,
          1963, 151 pp.
               An authoritative social history of the Creole commun-
          ity, which has played a role in the development of the
          city far out of proportion to its present numbers.

113.2.13 RIDDELL, J.B. The Spatial Dynamics of Modernization in
          Sierra Leone. Northwestern University Press, Evanston,
          Ill., 1970. Pp. 95-127, "Migration to Freetown."
               An examination of the spatial pattern of migration
          towards Freetown, seen as a response to the diffusion of
          the institutions of modernization, such as transport
          facilities and education, discussed earlier in the book.

113.2.14 STEADY, F.C. "Protestant women's associations in Freetown,
          Sierra Leone." In Hafkin, N.J. and Bay, E.G., (eds.),
          Women in Africa. Stanford University Press, 1976,
          213-237.
               Examines the significance of religious associations
          among Creole women in Freetown, both for the Church it-
          self and for society more generally.

A notable earlier study is:

113.2.15 BANTON, M.P. West African City: a study of tribal life in
          Freetown. Oxford University Press, London, 1957, 228 pp.

Unpublished theses include:

113.2.16 ADEOKUN, L.A. Aspects of the Population Geography of the
          Western Area, Sierra Leone. Ph.D. thesis, University
          of Durham, U.K., 1974.

113.2.17 PETERSON, J.E. Freetown: a study of the dynamics of a
          liberated African society, 1807-1870. Ph.D. thesis,
          Northwestern University, Evanston, Ill., 1963.

113.2.18 STEADY, F.C. The Structure and Functions of Women's
          Voluntary Associations in an African City: a study of
          the associative process among women in Freetown.
          D.Phil. thesis, Oxford University, 1974.

Kabala (Provincial town. Population in 1974: 10,000.)

113.3.1   HARVEY, M.E. "Kabala: the northern frontier town."
          Sierra Leone Studies, 21, 1967, 63-79.
               Describes the town's origin, growth, population
          structure, and land-use pattern.

Kenema (Headquarters of Eastern Province. Population in 1974: 31,000.)

113.4.1 GAMBLE, D.P. "Kenema." The Bulletin: Journal of the
Sierra Leone Geographical Association, 7, 1964, 9-12.
A brief description of the town.

113.4.2 GAMBLE, D.P. "The population of Kenema." Sierra Leone
Geographical Journal, 11, 1967, 15-24.
Presents the results of a 1962 sample survey of households covering topics such as ethnic composition, demographic structure, and occupations.

See also 113.0.10, 113.0.16, 113.0.19.

Koidu (Diamond-mining center that has lately displaced Bo as the
largest provincial town. Population in 1974: 76,000.)

113.5.1 GERVIS, G. "Koidu, Sierra Leone's second city." In Oliver,
P. (ed.), Shelter in Africa. Barrie and Jenkins, London,
1971, 210-216.
An account of the rapid, largely unplanned, growth of
the town since the mid-1950s, resulting from the boom in
small-scale mining in the vicinity, with an emphasis on
the forms and layout of the spontaneous housing.

Lunsar (Provincial town adjacent to the now-defunct Marampa iron ore
mine. Population in 1974: 21,000.)

113.6.1 DAWSON, J. "Urbanization and mental health in a West
African community." In Kiev, A. (ed.), Magic, Faith and
Healing. Free Press of Glencoe, New York, 1964, 305-342.
Provides some social background on the Mende and Temne,
then examines for the mine workers the psychological
effects of urbanization and the therapeutic function of
traditional African psychiatry in an urban situation.

113.6.2 GAMBLE, D.P. "Sociological research in an urban community
in Sierra Leone." Sierra Leone Studies, 17, 1963,
254-268.
An account of a social survey of the town.

113.6.3 GAMBLE, D.P. "Lunsar." The Bulletin: Journal of the
Sierra Leone Geographical Association, 7, 1964, 13-17.
A brief description of the town.

113.6.4 GAMBLE, D.P. "Occupational prestige in an urban community
in Sierra Leone." Sierra Leone Studies, 19, 1966, 98-108.
Reports on a survey to discover which occupations are
most highly regarded by the people of Lunsar.

113.6.5 MILLS, A.R. "A comparison of urban and rural populations in
the Lunsar area: I, Lunsar." Sierra Leone Studies, 20,
1967, 173-190.
Presents the results of a 10 percent sample census,
dealing with demographic characteristics, occupations,
and housing, undertaken in 1959 as a basis for a study
of health conditions.

Unpublished theses include:

113.6.6 BUTCHER, D.A.P. The Role of the Fulbe in the Urban Life
and Economy of Lunsar, Sierra Leone. Ph.D. thesis,
University of Edinburgh, 1965.

113.6.7 MILLS, A.R. Effect of Urbanization on Health in a Mining
Area of Sierra Leone. Ph.D. thesis, University of
Edinburgh, 1962.

Magburaka (District headquarters in central Sierra Leone. Population in 1974: 10,500.)

113.7.1 DORJAHN, V.R. "Tailors, carpenters and leather workers in
Magburaka." Sierra Leone Studies, 20, 1967, 158-172.
Examines the nature of these trades in Magburaka, the
incomes obtained in them, and the attitudes of the parti-
cipants, mainly self-employed or apprentices, towards
their work.

113.7.2 DORJAHN, V.R. "The extent and nature of political knowledge
in a Sierra Leone town." Journal of Asian and African
Studies, 3, 1968, 203-215.
Presents the results of an inquiry into the extent of
knowledge of political affairs by both literates and non-
literates, the extent being very low among the latter
group.

113.7.3 DORJAHN, V.R. "Some rural-urban marriage differentials:
the Temne of Magburaka town and its environs." Urban
Anthropology, 2, 1973, 161-181.
Examines contrasts in marriage patterns between towns-
people and rural dwellers, especially the role of go-
betweens, bridewealth, and male attitudes regarding a
suitable spouse.

113.7.4 DORJAHN, V.R. and HOGG, T.C. "Job satisfactions, dissatis-
factions and aspirations in the wage labour force of
Magburaka, a Sierra Leone town." Journal of Asian and
African Studies, 1, 1966, 261-278.
A detailed survey of attitudes of unskilled laborers,
skilled laborers, and teachers, based on questionnaires.
Makes comparisons with an earlier study in Stanleyville.

113.7.5 KHURI, F.I. "Kinship, emigration and trade partnership among
         the Lebanese of West Africa." Africa, 35, 1965, 385-395.
              Describes the kinship structure of Lebanese in Magburaka
         and in Ouagadougou, shows how kinship ties promote emigra-
         tion from Lebanon, and examines the trade partnerships
         common among kinsmen.

Unpublished theses include:

113.7.6 KHURI, F.I. The Influential Men and the Exercise of
         Influence in Magburaka, Sierra Leone. Ph.D. thesis,
         University of Oregon, 1964.

Makeni (Headquarters of Northern Province. Population in 1974:
         26,000.)

113.8.1 HARVEY, M.E. "Makeni: a geographical study of a growing
         northern town and its environs." Sierra Leone Geographical
         Journal, 11, 1967, 26-42.
              Describes the town's site, growth, land-use pattern,
         and relationships with its surrounding area.

         See also 113.0.10, 113.0.16, 113.0.19.

TOGO

General

114.0.1 AGBLEMAGNON, F.N. "Le rôle social, économique et politique des agglomérations urbaines: le cas du Togo." In INCIDI, Urban Agglomerations in the States of the Third World. Brussels, 1971, 367-383.
Outlines the extent and distribution of urban development in Togo, examines the economic activities of the urban population, and discusses the towns as centers of economic, social, and political change.

114.0.2 GUILLAUD, G. "Le Togo." Urbanisme, 159, 1977, 74-79.
Wide-ranging discussion of regional planning issues and the process of urbanization in Togo and of plans both for Lomé and for urban development elsewhere in the country.

114.0.3 PIRAUX, M. Le Togo Aujourd'hui. Jeune Afrique, Paris, 1977, 239 pp.
Includes lavishly illustrated descriptions of sixteen towns (pp. 112-194), stressing aspects of tourist interest.

*114.0.4 TOGO. Recensement Général de la Population du Togo, 1958-1960. Fasc. 1. Résultats provisoires pour la population urbaine. Lomé, 1961, 107 pp.

114.0.5 TOGO. Recensement Général de la population du Togo, 1958-1960. Fasc. 5. Résultats définitifs pour les communes urbaines. Lomé, 1962, 135 pp.
Presents and analyzes data on age and sex, marital status, household structure, fertility, mortality, education, occupations, and housing, in many cases giving separate figures for seven towns.

114.0.6 TOGO. Recensement Général de la Population (1970). Vol 2, Résultats détailles par circonscription. Lomé, 1975, 661 pp.
Provides detailed figures on age and sex structure, ethnic groups, birthplace, marital status, religion, education, and occupation for each town, as well as for rural areas.

Unpublished theses include:

114.0.7 LE BOURDIEC, F. Etude Géographique des Circuits Commerciaux du Togo. Thèse 3e cycle, Université de Strasbourg, 1962.

West Africa

Lomé (Capital city. Population at 1970 census: 148,000. Estimate
for 1975: 215,000.)

114.1.1 ATTIGNON, H. "Lomé." Revue Française d'Etudes Politiques
Africaines, 81, 1972, 49-57.
Describes the origins, growth, character, and functions
of the town.

114.1.2 AZIAHA, Y.A. Organisation et Aménagement de l'Espace au
Togo: la région de Lomé. Institut de Géographie,
Université de Toulouse, 1978, 333 pp.
Mimeographed version of a thesis on regional planning
for Lomé and its surroundings, providing discussions of
the city's site, morphology, land-use and land-tenure
patterns, and urban-rural relationships.

114.1.3 FELI, D. Problèmes Urbains au Togo: problématique de la
circulation à Lomé. Institut National de la Recherche
Scientifique, Lomé, 1977, 100 pp.
A mimeographed geographical study examining the transport systems and traffic patterns in the city, noting
major problems and making recommendations.

*114.1.4 KONOU, E. "Le port de Lomé." Bulletin de l'Institut
d'Enseignement Supérieur du Bénin, 6, 1968, 35-47.

114.1.5 NIHAN, G.; DEMOL, E.; and JONDOH, C. "The modern informal
sector in Lomé." International Labour Review, 118, 1979,
630-644.
Examines the results of an ILO 1977-1978 survey focusing on wood- and metal-working and mechanical repairs
and outlines a program of action. (Full details are in
a restricted 1978 ILO paper.)

*114.1.6 STEINBACH, M. and ALLEGRET, . Ville de Lomé: étude
d'Urbanisme, 5 vols. SMUH, Paris, 1967.

114.1.7 ANON. Lomé, Capitale du Togo. Editions Delroisse, Boulogne,
1975, 128 pp.
A volume of colored photographs with a brief text in
French, English, and German focusing on aspects of tourist
interest.

Unpublished theses include:

114.1.8 KENKOU, G. Urbanisation et Développement de Lomé. Thèse
3e cycle, Université de Paris V, 1973.

West Africa

UPPER VOLTA

General

*115.0.1 ARNAUD, M., ROURE and VEDRENNE. Aménagement Urbain à Ouagadougou et Bobo-Dioulasso. SMUH, Paris, 1961, 164 pp.

115.0.2 GREGORY, J.W. "Urbanisation et développement: le cas de la Haute Volta." Notes et Documents Voltaiques, 7 (1), 1973, 34-47.
Discusses the rate and nature of urban growth in Upper Volta, notes the paradox between stated rural development priorities and actual urban concentration of government investment, and argues for more real emphasis on rural development.

115.0.3 GREGORY, J.W. "Development and in-migration in Upper Volta." In Amin, S. (ed.), Modern Migrations in Western Africa. Oxford University Press, London, 1974, 305-318.
English version of the above paper.

115.0.4 GREGORY, J.W. "Urbanization and development planning in Upper Volta: the 'education variable.'" In El-Shakhs, S. and Obudho, R.A. (eds.), Urbanization, National Development and Regional Planning in Africa. Praeger, New York, 1974, 130-142.
Briefly outlines the pattern of urbanization and rural out-migration in Upper Volta and shows that the rural education program is hindered by bias towards urban areas in other aspects of development.

115.0.5 GREGORY, J.W. "Level, rates and patterns of urbanization in Upper Volta." Pan-African Journal, 9, 1976, 125-134.
Reviews the evolution of the pattern of urban centers in Upper Volta and poses various questions on the future path and role of urbanization.

115.0.6 GUISSOU, H. "Le rôle des agglomérations urbaines dans les états du Tiers-monde: Haute Volta." In INCIDI, Urban Agglomerations in the States of the Third World. Brussels, 1971, 192-204.
A very general discussion of the towns as foci for the rural economy and as agents of social change, noting both positive and negative aspects.

115.0.7 PALLIER, G. "L'approvisionnement en viande des villes de la Haute-Volta." In CEGET, Dix Etudes sur l'Approvisionnement des Villes. Bordeaux, 1972, 191-206.
Shows how livestock are brought to supply the towns with meat, noting satisfactory supplies in Bobo-Dioulasso

and smaller towns but increasing shortage and reduced consumption in Ouagadougou.

115.0.8 PERON, Y. and ZALACAIN, V. Atlas de la Haute-Volta. Jeune Afrique, Paris, 1975.
Multicolored maps of the main towns and a brief text are provided on pp. 44-66.

*115.0.9 POUBEL, M. Construction et Urbanisme en République Voltaique. SMUH, Paris, 1966, 54 pp.

Bobo-Dioulasso (Second town, rivalling Ouagadougou as a commercial center. Population at 1975 census: 115,000.)

*115.1.1 HAUTE VOLTA. Etude Démographique et Socio-économique du Centre Urbain de Bobo-Dioulasso. SEDES, Paris, 1961, 103 + 111 pp.

115.1.2 SOUILLAT, M.J. and VARNIER, J.M. Bobo-Dioulasso: étude urbaine. Institut de Géographie, Reims, 1971, 188 pp.
A mimeographed study providing a comprehensive examination of the town's site, morphology, population structure, functions, and relations with its hinterland.

115.1.3 VAN WETTERE-VERHASSELT, Y. "Bobo-Dioulasso: le développement d'une ville d'Afrique occidentale." Cahiers d'Outre-Mer, 22, 1969, 88-94.
A brief account of the site, origins, growth, layout, and economy of the town.

Ouagadougou (Capital city. Population at 1975 census: 173,000.)

115.2.1 BRICKER, G. and TRAORE, S. Transitional urbanization in Upper Volta: the case of Ouagadougou, a savannah capital." In Obudho, R.A. and El-Shakhs, S. (eds.), Development of Urban Systems in Africa. Praeger, New York, 1979, 177-195.
Examines the pattern of neighborhoods in the city, prospective problems from population growth, and the Cissin site-and-service and settlement upgrading projects.

115.2.2 DENIEL, R. Croyances Réligieuses et Vie Quotidienne: islam et christianisme à Ouagadougou. CNRS, Paris; CVRS, Ouagadougou, 1970, 356 pp.
Presents the results of a detailed investigation of religious belief and practice in the city and of its relationships to social and economic life.

*115.2.3 HAUTE VOLTA. Etude Economique de la Ville de Ouagadougou.

Société Centrale pour l'Equipement du Territoire, Paris, 1962, 162 pp.

115.2.4 HAUTE VOLTA. <u>Recensement Démographique de Ouagadougou 1961-1962: résultats définitifs</u>. INSEE, Paris, 1964, 93 pp.
Provides data on age and sex, marital status, ethnic groups, education, occupations, fertility, and migration, in each case for the city as a whole only.

115.2.5 HAUTE VOLTA. <u>Les Quartiers Spontanés de Ouagadougou</u>. Ministère des Travaux Publics, des Transports et de l'Urbanisme, Ouagadougou, 1973, 34 pp.
Examines the growth of spontaneous settlement, the nature of the houses, and the characteristics of their occupants, with data on nine specific areas.

115.2.6 KHURI, F.I. "Kinship, emigration and trade partnership among the Lebanese of West Africa." <u>Africa</u>, 35, 1965, 385-395.
Shows how the kinship structure and business relationships of the Lebanese traders in Ouagadougou and in Magburaka (Sierra Leone) reflect patterns in their homeland.

115.2.7 LEMARCHANDS, G. "Un projet urbain d'habitat en Haute-Volta." <u>Urbanisme</u>, 159, 1977, 82-87.
Notes the uncontrolled nature of much recent settlement in Ouagadougou and describes the Cissin upgrading project, with many photographs and plans of its improved housing.

115.2.8 LEMARCHANDS, G. "An urban housing policy project in Upper Volta." <u>Habitat International</u>, 3, 1978, 113-119.
An English version of the above paper, but with less detail and illustration and more reflection on its significance as a pilot project.

115.2.9 OUEDRAOGO, O.D. "People's participation in the improvement of their environment: the Cissin project." <u>African Environment</u>, 2 (1-2), 1976, 125-134.
An account of this housing improvement project with an emphasis on the importance of self-help and self-management.

115.2.10 OUEDRAOGO, M-M. and VENNETIER, P. "Quelques aspects de l'approvisionnement d'une ville d'Afrique noire: l'exemple de Ouagadougou." In CEGET, <u>Nouvelles Recherches sur l'Approvisionnement des Villes</u>. Bordeaux, 1977, 204-228.
Shows how the people of the city provide most of their own food by cultivating locally or obtaining it from

rural relatives, but face increasing scarcity of both firewood and water.

115.2.11 PALLIER, G. "Les activités du secteur secondaire à Ouagadougou." In CNRS, La Croissance Urbaine en Afrique Noire et à Madagascar. Paris, 1972, 905-919.
Provides a survey of craft industries, the building industry, and the few large manufacturing industries in the city, with maps of the distribution of each.

115.2.12 PALLIER, G. "Les dolotières de Ouagadougou." In CEGET, Dix Etudes sur l'Approvisionnement des Villes. Bordeaux, 1972, 119-139.
Reports on a study of the small-scale manufacture of millet beer (dolo) in Ougadougou, describing the process and discussing the economic gains to the women involved.

115.2.13 POUSSI, M. "Ouagadougou, études urbaines." Notes et Documents Voltaiques, 6 (2), 1973, 3-11.
Summarizes and reviews the thesis by Dao noted below.

*115.2.14 SEDES. Flux Commerciaux dans la Grande Région de Ouagadougou. Paris, 1964, 257 pp.

115.2.15 SKINNER, E.P. "Political conflict and revolution in an African town." American Anthropologist, 74, 1972, 1208-1217.
Shows how diverse factions had to compete for rights, resources, and power within the city following independence and how its status as national capital presented special problems for municipal government.

115.2.16 SKINNER, E.P. African Urban Life: the transformation of Ouagadougou. Princeton University Press, 1974, 487 pp.
A very comprehensive survey of life in the city in the mid-1960s. After an outline of its evolution and a review of its formal and informal economic activities, further chapters cover kinship, marriage and family life, associations, education, recreation, religion, law, and politics.

115.2.17 SKINNER, E.P. "Voluntary associations in Ouagadougou: a re-appraisal of the function of voluntary associations in African urban centres." African Urban Notes, B, 1, 1975, 11-20.
Examines the formation and character of associations in Ougadougou in the 1950s and argues that there--as elsewhere--they were really intended more for political mobilization against colonial rule than for mutual aid in the urban environment.

115.2.18 SKINNER, E.P. "Voluntary associations and ethnic competition
          in Ouagadougou." In Du Toit, B.M. (ed.), Ethnicity in
          Modern Africa. Westview, Boulder, Colo., 1978, 191-211.
               Examines the rise and fall of associations in the
          city, again noting their primary role as political mo-
          bilizers, which discouraged their survival after
          independence.

*115.2.19 SMUH. Programme d'Action de Développement et d'Aménagement
          dans la Région de Ouagadougou. Paris, n.d., 259 pp.

Unpublished theses include:

115.2.20 DAO, O. Ouagadougou, Etude Urbaine. Thèse 3e cycle,
          Université de Montpelier, 1973.

115.2.21 OUEDRAOGO, M-M. L'Approvisionnement de Ouagadougou en
          Produits Vivrières, en Eau et en Bois. Thèse 3e cycle,
          Université de Bordeaux III, 1974.

115.2.22 PALLIER. G. L'Artisanat et les Activités Industrielles à
          Ouagadougou. Thèse 3e cycle, Université de Paris X,
          1970.

Equatorial Africa

GENERAL

2.0.1   DENIS, J. Le Phénomène Urbain en Afrique Centrale.
         Académie Royale des Sciences Coloniales. Brussels, 1958,
         407 pp.
             The only work dealing with Equatorial Africa as a
         whole. Very substantial and still valuable.

BURUNDI

Bujumbura (Capital city and the only major urban center. Population
           estimate for 1975: 150,000. Former name: Usumbura.)

201.1.1 BURUNDI. Enquête auprès des Ménages de Bujumbura. Ministère
         du Plan, Bujumbura, 1979, 58 pp. + appendices.
             Presents and analyzes data from a 1978 household ex-
         penditure survey in twelve distinct quarters of the city.

201.1.2 ROBATEL, J-P. "La condition ouvrière à Bujumbura." Revue
         Universitaire du Burundi: Sciences Economiques et
         Sociales, 1, 1972, 1-15.
             Examines the qualifications, stability, working con-
         ditions, wages, and expenditure patterns of workers in
         the city and makes recommendations for improvement.

201.1.3 UNIVERSITE DU BURUNDI. Atlas du Burundi. CEGET, Bordeaux,
         1979.
             Sheets 26, 27, and 28 portray the physical structure,
         the economic activities, and the food supplies of the
         city.

201.1.4 VAN DE WALLE, E. "Chômage dans une petite ville d'Afrique:

Usumbura." <u>Zaire</u>, 14, 1960, 341-359.
   Examines the extent and nature of unemployment in the
town in 1958.

201.1.5 VAN DE WALLE, E. "Un essai de resorption de chômage:
         Usumbura, 1959." <u>Zaire</u>, 14, 1960, 467-480.
            Discusses the public works program begun in 1959 to
         reduce the unemployment problem and also the workers'
         response to it.

*201.1.6 VAN DE WALLE, E. "Facteurs et indices de stabilisation et
         d'urbanisation à Usumbura." <u>Recherches Economiques de
         Louvain</u>, 27 (2), 1961, 97-121.

201.1.7 VAN DER VELPEN, C. <u>Manuel de Géographie du Burundi</u>. De
         Boeck, Brussels, 1973, 136 pp.
            Includes a brief description of Bujumbura, pp. 63-70.

A notable earlier study is:

201.1.8 BAECK, L. <u>Etude Socio-économique du Centre Extra-coutumier
         d'Usumbura</u>. Académie Royale des Sciences Coloniales,
         Brussels, 1957, 156 pp.

CAMEROON

General

202.0.1 BILLARD, P. <u>Le Cameroun Fédéral</u>. Vol. 2, Essai de
         <u>Géographie Humaine et Economique</u>. Imprimerie des Beaux-
         Arts, Lyon, 1968, 399 pp.
            Includes an account of commerce and industry in Douala,
         Yaoundé, and other towns, pp. 207-239.

202.0.2 BIYONG, B. "La croissance urbaine: l'exemple du Cameroun."
         In CNRS, <u>La Croissance Urbaine en Afrique Noire et à
         Madagascar</u>. Paris, 1972, 339-356.
            Evaluates the sources of data on urban population
         growth, enumerates the population of all urban settle-
         ments in 1965 and 1970, and discusses migration as the
         main contributor to urban growth.

202.0.3 CAMEROUN. <u>La Population du Cameroun Occidental</u>. Résultats
         <u>de l'enquête démographique de 1964</u>, 2 vols. INSEE,
         Paris, 1969.
            Includes data on the population of each quarter of
         six major towns in volume 2.

202.0.4   CHAMPAUD, J. "L'utilisation des équipements tertiaires dans l'ouest du Cameroun." In CNRS, <u>La Croissance Urbaine en Afrique Noire et à Madagascar</u>. Paris, 1972, 401-413.
    Examines the areas served by the hospitals and schools of the towns of the Western Region of the former East Cameroon.

202.0.5   CHAMPAUD, J. "Genèse et typologie des villes du Cameroun de l'ouest." <u>Cahiers ORSTOM, Série Sciences Humaines</u>, 9, 1972, 325-336.
    Traces the origins and growth of towns in the former West Cameroon and the Western Region of former East Cameroon, discussing contrasts in size, functions, and situation in relation to the total spatial systems of the area.

202.0.6   CLIGNET, R. "Quelques remarques sur le rôle des femmes africaines en milieu urbain: le cas du Cameroun." <u>Canadian Journal of African Studies</u>, 6, 1972, 303-316.
    Shows that in Douala and Yaoundé urbanization has not led to the dominance of the nuclear family in social organization, both the extended family and female solidarity remaining very important.

202.0.7   CLIGNET, R. and JORDAN, F. "Urbanization and social differentiation in Africa: a comparative analysis of the ecological structures of Douala and Yaoundé." <u>Cahiers D'Etudes Africaines</u>, 11, 1971, 261-297.
    Examines patterns of social differentiation in relation to the Shefky and Bell theory of increase in scale, with some comparison of the two cities and some discussion of spatial patterns within each.

*202.0.8   COQUEREL, R. and COURTIER, M. <u>Principes Géneraux pour une Politique d'Urbanisme au Cameroun</u>. SMUH, Paris, 1961, 147 pp.

202.0.9   COTTEN, A-M. and MARGUERAT, Y. "Deux réseaux urbains africains: Cameroun et Côte d'Ivoire." <u>Cahiers d'Outre-Mer</u>, 29, 1976, 348-385; and 30, 1977, 348-382.
    The two countries are compared first in terms of the origins and evolution of their urban systems and then in terms of the functioning of the systems, with special reference to administration, commerce, and industry.

202.0.10 DEBEL, A. <u>Cameroon Today</u>. Jeune Afrique, Paris, 1977, 255 pp.
    Includes illustrated descriptions of Douala (pp. 126-134), Yaoundé (pp. 185-199), and thirty other towns, emphasizing aspects of tourist interest.

202.0.11 KOFELE-KALE, N. "Patterns of political orientations towards the nation: a comparison of rural-urban residents in anglophone Cameroon." African Social Research, 26, 1978, 469-488.
  Compares rural and urban dwellers' degree of identification with the nation as an entity on the basis of a 1972-1973 questionnaire survey.

202.0.12 MARGUERAT, Y. "Réflexions provisoires sur la décadence des villes secondaires au Cameroun." In CNRS, La Croissance Urbaine en Afrique Noire et à Madagascar. Paris, 1972, 841-845.
  Shows that while the largest cities and some very small towns are expanding rapidly, many of the intermediate towns are experiencing relative decline.

202.0.13 MARGUERAT, Y. Analyse Numérique des Migrations vers les Villes du Cameroun. ORSTOM, Paris, 1975, 107 pp.
  A detailed analysis of birthplace data for the population of all towns from the 1967-1969 census, with numerous maps. Relates rates of out-migration to various characteristics of each area and plots the migration hinterland of each town. Includes an appendix on the distribution of ethnic groups within Douala.

202.0.14 MARGUERAT, Y. Atlas du Cameroun, Planche XVII: les villes et leurs fonctions. ORSTOM, Paris, 1975, 131 pp.
  Intended as an accompaniment to a set of twelve maps in the national atlas, this monograph provides a comprehensive survey of the urban system, covering population growth, migration patterns, urban functions, and patterns of interaction among the towns.

202.0.15 MORINIERE, J-L. L'Organisation de l'Espace dans un Pays en Voie de Développement: le Cameroun. Institut de Géographie, Université de Nantes, 1975, 335 pp.
  A study of the evolution of spatial patterns and systems of economic, social, and political activity in Cameroon, with emphasis throughout on the towns and their role in spatial organization.

202.0.16 NZOUANKEU, J.M. "Le rôle des villes dans la modernisation du Cameroun." In INCIDI, Urban Agglomerations in the States of the Third World. Brussels, 1971, 37-93.
  Discusses urban definition, demographic structures, urban-rural disparities in welfare, and especially government efforts to integrate urban and rural areas and to spread social services to rural areas.

202.0.17 TANDAP, L.T. "Evaluation of the sequence of urbanization and population redistribution in Cameroon." Abbia,

34-37, 1979, 391-422.
    Reviews changes in population distribution in Cameroon
since 1963, especially changes in the urban population
and the urban share of the total in each division. Many
tables and maps.

202.0.18 TISSANDIER, J. "Aspects des relations villes-campagnes
          dans le départment de la Haute-Sanaga." In CNRS, La
          Croissance Urbaine en Afrique Noire et a Madagascar.
          Paris, 1972, 1029-1045.
              A microstudy of the role of small urban centers with-
          in a district just northeast of Yaoundé, even the largest
          of which is heavily overshadowed by the capital city.

202.0.19 TJEEGA, P. "Villes." In Laclavère, G. (ed.), Atlas de la
          République Unie de Cameroun. Jeune Afrique, Paris,
          1979, 40-43.
              Colored maps of the distribution of urban population
          and its 1967-1976 growth, of Douala and of Yaoundé, and
          a brief text.

Unpublished theses include:

202.0.20 FITZGERALD, M.C. The Content and Structure of Friendship:
          an analysis of the friendships of urban Cameroonians.
          Ph.D. thesis, Northwestern University, Evanston, Ill.,
          1978.

202.0.21 NGASSA KAMGA, M. Urbanisation et Pôle de Développement
          Economique dans un Pays Sous-Developpé: exemple du
          Cameroun. Thèse Doctorat d'Etat, Université de Paris I,
          1975.

Buea   (Headquarters of West Cameroon before full unification.
       Population in 1970: 12,000.)

202.1.1   COURADE, G. "L'espace urbain de Buea." In CNRS, La
          Croissance Urbaine en Afrique Noire et à Madagascar.
          Paris, 1972, 475-492.
              In the context of the town's origin as a German ad-
          ministrative capital, the sharp contrasts among its
          various quarters are examined.

Douala (Largest city, commercial center, and chief port. Population
        at 1976 census: 458,000.)

202.2.1   CAMEROUN. Analyse des Principaux Résultats du Recensement
          de Douala 1964-1965. INSEE, Paris, 1975, 131 pp.
              Analyzes age and sex structures, ethnic origins,

educational levels, employment, and migration for the
city as a whole, with many detailed tables.

202.2.2   CLARKE, J.I.   "Aerial photograph of Douala, Cameroun." Die
          Erde, 99, 1968, 205-208.
               An analysis of the structure of the city as revealed
          by an air photograph.

202.2.3   DIZIAIN, R. and CAMBON, A.   "Etude sur la population du
          quartier New Bell à Douala." Recherches et Etudes
          Camerounaises, 3, 1960, 1-210.
               A re-issue of a 1957 ORSTOM report presenting the
          results of a detailed survey of demographic characteris-
          tics, household structures, educational levels, occupa-
          tions, incomes, and housing conditions in one of the
          major residential areas of the city.

202.2.4   EYIDI, B.   "Une enquête sur l'alimentation à Douala (quartier
          New-Bell)." Recherches et Etudes Camerounaises, 5, 1961,
          3-45.
               Presents the results of a detailed survey of food con-
          sumption patterns and resulting nutritional levels.

202.2.5   GARDINIER, D.   "Urban politics in Douala, Cameroun."
          African Urban Notes, 4 (3), 1969, 20-27.
               Examines popular reaction to proposed municipal re-
          forms in the 1950s.

202.2.6   GOUELLAIN, R.   "Parenté et affinités ethniques dans l'écologie
          du 'Grand Quartier' de New-Bell, Douala." In Southall,
          A. (ed.), Social Change in Modern Africa.   Oxford University
          Press, London, 1961, 254-272.
               Outlines the evolution of this residential area and
          draws on a sample survey to show how kinship and ethnic
          ties have affected migrants' patterns of adaptation to
          the urban environment.

202.2.7   GOUELLAIN, R.   "Douala: formation et développement de la
          ville pendant la colonisation." Cahiers d'Etudes
          Africaines, 13, 1973, 442-468.
               Evaluates the local Duala and European contributions
          to the development of the city and considers the effects
          of their juxtaposition on its spatial structure.

202.2.8   GOUELLAIN, R.   Douala: ville et histoire.   Institut
          d'Ethnologie, Paris, 1975, 402 pp.
               A comprehensive study of the growth of the city up to
          the time of independence. Discusses precolonial settle-
          ment and traditions and early contacts with Europeans,
          before tracing the evolution of the city under German
          and French rule. Special attention is given to changing

demographic structures and to change in the spatial patterns of distinct social groups.

202.2.9 HAERINGER, P. "Propriété foncière et politiques urbaines à Douala." Cahiers d'Etudes Africaines, 13, 1973, 469-496.

Examines the effects of both traditional Duala landtenure and European forms of land occupance on the organization of space within the city. Includes many illustrations of housing types.

202.2.10 LIPPENS, P. "Les relations entre la population et les pouvoirs publics dans la ville de Douala." Penant, 84, 1974, 204-223.

Discusses the problems of adapting administrative structures to changing situations since independence, with special reference to one residential quarter where relations between the administration and the local population are very strained.

202.2.11 MAINET, G. "Quelques aspects du ravitaillement de Douala en nourriture d'origine animale." In CEGET, Recherches sur l'Approvisionnement des Villes. CNRS, Paris, 1976, 81-113.

Reports on a study concerned with both patterns of meat consumption within the city and sources and distribution channels of animals and meat.

202.2.12 MAINET, G. "Douala, le port et la ville." Cahiers d'Outre-Mer, 29, 1976, 49-69.

Shows how Douala's port function influences its other economic activities, including their rates of growth and their specific locations within the city.

202.2.13 MAINET, G. "Mobilité résidentielle et dynamique urbaine à Douala." Cahiers d'Outre-Mer, 32, 1979, 139-157.

Reports on a study of residential mobility within the city, mapping patterns of movement, discussing factors affecting it, and noting the enduring importance of ethnic ties.

202.2.14 M'BASSI ELONG, P. "The water problem at Douala." Planification Habitat Information, 74, 1973, 5-68.

Examines the water needs of the city's population, the present system by which these are supplied, and the prospects for increasing the supply. In English and French.

202.2.15 SWEEN, J. and CLIGNET, R. "Urban unemployment as a determinant of political unrest: the case study of Douala, Cameroon." Canadian Journal of African Studies,

3, 1969/70, 463-487.
Discusses the political influence exerted by all forms
of unemployment in African cities, with special reference
to Douala and drawing on data on various characteristics
of the unemployed from 1964 municipal census returns.

*202.2.16   VAN SLAGEREN, J.   "Les immigrants à Douala."   Christianisme
Social, 73, 1965, 191-198.

Unpublished theses include:

202.2.17   KENGNE, F.   Bonaberi dans Douala: autonomie et inter-
dépendance.   Thèse 3e cycle, Université de Bordeaux III,
1977.

202.2.18   LACAN, M.   La Population de Douala: structures internes
et mouvements migratoires.   Thèse 3e cycle, Université
de Toulouse II, 1974.

202.2.19   MOBY-ETIA, P.   Les Pays du Bas Mungo--Bas Wouri: étude
géographique de la vie rurale et des relations avec
Douala.   Thèse 3e cycle, Université de Paris I, 1976.

202.2.20   MPONDO NSANGUE AKWA, L.P.   Urbanisation et traditions chez
les duala du Cameroun.   Thèse 3e cycle, Université de
Paris V, 1974.

Garoua   (Old provincial town in the north. Population at 1976
census: 69,000.)

*202.3.1   BASSORO, A. and ELDRIDGE, M.   Histoire de Garoua, Cité
Peule du XIXe siècle.   ONAREST, Yaoundé, 1977, 303 pp.

Kumba   (Provincial town in former West Cameroon. Population at 1976
census: 59,000.)

202.4.1   LAGERBERG, C.S.I.J. and WILMS, G.J.   Profile of a Commercial
Town in West-Cameroon.   Tilburg University Press,
Netherlands, 1974, 76 pp.
An analysis of the demographic structure, educational
levels, and pattern of occupations in Kumba, on the basis
of a detailed sample survey.

N'Gaoundéré   (Old provincial town, now terminus of the new Trans-
Cameroon railway. Population at 1976 census: 25,000.)

202.5.1   GONDOLO, A.   "Evolution économique de la ville de N'Gaoundéré
(Cameroun)."   Cahiers d'Outre-Mer, 32, 1979, 179-193.

Notes the town's early nineteenth-century origins, early twentieth-century stagnation, and postindependence revival, examines its present economy, and discusses the duality now evident in its economic and physical structure.

A notable earlier publication is:

202.5.2 FROELICH, J.C. "N'Gaoundéré: la vie économique d'une cité Peule." Etudes Camerounaises, 43/44, 1954, 3-65.

An unpublished thesis is:

202.5.3 GONDOLO, A. N'Gaoundéré: évolution d'une ville peule. Thèse 3e cycle, Université de Rouen, 1978.

Victoria (Secondary port in the former West Cameroon. Population at 1976 census: 35,000.)

202.6.1 COURADE, G. Victoria-Bota: croissance urbaine et immigration. ORSTOM, Paris, 1975, 135 pp.
         Examines the evolution of the town, migration patterns, its social structures, employment, its shrinking functions, and its sphere of influence.

Yaoundé (Capital city. Population at 1976 census: 314,000.)

202.7.1 AROUNA, N. Offre et Demande des Produits Vivriers dans la Région de Yaoundé. ONAREST, Yaoundé, 1977, 77 pp.
         Examines the pattern of demand for food within and around the expanding city and the evolving pattern of supply.

202.7.2 CAMEROUN. La Population de Yaoundé. Résultats définitifs du recensement de 1962. INSEE, Paris, 1970, 376 pp.
         Provides data on age and sex, ethnic groups, education, employment, migration, fertility, etc., in some cases for twenty-three subdivisions of the city.

202.7.3 CLARKE, J.I. "Aerial photograph: Yaoundé." Die Erde, 98, 1967, 1-4.
         An analysis of the structure of the city, as revealed by an air photograph.

202.7.4 FRANQUEVILLE, A. "Le paysage urbain de Yaoundé." Cahiers d'Outre-Mer, 21, 1968, 113-154.
         A detailed account of the site, physical growth, present morphology, and planning problems of the city, with many illustrations.

*202.7.5   FRANQUEVILLE, A. <u>Deux Essais sur les Relations Ville-</u>
            <u>Campagne au Nord de Yaoundé</u>. ORSTOM, Yaoundé, 1971.

202.7.6   FRANQUEVILLE, A. "Les relations ville-campagne sur la
            route de Yaoundé." <u>Cahiers ORSTOM, Série Sciences</u>
            <u>Humaines</u>, 9, 1972, 337-387.
                A detailed study of urban-rural relations with respect
            to settlements along the first 60 km of the road north
            from Yaoundé, including migration, use of urban services,
            and supplies to urban markets.

202.7.7   FRANQUEVILLE, A. "Les immigrés du quartier de la Briqueterie
            à Yaoundé." In CNRS, <u>La Croissance Urbaine en Afrique</u>
            <u>Noire et à Madagascar</u>. Paris, 1972, 567-590.
                Analyzes 1967 census results for the Briqueterie
            quarter of Yaoundé and its three constituent parts, in
            terms of demographic structure, area of origin, and
            occupations.

202.7.8   FRANQUEVILLE, A. "L'évolution du marché central de Yaoundé:
            comparison de deux enquêtes." In CEGET, <u>Recherches sur</u>
            <u>l'Approvisionnement des Villes</u>. CNRS, Paris, 1976,
            115-129.
                Reports on 1968 and 1973 studies of the central market,
            noting little change in its role in selling fruit and
            vegetables drawn from a wide area and noting that the
            needs of an expanding population are being met by the
            opening of new suburban markets.

202.7.9   FRANQUEVILLE, A. "Croissance démographique et immigration
            à Yaoundé." <u>Cahiers d'Outre-Mer</u>, 32, 1979, 321-354.
                Discusses the city's rapid population growth and
            present demographic structure, immigrant origins and
            the present ethnic structure, and the changing distribu-
            tion of ethnic groups within the city.

202.7.10   MORINIERE, J-L. "La régime maraîchère intra et peri-urbaine
            de Yaoundé." In CEGET, <u>Dix Etudes sur l'Approvisionnement</u>
            <u>des Villes</u>. Bordeaux, 1972, 47-81.
                Examines the small-scale cultivation and marketing
            of "European" vegetables on the swampy valley floors
            within and close to the city.

202.7.11   ROUSSEL, L.; TURLOT, F.; and VAURS, R. "La mobilité de la
            population urbaine en Afrique noire: deux essais de
            mesure, Abidjan et Yaoundé." <u>Population</u>, 23, 1968,
            333-352.
                Compares the results of 1963-1965 surveys in the two
            cities, which provided much information on population
            movements into, out of, and within each of them.

202.7.12   STEEL, W.F.   "Development of the urban artisanal sector in
           Ghana and Cameroun."   Journal of Modern African Studies,
           17, 1979, 271-284.
               A comparative study of the structure and composition
           of small-scale industry and services in Yaoundé and
           Accra, based on 1973 and 1976 surveys, stressing the
           similarities between the two cities.

202.7.13   ZE NGUELE, R.   "Problèmes démographiques de la croissance
           urbaine à Yaoundé."   In CNRS, La Croissance Urbaine en
           Afrique Noire et à Madagascar.   Paris, 1972, 1089-1103.
               Discusses the city's rapid growth between 1957 and
           1969, the role of in-migration in this growth, the re-
           sulting demographic structure, and the employment
           situation.

Unpublished theses include:

202.7.14   N'DIFO, M.E.   Contribution à l'Etude des Problèmes
           d'Urbanisme et d'Habitat du plus Grand Nombre en Afrique.
           Cas concret de Yaoundé.   Thèse, Institut d'Urbanisme,
           Paris, 1966.

202.7.15   N'GUIONZA, .   Yaoundé: étude de géographie urbaine.   Thèse
           3e cycle, Université de Strasbourg, 1969.

202.7.16   ONAMBELE, X.   La Distribution des Biens de Consommation et
           les Problèmes Urbains a Yaoundé.   Thèse 3e cycle,
           Université de Paris, 1969.

202.7.17   ONGLA, J.   Structure, Conduct and Performance of the Food
           Crop Marketing System in Cameroon: a case study of
           Yaoundé and adjacent areas.   Ph.D. thesis, University
           of Florida, Gainesville, 1978.

CENTRAL AFRICAN REPUBLIC

General

203.0.1   PRIOUL, C. "Les caractères démographiques des centres
            urbains provinciaux en République Centrafricaine." In
            CNRS, La Croissance Urbaine en Afrique Noire et à
            Madagascar. Paris, 1972, 961-970.
                Analyzes the results of a 1968 demographic survey of
            thirty-one urban centers outside the capital, noting
            contrasts among them, and examines the massive inter-
            regional migration, both rural-urban and rural-rural.

203.0.2   PRIOUL, C. "Villes et agriculture vivrière en République
            Centrafricaine." In CEGET, Dix Etudes sur l'Approvisionne-
            ment des Villes. Bordeaux, 1972, 83-117.
                Shows that satisfactory systems of food supply have
            evolved spontaneously both in Bangui, where most people
            depend largely on food supplies by rural relatives, and
            in smaller towns, where most can grow their own on the
            surrounding land.

203.0.3   REPUBLIQUE CENTRAFRICAINE. Enquête Démographique en
            République Centrafricaine, 1959-1960: résultats
            définitifs. INSEE, Paris, 1964, 262 pp.
                Presents and analyzes data on the structure and the
            movement of the population, distinguishing throughout
            between urban and rural areas.

*203.0.4   REPUBLIQUE CENTRAFRICAINE. Enquête Démographique par Sondage
            sur les Centres Urbains Secondaires: rapport synthétique.
            Bangui, 1968, 76 pp.

203.0.5   ZARHY, M. Les Centres Urbains et Régionaux de la République
            Centrafricaine. Planning and Development Institute,
            Jerusalem, 1963, 32 pp.
                Outlines the population characteristics and physical
            infrastructure of each of the main towns.

Bangui   (Capital city. Population estimate 1975:   250,000.)

203.1.1   BINET, J. "Image of the town as seen by schoolchildren of
            Bangui." Bulletin du SMUH, 68, 1972, 3-18.
                Analyzes the knowledge and perception of the city and
            its various parts as indicated in essays written by 484
            children from a variety of its schools. In French and
            English.

*203.1.2   DEPRET, R. Bangui: urbanisme et habitat. SMUH, Paris,
            1967, 55 pp.

*203.1.2a GOSSEYE, S. Un Espace Urbain et Africain: recherches à
           Bangui. Gosseye, Paris, 1978, 190 pp.

 203.1.3   GOUTALIER, R. "Les débuts difficiles de la capitale de la
           République Centrafricaine: Bangui de 1889 à 1893."
           Cahiers d'Etudes Africaines, 14, 1974, 299-316.
             Drawing on many contemporary documents, examines the
           origins of Bangui as a colonial outpost and the great
           problems experienced by the French there.

*203.1.4   LEGRAND, J.M. "Le plan directeur de Bangui." Industries
           et Travaux d'Outremer, 10, 1962.

 203.1.5   PRIOUL, C. "Les cultures maraîchères à Bangui." Cahiers
           d'Outre-Mer, 22, 1969, 191-202.
             Examines market gardening in and around the city,
           discussing the people involved, their cultivation prac-
           tices, and the marketing system.

 203.1.6   PRIOUL, C. "Le rôle des relations familiales entre Bangui
           et les villages centrafricaines." Canadian Journal of
           African Studies, 5, 1971, 61-78.
             Examines the extent of visiting between the urban
           population and their rural kinsfolk and the transfers
           of cash and goods resulting from the visits.

 203.1.7   SORET, M. Bangui, Etudes Socio-Démographiques de l'Habitat,
           2 vols. ORSTOM, Bangui, 1961.
             Reports on a sample survey providing data on demography,
           migration, and employment as well as much detail on hous-
           ing conditions.

A notable earlier study is:

 203.1.8   LEBEUF, J-P. Bangui. Editions de l'Union Française,
           Paris, 1954, 66 pp.

Unpublished theses include:

 203.1.9   LEMOTOMO, E. Bangui, Etude Urbaine. Thèse 3e cycle,
           Université de Paris I, 1977.

 203.1.10 PRIOUL, C. Alimentation, Agriculture et Approvisionnement
           à Bangui. Thèse 3e cycle, Université de Bordeaux, 1971.

CHAD

General

204.0.1   CABOT, J. and CLANET, J.   "Fort-Lamy; Fort-Archambault;
          Moundou; Abéché." In Cabot, J. and Bouquet, C. (eds.),
          Atlas Pratique du Tchad. Institut National Tchadien
          pour les Sciences Humaines, Fort-Lamy, 1972, pp. 62-67.
              Provides detailed maps, air photographs, and brief
          descriptions for each of these towns.

204.0.2   TCHAD. Enquête Démographique au Tchad, 1964, 2 vols.
          INSEE, Paris, 1966, 309 and 196 pp.
              Largely a rural sample survey, but includes also the
          results of a full census of Abéché, Bongor, Doba, Houmra,
          Moundou, and Sarh, giving data on demography, household
          structure, and employment.

204.0.3   TCHAD. Enquête Socio-Economique au Tchad, 1965. INSEE,
          Paris, 1969, 333 pp.
              A detailed study in urban and rural areas of southern
          Chad, with an analysis of household budgets in Sarh (pp.
          87-151) and Moundou (pp. 153-210) and an analysis of food
          consumption in these towns and rural areas (pp. 211-302).

204.0.4   TEISSERENC, P. "Milieu urbain et recherche d'une identité
          culturelle: les lycéens de Fort-Archambault et d'Abéché
          (Tchad)." Cahiers d'Etudes Africaines, 13, 1973, 511-548.
              Summarizes the results of a study of reactions of
          secondary school children to the culture conflict pro-
          vided by urban Western education against a rural tradi-
          tional background, noting differences between the two
          towns.

204.0.5   WORKS, J.A.   Pilgrims in a Strange Land: Hausa Communities
          in Chad. Columbia University Press, New York, 1976,
          280 pp.
              Examines the settlement of Hausa people in Chad,
          especially in the towns of Abéché and Fort-Lamy (now
          N'Djamena), largely to provide services for pilgrims
          travelling to Mecca. Includes chapters on each town,
          largely historical in approach, but also contrasting the
          compact and now declining Hausa community in Abéché with
          the more scattered and flourishing Hausa groups in the
          capital. The published version of a 1972 University of
          Wisconsin Ph.D. thesis.

204.0.6   ZARHY, M. Les Centres Urbains et Régionaux de la République
          du Tchad. Institute of Planning and Development,
          Jerusalem, 1963, 63 pp.

208

Surveys the distribution of urban centers, their demographic characteristics, their physical infrastructure,
and their problems.

Unpublished theses include:

204.0.7 TEISSERENC, P. De la Communauté Ethnique à la Communauté
Nationale: les lycéens d'Abéché et de Sarh (Tchad).
Thèse 3e cycle, Université de Paris V, 1973.

Abéché (Provincial town in the east. Population in 1975: 40,000.)

*204.1.1 MARNAY, P. and THEVENIN, P. Etude Socio-économique de la
Ville d'Abéché. SEDES, Paris, 1965, 269 pp.

N'Djamena (Capital city. Population estimate 1975: 250,000. Former
name: Fort-Lamy.)

204.2.1 BARDINET, C. "La population des vendeurs du Grande-Marché
de N'Djamena en 1976." Cahiers d'Outre-Mer, 31, 1978,
225-250.
Outlines the structure of the city's central business
area, indicates the trades represented in the central
market, and examines the age, origins, and present area
of residence of the traders.

204.2.2 BOUQUET, C. "Les champs extra-urbains des citadins de
N'Djamena (Tchad)." In CEGET, Nouvelles Recherches sur
l'Approvisionnement des Villes. Bordeaux, 1977, 181-201.
Reports on a study of food supplies in three residential
areas, finding most households having fields on the periphery and some having farms with paid laborers producing
supplies for the town markets.

*204.2.3 COURTIER, M. and GOSSELIN, M. Etude sur l'Urbanisation et
l'Amélioration de l'Habitation dans les Quartiers Africains
de Fort-Lamy. SMUH, Paris, 1961.

204.2.4 ECKERT, H. Enquêtes Socio-économiques de l'Habitat à
N'Djamena 1975 à 1976. United Nations Development
Programme, N'Djamena, 1977, 113 pp.
A mimeographed report on urban housing, providing in-
formation on demographic structures and incomes as well
as on rents, housing conditions, and household facilities.

204.2.5 TCHAD. Recensement Démographique de Fort-Lamy, 1962:
résultats provisoires. INSEE, Paris, 1964, 78 pp.
Presents and analyzes data on age and sex, ethnic
groups, birthplace, occupations, fertility, mortality,

migration, and housing, with some figures for twenty-three zones within the city.

Notable earlier studies include:

204.2.6 DENIS, J. "Fort-Lamy: croissance et destin d'une ville africaine." Bulletin de la Société Belge d'Etudes Géographiques, 27, 1958, 35-54.

204.2.7 LEBEUF, J-P. Fort-Lamy. Editions de l'Union Française, Paris, 1950, 62 pp.

Unpublished theses include:

204.2.8 LAVELLE, A. Mutations Villageois et Développement Urbain au Tchad: l'absorption de Milezi-Farcha par Fort-Lamy. Thèse 3e cycle, Université de Bordeaux, 1971.

204.2.9 MORIN, M. Fort-Lamy: capitale et métropole incomplète du Tchad. Thèse 3e cycle, Université de Lyon, 1972.

Sarh (Provincial town in the south. Population in 1975: 60,000. Former name: Fort-Archambault.)

*204.3.1 BODIN, F. and HANSBERGER, R. Fort-Archambault. SMUH, Paris, 1964, 30 pp.

204.3.2 BOISSON, J. L'Histoire du Tchad et de Fort Archambault. Scorpion, Besançon, 1966, 249 pp.
    A chronological account of the origins and fluctuating fortunes of the town, with special reference to military and administrative matters, but with something on its form and functions also.

204.3.3 CHAUVET, J. "Tradition et modernisme dans les quartiers de Sarh." Cahiers d'Outre-Mer, 30, 1977, 57-82.
    Defines and differentiates African residential areas, contrasting some stable and homogeneous communities with others that are more mixed and more unstable.

Unpublished theses include:

204.3.4 BARAKE, M. La Fonction Commerciale de Sarh. Thèse 3e cycle, Université de Paris I, 1974.

204.3.5 CHAUVET, J. Les Quartiers de Sarh (Tchad). Thèse 3e cycle, Université de Bordeaux III, 1974.

CONGO

General

205.0.1 ARNAUD, M.; LAURENT, O.; and SPIRE, B. Habitat et Urbanisme en République du Congo. SMUH, Paris, 1961, 99 pp.
An examination of existing housing conditions in Brazzaville, Pointe Noire, and six smaller towns, with detailed plans for housing development. Includes numerous maps and photographs.

205.0.2 AUGER, A. "Notes sur les centres urbains secondaires au Congo-Brazzaville." Cahiers d'Outre-Mer, 21, 1968, 29-55.
An account of the demographic and socioeconomic structure of the fifteen centers with 2000 to 5000 inhabitants and a discussion of their economic role in relation to surrounding areas.

205.0.3 AUGER, A. "Villes." In Vennetier, P. (ed.), Atlas de la République Populaire du Congo. Jeune Afrique, Paris, 1977, 28-29.
Colored maps of Brazzaville and Pointe-Noire, with a brief text.

205.0.4 VENNETIER, P. "L'urbanisation et ses conséquences au Congo-Brazzaville." Cahiers d'Outre-Mer, 16, 1963, 263-280.
Discusses patterns of internal migration, the consequences of the exodus for the rural areas, and the implications of rapid population growth for the economy and physical form of the towns.

205.0.5 VENNETIER, P. Géographie du Congo-Brazzaville. Gauthier-Vilars, Paris, 1966, 169 pp.
Discusses the structure and growth of urban centers on pp. 65-69 and urban unemployment problems on pp. 109-112, with various references to the towns elsewhere.

Brazzaville (Capital city. Population at 1974 census: 290,000.)

205.1.1 ALTHABE, G. "Etude du chômage à Brazzaville en 1957: étude psychologique." Cahiers ORSTOM, Série Sciences Humaines, 1 (4), 1963, 106 pp.
Presents the results of a social survey among the unemployed in the Poto-Poto area, with a discussion focused on attitudes to city life and to rural homes.

205.1.2 AUGER, A. "Le ravitaillement vivrier traditionnel de la population Africaine de Brazzaville." In CNRS, La

<blockquote>
Croissance Urbaine en Afrique Noire et à Madagascar,
Paris, 1972, 273-298.

Examines the food products supplied to the city, the
patterns of flow by river, road, and rail, and the marketing systems by which the supplies are organized.
</blockquote>

205.1.3   AUGER, A. and VENNETIER, P. "La croissance périphérique des
villes: naissance et développement d'une banlieue
brazzavilloise." In Durand-Lasserve, A.; Auger, A.; and
Vennetier, P., Croissance Périphérique des Villes: cas
de Bangkhok et de Brazzaville. CEGET, Bordeaux, 1976,
225-286.

A detailed study of former land-use, processes of land
subdivision and occupation, house construction, demographic structure, occupations, and lack of municipal services
in the newly-settled Mfilou area on the western edge of
the city.

205.1.4   BALANDIER, G. "Le travailleur africain dans les 'Brazzavilles
noires.'" Présence Africaine, special issue, 1962, 315-330.

205.1.5   CONGO. Recensement de Brazzaville 1961. Résultats
définitifs. INSEE, Paris, 1965, 113 pp.

Provides and analyzes data on age and sex, marital
status, ethnic groups, education, occupations, migration,
and fertility, with some data for different residential
quarters.

205.1.6   CONGO. Mouvement Naturel de la Population à Brazzaville,
1960-1974. Brazzaville, 1975, 149 pp.

A detailed analysis of registration figures for births
and deaths over the fifteen-year period, making comparisons with provisional 1974 census data.

205.1.7   CONGO. Recensement Général de la Population de 1974:
Commune de Brazzaville. Résultats Définitifs. Brazzaville,
1975, 96 pp.

Provides much data and extensive commentary on demographic structure, ethnic composition, and household
structures for the city as a whole.

205.1.8   CONGO. Recensement Général de la Population de 1974:
Commune de Brazzaville. 5 further volumes, Brazzaville,
1976, 59+57+61+56+103 pp.

Provides detailed data for seven districts covering
demography, migration, occupations, and housing.

205.1.9   DEVAUGES, R. "Urban unemployment in Africa South of the
Sahara: II--unemployment in Brazzaville." Inter-
African Labour Institute Bulletin, 7 (3), 1960, 8-48.

Presents the results of a 1957 survey of the extent

and nature of unemployment in the city, discussing also the living conditions of the unemployed and possible remedial measures. (In English and French.)

205.1.10 DEVAUGES, R. "Mieux-être et promotion sociale chez les salariés africains de Brazzaville." In Southall, A. (ed.), Social Change in Modern Africa. Oxford University Press, London, 1961, 182-204.

Describes a social survey of the Poto-Poto area, investigating the size and distribution of different income groups, factors affecting living standards, and the extent of shifts to European patterns of consumption.

205.1.11 DEVAUGES, R. "Etude du chômage à Brazzaville en 1957: étude sociologique." Cahiers ORSTOM, Série Sciences Humaines 1 (4), 1963, 201 pp.

Drawing upon the results of the survey noted in item 205.1.1, discusses the migration and employment situation revealed, some social characteristics of the unemployed, and possible solutions to the problem.

205.1.12 DEVAUGES, R. L'Oncle, le Ndouki et l'Entrepreneur: la petite entreprise congolaise à Brazzaville. ORSTOM, Paris, 1977, 187 pp.

An intensive study of small-scale enterprise in Brazzaville, including builders, traders, tailors, etc., in terms of characteristics of the entrepreneurs, the scale and economics of the enterprises, success and failure, and the important role of traditional magico-religious practice.

*205.1.13 HAERINGER, P. Le Phénomène Suburbain à Brazzaville. ORSTOM, Brazzaville, 1965, 128 pp.

205.1.14 JEANNIN, M. "L'agriculture et les habitants de Makélékélé (un quartier récent de Brazzaville)." In CEGET, Dix Etudes sur l'Approvisionnement des Villes. Bordeaux, 1972, 17-46.

Shows how the great majority of women in this new western suburb either find some local land for cultivation or maintain a farm in their home village and describes the local farms where cassava is the main crop.

205.1.15 JEANNIN, M. "Les activités agricoles des femmes de Brazzaville: l'exemple de Makélékélé et de la terre Kimpouomo." In CEGET, Recherches sur l'Approvisionnement des Villes. CNRS, Paris, 1976, 133-257.

Includes a discussion of the demographic and social background of the area and then examines in detail cultivation practices, crop production, and the channels of supply especially of cassava to the city markets,

concluding that the resulting income gives wives significant economic independence.

*205.1.16 LEGRAND, M. "L'urbanisme de Brazzaville." Industries et
Travaux d'Outremer, 74, 1960, 27-35.

205.1.17 POATY, J-P. "Contradictions sociales et formes de conflits
sociaux dans une ville africaine: Brazzaville." Espaces
et Sociétés, 10/11, 1973/4, 139-151.
      Argues that conflicts often labelled "tribal" among
the Brazzaville population are in fact due to the economic and social structure associated with dependency
and to increasing marginality of much of the population.

205.1.18 SAUTTER, G. De l'Atlantique au Fleuve Congo: une géographie
de sous-peuplement. Mouton, Paris, 1966, Ch.V 'Le Stanley
Pool', pp. 327-466.
      The whole volume is concerned largely with rural popu-
lation and land-use, but within this chapter pp. 387-417,
"Les nouveaux riverains," examines African settlement in
Bacongo and Poto-Poto areas of the city.

205.1.19 VENNETIER, P. "Un quartier suburbain de Brazzaville:
Moukondji-Ngouaka." Bulletin de l'Institut d'Etudes
Centrafricaines, 19/20, 1960, 91-124.
      Examines a village near the western edge of the city
that grew rapidly as a suburban settlement in the 1950s,
with details of demographic structure, economic activities, and house types and layout.

205.1.20 VINCENT, J-F. Femmes Africaines en Milieu Urbain. ORSTOM,
Paris, 1966, 287 pp.
      Presents the results of an intensive study of patterns
of marriage and family life for women in Brazzaville,
with discussions also of the development of education
for girls, the influence of religion, and the increase
in income-earning opportunities for women.

A notable earlier study is:

205.1.21 BALANDIER, G. Sociologie des Brazzavilles Noires. Colin,
Paris, 1955, 274 pp.

Unpublished theses include:

205.1.22 GOMA-LOUSSAKOU, F. Essai d'une Etude Urbaine et Sanitaire:
infrastructure d'assainissement et problèmes de protec-
tion sanitaire dans la collectivité de Brazzaville.
Thèse 3e cycle, Université de Paris, EHESS, 1979.

205.1.23   KONGO, M.   Petits Métiers et Commerce de l'Artisanat à
           Brazzaville.   Thèse 3e cycle, Université de Bordeaux III,
           1975.

205.1.24   MAYINDOU, F.   Le rôle de Brazzaville dans l'Organisation
           de l'Espace National Congolais.   Thèse 3e cycle,
           Université de Paris VIII, 1976.

205.1.25   MOUNIKOU, M.   La Société Brazzavilleoise: tradition et
           réalité urbaine.   Thèse 3e cycle, Université de Paris,
           1969.

Pointe-Noire   (Second city and chief port.   Population at 1974
               census: 140,000.)

205.2.1   CONGO.   Recensement Démographique de Pointe-Noire, 1958:
           résultats définitifs.   INSEE, Paris, 1961, 126 pp.
               Presents and analyzes data on age and sex, ethnic
           groups, marital status, household structure, birthplace,
           migration, and occupations, in some cases for twenty-
           three distinct zones.

*205.2.2   DHONT, Y.   Les Marchés Africains de Pointe-Noire.   ORSTOM,
           Brazzaville, 1963, 98 pp.

*205.2.3   LIERDEMAIN, J.L.   Analyse Socio-démographique de la
           Population de Pointe-Noire.   4 vols.   ORSTOM, Brazzaville,
           1965, 360 pp.

205.2.4   LIERDEMAIN, J.L.   "Pointe-Noire: évolution d'un modèle de
           croissance démographique urbaine (1958-1970)."   In CNRS,
           La Croissance Urbaine en Afrique Noire et à Madagascar.
           Paris, 1972, 785-802.
               Notes the rapid growth of the town and examines its
           demographic structure, estimating that natural increase
           adds 2 percent a year and migration 5 percent, and
           stressing the need to plan for continued growth.

205.2.5   VENNETIER, P.   "La vie agricole urbaine à Pointe-Noire."
           Cahiers d'Outre-Mer, 14, 1961, 60-84.
               Examines the farming taking place within the urban
           and peri-urban areas and emphasizes its importance.

205.2.6   VENNETIER, P.   "La population de Pointe-Noire."   Cahiers
           d'Outre-Mer, 17, 1964, 235-238.
               Summarizes the results of a survey of population
           structure and origins undertaken in 1962, reported more
           fully by Lierdemain (above).

205.2.7   VENNETIER, P.   Pointe-Noire et la Façade Maritime du

Congo-Brazzaville. ORSTOM, Paris, 1968, 458 pp.
Part 1 on physical and cultural geography includes a
brief discussion of migration and a section on the demography of the urban population. Part 3 on the city and
its problems (pp.261-418) examines in detail its origins
and growth, physical form, social problems, food supplies,
and functions as a commercial and industrial center and
as a port.

205.2.8   VENNETIER, P. "Les ports du Gabon et du Congo-Brazzaville."
Cahiers d'Outre-Mer, 22, 1969, 337-355.
Includes a discussion of the growth of port activity
at Pointe-Noire and examines its traffic and the extent
of its hinterland in the 1960s.

205.2.9   VENNETIER, P. "Problems of port development in Gabon and
Congo-Brazzaville." In Hoyle, B.S. and Hilling, D. (eds.),
Seaports and Development in Tropical Africa. Macmillan,
London, 1970, 183-201.
An English version of the above paper.

A notable earlier paper is:

205.2.10   DENIS, J. "Pointe-Noire." Cahiers d'Outre-Mer, 8, 1955,
350-368.

EQUATORIAL GUINEA

Nothing of substance has been found on the urban centers of this country, all of which are very small. A national encyclopaedia with a brief entry on each town is:

206.0.1 LINIGER-GOUMAZ, M. La Guinée Equatoriale: un pays méconnu. Harmattan, Paris, 1979, 507 pp.

A bibliography (in Spanish) including many items that make some reference to the towns is:

206.0.2 LINIGER-GOUMAZ, M. Guinea Ecuatorial: Bibliografía general. Commission Nationale Suisse pour l'UNESCO, Berne, 1976, 335 pp. (An earlier edition of 171 pp. appeared in 1974.)

GABON

General

207.0.1 BOUET, C. "Pour une introduction a l'étude des migrations modernes en milieu sous-peuplé: situation actuelle du salariat et de l'emploi au Gabon." Cahiers ORSTOM, Série Sciences Humaines, 10, 1973, 295-306.
         Examines the nature and distribution of wage-employment in Gabon, its concentration in Libreville and Port-Gentil, and the resulting migration flows, which exceed the employment opportunities.

207.0.2 HANCE, W.A. and VAN DONGEN, I.S. "Gabon and its main gateways: Libreville and Port Gentil." Tijdschrift voor Economische en Sociale Geografie, 11, 1961, 286-295.
         After a broad discussion of economic development in Gabon, the physical characteristics and traffic patterns of the two ports are examined.

207.0.3 POURTIER, R. "Ville et espace en Afrique noire: exemple du Gabon." L'Espace Géographique, 8, 1979, 119-130.
         Examines changes in the space economy of Gabon resulting from export-oriented economic growth, the role of urban centers in these changes, and the increasing dominance of Libreville.

207.0.4 REMY, M. Gabon Today. Jeune Afrique, Paris, 1977, 263 pp.
         Includes lavishly illustrated descriptions of

Libreville and other towns, emphasizing aspects of
tourist interest.

207.0.5 VENNETIER, P. "Les ports du Gabon et du Congo-Brazzaville."
Cahiers d'Outre-Mer, 22, 1969, 337-355.
Includes discussions of the growth of port activity
at Libreville and Port Gentil and examines their traffic
patterns in the 1960s.

207.0.6 VENNETIER, P. "Problems of port development in Gabon and
Congo-Brazzaville." In Hoyle, B.S. and Hilling, D. (eds.),
Seaports and Development in Tropical Africa. Macmillan,
London, 1970, 183-201.
An English version of the above paper.

Unpublished theses include:

207.0.7 ADANDE, J-F. Recherches sur l'Approvisionnement des Pôles
de Consommation du Gabon. Thèse 3e cycle, Université de
Paris, 1968.

Libreville (Capital city. Population estimate 1975: 150,000.)

207.1.1 BASCOU-BRESCANE, R. "L'étude de la population de Libreville
de 1960 à 1970." In CNRS, La Croissance Urbaine en Afrique
Noire et à Madagascar. Paris, 1972, 299-315.
Reviews seven population censuses and surveys undertaken in Libreville between 1960 and 1970, discussing
their aims and methods and summarizing the information
obtained.

207.1.2 GABON. Recensement et Enquêtes Démographiques 1960-1961:
résultats pour Libreville. INSEE, Paris, 1962, 52 pp.
Provides data on age, sex, birthplace, tribe, marital
status, and occupations, in some cases for five distinct
zones of the city.

207.1.3 GABON. Recensement de la Population de la Commune de
Libreville, 1964. Service National de la Statistique,
Libreville, 1965, 56 pp.
Provides and analyzes data on age and sex, household
size, tribe and nationality, birthplace and length of
residence, and occupations, in some cases for five
districts.

207.1.4 GABON. Etude des Conditions de Vie à Libreville, 1961-1962.
INSEE, Paris, 1969, 142 pp.
Presents and analyzes data on household income, expenditure, subsistence consumption, and housing conditions,
on the basis of a survey of 304 households.

207.1.5   GHENASSIA, J-C. (ed.) <u>Libreville, Capitale de la République</u>
          <u>Gabonaise</u>. Société Gabonaise d'Edition, Libreville, 1973,
          131 pp.
                A collection of old and recent photographs of the
          city and its surroundings.

207.1.6   LASSERRE, G. "La dynamique de l'espace urbain à Libreville:
          règlement foncière et morphologie des quartiers." In
          CNRS, <u>La Croissance Urbaine en Afrique Noire et à</u>
          <u>Madagascar</u>. Paris, 1972, 739-761.
                Examines the physical structure of the city, stressing
          the significance of land-tenure for patterns of land-
          value, housing types, etc. Incorporates several maps
          and air photographs.

207.1.7   LASSERRE, G. "Les mécanismes de la croissance et les
          structures démographiques de Libreville (1953-1970)."
          In CNRS, <u>La Croissance Urbaine en Afrique Noire et à</u>
          <u>Madagascar</u>. Paris, 1972, 718-738.
                Examines rates of population growth, the contribution
          of migration, the origins of migrants, and the ethnic
          and demographic structure of the city's population at
          various dates.

The major work on Libreville remains:

207.1.8   LASSERRE, G. <u>Libreville: la ville et sa région</u>. Colin,
          Paris, 1958, 348 pp.

Still of use also is:

207.1.9   LASSERRE, G. "Le paysage urbain des Librevilles Noires."
          <u>Cahiers d'Outre-Mer</u>, 9, 1956, 363-388.

Unpublished theses include:

207.1.10 WALTER, R. Le Développement de Libreville. Thèse 3e cycle,
          Université de Aix-Marseille II, 1976.

<u>Port-Gentil</u> (Second town and port. Population estimate in 1975:
          75,000.)

207.2.1   BOUQUEREL, J. "Port-Gentil, centre économique du Gabon."
          <u>Cahiers d'Outre-Mer</u>, 20, 1967, 247-274.
                Examines the town's port activity, commercial func-
          tions, and industries; its physical form and demographic
          structure; and its future prospects.

207.2.2   ROUMEGOUS, M. "Port-Gentil: quelques aspects sociaux du
          développement industriel." <u>Cahiers d'Outre-Mer</u>, 19,

1966, 321-353.
Discusses the town's growth, the origins of its population, the social and economic conditions of its labor
force, and the policies of the major companies providing
employment.

RWANDA

General

208.0.1   GOTANEGRE, J-F; PRIOUL, C.; and SIRVEN, P.   Géographie du
          Rwanda.   De Boeck, Brussels, 1974, 142 pp.
              Chapter 15, "Les villes" (pp. 123-130) provides brief
          accounts of the growth and character of Kigali and smaller
          towns; there is some relevant material elsewhere, e.g.,
          chapter 17 on commerce.

208.0.2   RWANDA.   Enquête Démographique de Rwanda, 1970.   INSEE,
          Paris, 1973, 280 pp.
              Includes information on the population of the towns.

208.0.3   SIRVEN, P.   "Transports et urbanisation au Rwanda."   In
          CEGET, Transports et Croissance Urbaine dans les Pays
          Tropicaux.   Bordeaux, 1976, 89-99.
              Indicates the very limited extent of urbanization in
          Rwanda, yet the high concentration of vehicles in the
          emerging towns; suggests that the road system will great-
          ly affect the pattern of future urban growth.

Kigali   (Before independence a very small town, but now growing as
          the national capital, the population reaching 90,000 by 1977.)

*208.1.1 GATSIMBANYI, G.   "Kigali: capitale naissante."   Rwanda
          Carrefour d'Afrique, 70, 1967, 4-11 and 71; 1967, 8-11.

208.1.2   SIRVEN, P.   "Note sur la croissance urbaine de Kigali."
          Etudes Rwandaises, 12, 1979, 134-147.
              Examines the town's site, slow colonial growth, rapid
          recent expansion, population structure, origins and dis-
          tribution, and employment structure.

208.1.3   VANDERSYPEN, M.   "Femmes libres de Kigali."   Cahiers d'Etudes
          Africaines, 17, 1977, 95-120.
              A broad review of prostitution in Kigali, discussing
          the women's haunts, age, social origins, etc., and also
          their attitudes and the attitudes of others towards them.

ZAIRE

General

209.0.1 DE SAINT MOULIN, L. "Histoire des villes du Zaire: notions
et perspectives fondamentales." Etudes d'Histoire
Africaine, 6, 1974, 137-167.
Discusses the creation of towns between 1895 and 1914,
subsequent changes in their legal status, the urban system in 1970, variations in 1938-1970 growth rates, and
prospects for urban growth up to 1980. An appendix
specifies the dates of designation of all urban centers.

209.0.2 DE SAINT MOULIN, L. "Les villes et le développement
économique du Zaire." In Breitengross, J.P. (ed.),
Planification et Développement Economique au Zaire.
Deutsches Institut für Afrika Forschung, Hamburg, 1974,
63-74.
Shows that per capita income is far higher in towns
than in rural areas, though less high in Kinshasa than in
Shaba towns, and suggests that while towns can play a
vital role in economic growth their potential must be
integrated with that of rural areas.

209.0.3 DE SAINT MOULIN, L. Atlas des Collectivités du Zaire.
Presses Universitaires du Zaire, Kinshasa, 1976, 65 pp.
Includes a map of the distribution of the urban popu-
lation and 1970 census figures for each locality, noting
Zairian and foreign population.

209.0.4 DE SAINT MOULIN, L. "Perspectives de la croissance urbaine
au Zaire." Zaire-Afrique, 111, 1977, 35-52.
Provides population figures for each urban center for
1938, 1948, 1958, and 1970, and makes projections up to
A.D. 2000, when Kinshasa may have almost seven million
inhabitants and Lubumbashi one and one-half million.

209.0.5 DIALLO, S. Zaire Today. Jeune Afrique, Paris, 1977, 263 pp.
Includes illustrated descriptions of forty towns and
cities, pp. 108-206, emphasizing aspects of tourist
interest.

209.0.6 GREVISSE, F. "Les aspects multiples et changeants du
problème du logement des populations katangaises."
Civilisations, 12, 1962, 88-110.
Discusses changes over twenty-five years in the housing
situation of the Katanga (now Shaba) population, rural
and urban, with special reference to government and mining
company responses to urban housing needs.

209.0.7   KAPUTO, S. "Phénomène d'ethnicité et de conflits ethno-
           politiques dans les centres urbains du Zaire." Etudes
           Zairoises, 3, 1975, 3-12.
               Examines the significance of ethnicity in the conflicts
           that occurred within the urban centers of Zaire in the
           1960s, in relation to other divisive forces.

209.0.8   KNOOP, H. "Aspects socio-économiques de l'urbanisation au
           Congo." In INCIDI, Urban Agglomerations in the States
           of the Third World. Brussels, 1971, 94-132.
               Notes the rapid growth of the urban population both
           before and after independence, discusses the increasing
           disequilibrium between urban and rural areas and the
           resulting pressures for migration, and stresses the
           urgency for action to reduce urban-rural disparities in
           income and welfare.

209.0.9   LEBLANC, M. Personnalité de la Femme Katangaise: contribu-
           tion à l'étude de son acculturation. Nauwelaerts,
           Louvain, 1960, 403 pp.
               Presents the results of an intensive study of psycho-
           logical and behavioral change among female migrants in
           the former Elizabethville and Kolwezi, in relation to
           much theoretical work in psychology.

209.0.10   LINIGER-GOUMAZ, M. Villes et Problèmes Urbains de la
           République Démocratique du Congo: bibliographie.
           Editions du Temps, Geneva, 1968, 86 pp.
               A mimeographed list of items for each urban center,
           most dating from the period before 1960 and thus not
           included in the present list. Lists 717 items in all,
           including some relating to Africa in general.

209.0.11   MATYABO ASAKILA. "Le système de filiation matrilinéaire
           face à une société en transition: case de la société
           urbaine zairoise." Antennes: Bulletin du CERUKI,
           Bukavu, 4 (1), 1976, 3-50.
               A sociological study of family and marriage patterns
           in Zaire cities, especially concerned with relations
           between traditional practice and modern civil law.

209.0.12   MIRACLE, M.P. "African markets and trade in the Copperbelt."
           In Bohannan, P. and Dalton, G. (eds.), Markets in Africa.
           Northwestern University Press, Evanston, Ill., 1962,
           698-738.
               Examines the marketing of agricultural produce in
           the Copperbelt towns of Zaire and Zambia, both in histor-
           ical perspective and in terms of the scale and organiza-
           tion of such trade in the late 1950s.

209.0.13   MONNIER, F. "L'hierarchie des villes: le cas des villes

de la République du Zaire." <u>Revue de l'Institut de
Sociologie</u>, 47, 1974, 275-298.
  Examines the spatial distribution and the hierarchical arrangement of urban centers in Zaire, noting changes
between 1958 and 1970 and using Haut-Zaire province to
exemplify the local hierarchies.

209.0.14 MPINGA, H. "Les mécanismes de la croissance urbaine en
  République Démocratique du Congo." <u>Etudes Congolaises</u>,
  11 (3), 1968, 95-103.
    Briefly examines economic and especially political
  factors contributing to rapid urban growth in Zaire in
  the early 1960s.

209.0.15 MPINGA, H. "Rôle sociale, économique et politique des
  agglomérations urbaines en République Démocratique du
  Congo." In INCIDI, <u>Urban Agglomerations in the States
  of the Third World</u>. Brussels, 1971, 133-145.
    Discusses the administrative structure of the towns
  before and after independence and the ways in which
  close ties with rural areas remain while many gross
  disparities exist.

209.0.16 MWEPU-KYABUTHA, G. "Quelques aspects des conséquences
  sociales de l'industrialisation au Katanga." <u>Civilisations</u>.
  17, 1967, 53-71.
    Discusses the cultural disequilibrium that has arisen
  out of the social consequences of industrialization in
  former Katanga, stressing the breakdown of traditional
  structures.

209.0.17 RAYMAEKERS, P. "Les taudis de nos grandes villes, leur
  reconversion et la création de cités satellites."
  <u>Problèmes Sociaux Congolais</u>, 50, 1960, 27-56.
    Outlines the rapid urban growth up to 1957, the re-
  sulting shanty development, and the scope for government
  action either to improve such areas or to replace them
  with planned satellite towns.

209.0.18 VENNETIER, P. "Villes." In Laclavère, G. (ed.), <u>Atlas de
  la République du Zaire</u>. Jeune Afrique, Paris, 1978,
  37-39.
    Multicolored maps of Kinshasa, Lubumbashi, and
  Kisangani, with a brief text.

209.0.19 VERHAEGEN, B. and LOVENS, M. "La fonction politique des
  villes au Congo." <u>Cahiers Economiques et Sociaux</u>, 2,
  1964, 271-279.
    On the basis of studies of the former Coquilhatville,
  Luluabourg, and Stanleyville, provides a general discussion of the role of provincial urban centers in social
  and political change.

209.0.20   VUNDOWE, F. "La réforme politique et administrative des
                villes et communes du Congo-Kinshasa." Etudes Congolaises,
                11 (3), 1968, 71-94.
                Outlines the administrative status of urban centers
            from 1923 onwards and gives full details of the new
            administrative structures set up in January 1968.

209.0.21   ANON. "Urban unemployment in Africa South of the Sahara:
                1--Unemployment in the Belgian Congo." Inter-African
                Labour Institute Bulletin, 7 (2), 1960, 8-38.
                Report provided by the government labor service,
            providing a general review of the extent and nature of
            unemployment, and indicating some measures taken to
            reduce the problem. (In English and French.)

Notable earlier works include:

209.0.22   BAUMER, G. Les Centres Indigènes Extracoutumiers au Congo
                Belge. Domat-Montchrestien, Paris, 1939, 235 pp.

209.0.23   CLEMENT, P.; PONS, V.G.; and XYDIAS, N. Contributions to
                Social Implications of Industrialization and Urbanization
                in Africa South of the Sahara. UNESCO, Paris, 1956.

209.0.24   HEYMAN, M. L'Urbanisme au Congo Belge. De Visscher,
                Brussels, 1951, 223 pp.

Unpublished theses include:

209.0.25   BERTOLINI, G. La Femme Zairoise en Milieu Urbain. Thèse
                3e cycle, Université de Nice, 1972.

Bukavu   (Headquarters of Kivu Province, in the extreme east.
            Population at 1970 census: 135,000.)

209.1.1   FRANSEN, J. Enquêtes Démographiques: Bukavu. Bureau
                d'Etudes d'Aménagements Urbains, Kinshasa, 1978, 437 pp.
                Examines the origins and growth of the town, Belgian
            colonial policy towards it, etc., as well as providing
            a mass of data on its demographic and ethnic structure,
            migration patterns, housing, and employment.

Unpublished theses include:

209.1.2   CALCIO-GAUDINO, J-C. Essai de Monographie Urbaine de la
                Ville de Bukavu. Thèse 3e cycle, Université de Grenoble
                I, 1973.

<u>Isiro</u> (Town in Haut-Zaire Province, in the far northeast, formerly
Paulis. Population in 1970: 50,000.)

209.2.1 CHOPRIX, G. <u>La Naissance d'une Ville: étude géographique
de Paulis (1934-1957)</u>. CEMUBAC, Brussels, 1961, 112 pp.
A detailed historical and geographical study of the
origin and growth of the town, its site and situation,
its economic functions, and its physical form.

<u>Kananga</u> (The headquarters of Kasai Occidentale Province, which grew
rapidly in the 1960s to become the country's second largest
city, with a population of 430,000 in 1970. Former name:
Luluabourg.)

209.3.1 LUX, A. "Le niveau de vie des chômeurs de Luluabourg."
<u>Zaire</u>, 14, 1960, 3-34.
Presents the results of a 1958 survey of unemployed
men in the city, investigating past and present sources
of finance and patterns of expenditure, with case studies
of various individuals.

A notable earlier study was:

209.3.2 LUX, A. "Migrations, accroissement et urbanisation de la
population congolaise de Luluabourg." <u>Zaire</u>, 12, 1958,
675-724 and 819-877.

Unpublished theses include:

209.3.3 NZONGOLA-NTALAJA. Urban administration in Zaire: a study
of Kananga, 1971-73. Ph.D. thesis, University of
Wisconsin, 1975.

<u>Kikwit</u> (Town in Bandundu Province. Population in 1970: 110,000.)

209.4.1 NICOLAI, H. "Naissance de la ville urbaine: Kikwit." In
Nicolai, H., <u>Le Kwilu</u>. CEMUBAC, Brussels, 1963,
379-399.
Examines the town's origins, growth, physical form,
functions, relations with the surrounding area, and
future prospects.

<u>Kinshasa</u> (Capital city. Population in 1970: 1.3 million. Former
name: Leopoldville.)

209.5.1 BAECK, L. "An expenditure study of the Congolese 'évolués'
of Leopoldville, Belgian Congo." In Southall, A. (ed.),
<u>Social Change in Modern Africa</u>. Oxford University Press,

London, 1961, 159–181.
Investigates expenditure patterns of the more affluent
African households in the mid-1950s, noting a high propensity to spend rather than save, close copying of
European consumption patterns, but also the continuing
importance of traditional elements such as kinship
obligations.

209.5.2 BARRIERE-CONSTANTIN, J. "Intervention en matière d'urbanisme
à Kinshasa." Bulletin du SMUH, 63, 1970, 4–27; and
Coopération et Développement, 33, 1970, 10–21.
Notes the rapid growth of the city and summarizes
plans prepared in 1966-1967 to guide its future physical
growth.

209.5.3 BERNARD, G. Ville Africaine, Famille Urbaine: les
enseignants de Kinshasa. Mouton, Paris, 1968, 173 pp.
Provides a brief outline of the city and of the basis
for selecting teachers for a case study and then analyzes
in detail the results of a survey of their economic status
and their social relationships, especially various aspects
of marriage.

209.5.4 BERNARD, G. "Conjugalité et rôle de la femme à Kinshasa."
Canadian Journal of African Studies, 6, 1972, 261–274.
Shows that far from aiding women's liberation, city
life is increasing their dependence on men as a result
of the loss of their major role in the farming economy.

209.5.5 BERNARD, G. "L'africain et la ville." Cahiers d'Etudes
Africaines, 13, 1973, 575–586.
Discusses the rapid growth of Kinshasa, emerging
social structures and patterns of social relationships,
and the citizens' attitudes to urban life.

*209.5.6 BUREAU D'ETUDES ET D'AMENAGEMENTS URBAINS. Kinshasa:
croissance urbaine. Kinshasa, 1975, 123 pp.

209.5.7 BUREAU D'ETUDES ET D'AMENAGEMENTS URBAINS. "Croissance
Urbaine de Kinshasa." Planification Habitat Information,
81, 1975, 1–98.
Includes discussions of the city's physical growth,
demographic structure, economic activities, infrastructure,
and planning problems, with numerous maps and photographs.
Text in English and French.

209.5.8 CAPRASSE, P. and BERNARD, G. "Le mariage chez les enseignants
à Leopoldville." Cahiers Economiques et Sociaux, 1 (3),
1963, 64–79.
Outlines a study in progress on marriage patterns among
primary school teachers and reviews a wide range of relevant literature.

209.5.9   CAPRASSE, P. and BERNARD, G.   "Analysis of a marriage in a
           Congolese urban setting." Cahiers Economiques et Sociaux,
           2, 1964, 75-90.
               Examines many aspects of one marriage as a case study
           within a broader inquiry on urbanization processes.
           Also in French, pp. 59-74.

209.5.10   CAPRASSE, P. and BERNARD, G.   "Les conditions de vie des
           familles d'enseignants à Leopoldville." Cahiers
           Economiques et Sociaux, 3, 1965, 411-454.
               Summary of the main findings of the study reported
           more fully in the Bernard monograph noted above.

209.5.11   COMHAIRE, J.L.L.   "Leopoldville and Lagos: comparative
           study of conditions in 1960." U.N. Economic Bulletin
           for Africa, 1 (2), 1961, 50-65; reprinted in Breese,
           G. (ed.), The City in Newly Developing Countries.
           Prentice-Hall, Englewood Cliffs, N.J., 1969, 436-460.
               Compares the two cities with respect to a wide range
           of issues, from age and size to patterns of in-migration,
           ethnicity, foreign influence, economic activities, public
           services, housing, and administration.

209.5.12   COMHAIRE-SYLVAIN, S.   Femmes de Kinshasa, Hier et Aujourd'hui.
           Mouton, Paris, 1968, 383 pp.
               The first part examines the life-style and social
           relationships of women in the city in 1945; the second
           discusses how the situation had changed by 1965; the
           third considers opportunities for wage employment and
           self-employment; and the fourth examines both female
           education and women's voluntary associations.

*209.5.13 CONGO.   Etude Socio-démographique de Kinshasa, 1967.
           Institut National de la Statistique, Kinshasa, and
           Société Françaises d'Etudes et de Développement, Paris,
           1969, 192 pp.

209.5.14   DE SAINT MOULIN, L.   "Esquisse sociologique de Kinshasa."
           Congo-Afrique, 9, 1969, 309-317.
               Brief discussion of aspects of social relationships
           in Kinshasa, with special reference to their spatial
           expression.

209.5.15   DE SAINT MOULIN, L.   "Quelle est la population de Kinshasa?"
           Congo-Afrique, 10, 1970, 65-77.
               Sketches the growth of the urban population and shows
           that the 1967 sociodemographic survey, noted above, pro-
           vides clear evidence for a population figure of 1.1
           million for 1970.

209.5.16   DE SAINT MOULIN, L.   "Ndjili, première cité satellite de

Kinshasa." Cahiers Economiques et Sociaux, 8, 1970, 295–316.

    Describes the rapid growth of this community on the southeast edge of Kinshasa in the 1950s and 1960s and examines housing conditions, origins of the population, their economic activities, and their daily patterns of movement.

209.5.17 DE SAINT MOULIN, L. "Unité et diversité des zones urbaines de Kinshasa." Cultures et Développement, 2, 1970, 363–387.

    Using the 1967 sociodemographic survey, six socio-economic zones of the city are distinguished; the physical form and population composition of each is examined; and factors influencing patterns of residential distribution are discussed.

209.5.18 DE SAINT MOULIN, L. "Les anciens villages des environs de Kinshasa." Etudes d'Histoire Africaine, 2, 1971, 83–119.

    Examines precolonial patterns of settlement in the area now occupied by the expanding city, noting how far indigenous communities have survived.

209.5.19 DE SAINT MOULIN, L. "Kinshasa." Revue Française d'Etudes Politiques Africaines, 69, 1971, 43–61.

    Discusses the rapid growth of the city, its place in the national economy, and its role in social and cultural change.

209.5.20 DE SAINT MOULIN, L. "La place de Kinshasa dans l'evolution nationale." Zaire-Afrique, 11, 1971, 367–382; and Nations Nouvelles, 29, 1971, 12–18.

    Examines the contribution of the city to the national economy, concluding that this matches its share of government expenditure but that the city is still insufficiently integrated with the rest of the country.

209.5.21 DE SAINT MOULIN, L. and DUCREUX, M. "La technique et le déroulement de l'étude socio-démographique de Kinshasa, 1967." Etudes Congolaises, 11 (4), 1968, 20–30.

    Discusses the methodology of the survey of which the main report was noted above.

209.5.22 DE SAINT MOULIN, L. and DUCREUX, M. "Le phénomène urbain à Kinshasa: évolution et perspectives." Etudes Congolaises, 12 (4), 1969, 117–142.

    A review of the distribution of the city's population, its demographic characteristics, patterns of in-migration, school attendance, occupations, and housing conditions, drawing largely upon the 1967 sociodemographic survey.

209.5.23 DUCREUX, M. "La croissance urbaine et démographique de

Kinshasa." In CNRS, <u>La Croissance Urbaine en Afrique</u>
<u>Noire et à Madagascar</u>. Paris, 1972, 549-565.
Describes the 1967 sociodemographic survey, presents
some of the results, makes comparisons with 1955, and
discusses the problems of rapid growth.

209.5.24 FLOURIOT, J.; DE MAXIMY, R.; and PAIN, M. <u>Atlas de Kinshasa</u>.
Institut Géographique du Zaire, Kinshasa, 1976, 88 pp.
A large-format atlas of multicolored maps with accompanying texts, covering terrain, climate, the city's
physical growth, population densities, population change,
housing types, economic activities, traffic, public services, education, and plans for the spatial pattern of
future urban growth.

209.5.25 HERBOTS, J.A. "Les droits fonciers et l'administration à
Léopoldville." <u>Etudes Congolaises</u>, 6 (3), 1964, 22-40.
A review of patterns and problems of land-tenure in
the city, in relation to changing administrative measures.

209.5.26 HOUYOUX, J. <u>Budgets Ménagers, Nutrition et Mode de Vie à</u>
<u>Kinshasa</u>. Presses Universitaires du Zaire, Kinshasa,
1973, 303 pp.
Presents the results of a detailed 1969 survey of
income and expenditure among a wide sample of households,
relating expenditure patterns to occupation, residential
area, education, etc., with numerous tables; also discusses working conditions, family life, and nutrition
levels within the city in the light of the survey results.

209.5.27 HOUYOUX, C. and J. "Les conditions de vie dans soixante
familles à Kinshasa." <u>Cahiers Economiques et Sociaux</u>,
8, 1970, 99-132.
Presents the results of a survey of the income and
expenditure of families in diverse circumstances, e.g.,
with head of household salaried, self-employed, unemployed, etc.

209.5.28 KAYITENKORE, E. "La construction dans les zones de
squatting de Kinshasa." <u>Cahiers Economiques et Sociaux</u>,
5, 1967, 327-353.
Discusses the extent and causes of squatting and examines the methods and costs of house construction, on
the basis of a survey in six areas of such settlement.

209.5.29 KNOOP, H. "Some demographic characteristics of a suburban
squatting community of Leopoldville." <u>Cahiers Economiques</u>
<u>et Sociaux</u>, 4, 1966, 119-146.
Reports on a 1965 survey of Kinsenso, a squatter
settlement then of 13,000 on the southeast fringe of the
city, showing much evidence of demographic balance and

social and economic stabilization in a population who
have largely moved in from elsewhere in the city.

209.5.30　KNOOP, H. "Une étude socio-démographique de Kinshasa."
Cultures et Développement, 1, 1968, 178-183.
　　　　A brief account of the aims and methods of the 1967
survey noted above.

209.5.31　LA FONTAINE, J.S. "Two types of youth group in Kinshasa
(Léopoldville)." In Mayer, P. (ed.), Socialization.
Tavistock, London, 1969, 191-213.
　　　　Investigates the proliferation of youth groups in
the city after independence, on the basis of a 1962-1963
survey, and their implications for social change.

209.5.32　LA FONTAINE, J.S. City Politics: a study of Leopoldville,
1962-63. Cambridge University Press, 1970, 247 pp.
　　　　Part one outlines the city's growth and form, its
population structure and economic life, and its administration and religious organization; part two examines
social relationships, including kinship, friendships,
and voluntary associations; part three discusses political parties, leaders, and processes in the city just
after independence.

209.5.33　LA FONTAINE, J.S. "The free women of Kinshasa: prostitution
in a city in Zaire." In Davis, J. (ed.), Choice and
Change: essays in honour of Lucy Mair. Athlone Press,
London, 1974, 89-113.
　　　　Shows that urbanization has produced a large group
of "femmes libres," who include both prostitutes and
women with longer-lasting liaisons, and discusses the
social and economic situation of different groups.

209.5.34　LIKANGA ANGBALU. "Quelques considérations sur la réforme
de 1968 et les finances communales de la ville de
Kinshasa." Cahiers Zairois d'Etudes Politiques et
Sociales, 3, 1974, 147-153.
　　　　Examines the operation of municipal government finance
in Kinshasa before and after the administrative reforms
of 1968.

209.5.35　M'BAYA, K. "Les industries du pôle de Kinshasa." Cahiers
du CEDAF, 1977, No. 1/2, 163 pp.
　　　　A detailed review of individual industries, an analysis of the total industrial structure, and a discussion
of the role of Kinshasa as an industrial growth pole in
relation to national development.

209.5.36　M'BUY, L.V. "Habitat et urbanisme à Kinshasa." Bulletin
du SMUH, 59, 1970, 16-87.

A study of social conditions, housing, and physical
infrastructure in areas of spontaneous settlement that
were rapidly developing in the 1960s.

209.5.37 MPETI, M.N. L'Evolution de la Solidarité Traditionnelle en
Milieu Rural et Urbain au Zaire. Presses Universitaires
du Zaire, Kinshasa, 1974, 287 pp.
Examines the family and clan solidarity of the Ntomba
and Basengele people in their home area, in the small
local town of Inongo, and in Kinshasa; also discusses
other relationships in the city, such as those within
small neighborhoods.

*209.5.38 MPINGA, H. Ville de Kinshasa: organisation politique et
administration actuelle. CEAN, Bordeaux, 1967, 124 pp.

209.5.39 MPINGA, H. "La coexistence des pouvoirs 'traditionnel' et
'moderne' dans la ville de Kinshasa." Cahiers Economiques
et Sociaux, 7, 1969, 67-90.
Examines the structure of local government within
Kinshasa, with special references to changes in the late
1960s and to the relationships between new communes on
the periphery and traditional patterns of authority in
the area.

*209.5.40 RAYMAEKERS, P. "Conjonctures socio-économiques à
Léopoldville." Notes et Documents de l'IRES de
l'Université de Léopoldville, 1 (2), 1960, 61 pp; 1 (4),
1960, 43 pp; 1 (6), 1960, 45 pp; 1 (16), 1961, 44 pp;
2 (2), 1961, 37 pp.

209.5.41 RAYMAEKERS, P. "Le squatting à Léopoldville." Inter-
African Labour Institute Bulletin, 8 (4), 1961, 22-53.
Reports on a survey of the extent, nature, and distribution of squatter settlement in the city in 1960-1961,
discussing the origins, employment situation, social
problems, and attitudes of the squatters. (English
summary.)

209.5.42 RAYMAEKERS, P. "Pre-delinquency and juvenile delinquency
in Leopoldville." Inter-African Labour Institute Bulletin,
10, 1963, 298-357.
Discusses the forms and causes of antisocial behavior
by young people in the city, with special reference to
drug-taking and the formation of gangs. (In English
and French.)

209.5.43 RAYMAEKERS, P. L'Organisation des Zones de Squatting:
application au milieu urbain de Léopoldville. Editions
Universitaires, Paris, 1964, 283 pp.
Begins with a discussion of the scale and nature of

unemployment in the city and of the sociology of the
unemployed; then proceeds to an examination of the extent of squatter settlement and especially of the organization of the squatters.

209.5.44 SCHWARZ, A. "Croissance urbaine et chômage à Kinshasa."
          Manpower and Unemployment Research in Africa, 2 (1),
          1969, 37–44.
          Largely concerned with the difficulties of measuring
          unemployment in Kinshasa, but indicating that it is a
          problem of increasing magnitude.

209.5.45 SCHWARZ, A. "Solidarité clanique, intégration urbaine et
          chômage en Afrique noire." Canadian Journal of African
          Studies, 3, 1969, 377–394.
          Reports on studies of Kinshasa's unemployed in the
          mid-1960s, which show the importance of kinship and clan
          ties in enabling them to survive in the city.

209.5.46 SPITAELS, G. "Considérations sur le chômage à Léopoldville."
          Inter-African Labour Institute Bulletin, 8 (3), 1961,
          81–97.
          Examines the extent of recorded unemployment in the
          city in 1959, reviews a government survey showing how
          far these data reflected the true picture, and considers
          employment prospects for the 1960s (English summary.)

209.5.47 TSHINYONGOLO-MULUNDA. "Le chômage masculin à Kinshasa."
          Cahiers Zairois de la Recherche et du Développement,
          16 (1), 1973, 59–80.
          Analyzes information on unemployment from a 1967–1968
          sociodemographic survey of the city, with nine pages of
          tables providing data for twenty zones.

209.5.48 VERHASSELT-VAN WETTERE, Y. "Quelques aspects de l'expansion
          de la ville de Kinshasa." In CNRS, La Croissance Urbaine
          en Afrique Noire et à Madagascar. Paris, 1972,
          1047–1054.
          Outlines the growth of the city, notes the huge recent
          spread of squatter settlement, and shows how air photo-
          graphs can provide information on them.

209.5.49 WILMET, J. "Observations sur l'évolution récente de
          l'urbanisation à Kinshasa." In CNRS, La Croissance
          Urbaine en Afrique Noire et à Madagascar. Paris, 1972,
          1073–1077.
          General account of the population growth and physical
          spread of the city and of the failure of jobs and infra-
          structure to keep pace with the growth.

209.5.50 WRZESINSKA, A. "Kinshasa female students speak about

themselves." Africa (Rome), 34, 1979, 373-390.
    Analyzes the responses to an inquiry on motives for attending school and aspirations in later life among female secondary school students.

209.5.51 ZAIRE. Activités Socio-économiques des Petites et Moyennes Entreprises de Kinshasa: étude statistique et cartographique. Office de Promotion des Petites et Moyennes Entreprises, Kinshasa, 1974, 143 pp.
    Provides data on small- and medium-scale economic activities in each of thirty-two zones of the city and maps the distribution of such activities within each zone.

Notable earlier studies include:

209.5.52 CAPELLE, E. La Cité Indigène de Léopoldville. CEPSI, Elizabethville, 1947, 110 pp.

209.5.53 DENIS, J. "Léopoldville: étude de géographie urbaine et sociale." Zaire, 10, 1956, 563-611.

Unpublished theses include:

209.5.54 BUKASA, A. Les Effets Economiques et Sociaux de la Concentration de la Population dans la Ville de Kinshasa. Thèse 3e cycle, Université de Paris I, 1975.

209.5.55 CREPIN, X. Occupation de l'Espace et Appropriation du Sol: évolution de l'habitat urbain en Afrique, Kinshasa Ndjili. Thèse Université de Paris VIII, 1977.

209.5.56 NELSON, E.R. African rural-urban migration: economic choice theory and Kinshasa evidence. Ph.D. thesis, Yale University, 1976.

209.5.57 NSHIMBA-LUBILANJI, L. Etude de l'Approvisionnement en Poisson de Kinshasa (Zaire): un problème de croissance urbaine en Afrique noire. Thèse 3e cycle, Université de Bordeaux III, 1973.

209.5.58 PAIN, M. Kinshasa: étude cartographique des petites activités. Thèse 3e cycle, Université de Toulouse II, 1975.

Kisangani (Headquarters of Haut-Zaire Province. Population in 1970: 230,000. Former name: Stanleyville.)

*209.6.1 HOUYOUX, J. Kisangani: étude des budgets ménagers. SICAI, Rome, 1972, 127 pp.

209.6.2 JEWSIECKI, B. "Histoire économique d'une ville coloniale:
         Kisangani, 1877-1960." Cahiers du CEDAF, 1978, No. 5,
         44 pp.
             Discusses the origins of the city; its role as a com-
         mercial, industrial and transport center from 1913 to
         1940; and its role in these respects from 1941 to 1960.

209.6.3 KORNFIELD, R. "The colonial situation and differential use
         of the city of Kisangani by Europeans and Zairians."
         African Urban Notes, B 1 (3), 1975, 101-116.
             Describes the city's physical layout and shows how the
         large degree of social segregation in the colonial period
         determined each racial group's spatial patterns of activity
         and movement and the differential use of urban amenities.

209.6.4 PONS, V.G. "Two small groups in Avenue 21: some aspects
         of the system of social relationships in a remote corner
         of Stanleyville, Belgian Congo." In Southall, A. (ed.),
         Social Change in Modern Africa. Oxford University Press,
         London, 1961, 205-216.
             Reports on a microstudy of the residents of twenty-
         three compounds in a low-income neighborhood, with special
         reference to relationships in two leisure time groups.

209.6.5 PONS, V.G. Stanleyville: an African urban community under
         Belgian administration. Oxford University Press, London,
         1969, 356 pp.
             Provides a brief account of the town and its population
         in the early 1950s, discusses patterns of in-migration,
         and examines the demographic structures and spatial dis-
         tributions of different ethnic groups. Then proceeds to
         a closer examination of particular neighborhoods and a
         detailed analysis of social relationships within a single
         street.

209.6.6 VERHAEGEN, B. (ed.) Kisangani, 1876-1976: histoire d'une
         ville. Vol. 1, la population. Presses Universitaires
         du Zaire, Kinshasa, 1976, 287 pp.
             A paper by L.De Saint Moulin on the growth and struc-
         ture of the population is followed by papers on individual
         ethnic groups by L. Baruti, W. De Mahieu, B. Yeikelo,
         A. Droogers, and G. Bibeau, and a paper on traditional
         medicine by E. Corin.

A notable paper in German is:

209.6.7 WIESE, B. "Kisangani--Probleme einer zentralafrikanischen
         Grosstadt." Kölner Geographische Arbeiten (Afrika), 5,
         1973, 35-78.

Unpublished theses include:

209.6.8 KORNFIELD-GILMAN, R. Relations between Zaireans and
         Europeans in the city of Kisangani: a symbolic inter-
         actionist approach. Ph.D. thesis, University of Manchester,
         U.K., 1974.

Lubumbashi (Headquarters of Shaba Province and third largest city.
            Population in 1970: 320,000. Former name: Elisabethville.)

209.7.1 ALEXANDRE-PYRE, S. "L'origine de la population du centre
         urbain de Lubumbashi." Publications de l'Université
         Officielle du Congo à Lubumbashi, 19, 1969, 141-150.
           Maps and discusses the areas of origin of the migrant
         population of the city, distinguishing temporary and
         permanent residents, and noting the effects of political
         crises in the 1960s.

209.7.2 ANSELIN, M. "La classe moyenne indigène à Elisabethville."
         Problèmes Sociaux Congolais, 53, 1961, 99-110.
           Describes the emergence of a class of small-scale
         entrepreneurs and discusses their role in the economic
         and social life of the city.

209.7.3 BENOIT, J. "Contribution à l'étude de la population active
         d'Elisabethville." Problèmes Sociaux Congolais, 54, 1961,
         3-53.
           Presents the results of a 1958 survey of over 4,000
         household heads, covering age, date of arrival, district
         of origin, type of employment, frequency of change of
         employment, and incidence of unemployment, and relation-
         ships among these characteristics.

209.7.4 BENOIT, J. La Population Africaine à Elisabethville à la
         Fin de 1957: son état, sa structure, ses mouvements et
         ses perspectives d'évolution prochaine. CEPSI,
         Elisabethville, 1962, 120 pp.
           A fuller presentation of the results of the survey
         noted above.

209.7.5 COMHAIRE, J. "Lubumbashi et Nairobi: étude comparée de
         leur évolution. 1) Lubumbashi." Revue Française d'Etudes
         Politiques Africaines, 67, 1971, 54-63.
           An account of the origins and growth of the city and
         the effects of government and mining company policies on
         its physical form.

209.7.6 DE WILDE, J. "Quelques aspects du ravitaillement en produits
         vivriers de Lubumbashi." In CEGET, Dix Etudes sur
         l'Approvisionnement des Villes. Bordeaux, 1972, 217-224.
           Discusses the problems of food supply arising from
         the city's poor agricultural environment and the

disorganization of farming in the 1960s, noting the need for restoring irrigated crop production.

209.7.7   FETTER, B. "Elisabethville." African Urban Notes, Bibliographical Supplement 7, 1968, 33 pp.
A listing of sources for the study of the history of the city.

209.7.8   FETTER, B. "Immigrants to Elisabethville: their origins and aims." African Urban Notes, 3 (2), 1968, 17-34.
Examines the nature and pattern of in-migration from the city's origin up to 1945.

209.7.9   FETTER, B. "African associations in Elisabethville, 1910-1935: their origins and development." Etudes d'Histoire Africaine, 6, 1974, 205-223.
Shows how the African population took traditional forms of association to the city, adapting them to assist with problems there, and continuing to adapt them as various circumstances changed.

209.7.10   FETTER, B. The Creation of Elisabethville, 1910-1940. Hoover Institution Press, Stanford, 1976, 211 pp.
A chronological account of the growth of the city, with chapters devoted to particular phases, such as the boom of the late 1920s and the subsequent depression. The main theme is that it was a city built by Europeans to serve European interests, with Africans moving in under pressure and experiencing many hardships.

209.7.11   HENNIN, R. "Les structures familiales en milieu urbain." Problèmes Sociaux Congolais, 68, 1965, 3-90.
Examines how urban life is affecting family and kin relations, and marriage in particular, on the basis of an extensive questionnaire survey.

209.7.12   HOUYOUX, J. and LECOANET, Y. Lubumbashi: démographie, budgets ménagers et étude du site. Bureau d'Etudes d'Aménagements Urbains, Kinshasa, 1975, 144 pp.
Examines the city's site, morphology, demography, land ownership, housing, employment, household budgets, and urban transport patterns, on the basis of an intensive statistical survey.

209.7.13   KAJIKA LUPUNDU. "Les manifestations de la solidarité dans une ville négro-africaine: le cas de Lubumbashi." Problèmes Sociaux Zairois, 104/5, 1974, 53-58.
Brief discussion of patterns of social relationships in the city.

209.7.14   LEBLANC, M. and MALAISSE, F. Lubumbashi, un Ecosystème

Urbain Tropical. Université Nationale du Zaire,
Lubumbashi, 1978, 166 pp.
 Examines the city's population and economy within
the context of the physical environment and as part of
a total ecosystem. Individual topics covered range from
the city's plant life to its transport flows. Numerous
maps and photographs are included.

209.7.15 LE BRUN, E. "Délinquence africaine en milieu urbain."
 Problèmes Sociaux Congolais, 58, 1962, 3-92.
 A wide-ranging study of crime in the city in the late
1950s, of the characteristics of criminals and delinquents,
and of factors contributing to a high crime rate.

209.7.16 MINON, P. Katuba: étude quantitative d'une communauté
 urbaine africaine. Faculté de Droit, Liège, Belgium,
1960, 90 pp.
 Presents the results of a detailed census undertaken
in 1957 in this new quarter of Lubumbashi, covering
demographic characteristics, marital status, size of
family, area of origin, date of arrival in town, etc.

209.7.17 POLOME, E.C. "Multilingualism in an African urban centre:
 the Lubumbashi case." In Whiteley, W.H. (ed.), Language
 Use and Social Change. Oxford University Press,
 London, 1971, 364-375.
 Provides a brief sketch of the growth of the city
as well as analyzing present patterns of language use
within it.

209.7.18 VAN ASSCHE, F. "La consommation indigène à Elisabethville."
 Problèmes Sociaux Congolais, 50, 1960, 117-138.
 Summarizes the results of a 1958 survey of household
budgets among a sample of 245 low- and middle-income
households.

209.7.19 WILMET, J. "Observations sur la géographie industrielle
 des pays en développement recemment décolonisés:
 l'exemple de Lubumbashi." In Mélanges de Géographie
 Offerts à M.O. Tulippe. Duculot, Gembloux, 1967,
 97-119.
 An analysis of the extent, nature, and location of
industrial development within Lubumbashi.

Notable earlier studies include:

209.7.20 CHAPELIER, A. Elisabethville: essai de géographie urbaine.
 Academie Royale des Sciences Coloniales, Brussels, 1957,
 167 pp.

209.7.21 DENIS, J. "Elisabethville: materiaux pour une étude de la
 population africaine." Bulletin du CESPI, 34, 1956, 137-195.

209.7.22 GREVISSE, F. Le Centre Extra-coutumier d'Elisabethville.
          CEPSI, Elisabethville; Duculot, Gembloux, 1951, 456 pp.

209.7.23 MINON, P. "Quelques aspects de l'évolution du centre
          extra-coutumier d'Elisabethville." Problèmes Sociaux
          Congolais, 36, 1957, 5-51.

Papers in German include:

209.7.24 MULLER, K.J. "Luftbilder Lubumbashi--ehemals Elisabethville."
          Die Erde, 110, 1979, 1-31.

Unpublished theses include:

209.7.25 FETTER, B.S. Elisabethville and Lubumbashi: the
          segmentary growth of a colonial city, 1910-1945. Ph.D.
          thesis, University of Wisconsin, 1968.

209.7.26 GOULD, T.F. The educated woman in a developing country:
          professional Zairian women in Lubumbashi. Ph.D. thesis,
          Union Graduate School, 1976.

209.7.27 KAJIKA-LUPUNDI, J. Les Manifestations de la Solidarité
          dans une Ville Négro-Africaine: Lubumbashi, République
          du Zaire. Thèse 3e cycle, Université de Paris V, 1972.

209.7.28 MWABILA-MALELA. Prolétariat et Conscience de Classe au
          Zaire: l'exemple des travailleurs de la ville industrielle
          de Lubumbashi. Thèse Doctorat, Université de Bruxelles,
          1973.

       See also 209.0.9.

Matadi (The country's chief port, between Kinshasa and the Atlantic.
        Population in 1970: 110,000.)

Nothing appears to have been published since:

209.8.1   MATHIEU, M. "Le port de Matadi." Bulletin de la Société
          Royale Belge de Géographie, 83, 1959, 41-65.

Mbandaka (Headquarters of Equateur Province. Population in 1970:
          110,000. Former name: Coquilhatville.)

Nothing appears to have been published since:

209.9.1   DE THIER, F.M. Le Centre Extra-Coutumier de Coquilhatville.
          Institut de Sociologie Solvay, Université Libre de
          Bruxelles, 1956, 143 pp.

<u>Mbuji-Mayi</u> (Headquarters of Kasai Oriental Province, growing rapidly
in the 1960s to reach 256,000 in 1970.)

209.10 No publications have been found.

North-East Africa

No works dealing with this area as a whole have been traced, but

See 4.0.20.

DJIBOUTI

Djibouti   (The town accounts for 100,000 of the 220,000 total
           population (1975 estimate) of this ministate.)

301.1.1 AUGUSTIN, P. "Quelques dénombrements de la population du
            Territoire Français des Afars et des Issas." Pount, 13,
            1974, 27-38.
               Reviews various population counts and estimates from
            1885 to 1927, with some figures specific to the town.
            Due to be followed by a second paper on later counts.

301.1.2 HAILU WOLDE EMMANUEL. "Major ports of Ethiopia." Ethiopian
            Geographical Journal, 3, 1965, 35-47.
               Covers Djibouti as well as Aseb and Mesewa, examining
            its site, history, present port facilities, traffic pat-
            tern, and hinterland.

301.1.3 MARTINEAU, A. et al. Djibouti. Delroisse, Paris, 1977,
            128 pp.
               A book of colored photographs of the town and the rest
            of the territory, with a brief text.

301.1.4 STEINBACH, M. and ALLEGRET, . "Djibouti: le quartier du
            stade." Bulletin du SMUH, 46, 1966, 1-25.

A brief illustrated account of the city and its housing problems and a fuller description of a 1962–1966
housing project. In English and French.

301.1.5 THOMPSON, V. and ADLOFF, R. Djibouti and the Horn of Africa.
Stanford University Press, Calif., 1968, 246 pp.
A broad discussion of the preindependence political,
social, and economic life of the whole territory, but
with much on the town, especially in chapter 6, "Social
development" and chapter 8, "The modern economy."

301.1.6 ANON. La Côte Française des Somalis. La Documentation
Française, Paris, 1961, 52 pp.
A survey of land and population, economic and social
conditions, including much relating to the town.

A bibliography for the country, including many items wholly or partly
concerned with the town, is:

301.1.7 CLARKE, W.S. "The Republic of Djibouti: an introduction
to Africa's newest state and a review of related literature and sources." Current Bibliography of African
Affairs, 10, 1977/8, 1–31.

See also 302.0.18.

ETHIOPIA

General

302.0.1 AKALOU WOLDE MICHAEL. "Some thoughts on the process of
              urbanization in pre-twentieth century Ethiopia."
              Ethiopian Geographical Journal, 5 (2), 1967, 35-38.
                 Shows that past Ethiopian urbanization was a cyclical
              rather than cumulative phenomenon and was based primarily
              on political or military functions, but also that by the
              late nineteenth-century mobile tented camps were giving
              way to longer-term settlements around palaces.

302.0.2 AKALOU WOLDE MICHAEL. "Urban development in Ethiopia
              1889-1925." Journal of Ethiopian Studies, 11, 1973, 1-16.
                 Examines the spread of urbanization through Menelik's
              territorial conquests, most new towns of this period being
              garrisons, and notes also the significance of new communi-
              cations, especially the railway along which fifteen or
              more towns grew up.

302.0.3 COMHAIRE, J.L. "Urban growth in relation to Ethiopian
              development." Cultures et Développement, 1, 1968, 25-39.
                 Outlines the evolution and present distribution of the
              twenty-five centers with over 7,000 people, stressing the
              increasing primacy of Addis Ababa. Provides much informa-
              tion on the nature and function of the towns, with no
              clearly dominant theme.

302.0.4 COOPER, R.L. and HORVATH, R.J. "Language, migration and
              urbanization." In Bender, M.L. et al. (eds.), Language
              in Ethiopia. Oxford University Press, London, 1976,
              191-212.
                 Describes the language situation in Ethiopian towns,
              relates this to patterns of migration, assesses the ex-
              tent of recent change, and concludes that urbanization
              has assisted the diffusion of Amharic.

302.0.5 ETHIOPIA. Survey of Major Towns in Ethiopia. Central
              Statistical Office, Addis Ababa, 1968, 114 pp.
                 Tabulates the results of 1964-1966 demographic surveys
              in numerous towns, providing data on economic status and
              housing as well as demographic characteristics.

302.0.6 ETHIOPIA. Urbanization in Ethiopia. Central Statistical
              Office, Addis Ababa, 1972, 58 pp.
                 Presents and analyzes data on the growth of the urban
              population, on its demographic structure, and on housing.

302.0.7 ETHIOPIA. Results of Urban Survey, Second Round. 3 vols.

Central Statistical Office, Addis Ababa, 1975, 702 pp.
Tabulates results of 1969-1971 surveys in ninety-one towns, excluding Addis Ababa and Asmara. Records urban populations by sex and age, religion, language, nationality, length of urban residence, education, employment, and occupation.

302.0.8 FELLOWS, P.A. "Urbanism: engineering trends in Ethiopia." International Journal of Comparative Sociology, 4, 1963, 162-177.
A broad account of the evolution of urbanism in Ethiopia and a discussion of the implications of modern urban growth in terms of needs for engineering, properly applied.

302.0.9 GADAMU, F. "Urbanization, polyethnic group voluntary associations and national integration in Ethiopia." Ethiopian Journal of Development Research, 1 (1), 1974, 71-80.
Examines the origins, development, and nature of Idir, associations based on neighborhood rather than ethnic origin, mainly but not exclusively in Addis Ababa.

302.0.10 HAILU WOLDE EMMANUEL. "Major ports of Ethiopia." Ethiopian Geographical Journal, 3, 1965, 35-47.
Examines the site, history, present port facilities, traffic patterns, and hinterland of Aseb, Mesewa, and also Jibuti. Concludes that Aseb has the brightest future, especially due to political uncertainty in regard to Jibuti.

302.0.11 HORVATH, R.J. "Towns in Ethiopia." Erdkunde, 22, 1968, 42-50.
A study of the origins, growth, and functions of the small towns of Shoa Province. Most are of recent origin and function largely as retail centers.

302.0.12 HORVATH, R.J. "The wandering capitals of Ethiopia." Journal of African History, 10, 1969, 205-219.
Describes the shifting capitals of the sixteenth and seventeenth centuries and offers explanations for the movement largely in terms of their military role.

302.0.13 HORVATH, R.J. "The process of urban agglomeration in Ethiopia." Journal of Ethiopian Studies, 8 (2), 1970, 81-88.
Provides an outline of the pattern of urban centers, including over 1300 small towns, distinguishing their endogenous functions such as marketing, formerly spread through rural areas, and their exogenous functions such as administration and education, which emanate from Addis Ababa.

302.0.14 KOEHN, P. "Urban origins and consequences of national and
           local political transformation in Ethiopia." In Walton,
           J. and Masotti, L. (eds.), The City in Comparative
           Perspective. Sage, Beverly Hills, Calif., 1976, 155-178.
               Examines the role of the urban elite in political
           change and discusses the changing nature of municipal
           government and urban politics.

302.0.15 KOEHN, P. and E.F. "Urbanization and urban development
           planning in Ethiopia." In Obudho, R.A. and El-Shakhs,
           S. (eds.), Development of Urban Systems in Africa.
           Praeger, New York, 1979, 215-241.
               Outlines the evolution and present pattern of urban
           centers and reviews policies and procedures for urban
           planning under Haile Selassie and under the subsequent
           military government.

302.0.16 MESFIN WOLDE MARIAM. "Some aspects of urbanization in
           pre-twentieth century Ethiopia." Ethiopian Geographical
           Journal, 3 (2), 1965, 13-20.
               Shows that past urbanization was widespread but often
           short-lived, outstanding cases being Axum, Lalibela, and
           Gondar. The failure to maintain urban civilization led
           to cultural degeneration.

302.0.17 MESFIN WOLDE MARIAM. "The rural-urban split in Ethiopia."
           In INCIDI, Urban Agglomerations in the States of the
           Third World. Brussels, 1971, 168-179.
               Suggests that the stagnation of Ethiopian civilization
           was due to the decline of traditional urbanism and that
           contemporary urbanization is largely alien to the rural
           majority. A widening rural-urban rift is a great poli-
           tical liability and planning for both urban and rural
           development is urgently needed.

302.0.18 PANKHURST, R. "Notes on the demographic history of
           Ethiopian towns and villages." Ethiopian Observer, 9,
           1965, 60-83.
               Draws together the population estimates of many past
           observers to indicate rates of growth and decline of
           towns up to the 1930s. Covers Ethiopia region by region
           and extends to Djibouti and Somalia also.

302.0.19 PANKHURST, R. Economic History of Ethiopia 1800-1935.
           Haile Sellassie I University Press, Addis Ababa, 1968,
           772 pp. Chap. 15 "Urban developments and the establish-
           ment of Addis Ababa," 689-717.
               Outlines the origins and the nineteenth-twentieth
           century fortunes of Gondar, Asmara, Harar, and other
           towns and examines the establishment and growth of
           Addis Ababa and its widening economic functions.

302.0.20 PROST-TOURNIER, J-M. "Premières données sur la géographie
urbaine de l'Ethiopie." Revue de Géographie de Lyon,
49, 1974, 5-36.
  Examines the historical antecedents of Ethiopian
urbanization, nineteenth- and twentieth-century urban
growth, the present urban system, demographic and economic characteristics of the towns, and current problems.

302.0.21 VANDERLINDEN, J. L'Ethiopie et ses Populations. Editions
Complexe, Brussels, 1977, 260 pp. "L'Ethiopien des
villes," pp. 45-87.
  A very general discussion of urban life in Ethiopia,
including sections on the military, education, industrial
activity, and political change.

Papers in German include:

302.0.22 KULS, W. "Zur Entwicklung städtischer Siedlungen in
Äthiopien." Erdkunde, 24, 1970, 14-26.

Unpublished theses include:

302.0.23 AKALOU WOLDE MICHAEL. Urban Development in Ethiopia in
Time and Space Perspective. Ph.D. thesis, University
of California, Los Angeles, 1967.

302.0.24 GADAMU, F. Ethnic Associations in Ethiopia and the Maintenance of Urban/Rural Relationships. Ph.D. thesis,
University of London, 1972.

Addis Ababa (Capital city. Population in 1975: 1.1 million.)

302.1.1 ALEMAYEHU SEIFU. "Eder in Addis Ababa: a sociological
study." Ethiopian Observer, 12, 1969, 8-18, 31-33.
  The Eder is a voluntary association for mutual aid
in such matters as burials. The paper discusses their
origins, structures, membership, functions, and influence on social change.

302.1.2 AMOS, F.J.C. "A development plan for Addis Ababa."
Ethiopian Observer, 6, 1962, 5-16.
  Provides an outline of the city's morphology, land-
use zones, traffic flows, etc., on the basis of data
gathered in 1960-1961 for a plan prepared in 1962.

302.1.3 BERLAN, E. Addis-Abéba: La Plus Haute Ville d'Afrique.
Allier, Grenoble, 1963, 217 pp.
  A comprehensive geographical study, discussing the
city's site, origins, growth, population, and economy.
Its functions are examined in detail, with special refer-
ence to the locations of each activity within the city.

*302.1.4   COMHAIRE, J. "Les Grandes Villes d'Afrique et de Madagascar: Addis-Abéba." Notes et Etudes Documentaires, 3650, 1969, 36 pp.

302.1.5   DENIS, J. "Addis Ababa: genèse d'une capitale impériale." Revue Belge de Géographie, 88, 1964, 283-314.
            Discusses the city's growth, its population structure, its dominant role within the country, and the problems of poverty behind a facade of development.

302.1.6   DE YOUNG, M. "An African emporium: the Addis Markato." Journal of Ethiopian Studies, 5 (2), 1967, 103-122.
            Presents the results of a detailed 1966 survey of "the largest market in Africa," covering types of trade, numbers engaged, and the value of stocks, both in market stalls and in other enterprises in the vicinity.

302.1.7   ETHIOPIA. Population of Addis Ababa. Central Statistical Office, Addis Ababa, 1972, 84 pp.
            Presents the results of a 1967 population sample survey, covering demographic and social aspects, and also migration, with data for ten districts.

302.1.8   GOULD, W.T.S. "The provision of secondary schools in African cities: a study of Addis Ababa." Town Planning Review, 44, 1973, 391-403.
            Examines the characteristics of secondary schools in the city and especially their location in relation to the distribution of population.

302.1.9   HOLLOWAY, R. "Street boys in Addis Ababa." Community and Development Journal, 5, 1970, 139-144.
            Examines the situation of Gurage migrants working as shoeshine boys, seen as casualties of the social and economic system, and calls for government aid both in the city and in the rural homeland.

302.1.10   HORVATH, R.J. "Von Thunen's isolated state and the area around Addis Ababa." Annals of the Association of American Geographers, 59, 1969, 308-323.
            Compares the land-use pattern around the city with Von Thunen's theoretical model, finding intensive vegetable production close by and a girdle of eucalyptus forest, which provides fuel and building material, but noting the feeble development of milk production.

302.1.11   JOHNSON, M. "Addis Ababa from the air." Ethiopian Observer, 6, 1962, 17-32.
            A set of air photographs, vertical and oblique, with brief comments on the site and the different zones of the city.

302.1.12 KLOOS, H. "The geography of pharmacies, druggist shops
and rural medicine vendors, and the origin of customers
of such facilities in Addis Ababa." Journal of Ethiopian
Studies, 12 (2), 1974, 77-94.
   Analyzes the distribution of seventy-three establishments and concludes that they are overconcentrated in
limited areas, leaving many potential customers lacking
such facilities.

302.1.13 KOEHN, P.H. "Selected bibliography: the municipality of
Addis Ababa, Ethiopia." African Urban Notes, B 1 (2),
1975, 133-147.
   The full bibliography from a Ph.D. thesis, only a
minority of the items relating specifically to Addis
Ababa.

302.1.14 OSTBY, I. and GULILAT, T. "A statistical study of household
expenditure in Addis Ababa." Eastern Africa Economic
Review, 1 (2), 1969, 63-74.
   Shows how consumption patterns differ according to
income, family size, age, etc., drawing upon a 1968
Central Statistical Office household survey.

302.1.15 PALEN, J.J. "Housing in a developing nation: the case of
Addis Ababa." Land Economics, 50, 1974, 428-434.
   Observes that in face of a 7 percent annual increase
of population the housing stock is remaining almost sta-
tic and that government's response to this crisis situation has been minimal.

302.1.16 PALEN, J.J. "Urbanization and migration in an indigenous
city: the case of Addis Ababa." In Richmond, A.H. and
Kubat, D. (eds.), Internal Migration: the New World and
the Third World. Sage, London, 1976, 205-223.
   Brief review of the city's form, growth, population,
patterns of in-migration and cultural assimilation, and
educational provision. Addis Ababa is seen as very dis-
tinctive--a fairly new city, yet of preindustrial type
with minimal colonial influence.

302.1.17 PANKHURST, R. "Menelik and the foundation of Addis Ababa."
Journal of African History, 2, 1961, 103-117.
   Discusses the decision by Menelik to establish a
capital first at Entoto in 1881, then a few miles south
at Addis Ababa in 1890, and also the resolving of the
problems of the early growth of the city.

302.1.18 PANKHURST, R. "The foundation and growth of Addis Ababa
to 1935." Ethiopian Observer, 6, 1962, 33-61.
   After noting the existence of an earlier capital at
Entoto, just to the north, the paper describes the 1886

origin of Addis Ababa, its evolution around the palace
and markets, its population growth, and its food and
fuel supplies in early years. Commercial growth boosted
by the arrival of the railway in 1917 is also considered.
Includes many maps and plans.

302.1.19   PANKHURST, S. "Changing face of Addis Ababa." Ethiopian
           Observer, 4 (5), 1960, 134-176.
                Describes many of the newer buildings, such as hotels,
           hospitals, and air terminals, and mentions some older
           ones, with many photographs and a detailed map.

302.1.20   ROSS, J. and BERHE, Z. "Legal aspects of doing business in
           Addis Ababa: a profile of mercato businessmen and their
           reception of new laws." African Law Studies, 10, 1974,
           1-46.
                Reports the results of a 1970-1971 survey in the main
           city market to discover how far merchants had accepted
           and absorbed imported business law concepts.

302.1.21   SHACK, W.A. "Urban ethnicity and the cultural process of
           urbanization in Ethiopia." In Southall, A. (ed.), Urban
           Anthropology. Oxford University Press, New York, 1973,
           251-285.
                Examines the economic and social position of Gurage
           migrants in Addis Ababa, emphasizing their continuing
           identity with their rural origins rather than any assimi-
           lation in a so-called urban melting pot.

302.1.22   SHACK, W.A. "Notes on voluntary associations and urbaniza-
           tion in Africa, with special reference to Addis Ababa,
           Ethiopia." African Urban Notes, B, 1, 1975, 5-10.
                Describes various associations in Addis Ababa, noting
           that while representing a response to urban life their
           form owes much to traditional social patterns and appli-
           cation of European models to them may be misleading.

302.1.23   SHACK, W.A. "Occupational prestige, status, and social
           change in modern Ethiopia." Africa, 46, 1976, 166-181.
                Discusses ethnic differentiation and social stratifi-
           cation in Addis Ababa and provides data on the prestige-
           ranking by eight ethnic groups of a set of occupations.

Papers in German include:

302.1.24   BEHRENDT, K.B. "Addis Abeba." Geographische Rundschau,
           15, 1963, 397-406.

302.1.25   ENGELHARD, K. "Addis Abeba, Probleme seiner Entwicklung."
           Erdkunde, 24, 1970, 207-219.

Unpublished theses include:

302.1.26   DIRASSE, L.   The Socioeconomic Position of Women in Addis
           Ababa: the case of prostitution. Ph.D. thesis, Boston
           University, 1978.

302.1.27   GARRETSON, P.P.   A History of Addis Ababa from its
           Foundation in 1886 to 1910. Ph.D. thesis, University
           of London, 1974.

302.1.28   HORVATH, R.J.   Around Addis Ababa: a geographical study
           of the impact of a city on its surroundings. Ph.D.
           thesis, University of California, Los Angeles, 1966.

302.1.29   JOHNSON, M.E.   The Evolution of the Morphology of Addis
           Ababa, Ethiopia. Ph.D. thesis, University of California,
           Los Angeles, 1974.

302.1.30   KOEHN, P.H.   The Municipality of Addis Ababa, Ethiopia:
           performance, mobilization, integration and change.
           Ph.D. thesis, University of Colorado, 1973.

Asmara   (Second city and Eritrean provincial capital. Population
         in 1975:   300,000.)

*302.2.1   ETHIOPIA. Results of the 1968 Population and Housing
           Censuses: Population and Housing Characteristics of
           Asmara. Central Statistical Office, Addis Ababa, 1974.

Gondar   (Provincial town of ancient origin. Population in 1975:
         44,000.)

302.3.1   GHIORGHIS MELLESSA. "Gondar yesterday and today."
          Ethiopian Observer, 12, 1969, 164-227.
             Provides a detailed history of the town and a full
          description of its main historic buildings.

302.3.2   MESSING, S.D. "The Abyssinian market town." In Bohanan,
          P. and Dalton, G. (eds.), Markets in Africa. Northwestern
          University Press, Evanston, Ill., 1962, 386-408.
             Examines the market system among the Amhara of central
          Ethiopia, focusing on the markets and other commerce in
          the town of Gondar, which are described in detail.

302.3.3   PANKHURST, R. "Notes for the history of Gondar." Ethiopia
          Observer, 12 (3), 1969, 177-227.
             Draws on numerous documentary sources to present a
          picture of Gondar from its seventeenth-century rise to
          prominence to its nineteenth-century decline.

<u>Harar</u> (Provincial town of ancient origin. Population in 1975:
    56,000.)

No publications traced, but an unpublished thesis is:

302.4.1 WALDRON, S.R. Social Organization and Social Control in
             the Walled City of Harar, Ethiopia. Ph.D. thesis,
             Columbia University, New York, 1974.

                              SOMALIA

General

303.0.1 HADJI GA'AL, A. "Problème des agglomérations urbaines en
             Somalie." In INCIDI, <u>Urban Agglomerations in the States</u>
             <u>of the Third World</u>. Brussels, 1971, 316-321.
                Discusses the widening gulf between the urban and
             rural populations, especially severe where so many rural
             dwellers are nomadic, and the need for closer integration
             for national development.

303.0.2 PANKHURST, R. "Notes on the demographic history of Ethiopian
             towns and villages." <u>Ethiopian Observer</u>, 9, 1965, 60-83.
                Covers the main towns of Somalia, as well as those of
             Ethiopia, reviewing the rates of growth and decline of
             individual towns up to 1930.

Publications in Italian include:

303.0.3 ARECCHI, A. "Somalia: problemi dell'insediamento urbano."
             <u>Africa</u> (Rome), 32, 1977, 93-105.

<u>Hargeisa</u> (Probably the second town of the country, lying inland in
    the north. Population estimate 1975: 70,000.)

303.1.1 SOMALI REPUBLIC. <u>A Multi-Purpose Statistical Survey of the</u>
             <u>Hargeisa Town, 1962</u>. Mogadishu, 1964, 42 pp.
                Reports on an extensive sample survey of the demo-
             graphic characteristics, educational levels, and economic
             activities of the population of Hargeisa.

<u>Mogadishu</u> (Capital city. Population estimate 1975: 350,000.)

303.2.1 NEGRE, A. "A propos de Mogadisco au Moyen Age." <u>Annales de</u>
             <u>l'Université d'Abidjan, Série Histoire</u>, 5, 1977, 5-38.

A discussion of the city's history from its seventh-century foundation up to the fifteenth-century visit of Vasco da Gama, covering settlement and political and economic life.

*303.2.2 SOMALI REPUBLIC. Report on the Demographic Survey of Mogadishu, July 1967. Mogadishu, 1970, 42 pp.

Unpublished theses include:

303.2.3 PUZO, W.D. Mogadishu, Somalia: geographic aspects of its evolution, population, functions and morphology. Ph.D. thesis, University of California, Los Angeles, 1972.

SUDAN

General

304.0.1 EL-ARIFI, S.A. "Urbanization and distribution of economic development in the Sudan." African Urban Notes, 6 (2), 1971, 115-140.
Outlines urban development in Sudan since the eighteenth century, discusses recent rural-urban migration, especially to Greater Khartoum, and stresses the dangers of excessive concentration of urbanization in one primary city.

304.0.2 EL-BUSHRA, EL-SAYED. "Occupational classification of Sudanese towns." Sudan Notes and Records, 50, 1969, 75-96.
Attempts a functional classification using data on occupations for thirty-five towns from the 1955-1956 census.

304.0.3 EL-BUSHRA, EL-SAYED. "Towns in the Sudan in the eighteenth and early nineteenth centuries." Sudan Notes and Records, 52, 1971, 63-70.
Reviews the sizes, functions, and forms of urban settlement during this period, showing that while precolonial urban centers existed in Sudan they were both few and small.

304.0.4 EL-BUSHRA, EL-SAYED. "The definition of a town in the Sudan." Sudan Notes and Records, 54, 1973, 66-72.
Discusses criteria used by Sudan census takers to distinguish urban and rural settlements and provides population figures for all settlements over 1000 in 1955-1956 and 1964-1965.

*304.0.5 EL-BUSHRA, EL-SAYED (ed.) Urbanization in the Sudan.
Philosophical Society of the Sudan, Khartoum, 1973,
199 pp.

304.0.6 EL-BUSHRA, EL-SAYED. "The Sudan." In Jones, R. (ed.),
Essays on World Urbanization. George Philip, London,
1975, 377-389.
   A broad review of contrasts in urban origins in Sudan,
the distribution of the urban population and of 1955-1970
urban growth, excessive rates of in-migration and resulting planning problems.

304.0.7 HALE, G.A. "Darfur towns: aspects of their growth."
African Urban Notes, 6 (2), 1971, 78-97.
   Examines the 1955-1970 growth in the urban population
of the province, in which lie Nyala, El Fasher, and El
Geneina, noting the contribution of natural increase,
in-migration, and designation of new urban centers.

304.0.8 HALE, S. "Migrants in Omdurman and Juba, Sudan." African
Urban Notes, 6 (2), 1971, 54-77.
   Outlines a proposed study of motives for rural-urban
migration, providing a theoretical framework and some
background data from the 1955-1956 census.

304.0.9 HALE, S. and G.A. "Sudan urban studies." African Urban
Notes, 6 (2), 1971, 1-7.
   Introduction to the special issue of this journal,
which included various contributions listed here.

304.0.10 HALE, S. and G.A. "An urban bibliography of the Sudan."
African Urban Notes, 6 (2), 1971, 150-181.
   Lists alphabetically about 500 items in English and
Arabic relating to the country's towns.

304.0.11 HENIN, R.A. "Economic development and internal migration
in the Sudan." Sudan Notes and Records, 44, 1963,
100-119.
   Discusses migration patterns revealed by the 1955-1956
census, including the relatively moderate rural-urban
flows, in relation to the broad pattern of economic
development.

304.0.12 INTERNATIONAL LABOUR OFFICE. Growth, Employment and Equity:
a comprehensive strategy for the Sudan. Geneva, 1976.
   Includes much material, much discussion, and many
proposals relevant to urbanization. Among the appended
technical papers, three deal with "Migration to Greater
Khartoum" (pp. 351-361), "Urban Labour Markets" (pp.
363-374), and "The informal sector in urban areas" (pp.
375-388). The ninth paper (pp. 319-343) presents in

seventeen tables the results of a wide-ranging household
socioeconomic survey in Greater Khartoum.

*304.0.13 KANNAPAN, S. "Urban labour market structure and employment
issues in the Sudan." In Kannapan, S. (ed.),
Studies of Urban Labour Market Behaviour in Developing
Areas. International Institute for Labour Studies,
Geneva, 1977, 85-106.

304.0.14 KAWABE, H. and NUR, O.A.M. "Urban growth and urbanward
migration in Sudan." In Urbanization and Migration in
some Arab and African Countries. Cairo Demographic
Centre, 1973, 125-149.
Analyzes levels and rates of urbanization in Sudan,
especially regional variations in 1956-1965 urban growth
rates, examines patterns of rural-urban migration, and
makes projections of urban population to 1985.

*304.0.15 KUHN, M.W. "The status of urbanization in the Republic of
the Sudan." California Geographer, 8, 1967, 1-7.

304.0.16 MUSTAFA, M. el M. "The Sudanese labour market." Manpower
and Unemployment Research, 9 (2), 1976, 29-54.
A wide-ranging review of the urban labor market, of
the scale and structure of employment, and of the failure
of jobs to keep pace with either migration or education.

304.0.17 SOMMER, J.W. "Spatial aspects of urbanization and political
integration in the Sudan." In El-Shakhs, S. and Obudho,
R.A. (eds.), Urbanization, National Development and
Regional Planning in Africa. Praeger, New York, 1974,
27-46.
Examines the patterns of migration to Sudan towns
and their varied ethnic structures and argues that by
drawing diverse groups together urbanization may assist
the process of national integration.

304.0.18 SUDAN. First Population Census of Sudan 1955/1956: town
planners' supplement. 2 vols. Khartoum, 1960, 1961.
Volume 1 provides tables of demographic data for
sixty-eight towns; volume 2 provides detailed plans of
each town, showing the enumeration areas.

304.0.19 SUDAN. Population and Housing Survey 1964/1965. Several
volumes. Khartoum, 1967, 1968.
One volume provides a general review of the data for
urban areas and there is a further volume for the urban
population of each province.

304.0.20 WINTERS, C. "Traditional urbanism in the north central
Sudan." Annals of the Association of American Geographers,

67, 1977, 500-520.
Examines the character of indigenous sixteenth- to nineteenth-century cities, most now in ruins, relating them to the archetype of the Muslim city.

304.0.21   YASSEIN, M.O.   "Social, economic and political role of urban agglomerations in developing states: the Sudan's experience."   In INCIDI, Urban Agglomerations in the States of the Third World.   Brussels, 1971, 335-355.
A wide-ranging discussion noting the dominance of towns in political life throughout this century, the strong centripetal economic forces, and the need for more rural development and rural-urban integration.

Unpublished theses include:

304.0.22   ELIAS, E.O.   Space Standards in Low-cost Housing with Specific Reference to Urban Areas of Central Sudan. Ph.D. thesis, University of Edinburgh, 1970.

El Obeid   (Headquarters of Kordofan Province, southwest of Khartoum. Population at 1973 census: 90,000.)

304.1.1   EL-DAWI, T.A.   "El Obeid: a Sudanese urban community in Kordofan Province."   African Urban Notes, 6 (2), 1971, 99-107.
Discusses the town's population, its diverse ethnic groups, and the features such as religion and leisure activities that bind these into a single community.

304.1.2   EL-DAWI, T.A.   "Social characteristics of big merchants and businessmen in El Obeid."   In Cunnison, I. and James, W. (eds.), Essays in Sudan Ethnography.   Hurst, London, 1972, 201-216.
Briefly describes the town and its commerce, summarizes the results of a survey of its wealthy merchants, and discusses the political power that their wealth has brought them.

A publication in German is:

304.1.3   BORN, M.   "El Obeid."   Geographische Rundschau, 20 (3), 1968, 87-97.

An unpublished thesis is:

304.1.4   EL-DAWI, T.A.   An Analysis of Cultural and Social Heterogeneity of a Sudanese Town.   Ph.D. thesis, University of Manchester, U.K., 1971.

Khartoum   (Capital city. Population at 1973 census including the
           administratively separate but physically adjacent Omdurman
           and Khartoum North: 780,000.)

304.2.1   BARCLAY, H.B. Buurri al Lamaab: a suburban village in the
          Sudan. Cornell University Press, Ithaca, N.Y., 1964,
          296 pp.
              An ethnographic account of a community living adjacent
          to the E boundary of Khartoum municipality, discussing
          its kinship structure, religious life, political organi-
          zation, and economy, but designed more to provide an in-
          sight into Arab Sudanese culture than to reveal the impact
          of the city.

*304.2.2 DOXIADIS ASSOCIATES. Khartoum, Khartoum North, Omdurman:
          a long term program and a master plan for the development
          of the town. Athens, 1960, 228 pp.

304.2.3   EL-BURSHRA, EL-SAYED. "The evolution of the three towns."
          African Urban Notes, 6 (2), 1971, 8-23.
              Reviews evidence of prehistoric settlement on the site,
          discusses the nineteenth-century origins and growth of
          both Khartoum and Omdurman, and briefly considers their
          further growth this century.

304.2.4   EL-BUSHRA, EL-SAYED. "The development of industry in Greater
          Khartoum, Sudan." East African Geographical Review, 10,
          1972, 27-50.
              Examines the range of industries represented in the
          city, their importance in terms of output and employment,
          and the factors influencing their location and growth.

304.2.5   EL-BUSHRA, EL-SAYED. "Sudan's triple capital: morphology
          and functions." Ekistics, 39, 1975, 246-250.
              Outlines the shape and structure of the agglomeration,
          the stages of its physical growth, and its functions as
          the national capital.

304.2.6   EL-BUSHRA, EL-SAYED. "The sphere of influence of Khartoum
          conurbation, Sudan." Erdkunde, 30, 1976, 286-294.
              Describes the city's centrality in bus and air routes
          and in telephone traffic and defines its hinterland at
          two levels in terms of wholesale and retail trade, medical
          facilities, etc.

304.2.7   EL-BUSHRA, EL-SAYED. An Atlas of Khartoum Conurbation.
          Khartoum University Press, 1976, 97 pp.
              Comprises forty-three maps and diagrams depicting the
          city's site and climate, origins and growth, land-use and
          housing types, demographic structure, and transport
          connections. There is an accompanying text on topics such
          as origins and land-use, and numerous photographs.

304.2.8   EL-BUSHRA, EL-SAYED. "Some demographic indicators for
          Khartoum conurbation, Sudan." Middle Eastern Studies,
          15, 1979, 295-309.
              Examines the growth, structure, and distribution of
          population within Khartoum, on the basis of the 1955-1956
          census and 1964-1965 surveys, with an emphasis on pat-
          terns of population density.

304.2.9   EL-DAWI, T.A. "Omdurman craftsmen: a preliminary report."
          Sudan Society, 2, 1963, 43-53.
              Describes the main craft industries in Omdurman, the
          social and economic organization of the craftsmen, and
          current changes affecting them.

304.2.10 GALAL-EL-DIN, M.A. "The factors influencing migration to
          the 'three towns' of the Sudan." Sudan Journal of
          Economic and Social Studies, 1 (1), 1974, 20-22.
              Discusses briefly the results of a 1971 survey of
          migrants in Greater Khartoum, investigating the timing
          of, and motives for, their migration.

304.2.11 HALE, S. "Nubians in the urban milieu: Greater Khartoum."
          Sudan Notes and Records, 54, 1973, 57-65.
              Analyzes the ways in which Nubian ethnic distinctive-
          ness is socially articulated in the city, with regard to
          both ideology and behavior.

304.2.12 HAMDAN, G. "The growth and functional structure of
          Khartoum." Geographical Review, 50, 1960, 21-40.
              Traces the physical growth of Khartoum proper during
          this century and analyzes the resulting arrangement of
          functional and residential areas.

304.2.13 HENIN, R.A. "The future population size of Khartoum,
          Khartoum North, Omdurman and Port Sudan." Sudan Notes
          and Records, 42, 1961, 85-90.
              Draws on the 1955-1956 census to estimate the shares
          of natural increase and migration in the urban popula-
          tion growth and makes projections up to 1996.

304.2.14 HILL, L. "The Tuti community." Sudan Society, 3, 1965,
          1-20.
              A social and economic study of the inhabitants of
          an island in the Nile in the center of Khartoum.

304.2.15 KAWABE, H. and FARAH, A.A.M. "An ecological study of
          Greater Khartoum." In Urbanization and Migration in
          some Arab and African Countries. Cairo Demographic
          Centre, 1973, 151-170.
              Examines the growth of the conurbation and spatial
          variations in demographic, economic, and housing

conditions indicated by the 1964-1965 population and
housing survey.

304.2.16 KUHN, M.W. "The central business function of Suq el Gabir,
Omdurman." African Urban Notes, 6 (2), 1971, 39-53.
Outlines the origins and form of Omdurman, discusses
the types of trade represented there, and indicates the
degree to which each is concentrated in the central
market.

304.2.17 LOBBAN, R. "The role of urban associations and social
networks in the "three town" area of the Sudan and their
relationship to urbanization." African Urban Notes, 5
(1), 1970, 37-46.
An outline of a research program, with a bibliography.

304.2.18 LOBBAN, R. "The historical role of the Mahas in the
urbanization of Sudan's 'three towns.'" African Urban
Notes, 6 (2), 1971, 24-38.
An account of the migration of the Mahas from the
north to the Khartoum area, of the influence of outstanding individuals, and of this community today in the
Tuti Island and Burri al Mahas areas.

304.2.19 LOBBAN, R. "Alienation, urbanisation and social networks
in the Sudan." Journal of Modern African Studies, 13,
1975, 491-500.
Largely concerned with the concepts of urbanization
and alienation, but on the basis of surveys of the old
settlements of Burri al Mahas and Tuti Island, both
now within the agglomeration.

304.2.20 LOBBAN, R.A. "Class, endogamy and urbanization in the
'Three Towns' of the Sudan." African Studies Review,
22 (3), 1979, 99-114.
Examines changing marriage patterns in Burri al Mahas
and Tuti Island and especially the extent to which endogamy persists, in terms of implications for class structure.

304.2.21 McLOUGHLIN, P.F.M. "The Sudan's three towns: a demographic
and economic profile of an African urban complex."
Economic Development and Cultural Change, 12, 1963/4,
70-83, 158-173, 286-304.
Part 1 summarizes 1955-1956 census data on the ethnic
and demographic structure; part 2 analyzes the economic
output of the city and the level of expenditure of its
population; part 3 examines the occupations and incomes
of the labor force.

304.2.22 McLOUGHLIN, P.F.M. "Labour market conditions and wages in
the three towns, 1900-1950." Sudan Notes and Records,

51, 1970, 105-118.
Examines historical trends in labor demand and supply,
with factors from the world economy to the Gezira development affecting the labor market, and leading to falling
real wages after 1931.

304.2.23 MAZARI, S. "Greater Khartoum." In Berger, M. (ed.), The
New Metropolis in the Arab World. Allied Publishers,
Delhi, 1963, 115-128.
A general account of the origins and growth of
Khartoum, Omdurman, and Khartoum North, and of their
planning problems, especially their housing needs.

304.2.24 OBERAI, A.S. "Migration, unemployment and the urban labour
market: a case study of the Sudan." International
Labour Review, 115, 1977, 211-223.
Draws on the ILO survey in Greater Khartoum to analyze
characteristics of migrants, causes of their migration,
and their contribution to the urban economy, showing that
most are effectively absorbed, but at disturbingly low
wages.

304.2.25 REHFISCH, F. "A study of some southern migrants in
Omdurman." Sudan Notes and Records, 43, 1962, 50-104.
Against the background of 1955-1956 census data on
the origins of the Omdurman population, the results of
a 1960 migrant survey are given, covering occupations,
earnings, leisure activities, reasons for moving, attitudes to town, and future intentions.

304.2.26 REHFISCH, F. "A sketch of the early history of Omdurman."
Sudan Notes and Records, 45, 1964, 35-47.
Summarizes what is known of the history of Omdurman
from the prehistoric period to 1898, most being on its
growth during the Mahdiya.

304.2.27 REHFISCH, F. "An unrecorded population count of Omdurman."
Sudan Notes and Records, 46, 1965, 33-39.
Provides details of a count including breakdown by
tribe that was made in 1921 but never published.

304.2.28 REHFISCH, F. "Omdurman during the Mahdiya." Sudan Notes
and Records, 48, 1967, 33-62.
A translated and edited version of an Italian account
by C. Rosignoli, originally published in 1898 and describing Omdurman in the 1880s.

304.2.29 REHFISCH, F. "A rotating credit association in the Three
Towns." In Cunnison, I. and James, W. (eds.), Essays in
Sudan Ethnography. Hurst, London, 1972, 189-200.
Examines the credit association known as Sandug

as it operates in greater Khartoum, especially in terms of its role as both an economic and a social institution.

*304.2.30 SIMPSON, M.C. Khartoum's Food Supplies; a study in the production and marketing of six basic foodstuffs. Department of Rural Economy, University of Khartoum, 1966, 196 pp.

304.2.31 STEVENSON, R.C. "Old Khartoum 1821-1885." Sudan Notes and Records, 47, 1966, 1-38.
An account of the settlement from its establishment in 1821 to its complete destruction by the Mahdi in 1885.

A notable earlier paper is:

304.2.32 HAMDAN, G. "Some aspects of the urban geography of the Khartoum complex." Bulletin de la Société de Géographie d'Egypte, 32, 1959, 89-120.

Unpublished theses include:

304.2.33 EL-BADAWI, O. Omdurman, la Vieille Ville Arabe du Soudan et ses Rapports avec la Ville Coloniale de Khartoum. Thèse 3e cycle, Université de Paris I, 1972.

304.2.34 EL-BUSHRA, EL-SAYED. The Khartoum Conurbation. Ph.D. thesis, University of London, 1970.

304.2.35 GALAL EL DIN, M. EL A. International Migration in the Sudan with Special Reference to Migration to Greater Khartoum. Ph.D. thesis, University of London, 1973.

304.2.36 KUHN, M.W. Markets and Trade in Omdurman, Sudan. Ph.D. thesis, University of California, Los Angeles, 1970.

304.2.37 LOBBAN, R.A. Social Networks in the Urban Sudan. Ph.D. thesis, Northwestern University, Evanston, Ill., 1973.

304.2.38 RAHMAN, A.B. Migration to Khartoum. Ph.D. thesis, University of Glasgow, 1979.

304.2.39 ZAHIR AL ZADATY, F. Political Mobilization in a Western Sudanese Immigrant Group in Khartoum. Ph.D. thesis, University of Manchester, U.K., 1972.

See also 304.0.12.

Port Sudan (Second city and chief port. Population at 1973 census: 130,000.)

304.3.1 BEDAWI, H.Y. and ELIAS, E.O. "Rehousing of squatters at
Diem Gilude, Port Sudan." In Self-help Practices in
Housing: selected case studies. United Nations, New
York, 1973, 111-129.
Outlines the general housing situation in Port Sudan
and examines the replacement of the spontaneous Diem
Gilude housing area by the planned Diem Mayu in the 1960s.

304.3.2 JAMES, W.R. "Port Sudan's overspill." Sudan Society, 4,
1969, 5-26.
Describes each of the fringe settlements of Port
Sudan, many being recent squatter communities, and examines social groupings within Deim Julud.

304.3.3 KHOGALI, M.M. "The development and problems of Port Sudan."
In Hoyle, B.S. and Hilling, D. (eds.), Seaports and
Development in Tropical Africa. Macmillan, London, 1970,
203-223.
Reviews the port's origins, growth, physical facilities,
and traffic patterns and discusses problems of congestion,
overland transport links, and fresh water supplies.

304.3.4 LEWIS, B.A. "Deim el Arab and the Beja stevedores of Port
Sudan." Sudan Notes and Records, 43, 1962, 16-49.
Results of a survey of the origins, household structure, employment, and budgets of the largely Beja people
of Deim el Arab, undertaken for the municipality that
wished to shift the settlement to make way for planned
urban development.

304.3.5 MILNE, J.C.M. "The impact of labour migration on the Amarar
in Port Sudan." Sudan Notes and Records, 55, 1974, 70-87.
Shows how one migrant group clings to many traditional
values and retains clear ethnic identity, even though
urban life is bringing great changes in social organization.

304.3.6 OLIVER, J. "Port Sudan: the study of its growth and
functions." Tijdschrift voor Economische en Sociale
Geografie, 57, 1966, 54-61.
Surveys the site, physical form, functions, and
future prospects of the town.

*304.3.7 SUDAN. Survey of Port Sudan. Department of Statistics,
Khartoum, 1965.

304.3.8 UNITED NATIONS ECONOMIC COMMISSION FOR AFRICA. Human
Settlements in Africa. United Nations, New York, 1976.
Pp. 103-111, "The resettlement in Port Sudan town."
Provides a brief outline of the town's growth and
describes a program whereby 40,000 people from its
squatter areas were rehoused between 1969 and 1975.

East Africa

4.0.1 ELKAN, W. "Circular migration and the growth of towns in East
       Africa." International Labour Review, 96, 1967, 581-589.
           Notes the continuing importance of short-term migration
       in East Africa and advocates measures to raise rural incomes
       and thus to reduce the incentive for movements to the towns.

4.0.2 ELKAN, W. "A note on urban unemployment with special reference
       to East Africa." Institute of Development Studies Bulletin,
       2 (4), 1970, 11-16.
           Examines reasons for increasing urban unemployment in
       East Africa, commenting upon Todaro's earlier analyses.

4.0.3 ELKAN, W. "Urban unemployment in East Africa." International
       Affairs, 46, 1970, 517-528.
           Examines recent employment trends in Kenya and Uganda
       and argues that the sluggish overall rate of growth is not
       inevitable but follows from government policies--or lack of
       them.

4.0.4 FUNNELL, D. "The role of small service centres in regional
       and rural development, with special reference to Eastern
       Africa." In Gilbert, A. (ed.), Development Planning and
       Spatial Structure. Wiley, Chichester, U.K., 1976, 77-111.
           Shows how throughout East Africa small service centers
       provide a crucial link between cities and countryside and
       argues for more study of ways in which the link may benefit
       or harm the rural population, in order to ensure more con-
       structive settlement planning.

4.0.5 GEORGULAS, N. An Approach to Urban Analysis for East African
       Towns. Maxwell Graduate School, Syracuse University, N.Y.,
       1963, 48 pp.
           Reviews the growth, demographic structure, and economic
       functions of East African towns, proposes a scheme for more

rigorous analysis, and outlines a prospective social survey of Dar es Salaam.

4.0.6   GREENSTONE, J.D.   "Corruption and self-interest in Kampala
and Nairobi."   Comparative Studies in Society and History,
8, 1966, 199-210.
Argues that self-interest may play a positive role in
the political life of these cities at their present stage
of development, responding to Werlin's paper on Nairobi
in the same issue.

4.0.7   GUGLER, J.   "Urbanization in East Africa."   In Hutton, J.
(ed.), Urban Challenge in East Africa.   East African
Publishing House, Nairobi, 1972, 1-26.
Outlines the extent of urbanization to date and the
characteristics of the urban population and examines the
growth and problems of Kampala more fully as a case study.

4.0.8   HARRIS, J.R. and TODARO, M.P.   "Urban unemployment in East
Africa."   East African Economics Review, 4 (2), 1968,
17-36.
Argues that rising unemployment is due to a rural-urban
earnings differential sufficient to induce excessive migration and that policies for rural as well as urban employment are needed.

4.0.9   HOYLE, B.S.   The Seaports of East Africa.   East African
Publishing House, Nairobi, 1967, 137 pp.
A geographical study examining Mombasa, Tanga, Dar es
Salaam, and Mtwara in terms of site and situation, origins
and port development, equipment and organization, traffic,
and hinterlands, with a separate chapter on the port of
Zanzibar.   The published version of a University of London
Ph.D. thesis.

4.0.10 HOYLE, B.S.   "The emergence of major seaports in a developing
economy: the case of East Africa."   In Hoyle, B.S. and
Hilling, D. (eds.), Seaports and Development in Tropical
Africa. Macmillan, London, 1970, 225-245.
Examines the evolution of the present pattern of port
development in relation to environmental factors, political and technological change, and economic pressures.

4.0.11 HUTTON, J. (ed.) Urban Challenge in East Africa.   East
African Publishing House, Nairobi, 1972, 285 pp.
A set of papers largely devoted to housing problems in
East African cities, most of them noted individually else-
where. The editor provides a brief concluding overview
of urban trends and research needs.

4.0.12 KANYEIHAMBA, G.W. and McAUSLAN, J.P.W.B. (eds.) Urban Legal

Problems in Eastern Africa. Scandinavian Institute of
African Studies, Uppsala, Sweden, 1978, 298 pp.
  A volume resulting from a workshop held in Nairobi in
1976, with papers on "Law, housing and the city in Africa,"
by McAuslan and on "Land banking" in East Africa by
Kanyeihamba, in addition to studies of legal aspects of
urbanization in Kenya, Uganda, and Zambia listed separately.

4.0.13 LARIMORE, A.E. "The Africanization of the colonial cities
         in East Africa." East Lakes Geographer, 5, 1969, 50-68.
           Discusses the shift of enterprises in East African towns
         from European and especially Asian to African ownership
         and relates this to Sjoberg's ideas on preindustrial and
         industrial urban societies.

4.0.14 O'CONNOR, A.M. "The cities and towns of East Africa:
         distribution and functions." In Berger, H. (ed.),
         Ostafrikanische Studien. Friedrich-Alexander-Universitat,
         Nuremberg, 1968, 41-52.
           Reviews the spatial pattern of urbanization within
         East Africa and notes the similarity in the functions of
         most urban centers--large and small.

4.0.15 O'CONNOR, A.M. "Expanding cities in a rural continent."
         Geographical Magazine, 44, 1971, 198-202.
           Discusses the character of urban centers in East Africa
         and the extent to which the colonial framework is guiding
         the pattern of contemporary growth.

4.0.16 OMINDE, S.H. The Population of Kenya, Tanzania and Uganda.
         Heinemann, Nairobi, 1975. Pp. 88-96, "Urbanization."
           Notes for each country the size and growth rate of
         the urban population and examines its distribution pat-
         tern, summarizing recent census data.

4.0.17 SAFIER, M. (ed.) The Role of Urban and Regional Planning in
         National Development for East Africa. Milton Obote
         Foundation, Kampala, 1970, 299 pp.
           The papers and proceedings of a seminar bringing together
         university and government personnel from Kenya, Tanzania,
         and Uganda. The more substantial papers on urban planning
         are listed separately; others deal with industrial growth,
         rural development, and regional planning activities within
         these countries.

4.0.18 SAFIER, M. "Urban problems, planning possibilities and
         housing policies." In Hutton, J. (ed.), Urban Challenge
         in East Africa. East African Publishing House, Nairobi,
         1972, 27-38.
           A broad review of the problems posed by rapid urban
         growth in East Africa and of present and prospective gov-
         ernment planning responses.

4.0.19   SEGAL, E.S.   "Ethnic variables in East African urban migration."
         Urban Anthropology, 2, 1973, 194-204.
              Shows the need for attention to the cultural context in
         studies of rural-urban migration, isolating five cultural
         variables that clearly affect such migration in East Africa.

4.0.20   SKAPA, B.A.   A Select Preliminary Bibliography on Urbanism
         in Eastern Africa.   Maxwell Graduate School, Syracuse
         University, N.Y., 1967, 45 pp.
              A comprehensive list of books, articles, and official
         publications in the fields of administration and sociology,
         including many slight or pre-1960 items not listed here.
         Extends to Sudan, Ethiopia, Zambia, and Malawi.

4.0.21   SOJA, E.W. and WEAVER, C.E.   "Urbanization and underdevelopment
         in East Africa."   In Berry, B.J.L. (ed.), Urbanization and
         Counterurbanization.   Sage, Beverly Hills, Calif., 1976,
         233-266.
              A broad survey of the distribution and character of
         contemporary urbanization in East Africa, emphasizing the
         colonial legacy and discussing the key planning problems
         for each of the capital cities.

4.0.22   SOUTHALL, A.W.   "The growth of urban society."   In Diamond,
         S. and Burke, G. (eds.), The Transformation of East Africa.
         Basic Books, New York, 1966, 462-493.
              Examines the origins and character of all the main
         towns, discusses Nairobi and Dar es Salaam more fully, and
         considers the effects of independence both on the broad
         pattern of urbanization and on change within the towns.

4.0.24   STREN, R.E.   "Urban policy."   In Barkan, J.D. and Okumu, J.J.
         (eds.), Politics and Public Policy in Kenya and Tanzania.
         Praeger, New York, 1979, 179-208.
              A revised and updated version of the paper noted above.

4.0.25   VAN ZWANNENBERG, R. and KING, A.   An Economic History of
         Kenya and Uganda.   Macmillan, London, 1975.   Chap. 13
         "Urbanisation," 253-274.
              Concentrates largely on Nairobi and Kampala, tracing
         their evolution through this century and stressing the per-
         sistence of dualistic patterns with one group commanding
         power and wealth, the other suffering oppression and
         poverty.

4.0.26 VENGROFF, R. "Urban growth and nation building in East
        Africa." Journal of Modern African Studies, 9, 1971,
        577-592.
            Examines postindependence municipal government in
        Nairobi, Mombasa, Kampala, and Dar es Salaam in terms of
        the administrators' perception and understanding of the
        social networks of the urban residents.

4.0.27 VINCENT, J. "The changing role of small towns in the agrarian
        structure of East Africa." Journal of Commonwealth and
        Comparative Politics, 12, 1974, 261-275.
            On the basis of fieldwork in Teso, Uganda, discusses
        the origin and social structure of small towns in East
        Africa and their political relationship to the surrounding
        rural societies.

4.0.28 VINCENT, J. "Room for manoeuvre: the political role of
        small towns in East Africa." In Owusu, M. (ed.),
        Colonialism and Change. Mouton, The Hague, 1975, 115-144.
            Expands on the previous paper in regard to small town
        politics, stresses the role of such towns in linking capi-
        tals and countryside, and argues for more study of them.

Note also several books dealing with the Asian community in East
Africa, relevant here because this group is highly concentrated in
the towns. They include:

4.0.29 BHARATI, A. The Asians in East Africa. Nelson-Hall, Chicago,
        1972, 362 pp.

4.0.30 DELF, G. Asians in East Africa. Oxford University Press,
        London, 1963, 74 pp.

4.0.31 GHAI, D.P. (ed.) Portrait of a Minority: Asians in East
        Africa. Oxford University Press, Nairobi, 1965, 154 pp.

4.0.32 MANGAT, J.S. A History of the Asians in East Africa. Oxford
        University Press, London, 1969, 234 pp.

See also 0.2.26.

East Africa

KENYA

General

401.0.1 BLOOMBERG, L.N. and ABRAMS, C. United Nations Mission to
Kenya on Housing: Report. United Nations, New York;
Government Printer, Nairobi, 1964, 79 pp.
    Reviews Kenya's short-term and long-term housing needs,
with special reference to the towns, and puts forward
various policy proposals.

401.0.2 CASSIDY, G. and RENSSEN, F. "Urban growth and population
distribution in Kenya." Journal of the Town Planning
Institute, 56, 1970, 175-179. Reprinted in Ekistics, 30,
1970, 387-392.
    Summarizes an analysis of Kenya's central-place hier-
archy prepared for the 1966-1970 Development Plan and a
projected distribution pattern for future urban growth.

401.0.3 ETHERINGTON, D.M. "Projected changes in urban and rural
population in Kenya and the implications for development
policy." East African Economics Review, 1, 1965, 65-83.
Reprinted in Sheffield, J.R. (ed.), Education, Employment
and Rural Development. East African Publishing House,
Nairobi, 1967, 54-74.
    Projects urban and rural population to 1990, shows
that urban areas cannot absorb most of the increase, and
points to the consequent urgency of rural development.

401.0.4 GAILE, G.L. "Processes affecting the spatial pattern of
rural-urban development in Kenya." African Studies
Review, 19 (3), 1976, 1-16.
    Analyzes rural-urban economic links in terms of govern-
ment financial flows, trade, migration, and the diffusion
of innovations, and considers each of these briefly for
Kenya.

401.0.5 GOLDS, J.M. "African urbanization in Kenya." Journal of
African Administration, 13, 1961, 24-28.
    Discusses whether the nucleated settlements established
in the Kikuyu areas during the Emergency might become real
urban centers, bringing urban ways of life to these areas.

401.0.6 HENKEL, R. Central Places in Western Kenya. Geographisches
Institut der Universitat, Heidelberg, 1979, 274 pp.
    The published version of a German doctoral thesis, ex-
amining quantitatively the system of central places in
Bungoma, Trans Nzoia, and West Pokot Districts, including
the town of Kitale, the smaller town of Bungoma, and many
minor settlements. The physical structure of some of these
is also described and mapped, e.g., Kitale on pp. 191-199.

401.0.7　INTERNATIONAL LABOUR OFFICE. Employment, Incomes and Equality:　a strategy for increasing productive employment in Kenya.　Geneva, 1972, 600 pp.
　　　　　Much of this highly influential study is concerned with urban employment and unemployment and it draws particular attention to the present importance and future potential of the urban informal sector of the economy.

401.0.8　JOHNSON, G.E. and WHITELAW, W.E.　"Urban-rural income transfers in Kenya." Economic Development and Cultural Change, 22, 1974, 473-479.
　　　　　Reports on a survey of 1140 rural-urban migrants, showing that almost 90 percent send regular remittances home and that these represent 20 percent of earnings.

401.0.9　KENYA.　Population Census 1962.　Advance Report of Volumes 1 and 2.　Ministry of Finance and Economic Planning, Nairobi, 1964, 94 pp.
　　　　　Provides a male/female, adult/child breakdown of the population of each race in eighteen towns.　Further details are provided, but in more scattered form, in the final voluems 1 and 2 (1965) and in volumes 3 and 4 (1966).

401.0.10　KENYA.　Development Plan 1970-1974.　Government Printer, Nairobi, 1969.　Chap. 3 "Economic and physical planning," 70-102.
　　　　　The discussion of physical planning notes the pattern of urban development in 1962, states that Nairobi and Mombasa must continue to expand, but also identifies thirty-five urban centers and larger numbers of rural centers, market centers, and local centers and proposes that this urban hierarchy should be planned as a whole.

401.0.11　KENYA.　Population Census 1969.　Volume 2, Data on Urban Population.　Ministry of Finance and Economic Planning, Nairobi, 1971, 82 pp.
　　　　　Provides data on age, sex, nationality, tribe, birthplace, and education for the population of each center with over 2,000 inhabitants.

401.0.12　KENYA.　Development Plan 1974-1978.　Government Printer, Nairobi, 1974.　Chap. 5 "Urban development," 114-147.
　　　　　Reviews very briefly the growth and distribution of the urban population and the 1970-1974 physical planning efforts.　Outlines an urban strategy including efforts to slow rural-urban migration and to spread urban growth more widely.　Provides a revised seventeen-page schedule of urban, rural, market, and local centers.

401.0.13　KIANO, J.G.　"The social, economic and political effects of

urban agglomerations in Kenya." In INCIDI, <u>Urban Agglomerations in the States of the Third World</u>. Brussels, 1971, 204-230.
A broad review of the colonial origins of most Kenya towns, their racial composition, employment and wage levels, unemployment, housing problems, and government policies.

401.0.14 LAURENTI, L. and GERHART, J. <u>Urbanization in Kenya</u>. Ford Foundation, New York. 1972, 45 pp. + 19 pp.
A paper by Laurenti on demographic trends and prospects in the towns and one by Gerhart on economic aspects of urban growth in relation to rural development.

401.0.15 McKEE, S.I.D. "Planning and urbanisation in Kenya." <u>The Planner</u>, 59, 1973, 321-325.
A broad review of urbanization processes in Kenya and of physical planning activities at both regional and local levels.

401.0.16 MOOCK, J.L. "The content and maintenance of social ties between urban migrants and their home-based support groups: the Maragoli case." <u>African Urban Studies</u>, 3, 1978/9, 15-31.
Discusses the nature of social and economic ties between urban migrants from a Maragoli village and their rural kinsfolk, showing how urban and rural networks are closely intertwined.

401.0.17 MORGAN, W.T.W. "Urbanization in Kenya: origins and trends." <u>Transactions, Institute of British Geographers</u>, 46, 1969, 167-177.
After noting the colonial origin of most Kenya towns, the paper analyzes the urban network both in relation to a set of population regions and in terms of an urban hierarchy. 1962 census figures for the demographic structure of each town are presented and rural-urban migration is briefly discussed.

401.0.18 MUSLIM, A.F. "The administration of justice in urban Kenya." In Kanyeihamba, G.W. and McAuslan, J.P.W.B. (eds.), <u>Urban Legal Problems in Eastern Africa</u>. Scandinavian Institute of African Studies, Uppsala, Sweden, 1978, 257-273.
Examines the extent to which the institutions for administering justice in Kenya towns have succeeded in adapting to the demands created by rapid urbanization and considers the role of law in the urbanization process.

401.0.19 NDETI, K. "Urbanization and regional planning in Kenya." In Mabogunje, A.L. and Faniran, A. (eds.), <u>Regional Planning and National Development in Tropical Africa</u>.

Ibadan University Press, Ibadan, 1977, 100-117.
Outlines the origins and present pattern of Kenya
urbanization, the economic functions of the towns, and
plans for future urban development in various regions.

401.0.20   OBUDHO, R.A. "The central places of Nyanza Province, Kenya:
a tentative study of urban hierarchy." African Urban
Notes, 5 (4), 1970, 71-88.
Reviews central place studies throughout Africa, shows
that separate hierarchies of traditional markets and
colonial centers coexist in Nyanza, and considers the
implications for planning the urban system.

401.0.21   OBUDHO, R.A. "Urbanisation and regional planning in
western Kenya." In El-Shakhs, S. and Obudho, R.A. (eds.),
Urbanization, National Development and Regional Planning
in Africa. Praeger, New York, 1974, 161-176.
Notes the disjunction between the pattern of traditional local markets and that of Asian-dominated towns
and trading centers established during the colonial
period and the consequent problem of how to incorporate
both in plans for the expansion of the urban network.

401.0.22   OBUDHO, R.A. "Urbanization and development planning in
Kenya: an historical appreciation." African Urban
Notes, B 1 (3), 1975, 1-56.
Traces the evolution of urban centers in Kenya from
the eleventh century, analyzes the present distribution
of towns, and discusses the recent development of urban
and regional planning throughout the country. Includes
a substantial bibliography.

401.0.23   OBUDHO, R.A. "Spatial dimensions and demographic dynamics
of Kenya's urban subsystem." Pan-African Journal, 9,
1976, 103-124.
Reviews various characteristics of forty-seven urban
centers and argues that these indicate an urban system
more oriented to overseas interests than to national
well-being.

401.0.24   OBUDHO, R.A. "The nature of Kenya's urban demography."
African Urban Studies, 4, 1979, 83-103.
Examines the growth and changing distribution of
Kenya's urban population, using 1948, 1962, and 1969
census data, and also the changing demographic and ethnic
structure of the main towns.

401.0.25   OBUDHO, R.A. "Urbanization and development planning in
Kenya." In Obudho, R.A. and El-Shakhs, S. (eds.),
Development of Urban Systems in Africa. Praeger, New
York, 1979, 242-257.

Outlines the evolution of the pattern of urban centers in Kenya, notes the extent of postcolonial urban growth, and discusses the country's urban and regional planning strategies.

401.0.26   OBUDHO, R.A. and WALLER, P.P. Periodic Markets, Urbanization and Regional Planning: a case study from western Kenya. Greenwood Press, Westport, Conn., 1976. Pt. 1, "The development of central place structure in western Kenya," 1-78.

Describes the establishment of the colonial network of towns and trading centers in western Kenya, largely unrelated to the previous pattern of indigenous markets; traces the evolution of urban settlement through the colonial period; and presents 1969 census data on demographic and ethnic structure of the towns. (Parts 2 and 3 deal with Kisumu and with regional planning.)

401.0.27   OGENDO, R.B. "Industrial role of the main Kenya towns." Journal of East African Research and Development, 3, 1973, 1-30.

A brief survey of the distribution of manufacturing among the towns and of the factors in industrial concentration, with maps of the location of industry and of land use in each of twelve urban centers.

401.0.28   OKOTH-OGENDO, H.W.O. "The urbanisation process in Kenya: research priorities." In Kanyeihamba, G.W. and McAuslan, J.P.W.B. (eds.), Urban Legal Problems in Eastern Africa. Scandinavian Institute of African Studies, Uppsala, 1978, 274-280.

Reviews alternative theoretical frameworks for the study of urbanization in Kenya and discusses priorities among the problems demanding attention, from lawyers and from others.

401.0.29   OMINDE, S.H. "Population movements to the main urban areas of Kenya." Cahiers d'Etudes Africaines, 20, 1965, 593-617.

Uses birthplace data from the 1962 census to map streams of migration to Nairobi and Mombasa, notes the effects of rapid in-migration on the urban age and sex structure, and shows diagrammatically the structure for each tribe in Nairobi and Mombasa.

401.0.30   OMINDE, S.H. Land and Population Movements in Kenya. Heinemann, London, 1968, 204 pp.

Chapter 4 (pp. 62-76), "Urbanisation," reviews the growth of the urban population up to 1962 and describes the location, functions, and population of the seven largest towns, with a map of each. Chapter 7 (pp. 108-181), "Migratory movements of population," examines

on the basis of census birthplace data the flow into
each province (including Nairobi Extra-Provincial District)
and shows the age-sex distribution of each tribe in each
district (including Nairobi and Mombasa).

401.0.31   REMPEL, H. "The rural to urban migrant in Kenya." African
Urban Notes 6 (1), 1971, 53-72.
Examines the background and social characteristics
of a sample of men who moved to any of eight urban centers in 1964-1968.

401.0.32   REMPEL, H. and TODARO, M.P. "Rural to urban labour
migration in Kenya." In Ominde, S.H. and Ejiogu, C.
(eds.), Population Growth and Economic Development in
Tropical Africa. Heinemann, London, 1972, 214-231.
Relates the data of the previous paper to the high
level of urban unemployment caused by migration at rates
far higher than new employment opportunities justify, but
induced by the high differential between expected earnings in rural and urban areas.

401.0.33   SOJA, E.W. The Geography of Modernization in Kenya.
Syracuse University Press, Syracuse, New York, 1968,
143 pp.
An analysis of the spatial diffusion of social, economic, and political change, which emphasizes the importance of urban centers in this process and particularly accessibility to the capital city.

401.0.34   STREN, R. "Evolution of housing policy in Kenya." In
Hutton, J. (ed.), Urban Challenge in East Africa. East
African Publishing House, Nairobi, 1972, 57-96.
Reviews official policy towards housing from the
interwar period through the later colonial years and
into independence. Notes the increasing scope of public
housing, especially through the National Housing
Corporation, but also the persisting dilemmas faced.

401.0.35   TAYLOR, D.R.F. "New central places in East Africa."
African Urban Notes, 3 (4), 1968, 15-29.
Examines the settlement patterns of the Kikuyu areas,
noting the traditional dispersed pattern, the creation
of large nucleated villages during the Emergency, and
the survival of some of these as central places that may
become small towns.

401.0.36   TAYLOR, D.R.F. "The role of the smaller urban place in
development: the case of Kenya." African Urban Notes,
6 (3), 1972, 7-23. Reprinted in El-Shakhs, S. and
Obudho, R.A. (eds.), Urbanization, National Development
and Regional Planning in Africa. Praeger, New York,

1974, 143-160.
Notes the dual spatial system of traditional markets and colonial administrative and trading centers and suggests that planning the growth of new small urban centers may bridge that division, as well as incorporating all rural areas more effectively in the processes of modernization and development.

*401.0.37 TENDBERG, O.G. "The Indo-Pakistanis' importance for the urbanization of Kenya." Pakistan Geographical Review, 17, 1962, 17-24.

401.0.38 TRIBE, M. "Aspects of urban housing development in Kenya." In Allen, C. and King, K. (eds.), Development Trends in Kenya. Centre of African Studies, University of Edinburgh, 1972, 243-268.
A review of government action regarding housing in the 1960s, with special reference to slum clearance schemes.

401.0.39 UCHE, U.U. "The law, policies and rural-urban migration in Kenya." In Kanyeihamba, G.W. and McAuslan, J.P.W.B. (eds.), Urban Legal Problems in Eastern Africa. Scandinavian Institute of African Studies, Uppsala, Sweden, 1978, 39-62.
Reviews the causes of rural-urban migration in Kenya, noting the influence of various government actions, examines past and present legal strategies to reduce its scale, and suggests alternative strategies.

401.0.40 WACHTEL, A. et al. Bibliography of Urbanisation in Kenya. Institute of Development Studies, University of Nairobi, 1974, 35 pp.
Lists various government documents, working papers, and unpublished dissertations, in addition to many items included here.

401.0.41 WACHTEL, E. "The urban image: stereotypes of urban life in Kenya." African Urban Notes, B 1 (3), 1975, 77-92.
Argues the importance of the interplay of image and reality in Kenyan urban development, with special reference to the social significance of recent Kenyan urban-based novels.

An earlier publication is:

401.0.42 VASEY, E.A. Report on African Housing in Townships and Trading Centres in Kenya, 1950. Government Printer, Nairobi, 1953.

Other works on Kenya that are largely concerned with activities in urban areas include:

401.0.43 CLAYTON, A. and SAVAGE, D.C. Government and Labour in
          Kenya, 1895-1963. Cass, London, 1974, 481 pp.

401.0.44 MARRIS, P. and SOMERSET, A. African Businessmen: a study
          of entrepreneurship and development in Kenya. Routledge
          and Kegan Paul, London, 1971, 288 pp.

401.0.45 OGENDO, R.B. Industrial Geography of Kenya. East African
          Publishing House, Nairobi, 1972, 308 pp.

401.0.46 REMPEL, H. and HOUSE, W.J. The Kenya Employment Problem:
          an analysis of the modern sector labour market. Oxford
          University Press, Nairobi, 1978, 194 pp.

401.0.47 SANDBROOK, R. Proletarians and African Capitalism: the
          Kenyan case, 1960-1972. Cambridge University Press,
          1975, 222 pp.

Unpublished theses include:

401.0.48 BENNETT, C.J. Persistence and Adversity: the growth and
          spatial distribution of the Asian population of Kenya,
          1902-1963. Ph.D. thesis, Syracuse University, Syracuse,
          N.Y., 1976.

401.0.49 HUNTINGDON, H.G. An Empirical Study of Ethnic Linkages in
          Kenya Rural-Urban Migration. Ph.D. thesis, State
          University of New York at Binghamton, 1975.

401.0.50 LILLYDAHL, J.G. Economic and Demographic Influences on
          Household Saving in Urban Kenya. Ph.D. thesis, Duke
          University, Durham, North Carolina, 1976.

401.0.51 McKIM, W.L. The Role of Interaction in Spatial Economic
          Development Planning: a case study from Kenya. Ph.D.
          thesis, Northwestern University, Evanston, Ill., 1974.

401.0.52 MEMON, P.A. Mercantile Intermediaries in a Colonial Spatial
          System: wholesaling in Kenya 1830-1940. Ph.D. thesis,
          University of Western Ontario, 1974.

401.0.53 OBUDHO, R.A. Development of Urbanization in Kenya: a
          spatial analysis and implication for regional development
          strategy. Ph.D. thesis, Rutgers University, New
          Brunswick, N.J., 1974.

401.0.54 PETTISS, S.T. Social Consequences of Rural-Urban Youth
          Migration in Two African Countries: Nigeria and Kenya.
          Ph.D. thesis, Brandeis University, Waltham, Mass., 1971.

401.0.55 REMPEL, H.   Labor Migration into Urban Centers and Urban
          Unemployment in Kenya. Ph.D. thesis, University of
          Wisconsin, Madison, 1971.

Kisumu (Fourth town of Kenya and headquarters of Nyanza Province.
        Population at 1969 census: 32,000. 1975 estimate within
        extended boundaries: 80,000.)

401.1.1   McCLINTOCK, H. "The planning of Kisumu's peri-urban areas."
          The Planner, 59, 1973, 328-329.
               Describes the problems of and policies for the peri-
          urban areas brought within the municipal boundary in
          1972.

401.1.2   MUGA, E. Crime in a Kenyan Town: a case study of Kisumu.
          East African Literature Bureau, Nairobi, 1977, 113 pp.
               A brief outline of the socioeconomic characteristics
          of the town's population is followed by an analysis of
          criminal convictions in 1972-1973 with special reference
          to the offenders' place of residence, showing marked
          variations in crime rates.

401.1.3   OBUDHO, R.A. "The urban geography of Kisumu: materials
          for research." Current Bibliography of African Affairs,
          4, 1971, 391-396.
               Mainly references on Kenya in general.

401.1.4   OBUDHO, R.A. Urbanization, City and Regional Planning of
          Metropolitan Kisumu: bibliographic survey of an East
          African city. Council of Planning Librarians, Monticello,
          Illinois, 1972, 26 pp.
               An even more wide-ranging set of references.

401.1.5   OBUDHO, R.A. and WALLER, P.P. Periodic Markets, Urbanization
          and Regional Planning: a case study from western Kenya.
          Greenwood Press, Westport, Conn., 1976. Pt. 2,
          "Urbanization and development planning of metropolitan
          Kisumu," 81-123.
               An account of the origin and growth of Kisumu, drawing
          on district reports and early censuses; an analysis of
          1969 census data on demographic and ethnic structure;
          and an examination of urban land use, functional and
          residential.

Unpublished theses include:

401.1.6   MUGENYI, M. Elite Participation in Decision-making:
          municipal Kisumu. Ph.D. thesis, Northwestern University,
          Evanston, Ill., 1976.

Kitale (Town in western Kenya. Population at 1969 census: 12,000.)

401.2.1 MULLER, M.S. <u>Action and Interaction: social relationships</u>
<u>on a low-income housing estate in Kitale, Kenya</u>. Afrika-
Studiecentrum, Leiden, Netherlands, 1975, 149 pp.
Provides a very brief background on the town, but
mainly gives the results of a detailed social survey
focused on people's relationships both with their neigh-
bors and with authorities.

See also 401.0.6.

Lamu (Coastal town with a long history, but of declining relative
importance. Population at 1969 census: 7000.)

401.3.1 GHAIDAN, U. "Lamu: case study of the Swahili town." <u>Town</u>
<u>Planning Review</u>, 45, 1974, 84-90.
An outline of the town's situation, history, spatial
layout, and typical house types.

401.3.2 GHAIDAN, U. <u>Lamu: a Study of the Swahili Town</u>. East
African Literature Bureau, Nairobi, 1975, 94 pp.
A fuller discussion, providing much detail on the design and arrangement of the buildings, with many illustrations.

Malindi (Coastal town to which tourism has brought some revival of
fortunes. Population at 1969 census: 11,000.)

401.4.1 MARTIN, E.B. <u>The History of Malindi: a geographical analysis</u>
<u>of an East African Coastal Town from the Portuguese Period</u>
<u>to the Present</u>. East African Literature Bureau, Nairobi,
1973, 301 pp.
An account of the town's history from the fifteenth
century to the present is followed by a detailed study
of its present retail and service trades, dhow traffic,
fishing industry, and tourist industry.

Mombasa (Second city and chief port. Population at 1969 census:
247,000; at 1979 census: 342,000.)

401.5.1 BERG, F.J. and WALTER, B.J. "Mosques, population and urban
development in Mombasa." In Ogot, B.A. (ed.), <u>Hadith I</u>.
East African Publishing House, Nairobi, 1968, 47-100.
Examines the pattern of mosque foundations from the
sixteenth century to the present and uses this and other
sources to show the growth and spread of population.

401.5.2   BERG, F.J. and WALTER, B.J. "The Swahili community of
          Mombasa, 1500-1900." Journal of African History, 9, 1968,
          35-56.
               Traces the evolution of the social and political struc-
          ture of precolonial Mombasa, through its rise to a city-
          state under the Mazrui dynasty and its subsequent rela-
          tive decline, with special reference to the grouping into
          the "Twelve Swahili Tribes," which in turn formed two
          confederations for much of the period.

401.5.3   DE BLIJ, H.J. Mombasa: an African city. Northwestern
          University Press, Evanston, Ill., 1968, 168 pp.
               A study of the city's urban morphology, concerned
          primarily with the contribution of each racial group and
          concluding that segregation was less marked than in most
          colonial cities. After a brief outline of the site and
          growth of the city, its functional zones are examined
          more fully and the spatial structure of the central busi-
          ness district is analyzed in great detail. Includes many
          maps and photographs.

401.5.4   DYER, H.T. Mombasa Master Plan. Municipal Council, Mombasa,
          1962, 78 pp.
               A thorough study of many aspects of the city, with
          detailed proposals for its future physical growth, some
          of which have now been implemented. Special attention is
          given to land-use, transport, and public services. In-
          cludes numerous maps and photographs.

401.5.5   EDARI, R.S. "Social change in Mombasa." In Walton, J. and
          Masotti, L.H. (eds.), The City in Comparative Perspective,
          Sage, Beverly Hills, Calif., 1976, 179-192.
               A study of railway employees shows that the more
          "urbanized" people (i.e., those longest resident in the
          city) are less "modernized" and have lower socioeconomic
          status than the later arrivals.

*401.5.6 JANMOHAMED, K.K. "African labourers in Mombasa, 1895-1940."
          In Ogot, B.A. (ed.), Economic and Social History of East
          Africa. East African Literature Bureau, Nairobi, 1975.

401.5.7   JANMOHAMED, K.K. "Ethnicity in an urban setting: a case
          study of Mombasa." In Ogot, B.A. (ed.), History and
          Social Change in East Africa. East African Literature
          Bureau, Nairobi, 1976, 186-206.
               Reviews the concept of "tribe" and considers how dif-
          ferent groups of migrants in Mombasa have reacted to the
          local Swahili culture and to each other.

401.5.8   KENYA. Atlas of Kenya. 3rd ed. Survey of Kenya, Nairobi,
          1970, pp. 80-81, "Mombasa."

A clear map of Mombasa Island at 1:20,000 and a brief
descriptive text.

401.5.9   PATEL, L. "Mombasa housing problems: legal and social
           aspects." In Hutton, J. (ed.), Urban Challenge in East
           Africa. East African Publishing House, Nairobi, 1972,
           235-257.
               Examines landlord-tenant relationships in terms of
           both the legal position and actual practice, largely
           through selected individual cases.

401.5.10   STREN, R.E. "Limitations on local planning in Kenya: the
           case of Mombasa Municipality." African Urban Notes,
           4 (4), 1969, 35-49.
               Analyzes some problems of local government in terms
           of postcolonial needs and priorities. Kenyan urban
           local government in general is reviewed and then atten-
           tion is directed to Mombasa's responses to town planning
           and housing problems.

401.5.11   STREN, R.E. "Functional politics and central control in
           Mombasa, 1960-1969." Canadian Journal of African Studies,
           4, 1970, 33-56.
               Shows that local political conflict and factionalism
           were so strong in Mombasa after independence that the
           dominant political party had little power, and effective
           control lay with the strong inherited civil service.

401.5.12   STREN, R.E. "A survey of lower income areas in Mombasa."
           In Hutton, J. (ed.), Urban Challenge in East Africa.
           East African Publishing House, Nairobi, 1972, 97-115.
               Presents the results of a 1968 survey of the Tudor
           housing estates and two sections of the Majengo "village
           layout," covering tribe, religion, age, household struc-
           ture, length of residence, and attitudes. Challenges the
           view of Majengo as a "slum."

401.5.13   STREN, R.E. Housing the Urban Poor in Africa: policy,
           politics and bureaucracy in Mombasa. Institute of
           International Studies, University of California, Berkeley,
           1978, 330 pp.
               A detailed study of how the municipal authorities
           responded to housing needs through the 1950s and 1960s.
           Discusses the local government system, local politics in
           a multiethnic situation, and the evolution of housing
           policy in Kenya as a whole. Examines planned and unplan-
           ned low-income housing and summarizes a 1968 social sur-
           vey of Majengo and Tudor neighborhoods, but the focus
           throughout is on political structures and decision-
           making processes.

401.5.14 STROBEL, M. "From lelemama to lobbying: women's associations
          in Mombasa, Kenya." In Hafkin, N.J. and Bay, E.G. (eds.),
          Women in Africa. Stanford University Press, Stanford,
          Calif., 1976, 183-211; and in Ogot, B.A. (ed.), History
          and Social Change in East Africa. East African Literature
          Bureau, Nairobi, 1976, 207-235.
                  Discusses the functions, continuities, and limited
          political significance of the Lelemama dancing groups
          of the 1920s and 1930s and the women's cultural associa-
          tions of the 1950s and 1960s.

401.5.15 STROBEL, M. Muslim Women in Mombasa 1890-1975. Yale
          University Press, New Haven, 1979, 258 pp.
                  A study of the ways in which life has changed for
          women in Mombasa and especially of the ways in which
          they have achieved greater autonomy, based on a 1975
          UCLA doctoral thesis. One chapter provides a general
          view of the evolution of Mombasa society, another focuses
          on female education, and two others expand the discussion
          from the paper noted above.

401.5.16 SWARTZ, M.J. "Religious courts, community and ethnicity
          among the Swahili of Mombasa: an historical study of
          social boundaries." Africa, 49, 1979, 29-41.
                  Examines the role of Koranic courts in asserting and
          maintaining the distinctiveness of the Swahili as a
          social group in Mombasa over several centuries.

401.5.17 TAYLOR, D.R.F. "The markets of Mombasa." African Urban
          Notes, 5 (2), 1970, 175-184.
                  Presents the results of a survey of nine markets,
          covering size, turnover, organization, goods handled,
          and areas served.

401.5.18 UNIVERSITY PRESS OF AFRICA. Mombasa: the Official Handbook.
          Nairobi, 1971, 168 pp.
                  A city guide providing information on history, indus-
          tries, amenities, etc.

401.5.19 VAN DONGEN, I.S. "Mombasa in the land and sea exchanges
          of East Africa." Erdkunde, 17, 1963, 16-38.
                  A study of the role of Mombasa as the leading port of
          East Africa, serving the whole of Kenya and Uganda and
          also Rwanda and parts of Zaire and Tanzania.

401.5.20 WALTER, B.J. "A spatial diffusion perspective of areal
          growth in African Islamic cities: the example of Mombasa."
          African Urban Notes, 7 (1), 1972, 95-110.
                  Applies the concept of spatial diffusion to the phy-
          sical growth of Mombasa since the 1830s, using the spread
          of mosques as the main indicator.

401.5.21 WILSON, G. "Mombasa: a modern colonial municipality."
          In Southall, A. (ed.), Social Change in Modern Africa.
          Oxford University Press, London, 1961, 98-112.
          A brief summary of a comprehensive social survey, now
          largely of historical interest.

Publications in German include:

401.5.22 SHEIKH-DILTHEY, H. "Alt-Mombasa: Interethnische Beziehungen
          einer ostafrikanischen Hafenstadt." Anthropos, 73, 1978,
          673-716.

Unpublished theses include:

401.5.23 BERG, F.J. Mombasa under the Busaidi Sultanate: the city
          and its hinterlands in the nineteenth century. Ph.D.
          thesis, University of Wisconsin, Madison, 1971.

401.5.24 JANMOHAMED, K.K. A History of Mombasa c. 1895-1939: some
          aspects of economic and social life in an East African
          port town during colonial rule. Ph.D. thesis, Northwestern
          University, Evanston, Ill., 1978.

          See also 4.0.9.

Nairobi (Capital city. Population at 1969 census: 509,000; at 1979
         census: 835,000.)

401.6.1 BUJRA, J. "Pumwani: language use in an urban Muslim
         community." In Whiteley, W.H. (ed.), Language in Kenya.
         Oxford University Press, Nairobi, 1974, 217-252.
         Examines patterns of language use in a multitribal
         setting with special reference to the influence of Islam,
         showing that Swahili is increasingly dominant, but more
         so for Muslims than for others.

401.6.2 BUJRA, J.M. "Women "entrepreneurs" of early Nairobi."
         Canadian Journal of African Studies, 9, 1975, 213-234.
         Shows how a group of women in Nairobi in the 1900s
         and 1910s acquired substantial income through beer brew-
         ing and prostitution, came to own much property, e.g.,
         in Pumwani, and played an important role in creating a
         stable urban community.

401.6.3 BUJRA, J.M. "Proletarianization and the "informal economy":
         a case study from Nairobi." African Urban Studies, 3,
         1978/9, 47-66.
         Shows how in the Pumwani neighborhood the capitalist
         economy has produced both a "formal sector" proletariat
         and more anomalous class fragments in the "informal

sector," and how the whole social environment affects working-class consciousness.

401.6.4   CAMINOS, H. et al. "A progressive development proposal: Dandora, Nairobi." Ekistics, 36, 1973, 205-213.
Provides details of the scheme for new residential areas at Dandora on the eastern edge of the city.

401.6.5   CARLEBACH, J. Juvenile Prostitutes in Nairobi. East African Institute of Social Research, Kampala, 1962, 50 pp.
A sociological study of this phenomenon.

401.6.6   CHANA, T. and MORRISON, H. "Housing systems in the low income sector in Nairobi." Ekistics, 36, 1973, 214-222.
A microstudy of the organization and nature of spontaneous house-building in Mathare Valley.

401.6.7   CLARK, D. "Unregulated housing, vested interest and the development of community identity in Nairobi." African Urban Studies, 3, 1978/9, 33-46.
Discusses the social organization of the long-established but expanding peripheral settlement of Kibera, showing the extent to which an internal economy and vested interests have built up within it.

401.6.8   COLLIER, V.C. and REMPEL, H. "The divergence of private from social costs in rural-urban migration: a case study of Nairobi, Kenya." Journal of Development Studies, 13, 1977, 199-216.
Shows how much total social costs of migration differ from costs to individuals for various groups of migrants, especially for those unemployed, and considers policy implications.

401.6.9   COMHAIRE, J. "Lubumbashi et Nairobi: étude comparée de leur evolution. 2) Nairobi." Revue Française d'Etudes Politiques Africaines, 67, 1971, 64-72.
A brief outline of the city's origins, population growth, physical expansion, and social problems.

401.6.10 DOW, T.E. "Attitudes towards family size and family planning in Nairobi." Demography, 4, 1967, 780-797.
Presents and analyzes the results of a 1966 survey of preferred family size and attitudes to family planning among 352 residents of the Shauri Moyo housing estate.

401.6.11 ELKAN, W. "Is a proletariat emerging in Nairobi?" Economic Development and Cultural Change, 24, 1976, 695-706.
Argues that increasing numbers of people in Nairobi have become permanently dependent on wage employment, largely severing ties with their rural origins.

401.6.12 ETHERTON, D. Mathare Valley: a case study of uncontrolled
          settlement in Nairobi. University of Nairobi, 1971,
          96 pp.
          Presents the results of a detailed survey of the main
          area of uncontrolled settlement in the city, covering
          the demographic and social characteristics of the popu-
          lation, forms of occupance of land and houses, and the
          physical structure of the houses.

401.6.13 FERGUSON, A.G. "Some aspects of urban spatial cognition in
          an African student community." Transactions, Institute
          of British Geographers, NS 4, 1979, 77-93.
          Shows that for students from mainly rural backgrounds,
          levels of cognition of the urban environment of Nairobi
          are lower and rise more slowly than Western-based theory
          would predict, implying limited integration into the life
          of the city.

401.6.14 FERRARO, G. "Tradition or transition? Rural and urban
          kinsmen in East Africa." Urban Anthropology, 2, 1973,
          214-231.
          Examines the nature and significance of kinship ties
          of Kikuyu in Nairobi and in rural Kiambu.

401.6.15 FERRARO, G.P. "Nairobi: overview of an East African city."
          African Urban Studies, 3, 1978/9, 1-13.
          Reviews the city's rapid population growth, the ubi-
          quity of rural-urban ties, and aspects of contemporary
          social change, as an introduction to other papers in the
          volume.

401.6.16 FUREDI, F. "The African crowd in Nairobi: popular movements
          and elite politics." Journal of African History, 14,
          1973, 275-290.
          An account of African political activity in the city
          in the 1940s and 1950s, concluding that the "crowd" that
          was then most important has now been eliminated as a
          political force by a small elite that was always well
          integrated into the ruling structures.

401.6.17 GUTKIND, P.C.W. "The energy of despair: social organization
          of the unemployed in two African cities." Civilisations,
          17, 1967, 186-214 and 380-405.
          A comparative study of Nairobi and Lagos, showing how
          in both cases family and kinship ties enable the unem-
          ployed to survive in town and prevent their becoming a
          force for revolution.

401.6.18 HAKE, A. African Metropolis: Nairobi's self-help city.
          Chatto & Windus, London, 1977, 284 pp.
          Three parts of roughly equal length examine the

development of the city as a whole from its origin in
the 1890s to independence; the spontaneous settlements
established mainly within the 1960s, south of Eastleigh,
in Kaburini, and in Mathare Valley, along with older
uncontrolled settlement in Pumwani, with special reference to negative official policies towards these settlements; and the nature of self-employment (legal and illegal), self-help social services, and self-help churches
within this sector of the city.

*401.6.19 HAKE, A. and ROSS, M.H. "Mathare Valley: a case of the
transitional urban sector." In Oloo, D. (ed.),
Urbanisation, its Social Problems and Consequences.
East Africa Literature Bureau, Nairobi, 1969, 99-122.

401.6.20 HARRIS, J.R. "A housing policy for Nairobi." In Hutton,
J. (ed.), Urban Challenge in East Africa. East African
Publishing House, Nairobi, 1972, 39-56.
Describes the balance between city council housing
and other forms of housing in Nairobi, noting the inadequacy of the former and the promise of site-and-service
schemes, and considers the options for the resettlement
of the population of Pumwani.

401.6.21 HUGHES, G. "Low-income housing: a Kenyan case study."
In Little, I.M.D. and Scott, M.F.G. (eds.), Using Shadow
Prices. Heinemann, London, 1976, 43-87.
Discusses the application of the Little-Mirrlees
method of social cost-benefit analysis to low-income
housing projects in Nairobi, especially the Dandora
site-and-service scheme.

401.6.22 KAMAU, L.J. "Social boundaries and public space." African
Urban Notes, B 2 (1), 1975, 67-84.
Notes the existence of sharply defined racial groups
in Nairobi and reports on a study of their contrasting
patterns of movement and activity within a central park,
observing more separation than interaction.

401.6.23 KAMAU, L.J. "Semipublic, private and hidden rooms:
symbolic aspects of domestic space in urban Kenya."
African Urban Studies, 3, 1978/9, 105-115.
Reports on a study of residents' attitudes to the
design of their houses in a government housing estate
in Kibera suburb.

401.6.24 KAYONGO-MALE, D. "Urban squatters in Nairobi and policies
for improving their condition." In Kanyeihamba, G.W.
and McAuslan, J.P.W.B. (eds.), Urban Legal Problems in
Eastern Africa. Scandinavian Institute of African
Studies, Uppsala, Sweden, 1978, 85-103.

Examines the extent of squatting in Nairobi, the
social and economic characteristics of the squatters,
factors contributing to the phenomenon, and government
responses to it.

401.6.25 KENYA. Atlas of Kenya. Survey of Kenya, Nairobi, 3rd ed.,
1970, pp. 78-79, "The city of Nairobi."
A clear map of central Nairobi at 1:20,000, and a
brief descriptive text.

401.6.26 KIMANI, S.M. "Spatial structure of land values in Nairobi."
Tijdschrift voor Economische en Sociale Geografie, 63,
1972, 105-114.
Shows how land values fell rapidly away from the city
center, but not at a regular rate in every direction.

401.6.27 KIMANI, S.M. "The structure of land ownership in Nairobi."
Canadian Journal of African Studies, 6, 1972, 379-402;
and Journal of East African Research and Development, 2,
1972, 101-124.
Analyzes the valuation rolls of the city council to
show the spatial pattern of land ownership around 1970
and demonstrates the very small proportion owned by
Africans, compared with that owned by government, by
individual Europeans, and in terms of value especially
by businesses and by individual Asians.

401.6.28 KING, K. The African Artisan: education and the informal
sector in Kenya. Heinemann, London, 1977, 226 pp.
A study of how Kenyans acquire the technical skills
that enable them to set up small manufacturing enterprises
and of how those skills are used. Covers skill acquisition in both the formal and the informal sector. Draws
some examples from diverse urban and rural areas, but
with a focus on Nairobi throughout.

401.6.29 KING, K. "Petty production in Nairobi: the social context
of skill acquisition and occupational differentiation."
In Bromley, R. and Gerry, C. (eds.), Casual Work and
Poverty in Third World Cities. Wiley, Chichester, U.K.,
1979, 217-228.
A general discussion of how skills for small-scale
manufacturing are acquired in various parts of Africa
is followed by an examination of small metal-working
enterprises in Nairobi, with special reference to limitations on upward mobility.

401.6.30 McVICAR, K.G. "Pumwani: the role of a slum community in
providing a catalyst for culture change in East Africa."
In Berger, H. (ed.), Ostafrikanische Studien. Friedrich-
Alexander-Universität, Nuremberg, 1968, 157-166.

A study of the social and economic character of the oldest area of African settlement in Nairobi, now demolished, emphasizing its positive features.

401.6.31 MANN, E. "Nairobi: from colonial to national capital." In Berger, H. (ed.), Ostafrikanische Studien. Friedrich-Alexander-Universität, Nuremberg, 1968, 141-155.
A summary of the city's history and its present morphology, emphasizing the effects of rigid physical planning, with a note on possible future directions of growth.

401.6.32 MORGAN, W.T.W. (ed.) Nairobi: City and Region. Oxford University Press, Nairobi, 1967, 154 pp.
Includes a clear outline of the growth of the city and of its population, economic activities and land-use pattern around 1962 by D.M. Halliman and W.T.W. Morgan; a review of its industries by R.B. Ogendo; and papers on the geology, physiography, climate, flora and fauna, and rural economy of the surrounding areas.

401.6.33 MORGAN, W.T.W. "The location of Nairobi." In Berger, H. (ed.), Ostafrikanische Studien. Friedrich-Alexander-Universität, Nuremberg, 1968, 136-140.
Examines briefly the factors influencing the choice of Nairobi first as a railway depot and then as the capital of Kenya.

401.6.34 MYERS, D. "Nairobi, first thirty years." Kenya Past and Present, 2, 1973, 13-21.
A well-illustrated brief account of the city's origins and early growth.

401.6.35 NAIROBI URBAN STUDY GROUP. Nairobi: metropolitan growth strategy. Vol. 1 Main report, vol. 2 Technical Appendices. City Council of Nairobi, 1973.
The main report reviews demographic and social issues, potential areas for physical growth, the recommended strategy, and implementation procedure. The technical appendices cover population, economic prospects, land-use, transport, housing, and city council revenue and expenditure, with a list of further technical papers available at City Hall.

401.6.36 NEALE, B. "Asians in Nairobi: a preliminary survey." In Whiteley, W.H. (ed.), Language Use and Social Change. Oxford University Press, London, 1971, 334-346.
A survey of the distribution and frequency of use of various languages among different components of the Nairobi Asian community.

401.6.37 NELSON, N. "'Women must help each other': the operation
          of personal networks among Buzaa beer brewers in Mathare
          Valley, Kenya." In Caplan, P. and Bujra, J.M. (eds.),
          Women United: Women Divided. Tavistock, London, 1978,
          77-98.
              Examines the production and marketing of maize beer
          in the Mathare squatter area, the networks of personal
          relations among the women engaged in it, and their fail-
          ure to use these networks to improve their conditions of
          life.

401.6.38 NELSON, N. "Female-centered families: changing patterns
          of marriage and family among Buzaa brewers of Mathare
          Valley." African Urban Studies, 3, 1978/9, 85-104.
              Shows that many unmarried women in this area are
          establishing female-centered households and examines
          their links with mothers, sisters, and children who may
          live either there or in the rural homeland.

401.6.39 NELSON, N. "How women and men get by: the sexual division
          of labour in the informal sector of a Nairobi squatter
          settlement." In Bromley, R. and Gerry, C. (eds.), Casual
          Work and Poverty in Third World Cities. Wiley, Chichester,
          U.K., 1979, 283-302.
              Discusses the economic activities undertaken in
          Mathare Valley, noting the incomes and the costs in-
          curred, and focusing on the relative involvement of men
          and women in each activity.

401.6.40 OGENDO, R.B. "Industrial location in the Nairobi area."
          Geojournal, 2, 1978, 451-462.
              Examines the structure and location of manufacturing
          within and around Nairobi, noting changes between 1965
          and 1975, and presenting much employment data for these
          years by sector and area.

401.6.41 OMINDE, S.H. "The city of Nairobi: population changes and
          pattern." Journal of East African Research and Development,
          1, 1971, 77-88.
              Analyzes some of the population patterns revealed by
          the 1969 census.

401.6.42 OMINDE, S.H. "Migration and the structure of population
          in Nairobi." In Cantrelle, P. (ed.), Population in
          African Development. Ordina, Dolhain, Belgium, 1974,
          537-550.
              Uses the 1969 census results to show variations with-
          in the city in population density and demographic struc-
          tures and also considers the pattern of birthplace of
          the city population.

401.6.43 PARKIN, D.J. "Congregational and interpersonal ideologies
in political ethnicity." In Cohen, A. (ed.), Urban
Ethnicity. Tavistock, London, 1974, 119-157.
Examines the bases of interpersonal ties among Luo
migrants in the Kaloleni area of Nairobi, stressing the
meaning of kinship and noting political implications,
and making comparisons with the Luo in Kampala, the
Hausa in Ibadan, and the Kru in Monrovia.

401.6.44 PARKIN, D.J. "Nairobi: problems and methods." In Whiteley,
W.H. (ed.), Language in Kenya. Oxford University Press,
Nairobi, 1974, 131-146.
Suggests an approach to the study of language choice
appropriate for present-day Nairobi.

401.6.45 PARKIN, D.J. "Status factors in language adding: Bahati
housing estate in Nairobi." In Whiteley (above), 147-165.
Examines for the largely Kikuyu population of a city
council estate the factors influencing the informal acquisition of other languages, notably Kamba and Swahili.

401.6.46 PARKIN, D.J. "Language shift and ethnicity in Nairobi:
the speech community of Kaloleni." In Whiteley (above),
167-187.
Compares the Kikuyu, Kamba, Luhya, and Luo in the
ethnically very mixed Kaloleni neighborhood with regard
to the frequency of use of different languages.

401.6.47 PARKIN, D.J. "Language switching in Nairobi." In Whiteley
(above), 189-216.
Examines the extent to which different languages are
used within conversations among people of different ethnic groups, for instance in the city's markets.

401.6.48 PARKIN, D.J. "Migration, settlement and the politics of
unemployment: a Nairobi case study." In Parkin, D.J.
(ed.), Town and Country in Central and Eastern Africa.
Oxford University Press, London, 1975, 145-155.
Focuses on the Luo in Nairobi, noting that their increasing dependence on urban jobs conflicts with their
feeling of exclusion from urban politics. Ethnic cleav-
age is aggravated by fear of unemployment.

401.6.49 PARKIN, D. The Cultural Definition of Political Response:
lineal destiny among the Luo. Academic Press, London,
1978, 347 pp.
An anthropological study of the implications of urban
residence and of socioeconomic change for family structures and social relationships among Luo migrants on the
Kaloleni housing estate. Individual chapters deal with
such topics as the significance of education, wage dependency, political uncertainty, and paradigms of leadership.

401.6.50 ROSS, M. "Measuring ethnicity in Nairobi." In O'Barr,
W.M. et al. (eds.), Survey Research In Africa.
Northwestern University Press, Evanston, Ill., 1973,
160-167.
Discusses the problems of conceptualizing and measuring ethnicity in Nairobi on the basis of field studies,
the results of which are reported in studies noted below.

401.6.51 ROSS, M.H. "Two styles of political participation in an
African city." American Journal of Political Science,
17, 1973, 1-22.
Distinguishes independence and postindependence styles
of political participation and evaluates factors affecting each, on the basis of surveys in two Nairobi housing
estates.

*401.6.52 ROSS, M.H. "Community formation in an African squatter
settlement." Comparative Political Studies, 6, 1973,
296-328.

401.6.53 ROSS, M.H. The Political Integration of Urban Squatters.
Northwestern University Press, Evanston, Ill., 1973,
228 pp.
Against a background of community organization and
political integration patterns found in squatter settlements around the world, these phenomena are examined for
the Mathare Valley settlements in Nairobi. The evolution
of spontaneous settlement and official African housing
throughout the city are reviewed, but there is a much
more detailed study of Mathare covering demographic
structure, tribe and birthplace, economic activities,
sense of community, and nature of community institutions,
as well as political integration.

401.6.54 ROSS, M.H. "Conflict resolution among urban squatters."
Urban Anthropology, 3, 1974, 110-136.
Examines the mechanisms for resolving disputes within
the squatter communities of Mathare Valley, noting simi-
larities to, and adaptations from, those in traditional
Kikuyu society.

401.6.55 ROSS, M.H. Grass Roots in An African City: political
behavior in Nairobi. MIT Press, Cambridge, Mass.,
1975, 169 pp.
Provides an outline of the political and social life
of Nairobi as a whole, but focuses primarily on two city
council housing estates at Shauri Moyo and Kariokor for
a study of life styles and social relationships, as well
as political attitudes and behavior.

401.6.56 ROSS, M.H. and WEISNER, T.S. "The rural-urban migrant

289

network in Kenya." American Ethnologist, 4, 1977, 359–375.
    Draws on earlier work in Nairobi by each author to
demonstrate the frequency of migration between urban and
rural homes, to review other urban-rural links, and to
show the significance of ethnic ties in social networks
within Nairobi.

401.6.57 TEMPLE, F.T. "Planning and budgeting for urban growth in
        Nairobi." Journal of East African Research and Development,
        3, 1973, 191–216.
            Assesses the capability of the city council to deal
        with the financial demands imposed by the city's rapid
        growth.

401.6.58 THADANI, V. "Women in Nairobi: the paradox of urban
        'progress'." African Urban Studies, 3, 1978/9, 67–83.
            Examines the circumstances in which women move to
        the city and suggests that urban life brings many of
        them a mixture of greater freedom and greater subservi-
        ence, the latter especially in the form of greater eco-
        nomic dependence upon men.

401.6.59 THORNLEY, A. "Rapid planning for rapid growth: Nairobi."
        The Planner, 59, 1973, 317–320.
            Describes a study projecting the likely direction of
        physical growth in Nairobi, arising from urgent airport
        planning.

401.6.60 TIWARI, R.C. "An analysis of the social agglomerations
        among Asians in Nairobi." Scottish Geographical Magazine,
        85, 1969, 141–149.
            Shows how both the Asians as a whole, and different
        communities within that group, are highly concentrated
        within certain parts of the city.

401.6.61 TIWARI, R.C. "Some aspects of the social geography of
        Nairobi." African Urban Notes, 7 (1), 1972, 36–61.
            Draws upon the 1962 and 1969 censuses to examine spa-
        tial patterns of population density, variations among
        the three main racial groups, and especially to trace
        changes in the residential distribution of the Asian
        population.

401.6.62 VAN ZWANENBERG, R. "History and theory of urban poverty in
        Nairobi." Journal of East African Research and Development,
        2, 1972, 165–203.
            Investigates the growth of an impoverished class in
        the 1920s and 1930s, with an emphasis on the failure of
        housing to match population growth and of wages to match
        housing costs.

401.6.63 WEISNER, T.S. "Studying rural-urban ties: a matched
          network sample from Kenya." In O'Barr, W.M. et al.
          (eds.), Survey Research in Africa. Northwestern
          University Press, Evanston, Ill., 1973, 122-134.
               Discusses the rationale of a matched sample of dwel-
          lers in Kariobangi, Nairobi and in rural Kakamega, and
          the techniques used in studying migration patterns on
          the basis of these samples. The research results are
          presented in a separate paper (below).

401.6.64 WEISNER, T.S. "Kariobangi: the case history of a squatter
          resettlement scheme in Kenya." In Arens, W. (ed.), A
          Century of Change in Eastern Africa. Mouton, The Hague,
          1976, 77-99.
               Discusses the planning and implementation of the
          Kariobangi site-and-service scheme intended for squatters
          evicted from the city center and how it has become a typ-
          ical landlord/tenant low-income housing area.

401.6.65 WEISNER, T.S. "The structure of sociability: urban
          migration and urban-rural ties in Kenya." Urban
          Anthropology, 5, 1976, 199-223.
               Data from a complex sociometric analysis of a matched
          rural-urban network sample, drawn from Kariobangi in
          Nairobi and a migrant source area in Kakamega District,
          show that the networks are highly interconnected and
          that clan affiliation is very significant.

401.6.66 WERLIN, H.H. "The Nairobi city council: a study in compara-
          tive local government." Comparative Studies in Society
          and History, 7, 1966, 181-198.
               A discussion of the development and operation of the
          city council during the colonial period.

401.6.67 WERLIN, H.H. Governing an African City: a Study of
          Nairobi. Africana, New York, 1974, 320 pp.
               A detailed study of the city administration both be-
          fore and after independence. Demonstrates the completely
          dominant role of the Europeans up to the 1960s and the
          consequent substantial problems as control rapidly passed
          into the hands of the African elite. The rivalry for
          power among different sectors of the population, the
          limited technical expertise available, and the intractable
          nature of problems such as the housing needs of the rapid-
          ly expanding population are all examined.

401.6.68 WERLIN, H.H. "The informal sector: the implications of the
          ILO's study of Kenya." African Studies Review, 17, 1974,
          205-212.
               Suggests that the ILO proposals for a more positive
          approach to informal sector traders and to squatter

settlement in Nairobi are unlikely to be accepted by
either national government or the city council.

A notable earlier publication is:

401.6.69 WHITE, L.W.T.; SILBERMAN, L.; and ANDERSON, P.R. Nairobi:
          master plan for a colonial capital. Colonial Office,
          London, 1948, 90 pp.

Unpublished theses include:

401.6.70 CHAE, H.K. Two Essays on the Residents of Nairobi, Kenya:
          (i) Intraurban migration; (ii) Schooling, earnings and
          experience. Ph.D. thesis, University of Oregon, 1976.

401.6.71 HENNEIN, S.S. The Study of Family Structure in Pumwani,
          Nairobi. Ph.D. thesis, Northwestern University, Evanston,
          Ill., 1972.

401.6.72 HUGHES, G.A. A Study of Housing Policy in Nairobi. Ph.D.
          thesis, Cambridge University, 1976.

401.6.73 KINNISON, S.M. Urbanization and Poverty in Africa. Case
          study: Nairobi, Kenya. Ph.D. thesis, Howard University,
          Washington, D.C., 1977.

401.6.74 McVICAR, K.G. Twilight of an East African Slum: Pumwani
          and the Evolution of an African Settlement in Nairobi.
          Ph.D. thesis, University of California, Los Angeles, 1968.

401.6.75 NELSON, D. Caste and Club: a study of the Goan politics
          in Nairobi. Ph.D. thesis, University of Nairobi, 1971.

401.6.76 NELSON, N. Dependence and Independence: female household
          heads in Mathare Valley, a squatter community in Nairobi,
          Kenya. Ph.D. thesis, University of London, 1978.

401.6.77 TEMPLE, F.T. Politics, Planning and Housing Policy in
          Nairobi. Ph.D. thesis, Massachusetts Institute of
          Technology, 1973.

401.6.78 THADANI, V. The Forgotten Factor in Social Change: the
          case of women in Nairobi, Kenya. Ph.D. thesis, Bryn
          Mawr College, Bryn Mawr, Pa., 1976.

401.6.79 TIWARI, R.C. Nairobi: A Study in Urban Geography. Ph.D.
          thesis, University of Reading, U.K., 1964.

401.6.80 WEISNER, T.S. One Family, Two Households: rural-urban ties
          in Kenya. Ph.D. thesis, Harvard University, 1973.

See also 4.0.6, 4.0.22, 4.0.25.

<u>Nakuru</u> (Headquarters of Rift Valley Province. Population at 1969
        census: 47,000.)

401.7.1 TAMARKIN, M. "Tribal associations, tribal solidarity and
            tribal chauvinism in a Kenya town." <u>Journal of African
            History</u>, 14, 1973, 257-274.
            The history of Nakuru from the 1920s suggests that
         town life has consolidated tribal identity and has ex-
         acerbated problems arising from tribal differences among
         its inhabitants.

401.7.2 WACHTEL, E. "Minding her own business: women shopkeepers
            in Nakuru, Kenya." <u>African Urban Notes</u>, B 1 (2), 1976,
            27-42.
            Shows how women are beginning to penetrate the small-
         scale formal business sector in Nakuru; reports on a
         survey of the backgrounds, economic circumstances, and
         problems of forty-seven women in such businesses.

Unpublished theses include:

401.7.3 TAMARKIN, M. Social and Political Change in a Twentieth
            Century African Urban Community in Kenya. Ph.D. thesis,
            University of London, 1973.

401.7.4 WACHTEL, A.A.D. Towards a Model of Urbanism in an African
            City: the dual focus career of formal sector workers in
            Nakuru, Kenya. Ph.D. thesis, Northwestern University,
            Evanston, Ill., 1978.

<u>Nyeri</u> (Headquarters of Central Province. Population at 1969 census:
       10,000.)

401.8.1 DUTTO, C.A. <u>Nyeri Townsmen</u>. East African Literature Bureau,
            Nairobi, 1975, 265 pp.
            Examines the administrative, commercial, and cultural
         framework of the town, and the social structure that has
         developed upon this. Topics investigated include employ-
         ment, living standards, religion, distinctiveness of
         residential areas, social relationships within the town,
         and links with the rural areas from which most people
         have come. Based on an American doctoral thesis.

TANZANIA

General

402.0.1 BARNUM, H.N. and SABOT, R.H. Migration, Education and Urban Surplus Labour: the case of Tanzania. OECD, Paris, 1976, 115 pp.
    Considers migrant behavior in terms of differentials between rural incomes and urban wages and of the influence of education, noting policy implications.

402.0.2 BIENEFELD, M. "The informal sector and peripheral capitalism: the case of Tanzania." Institute of Development Studies Bulletin, 6 (3), 1975, 53-73.
    Shows that people working in the "informal sector" are very diverse in activities and income, that many show vitality and responsiveness to opportunity, but that successful activities may be taken over by the large-scale sector.

402.0.3 BIENEFELD, M.A. "Occupational structure and industrial distribution of wage earners." In Kim, K.S. et al. (eds.), Papers on the Political Economy of Tanzania. Heinemann, Nairobi, 1979, 245-252.
    Summarizes the information on the distribution of wage earners among occupations and industries obtained in the 1971 surveys of seven towns, the full report of which is listed below.

402.0.4 BIENEFELD, M. and SABOT, R.H. The National Urban Mobility, Employment and Income Survey of Tanzania. Economic Research Bureau, University of Dar es Salaam, 1971.
    A mimeographed report presenting the results of an extensive survey of migration patterns, employment structure, and incomes in Dar es Salaam, Arusha, Dodoma, Mbeya, Mwanza, Tabora, and Tanga.

402.0.5 BROWN, B. and W.T. "East African trade towns: a shared growth." In Arens, W. (ed.), A Century of Change in Eastern Africa. Mouton, The Hague, 1976, 183-200.
    Discusses the nineteenth-century resurgence of urbanism in Tanzania, focusing on Bagamoyo, Tabora, and Ujiji, which all grew through caravan trade, aiding the spread of a common Swahili culture.

402.0.6 CLAESON, C.F. and EGERO, B. Population Movement in Tanzania: Movement to Towns. BRALUP, University of Dar es Salaam, 1971, 86 pp.
    Presents tables and maps showing the origins of each town's in-migrant population and the urban destinations

of each region's rural-urban migrants, on the basis of the 1967 census.

402.0.7 CLAESON, C.F. and EGERO, B. "Migration and the urban population: a demographic analysis of population census data for Tanzania." Geografisker Analer, B, 54, 1972, 1-18.
Uses 1967 census data to show demographic selectivity in migration and the implications of massive migration for the demographic structure of the urban population. Variables such as educational levels are also considered.

402.0.8 DOHERTY, J. "Ideology and town planning in Tanzania." Journal of the Geographical Association of Tanzania, 14, 1976, 79-104.
Discusses the evolution and present character of town planning in Tanzania, arguing that colonial approaches persist and that town planning practice therefore largely conflicts with the country's socialist development aims.

402.0.9 HAYUMA, A.M. "Training programme for the improvement of slums and squatter areas in Tanzania." Habitat International, 4, 1979, 119-129.
Outlines the current rate of urban growth, the shift in policy to site-and-service projects and squatter upgrading, and the task of training local personnel to manage these programs.

402.0.10 HIRST, M.A. "A functional analysis of towns in Tanzania." Tijdschrift voor Economische en Sociale Geografie, 64, 1973, 39-51.
Examines the functions of Tanzanian towns in relation to the evolving space economy, noting the small extent of functional differentiation. Includes an analysis of telephone traffic to show how Dar es Salaam dominates interurban interaction.

402.0.11 KIKENYA, J.D. "National Housing Corporation: progress in housing the masses." Tanzania Notes and Records, 76, 1975, 185-190.
Outlines the activities of the National Housing Corporation in the provision of urban housing during the 1960s.

402.0.12 MASCARENHAS, A.C. "Urban centres." In Berry, L. (ed.), Tanzania in Maps. University of London Press, 1971, 130-133.
Maps to show the 1967 population and the range of services in each urban center, and text discussing the origins, distribution, and functions of the towns.

402.0.13 MASCARENHAS, A.C. "Urban growth." In Egero, B. and Henin,
          R.A. (eds.), The Population of Tanzania. BRALUP,
          University of Dar es Salaam, 1973, 76-97.
              Outlines the evolution of the country's towns and
          analyzes urban population data from the 1948, 1957, and
          1967 censuses, noting contrasts in growth rates, patterns
          of in-migration, and employment, and anomalies of admin-
          istrative status.

402.0.14 MASCARENHAS, A.C. "Urban housing in mainland Tanzania."
          In Egero, B. and Henin, R.A. (eds.), The Population of
          Tanzania. BRALUP, University of Dar es Salaam, 1973,
          98-118.
              Analyzes the data on housing in all mainland towns
          from the 1967 census, covering house types, tenure and
          rents, electricity and water supplies, and occupancy of
          rooms, noting intertown variations in each case.

402.0.15 MASCARENHAS, A.C. and CLAESON, C.F. "Factors influencing
          Tanzania's urban policy." African Urban Notes, 6 (3),
          1972, 24-42.
              Contrasts the laissez faire attitude towards urban
          development of the early 1960s with the later policies
          of restraining urban growth and of decentralization tied
          to the rural development priorities formulated in the
          Arusha Declaration of 1967.

402.0.16 MKAMA, J. "Urban development policies and planning experience:
          Tanzania." In Safier, M. (ed.), The Role of Urban and
          Regional Planning in National Development of East Africa.
          Milton Obote Foundation, Kampala, 1970, 196-206.
              Outlines pre- and postindependence policies towards
          urban growth and comments on certain pieces of planning
          legislation and some specific schemes.

402.0.17 MLAY, W.F. "Checking the drift to towns." Journal of
          the Geographical Association of Tanzania, 14, 1976,
          182-203.
              Examines factors contributing to massive rural-urban
          migration in Tanzania, especially spread of education
          and contrasts in employment opportunities, and reviews
          recent efforts to check the flow.

402.0.18 MLAY, W.F.I. "Rural to urban migration and rural develop-
          ment." Tanzania Notes and Records, 81/82, 1977, 1-13.
              Similar to the paper noted above, but with more em-
          phasis on the results of a research project on migration
          into Arusha and Moshi towns.

402.0.19 SABOT, R.H. "The meaning and measurement of urban surplus
          labour." Oxford Economic Papers, 29, 1977, 389-411.

> Clarifies the definition of urban surplus labor and measures its magnitude in Tanzania on the basis of the 1971 National Urban Mobility, Employment and Income Survey noted above (402.0.4).

402.0.20   SABOT, R.H.   The Social Costs of Urban Surplus Labour. OECD, Paris, 1977, 104 pp.
> An assessment of the social costs of urban unemployment in the case of Tanzania, later incorporated as chapter 6 in the monograph noted below.

402.0.21   SABOT, R.H.   Economic Development and Urban Migration: Tanzania 1900-1971.   Oxford University Press, Oxford, 1979, 279 pp.
> An intensive study of rural-urban migration and of urban employment and unemployment in Tanzania, both as they have developed and in terms of present processes, based on a 1974 Oxford doctoral thesis, and incorporating many results from the National Urban Mobility, Employment and Income Survey noted above. Individual chapters deal with the evolving labor market as a determinant of migration, the characteristics of the migrants, the significance of education, the social costs of unemployment, the stability of migrants, and policy options.

402.0.22   SABOT, R.H.   "Education, income distribution and rates of urban migration in Tanzania." In Kim, K.S. et al. (eds.), Papers on the Political Economy of Tanzania.   Heinemann, Nairobi, 1979, 253-260.
> Assesses the significance of education as a factor affecting the incidence of rural-urban migration, with the aid of data from the 1971 survey noted above, noting the implications of sharply rising numbers of school-leavers.

402.0.23   SABOT, R.H.   "Open unemployment and the employed compound of surplus labour." In Kim, K.S. et al. (eds.), Papers on the Political Economy of Tanzania.   Heinemann, Nairobi, 1979, 261-271.
> A further paper drawing on the 1971 survey of seven towns, assessing the extent and nature of urban unemployment, and also the extent of surplus labor among the wage-employed and the self-employed.

402.0.24   SAMATTA, B.A.   "The social, economic and political role of urban agglomerations in the United Republic of Tanzania." In INCIDI, Urban Agglomerations in the States of the Third World.   Brussels, 1971, 356-367.
> A broad review of the patterns of recent social and political change, of the dangers of a rift between urban and rural populations, and of measures being taken by government to prevent this.

402.0.25 SANG, W.H. "Urban water supply problems and policy in
          Tanzania: a critical assessment." Journal of the
          Geographical Association of Tanzania, 14, 1976, 105-135.
               Outlines the problems of urban water supply, discusses
          recent action and plans in Dar es Salaam, Dodoma, and
          Tanga, and reviews the options open to the decision-
          makers in this field.

402.0.26 STREN, R.E. Urban Inequality and Housing Policy in
          Tanzania: the Problem of Squatting. University of
          California Institute of International Studies, Berkeley,
          1975, 112 pp.
               Provides a clear outline of the general pattern of
          urbanization in Tanzania, including the extent of rural-
          urban migration and the efforts made to provide housing,
          before undertaking a detailed analysis of the growth of
          squatting in Dar es Salaam and the social and economic
          characteristics of the squatters there. Concludes that
          even Tanzania's enlightened policies cannot overcome
          the pressures for migration and thus for squatting.

402.0.27 TANZANIA. Second Five-Year Plan for Economic and Social
          Development, 1969-1974. Vol. 1, General Analysis. Dar
          es Salaam, 1969. Chap. 12 "Urban development," 176-186;
          Chap. 13 "Housing policy," 187-192.
               Chapter 12 stresses the need to restrict the growth
          of Dar es Salaam and to direct urban development to nine
          other urban growth areas. Chapter 13 outlines the gov-
          ernment house-building program, which is largely confined
          to the towns.

402.0.28 TANZANIA. 1967 Population Census. Volume 2, Statistics
          for Urban Areas. Dar es Salaam, 1970, 304 pp.
               Includes data for each town on age, sex, ethnic origin,
          birthplace, citizenship, literacy, education, and eco-
          nomic activity, and on house type and size, provision
          of services, and level of rent. Also includes some data
          for wards within each town.

402.0.29 TANZANIA. 1969 Household Budget Survey. 2 vols. Dar es
          Salaam, 1972, 222 + 82 pp.
               Provides much data on household income, expenditure
          and consumption in volume 1, and on housing in volume 2,
          for Dar es Salaam and nine provincial towns, as well as
          for selected rural areas.

402.0.30 TANZANIA. Third Five-Year Plan for Economic and Social
          Development, 1976-1981. Dar es Salaam, 1978. Chap. 12
          "Construction, housing and urban development," 68-78.
               Outlines plans for the construction sector, the an-
          ticipated distribution of urban growth, and urban hous-
          ing and site-and-service programs.

402.0.31   YAHYA, S.S.   "Urban transportation and land use in Tanzania."
           Ekistics, 27, 1969, 144-147.
                Examines briefly the effects of road transport on
           patterns of land-use in Dar es Salaam and Zanzibar City.

402.0.32   ANON.   "Town planning revolves around the people: a record
           of ten years." Tanzania Notes and Records, 76, 1975,
           179-184.
                Briefly reviews government urbanization policies
           since independence and especially the activities of the
           Town Planning Division.

Publications in German include:

402.0.33   MEUER, P.; SIEBOLDS, P.; and STEINBERG, F.   Urbanisierung
     ‾   und Wohnungsbau in Tanzania.   Institut für Wohnungsbau
           und Stadtteilplanung, Technische Universität, Berlin,
           1979, 278 pp.

402.0.34   VORLAUFER, K.   "Die Funktion der Mittelstädte Afrikas im
           Prozess des sozialen Wandels: das Beispiel Tansania."
           Afrika-Spectrum, 1971, No. 2, 41-59.

Unpublished theses include:

402.0.35   MLAY, W.F.   Recent Rural-Urban Migration in Tanzania with
           reference to Movements into Moshi and Arusha towns.
           Ph.D. thesis, University of London, 1974.

Arusha   (Northern provincial town.   Population at 1967 census:
           32,000.)

402.1.1   PLANNING AND DEVELOPMENT COLLABORATIVE INTERNATIONAL.
           Arusha, Tanzania: master plan and five-year development
           program.   Washington, D.C., 1970.
                A comprehensive physical plan for the future growth
           of the town.   Not widely available.

       See also 402.0.18, 402.0.35.

Dar es Salaam   (Capital city until replaced by Dodoma in late 1970s.
           Population at 1967 census: 273,000.   Estimate for
           1975:   510,000.)

402.2.1   DE BLIJ, H.J.   Dar es Salaam, Northwestern University Press,
           Evanston, Ill., 1963, 95 pp.
                Subtitled A study in urban geography, it provides an
           outline of the city's site, situation, development, and
           functional structure, but the main focus is upon the

character and spatial structure of the central business
district, both of which clearly reflected the colonial
past. Numerous maps and photographs are included.

402.2.2 GROHS, G. "Slum clearance in Dar es Salaam." In Hutton, J.
(ed.), Urban Challenge in East Africa. East African
Publishing House, Nairobi, 1972, 157-176.
Reviews various improvement and replacement strategies
and concludes in favor of site-and-service schemes.

402.2.3 ILIFFE, J. "The creation of group consciousness among the
dockworkers of Dar es Salaam 1929-50." In Sandbrook, R.
and Cohen, R. (eds.), The Development of an African
Working Class. Longman, London, 1975, 49-72.
Shows how group feeling arose among this set of workers
out of their working conditions long before they were involved in national politics. A slightly longer version
appears in Sutton (below).

402.2.4 ILIFFE, J. A Modern History of Tanganyika. Cambridge
University Press, 1979. Chap. 12 "Townsmen and workers,"
381-404.
Largely concerned with the growth of Dar es Salaam
through the first half of this century, the social and
political organization of its population during this period, and especially the emerging labor movement.

402.2.5 LESLIE, J.A.K. A Survey of Dar es Salaam. Oxford University
Press, London, 1963, 280 pp.
Presents the results of a sociological survey of
African migrants living in the city in 1956-1957. The
emphasis is on social relationships, with much material
presented in an impressionistic rather than systematic
way. Extensive quotations from interviews are included.

402.2.6 LOWE, L.T. "The urban woman worker in Dar es Salaam."
African Urban Notes, B 2 (3), 1976, 11-19.
Discusses general employment problems for women in
African cities and reports on a 1968-1969 survey of women
workers in Dar es Salaam, concerned with both socioeconomic
characteristics and attitudes to work.

402.2.7 MASCARENHAS, A.C. "The impact of nationhood on Dar es Salaam."
East African Geographical Review, 5, 1967, 39-46.
Examines changes in the city resulting from the attain-
ment of national independence in 1961.

402.2.8 MASCARENHAS, A.C. "Dar es Salaam." In Berry, L. (ed.),
Tanzania in Maps. University of London Press, 1971,
134-139.
Maps and supplementary text on the growth of the city,
its present land-use, and its port.

402.2.9 MBILINYI, S.M. and MASCARENHAS, A.C. "Bananas and the Dar
es Salaam Market." East African Journal of Rural
Development, 6, 1973, 55-77. Reprinted in Kim, K.S. et
al. (eds.), Papers on the Political Economy of Tanzania.
Heinemann, Nairobi, 1979, 228-239.
Examines the trade in this local agricultural product
in the city's markets, with reference to source areas,
transport, market operations, and fluctuating prices.

402.2.10 PROJECT PLANNING ASSOCIATES. National Capital Master Plan,
Dar es Salaam. Toronto, 1968, 117 pp. plus seven technical supplements.
A comprehensive long-term plan, with detailed studies
of transport, public services, etc. Few copies printed
and thus not widely available, yet it contains much valuable information apart from its proposals for the future.

402.2.11 SEGAL, E.S. "Urban development planning in Dar es Salaam."
In Obudho, R.A. and El-Shakhs, S. (eds.), Development of
Urban Systems in Africa. Praeger, New York, 1979,
258-271.
Reviews the origins and growth of the city and discusses government policies influencing the rate and
direction of its development since independence.

402.2.12 SUTTON, J.E.G. (ed.) Dar es Salaam: City, Port and Region.
Tanzania Notes and Records, No. 71. Tanzania Society,
Dar es Salaam, 1970, 213 pp.
Includes a historical sketch by the editor, a lengthy
paper on the geomorphology of the area by P.H. Temple,
another on the port by A.C. Mascarenhas, and a third on
the dockworkers by J. Iliffe. Briefer papers deal with
climate, archaeology, social and political life, and
education, and there are short notes on other topics.
Many photographs are included.

402.2.13 TEISEN, M. "Dar es Salaam." In Svendsen, K.E. and Teisen,
M. (eds.), Self-reliant Tanzania. Tanzania Publishing
House, Dar es Salaam, 1969, 78-90.
A brief account of the city's history and a lively
description of its present character.

402.2.14 TANZANIA. Household Budget Survey of Wage-earners in Dar
es Salaam, 1965. Central Statistical Bureau, Dar es
Salaam, 1967, 29 pp.
Presents the results of a sample survey of household
income and expenditure patterns.

402.2.15 TANZANIA. Survey of Distributive Trades in Dar es Salaam,
1970. Bureau of Statistics, Dar es Salaam, 1972, 31 pp.
Presents the results of a survey of all trading

establishments in Dar es Salaam with any employees,
covering employment, sales, stocks, etc., for each type
of trade.

Publications in German include:

402.2.16 SCHNEIDER, K.G. Dar es Salaam: Stadtentwicklung unter dem
          Einfluss der Araber und Inder. Steiner, Wiesbaden, 1965,
          87 pp.

402.2.17 VORLAUFER, K. Dar es Salaam. Deutsches Institut für
          Afrika-Forschung, Hamburg, 1973, 230 pp.

Unpublished theses include:

402.2.18 FLANAGAN, W.G. The Extended Family as an Agent of
          Urbanization: a survey of men and women working in Dar
          es Salaam, Tanzania. Ph.D. thesis, University of
          Connecticut, 1977.

402.2.19 MASCARENHAS, A.C. Urban Development in Dar es Salaam.
          M.A. thesis, University of California, Los Angeles, 1966.

402.2.20 SWANTZ, L.W. The Role of the Medicine-man among the Zaramo
          of Dar es Salaam. Ph.D. thesis, University of Dar es
          Salaam, 1972.

          See also 4.0.5, 4.0.9, 4.0.22, 402.0.26.

Dodoma (Provincial town to be developed as the new national capital.
         Population at 1967 census: 23,000.)

402.3.1 HOYLE, B.S. "African socialism and urban development: the
          relocation of the Tanzanian capital." Tijdschrift voor
          Economische en Sociale Geografie, 70, 1979, 207-216.
              Examines the origins and growth of Dodoma, the factors
          influencing its selection as the new national capital,
          and the plans for its physical development.

402.3.2 KAHAMA, C.G. "A tailor-made city: Dodoma, future capital."
          Ceres, 8, 1975, 35-37.
              Outlines the physical plan for the new capital, with
          emphasis on anticipated patterns of movement within it,
          largely on foot, cycle, or public transport.

402.3.3 PERCIVAL, R.N. "Dodoma: a new capital city for Tanzania."
          Town and Country Planning Summer School, Report of
          Proceedings. 1975, 95-99.
              Discusses briefly the purpose of relocating the capi-
          tal, the choice of site, and the basic features of the
          plan for the new city.

402.3.4   TANZANIA CAPITAL DEVELOPMENT AUTHORITY. <u>A Portrait of</u>
          <u>Dodoma</u>. Dodoma, 1975, 55 pp.
              An illustrated account of the history of the town from
          its nineteenth-century origins to the time of its selec-
          tion as national capital.

402.3.5   TANZANIA CAPITAL DEVELOPMENT AUTHORITY, and PROJECT PLANNING
          ASSOCIATES. <u>Capital City Master Plan</u>. 8 vols. Dodoma,
          1975.
              A set of intensive studies of existing conditions in
          the Dodoma area and detailed plans for the physical devel-
          opment of the new city. Individual volumes provide de-
          tailed studies of specific topics such as transport, water
          supplies, and social services. Published, but with very
          limited circulation.

<u>Kigoma-Ujiji</u>   (Town on the shore of Lake Tanganyika, combining
                colonial and precolonial settlements. Population at
                1967 census: 21,000.)

402.4.1   HINO, S. "Social stratification in a Swahili town." <u>Kyoto</u>
          <u>University African Studies</u>, 2, 1968, 51-74.
              Examines the different ethnic groups represented, the
          fusion of most into a "Swahili" community, and its rela-
          tionship to nonintegrated groups.

402.4.2   HINO, S. "The occupational differentiation of a Swahili
          town." <u>Kyoto University African Studies</u>, 2, 1968, 75-107.
              A detailed account of the occupations of both the
          Swahili and other groups, each occupation discussed in
          turn.

402.4.3   HINO, S. "Neighbourhood groups in African urban society:
          social relations and consciousness of Swahili people in
          Ujiji, a small town of Tanzania, East Africa." <u>Kyoto</u>
          <u>University African Studies</u>, 6, 1971, 1-30.
              Describes the social structure of the town, in terms
          of relationships at three spatial scales, emphasizing
          the significance of Islam for the community's value
          system.

Unpublished theses include:

402.4.4   BROWN, B.B.   Ujiji: the history of a lakeside town,
          1800-1914. Ph.D. thesis, Boston University, 1973.

<u>Morogoro</u> (Provincial town in the east. Population at 1967 census:
           25,000.)

East Africa

402.5.1 AGBATEKWE, A. and HUSSEIN, M. Master Plan for Morogoro, United Republic of Tanzania. Ministry of Lands, Housing and Urban Development, Dar es Salaam, 1974, 39 pp.
Surveys the existing town, estimates population growth and infrastructural needs for twenty years, and proposes the form that physical growth might take.

402.5.2 LUNDQVIST, J. The Economic Structure of Morogoro Town. Scandinavian Institute of African Studies, Uppsala, Sweden, 1973, 70 pp.
Analyzes the economic activities of the town, its economic relationships with the rest of Tanzania, and changes in its economic structure during the 1960s, largely based on a questionnaire survey of all the town's commercial and industrial firms.

Moshi (Provincial town in the north. Population at 1967 census: 27,000.)

402.6.1 SAMOFF, J. Tanzania: local politics and the structure of power. University of Wisconsin Press, Madison, 1974, 286 pp.
A study of politics in Kilimanjaro District, showing the critical role of the town of Moshi in the political life of the district, as well as examining issues specific to the town, including the operation of the town council.

See also 402.0.18, 402.0.35.

Mwanza (Provincial town in the northwest. Population at 1967 census: 35,000.)

The only substantial study is an unpublished thesis:

402.7.1 GREBLE, R.E. Urban Growth Problems of Mwanza Township, Tanzania: a study of tributary relationships. Ph.D. thesis, Boston University, 1971.

Tanga (Port in the northeast, second in size among the mainland towns. Population at 1967 census: 61,000.)

402.8 No substantial publications have been traced, but see 4.0.9.

Zanzibar (The only major town of the Zanzibar component of the United Republic of Tanzania. Population at 1967 census: 68,000.)

402.9.1 MARTIN, E.B. Zanzibar: tradition and revolution. Hamish

304

Hamilton, London, 1978, 149 pp.
Describes the character and recent history of Zanzibar
and Pemba Islands in general, but with frequent references
to Zanzibar Town.

402.9.2 NILSSON, S.A. et al. Zanzibar: present conditions and
future plans. University of Lund, Sweden, Department of
Architecture, n.d. [1970?], 87 pp.
Provides the results of an architectural and planning
survey of the town as a whole, with many maps and photographs, and presents detailed plans for the Miembeni area.

See also 4.0.9.

UGANDA

General

403.0.1 BAKWESEGHA, C.J. "Towards a modelling strategy of spatial
development for Uganda." Pan-African Journal, 8, 1975,
297-318.
Notes that development policies tend to be either
urban- or rural-based and argues for a combined approach
in Uganda with a planned hierarchy of large and small
central places.

403.0.2 DAK, O. A Geographical Analysis of the Distribution of
Migrants in Uganda. Department of Geography, Makerere
University, Kampala, 1968, 213 pp.
A detailed review based on the 1959 census, presented
mainly at the district level and covering both rural-
rural and rural-urban migration.

403.0.3 ELKAN, W. Migrants and Proletarians: urban labour in the
economic development of Uganda. Oxford University Press,
London, 1960, 149 pp.
A study of the labor force in several industrial enterprises in Kampala, Jinja, and Mbale, covering labor demand and supply, wages, industrial relations, and management. The distinction between a minority, who commuted
from surrounding farms to permanent jobs, and the majority,
who were short-term long-distance migrants, is emphasized.

403.0.4 FUNNELL, D.C. Service Centres in Teso. Department of
Geography, Makerere University, Kampala, 1972, 64 pp.
Examines data for thirty-five functional attributes of
forty-five towns and trading centers in Teso District and

considers them as a network of central places especially
for retail trade.

403.0.5   GRILLO, R.D. "Anthropology, industrial development and
           labour migration in Uganda." In Brokensha, D. and
           Pearsall, M. (eds.), The Anthropology of Development in
           Subsaharan Africa. University of Kentucky, Lexington,
           1969, 77-84.
               Relates 1965 studies of railway workers to Elkan's
           study, stressing the benefits of continued rural ties
           and doubting the need for total urban commitment.

403.0.6   HIRST, M.A. "The changing patterns of district administra-
           tive centres in Uganda since 1900." Geographical
           Analysis, 3, 1971, 90-98.
               Examines the evolving pattern of local administrative
           centers from 1900 to 1970, assessing its efficiency in
           spatial terms by means of statistical nearest-neighbour
           analysis.

403.0.7   HUTTON, C.R. "Unemployment in Kampala and Jinja, Uganda."
           Canadian Journal of African Studies, 3, 1969, 431-440.
               Discusses the extent of urban unemployment, showing
           that seasonality of rural occupations causes marked
           seasonality in its extent.

403.0.8   HUTTON, C.R. Reluctant Farmers? East African Publishing
           House, Nairobi, 1973, 331 pp.
               Chapters on unemployment in Kampala and Jinja, the
           unemployed as rural-urban migrants, and rates of labor
           migration provide a background for detailed studies of
           schemes to resettle the urban unemployed and new school-
           leavers on the land.

403.0.9   KANYEIHAMBA, G.W. "Urban planning law in East Africa with
           special reference to Uganda." Progress in Planning,
           2 (1), 1973, 1-85.
               A review of traditional, colonial and postcolonial
           land law and policies, procedures for government acquisi-
           tion of land for development, and urban planning agencies
           and processes, largely focused upon Uganda.

403.0.10   McMASTER, D.N. "The colonial district town in Uganda."
           In Beckinsale, R.P. and Houston, J.M. (eds.), Urbanization
           and its Problems. Blackwell, Oxford, 1968, 330-351.
               Examines selected towns in terms of situation, site,
           form, and functions, observing sufficient similarity to
           formulate a model, e.g., of twin foci provided by the
           "boma" and the "bazaar."

403.0.11   MUWONGE, J.W. "Functions and characteristics of trading

centres in Uganda." East African Geographical Review, 11, 1973, 52-64.
Examines sixty-four trading centers in the area around Kampala, noting their shanty form resulting partly from land-tenure arrangements, their flourishing retail trade, and their emergence as nodes in the rural economy.

403.0.12 ODONGO, J. and LEA, J.P. "Home ownership and rural-urban links in Uganda." Journal of Modern African Studies, 15, 1977, 59-73.
Presents the results of surveys in the Kisenyi area of Kampala and the Kengere area of Soroti on attitudes to owning homes in either urban or rural areas. These indicate an emerging preference for an urban home in the former case, but a continued priority for maintaining rural ties by house building in the latter case.

403.0.13 SAFIER, M. and LANGLANDS, B.W. (eds.) Perspectives on Urban Planning for Uganda. Department of Geography, Makerere University, Kampala, 1969, 238 pp.
Fourteen papers consider past and prospective urban planning, some concerned with administrative or economic aspects, others with sectors such as housing, industry and water supplies. The longest paper, by Langlands, provides a broad review of urban forms and functions in Uganda, which would form an appropriate starting point for any study of urbanization in Uganda.

402.0.14 SCAFF, A.H. "Urbanization and development in Uganda." Sociological Quarterly, 8, 1967, 111-121.
Outlines the growth and social structure of urban centers in Uganda and argues that in contrast to some situations elsewhere, increased urbanization is there making a positive contribution to development.

403.0.15 SPLANSKY, J.B. "Some geographic characteristics of permanent retail institutions in Ankole." East African Geographical Review, 7, 1969, 61-78.
Presents data, much in map form, on the pattern of retail establishments in Mbarara town, two much smaller towns, and 380 other central places, most of which were established only within the 1960s.

403.0.16 SSEMPEBWA, E.F. "The law and problems of urban housing finance in Uganda." In Kanyeihamba, G.W. and McAuslan, J.P.W.B. (eds.), Urban Legal Problems in Eastern Africa. Scandinavian Institute of African Studies, Uppsala, Sweden, 1978, 163-183.
Reviews the increasing demand for urban housing, inadequate and inappropriate government responses, the

particular land-tenure problems of Uganda, the problem
of financing public and private housing, and implications
for future government policy.

403.0.17 TRIBE, M.A. "Patterns of urban housing demand in Uganda."
East African Economics Review, 4, 1968, 35-50. Reprinted
in Hutton, J. (ed.), Urban Challenge in East Africa.
East African Publishing House, Nairobi, 1972, 138-156.
Shows that the key factors affecting demand for urban
housing are ability to pay the rents charged, household
size, and the location of the houses, and suggests that
patterns have changed little in recent years with few
yet seeking to own houses. Based on a survey of government employees in Kampala, Entebbe, and Mbale.

403.0.18 TRIBE, M.A. "Housing finance in Uganda." In Hutton, J.
(ed.), Urban Challenge in East Africa. East African
Publishing House, Nairobi, 1972, 116-137.
Notes the dual nature of the housing market, with
government providing high-cost housing for the elite,
but failing to cope with the housing problem for the
great majority, despite the creation of housing estates
in the 1950s and tenant-purchase schemes in the 1960s.

403.0.19 UGANDA. Uganda Census 1959: non-African population. East
African Statistical Department, Nairobi, 1960, 110 pp.
Provides much information on the predominantly urban
non-African population for 1959, with data for each town
pp. 73-80. The equivalent volume for the African population provides very little urban data.

403.0.20 UGANDA. Report on the 1969 Population Census. 3 vols.
Kampala, 1971-73.
Volume 1, Population of Administrative Areas, records
total numbers and sex and age structure for each town
and for wards within Kampala, Jinja, and Mbale. Volume
3, Additional Tables, records for each race data on sex,
age, nationality, birthplace, and education, for Kampala,
Jinja, and Mbale as well as the districts.

403.0.21 UGANDA. Third Five-Year Development Plan, 1971/2-1975/6.
Government Printer, Entebbe, 1972. Chap. 19, "Housing,"
355-366.
Mainly on urban housing, noting National Housing
Corporation activity in the second plan period and outlining policy for 1971-1976. Little specifically on
urban development elsewhere in the plan.

403.0.22 WITTHUHN, B.O. "An imposed urban structure: Uganda."
In El-Shakhs, S. and Obudho, R.A. (eds.), Urbanization,
National Development and Regional Planning in Africa.

Praeger, New York, 1974, 67-74.
Shows how the development of urban centers in Uganda
was initiated mainly by the British and from a study of
the spread of postal facilities suggests that the timing
of such infrastructural investment largely determined
the structure of the present urban hierarchy.

Two volumes on the formerly large and predominantly urban Asian
community are:

403.0.23 MORRIS, H.S. The Indians in Uganda. Weidenfeld and
Nicolson, London, 1968, 230 pp.

403.0.24 TWADDLE, M. (ed.) Expulsion of a Minority: essays on
Ugandan Asians. Athlone Press, London, 1975, 240 pp.

Works published before 1960 include:

403.0.25 KENDALL, H. Town Planning in Uganda. Crown Agents, London,
1955, 91 pp.

403.0.26 LARIMORE, A.E. The Alien Town: Patterns of Settlement in
Busoga, Uganda. Department of Geography, University of
Chicago, 1959, 208 pp.

Works in German include:

403.0.27 KADE, G. Die Stellung der zentralen Orte in der
Kulturlandschaftlichen Entwicklung Bugandas. J.W. Goethe
Universität, Frankfurt, 1969, 334 pp.

Unpublished theses include:

403.0.28 BAKWESEGHA, C.J. Modernization and National Integration in
Uganda. Ph.D. thesis, Rutgers University, New Brunswick,
N.J., 1973.

403.0.29 BROWNLEE, R.J. An Empirical Investigation of Spatial Labor
Mobility within a Developing Economy: Uganda. Ph.D.
thesis, Syracuse University, Syracuse, N.Y., 1973.

403.0.30 FUNNELL, D.C. Service Centres in Teso District, Uganda.
D.Phil. thesis, University of Sussex, U.K., 1974.

403.0.31 HUTTON, C.R. Unemployment and Labour Migration in Uganda.
Ph.D. thesis, University of East Africa (Makerere
College), 1968.

403.0.32 MUWONGE, J.W. The Spatial Distribution of Trading Centers
in Central Buganda. Ph.D. thesis, University of
California, Los Angeles, 1972.

403.0.33 ODONGO, J. Urban Migrant and Slum Housing Systems in the Third World: a Ugandan study. Ph.D. thesis, University of Sydney, 1979.

403.0.34 SPLANSKY, J.B. Emergent Urban Places in Africa: the case of Ankole, Uganda. Ph.D. thesis, University of California, Los Angeles, 1971.

403.0.35 WITTHUHN, B.O. The Spatial Integration of Uganda as a Process of Modernization. Ph.D. thesis, Pennsylvania State University, 1968.

Gulu (Chief provincial town of northern Uganda. Population at 1969 census: 20,000.)

403.1.1 OCITTI, J.P. The Urban Geography of Gulu. Department of Geography, Makerere University, Kampala, 1973, 227 pp.
     Surveys the origin, growth, demography, and functions of Gulu, delineates its hinterland, and examines in detail its morphology. Includes numerous maps of the town and of its sphere of influence.

Jinja (Second town of Uganda, notable as an industrial center. Population at 1969 census including suburbs: 100,000.)

403.2.1 BRANDT, H.; SCHUBERT, B.; and GERKEN, E. The Industrial Town as a Factor of Economic and Social Development: the Example of Jinja, Uganda. Weltforum, Munich, 1972, 451 pp.
     Three separate essays examine the effect of the town on the small-scale farming in its vicinity, the supply of staple foodstuffs to the town, and processes of social change both in the town and in the area around it.

403.2.2 HOYLE, B.S. "The economic expansion of Jinja, Uganda." Geographical Review, 53, 1963, 377–388.
     Discusses the industrial development that took place at Jinja in the decade following the opening of the Owen Falls Dam across the Nile in 1954.

403.2.3 HOYLE, B.S. "Industrial development at Jinja, Uganda." Geography, 52, 1967, 64–67.
     Discusses the factors encouraging industrial development at Jinja and examines the location of industries within the urban area.

403.2.4 UGANDA. Atlas of Uganda. Entebbe, 1962, 1967. Pp. 78–79, "Jinja."
     A map of the town at a scale of 1:10,000 and a brief descriptive text.

A notable earlier study is:

403.2.5   SOFER, C. and R. Jinja Transformed. East African Institute
          of Social Research, Kampala, 1955, 120 pp.

      See also 403.0.26.

Kampala   (Capital city. Population at 1969 census, including a large
          peri-urban zone: 330,000. 1975 estimate: 450,000.)

403.3.1   BAROT, R. "The Hindus of Bakuli." In Twaddle, M. (ed.),
          Expulsion of a Minority: essays on Ugandan Asians.
          Athlone Press, London, 1975, 70-80.
              Examines the nature of the Indian community in one
          neighborhood of the city, with special reference to the
          significance of folk categories and caste within this
          community.

403.3.2   CLINARD, M.B. and ABBOTT, D.J. Crime in Developing Countries:
          a comparative perspective. Wiley, New York, 1973, 319 pp.
              A volume presenting the results of 1968-1969 studies
          on crime in Kampala in the context of a wider discussion
          of crime in the cities of less developed countries.
          Specific topics covered include the characteristics of
          convicted offenders, the relationship of crime to migra-
          tion and to slum dwelling, and the role of the police in
          cities like Kampala.

403.3.3   GRILLO, R.D. African Railwaymen: solidarity and opposition
          in an East African labour force. Cambridge University
          Press, London, 1973, 215 pp.
              Shows how Kampala's railway workers form a distinct
          community within the city; explores their social rela-
          tionships, status and class structures, and social mobil-
          ity; and shows that they are so involved in both their
          specific industry framework and the social network of
          their rural homes that involvement in the city is limited.

403.3.4   GRILLO, R.D. "Ethnic identity and social stratification of
          a Kampala housing estate." In Cohen, A. (ed.), Urban
          Ethnicity. Tavistock, London, 1974, 159-185.
              Examines the importance of ethnic identity on the
          railway housing estate at Nsambya and discusses its re-
          lationships to social stratification.

403.3.5   GUTKIND, P.C.W. "Notes on the Kibuga of Buganda." Uganda
          Journal, 24, 1960, 29-43.
              An illustrated account of the settlement that formed
          the Buganda capital when the British arrived in the late
          nineteenth century.

*403.3.6   GUTKIND, P.C.W. "Accommodation and conflict in an African
            peri-urban area." Anthropologica NS, 4, 1962, 163-173.

403.3.7   GUTKIND, P.C.W. The Royal Capital of Buganda. Mouton,
            The Hague, 1963, 330 pp.
                A comprehensive study of the "traditional" part of
            Kampala, past and present, including its internal admin-
            istrative organization, its complex land-tenure pattern,
            recent efforts at urban improvement, and the evolution
            of relations between this area and the adjacent colonial
            city.

403.3.8   GUTKIND, P.C.W. "African urban marriage and family life:
            a note on some social and demographic characteristics
            from Kampala, Uganda." Bulletin de l'IFAN, B25, 1963,
            266-287.
                For a sample of wives, urban-resident and rural-
            resident, of men living in Kampala, marriage patterns
            and stability, numbers of children, etc., are investigated.

403.3.9   GUTKIND, P.C.W. "African urbanism, mobility and the social
            network." International Journal of Comparative Sociology,
            6, 1965, 48-60. Reprinted in Piddington, R. (ed.),
            Kinship and Geographical Mobility. Brill, Leiden,
            Netherlands, 1965. Also reprinted in Breese, G. (ed.),
            The City in Newly Developing Countries. Prentice-Hall,
            Englewood Cliffs, N.J., 1969, 389-400.
                Explores the social relationships of both Ganda and
            other Africans in Mulago neighborhood, stressing the
            distinction between kin-based and association-based
            social networks, and noting how these are shaped by
            patterns of rural-urban mobility.

403.3.10   HALPENNY, P. "Three styles of ethnic migration in Kisenyi,
            Kampala." In Parkin, D.J. (ed.), Town and Country in
            Central and Eastern Africa. Oxford University Press,
            London, 1975, 276-287.
                Discusses briefly the lifestyle of Asian/Arab and
            Kenya African minority groups and more fully that of
            immigrant Ganda, with an emphasis on the neglected role
            of independent women migrants.

*403.3.11   HIRST, M.A. "Essays on the social geography of Kampala."
            Geowest, 2. 1974, 1-72.

403.3.12   HIRST, M.A. "The distribution of migrants in Kampala."
            East African Geographical Review, 13, 1975, 37-55; and
            in Parkin, D.J. (ed.), Town and Country in Central and
            Eastern Africa. Oxford University Press, London, 1975,
            319-336.
                Quantitative analysis of birthplace data from the

1969 census shows some residential clustering of people from each area, but less than expected: factors other than origin have more influence on residential location.

403.3.13 JELLICOE, M. "Credit and housing associations among Luo immigrants in Kampala." In Hutton, J. (ed.), <u>Urban Challenge in East Africa</u>. East African Publishing House, Nairobi, 1972, 258-277.
  Shows how most Luo are members of voluntary associations linked to the Luo Union, which pay for transport of bodies for burial at home and for rural primary schools, and which provide credit for businesses and house-building in home areas, in Kisumu, and in Kampala. Suggests that such self-help efforts merit official support.

403.3.14 KAMPALA CITY COUNCIL. <u>Kampala</u>. University Press of Africa, Nairobi, 1970, 110 pp.
  A compendium of information on the city's amenities, industries, social services, etc.

403.3.15 KUPER, J. "The Goan community in Kampala." In Twaddle, M. (ed.), <u>Expulsion of a Minority: essays on Ugandan Asians</u>. Athlone Press, London, 1975, 53-69.
  Examines the nature of the Goan community in the city in the late 1960s, especially its distinctive features compared with other Asian groups and segmentation within the community itself.

403.3.16 MANDEVILLE, E. "The formality of marriage: a Kampala case study." <u>Journal of Anthropological Research</u>, 31, 1975, 183-195.
  Examines the contrasting circumstances, ideas, and marital roles of those whose marriages have been formalized and those who have not done this, within a predominantly Ganda peri-urban area of Kampala.

403.3.17 MANDEVILLE, E. "Poverty, work and the financing of single women in Kampala." <u>Africa</u>, 49, 1979, 42-52.
  Examines the financial position of female household heads in a peri-urban area, based on a 1968-1970 survey, and shows that they are badly off in comparison with married women, so that financial gain is not the reason for remaining unmarried.

403.3.18 MUKWAYA, A.B. "The marketing of staple foods in Kampala, Uganda." In Bohanan, P. and Dalton, G. (eds.), <u>Markets in Africa</u>. Northwestern University Press, Evanston, Ill., 1962, 643-666.
  A study of the areas of origin, means of transport, and trading organization for the supply of basic foods to the city in the early 1950s.

403.3.19   MULUMBA, S.S.   Underline: Urbanization in Developing Countries: a
           case study--Kampala.   MIT Press, Cambridge, Mass., 1974,
           122 pp.
               Analyzes land-use and house types in selected areas
           of Kampala, incorporating also data on demography, in-
           comes, etc.   Numerous maps and air photographs, providing
           a strong visual impression of the urban environment.

403.3.20   MUWONGE, J.W.   "Urban planning and the problem of uncontrolled
           settlements in Kampala."   In Kanyeihamba, G.W. and
           McAuslan, J.P.W.B. (eds.), Urban Legal Problems in
           Eastern Africa.   Scandinavian Institute of African
           Studies, Uppsala, Sweden, 1978, 148-162.
               Examines the nature and extent of colonial planning
           in Kampala, changed policies towards urban housing after
           independence, and the increasing amount of uncontrolled
           settlement.

403.3.21   OBBO, C.   "Women's careers in low income areas as indicators
           of country and town dynamics."   In Parkin, D.J. (ed.),
           Town and Country in Central and Eastern Africa.   Oxford
           University Press, London, 1975, 288-295.
               Shows that many women have migrated to self-employment
           in the Namuwongo and Wabigalo areas of Kampala and pro-
           vides a brief biography of one such woman.

403.3.22   O'CONNOR, A.M. and SEMUGOOMA, S.M.   The Peripheral Zone of
           Kampala.   Department of Geography, Makerere University,
           Kampala, 1968, 47 pp.
               Two essays, one attempting to define the urban limits
           of Kampala, which at that date bore no relation to ad-
           ministrative boundaries, the other providing an account
           of the origins and functions of the fringe settlement
           of Nateete.

403.3.23   PARKIN, D.J.   "Types of urban African marriage in Kampala."
           Africa, 36, 1966, 269-285.
               Analyzes the variety of marriage patterns in the east
           of Kampala, including degrees of permanence and the in-
           cidence of intertribal unions.

403.3.24   PARKIN, D.J.   "Urban voluntary associations as institutions
           of adaptation."   Man, 1, 1966, 90-95.
               Compares findings in Kampala with those of Banton in
           Freetown, suggesting that migrants from centralized
           tribes need associations less than others.

403.3.25   PARKIN, D.J.   Neighbours and Nationals in an African City
           Ward.   Routledge and Kegan Paul, London, 1969, 228 pp.
               Based on intensive fieldwork in Nakawa and Naguru
           municipal housing estates in 1962-1964, this study

analyzes ways in which tribal ties are maintained. The focus is on Luo and Luhya people from western Kenya living alongside people of diverse Ugandan ethnic groups.

403.3.26 PARKIN, D.J. "Tribe as fact and fiction in an East African city." In Gulliver, P.H. (ed.), Tradition and Transition in East Africa. Routledge and Kegan Paul, London, 1969, 273-296.
Examines the significance of tribal identity in social life and in economic and political organization. Status is slowly displacing tribe as a factor, e.g., in residential clustering, but anti-Kenyan feeling became important after independence.

403.3.27 PARKIN, D.J. "Language choice in two Kampala housing estates." In Whiteley, W.H. (ed.), Language Use and Social Change. Oxford University Press, London, 1971, 347-363.
Discusses the language problem on Nakawa and Naguru estates, especially for Kenyans who could use their own languages, Luganda, Swahili, or English.

403.3.28 RIGBY, P. "Ritual values and social stratification in Kampala, Uganda." In Arens, W. (ed.), A Century of Change in Eastern Africa. Mouton, The Hague, 1976, 115-127.
Discusses the relationship between the status of prophets or diviners in traditional religion, and their socioeconomic status in present-day Kampala, in the context of a review of the concept of social stratification in Africa.

403.3.29 RIGBY, P. and LULE, F.D. "Continuity and change in Kiganda religion in urban and peri-urban Kampala." In Parkin, D.J. (ed.), Town and Country in Central and Eastern Africa. Oxford University Press, London, 1975, 213-227.
Suggests that traditional religion has been largely ignored in African urban studies; yet in Kampala the consultation and propitiation of spirits is widespread, urbanization perhaps increasing its intensity as people face new problems.

403.3.30 SCAFF, A.H. "Urbanization and the labour force." In Beling, W.A. (ed.), The Role of Labor in African Nation Building. Praeger, New York, 1968, 73-94.
Presents the results of a 1964 socioeconomic survey of the Kisenyi neighborhood and compares them with those reported for 1954 by Southall and Gutkind, as a case study in African urbanization.

403.3.31 SOLZBACHER, R.M. "East Africa's slum problem: a question of definition." In Gugler, J. (ed.), Urban Growth in

Subsaharan Africa. Makerere University, Kampala, 1970, 45-52.

Summarizes a study of housing quality and social organization in the Kibuli area, suggesting that the slum problem may be wrongly conceived and that improvement may be preferable to re-housing.

403.3.32 SOUTHALL, A.W. "Kinship, friendship and the network of relations in Kisenyi, Kampala." In Southall, A.W. (ed.), Social Change in Modern Africa. Oxford University Press, London, 1961, 217-229.

Presents the results of a sociological study in 1953-1955 in an area of dense settlement, then just outside the city boundary.

403.3.33 SOUTHALL, A. "The concept of elites and their formation in Uganda." In Lloyd, P.C. (ed.), The New Elites of Tropical Africa. Oxford University Press, London, 1966, 342-366.

Within a broad discussion of the concept of elites, the significance of the coexistence of distinct tribal groups for elite formation in Kampala is examined.

403.3.34 SOUTHALL, A.W. "Kampala-Mengo." In Miner, H. (ed.), The City in Modern Africa. Praeger, New York; Pall Mall, London, 1967, 297-332.

A concise account of the precolonial origin of Mengo and later growth of the adjacent colonial city of Kampala, which overwhelmed it. Stresses ethnic separation between races and also between Ganda and other Africans.

403.3.35 SOUTHALL, A.W. "Urban migration and the residence of children in Kampala." In Mangin, W. (ed.), Peasants in Cities. Houghton Mifflin, Boston, 1970, 150-159.

Shows that in Kampala the poorest tend to have rather fewer children than the more affluent and to have them living in town to a far lesser extent. Thus a disproportionate number of town children are from the richer homes, with higher expectations.

403.3.36 TEMPLE, P.H. "Nakasero market, Kampala." Uganda Journal, 28, 1964, 165-178.

Presents the results of a detailed survey of the city's central market, African-controlled but with a largely non-African clientele.

403.3.37 TEMPLE, P.H. "The growth of Kampala: an historical-geographical review." In Berger, H. (ed.), Ostafrikanische Studien. Friedrich-Alexander-Universität, Nuremberg, 1968, 75-92.

Brief account of the city's origins and physical growth, with several maps and photographs.

403.3.38 TEMPLE, P.H. "The urban markets of greater Kampala."
Tijdschrift voor Economische en Sociale Geografie, 60,
1969, 346-359.
Surveys the distribution, size range, hierarchical
structure, and trading specialties of Kampala's many
markets, the complex network being closely related to
the spatial structure of the city as a whole.

403.3.39 THOMPSON, R.W. "Rural-urban differences in individual
modernization in Buganda." Urban Anthropology, 3, 1974,
64-78.
A survey in Kampala, a small trading center, and a
rural area suggests that rural dwellers express "modern"
values more often than urbanites, perhaps due to feelings
of insecurity and frustration in the city.

403.3.40 THOMPSON, R.W. "Fertility aspirations and modernization in
urban Uganda: a case of resilient cultural values."
Urban Anthropology, 7, 1978, 155-170.
Reports on a survey of urban and rural Baganda showing
that preferred number of children is yet little affected
by urban living or by other changes indicative of
"modernity."

403.3.41 UGANDA. Atlas of Uganda. Entebbe, 1962, 1967. Pp. 76-77,
"Kampala."
A map of central Kampala at a scale of 1:10,000 and
a brief descriptive text.

Notable studies published before 1960 include:

403.3.42 MUNGER, E.S. Relational Patterns of Kampala, Uganda.
Department of Geography, University of Chicago, 1951,
165 pp.

403.3.43 SOUTHALL, A.W. and GUTKIND, P.C.W. Townsmen in the Making:
Kampala and its Suburbs. East African Institute of
Social Research, Kampala, 1957, 248 pp.

Works in German include:

403.3.44 VORLAUFER, K. Physiognomie, Struktur und Funktion Gross-
Kampalas. J.W. Goethe Universität, Frankfurt, 1967,
556 pp. and map vol. This is the most comprehensive
geographical study of the city.

Unpublished theses include:

403.3.45 ABBOTT, D.J. Crime and Development in an African City.
Ph.D. thesis, University of Wisconsin, 1972.

403.3.46 FUSCH, R.D. Cultural Tradition and Innovation in the Urban
         Landscape of Kampala. Ph.D. thesis, University of Oregon,
         1972.

403.3.47 KIBUKA, E.P. Sociological Aspects of Juvenile Delinquency
         in Kampala from 1962 to 1969. Ph.D. thesis, University
         of East Africa, 1972.

403.3.48 KUPER, J.S. The Goan Community in Kampala, Uganda. Ph.D.
         thesis, University of London, 1973.

403.3.49 LUBEGA, A. The Financing and Production of Private Houses
         in an Urban District of Kampala. Ph.D. thesis, University
         of London, 1969.

403.3.50 MANDEVILLE, E. Failure and Conformity in an African City.
         D. Phil. thesis, University of Sussex, U.K., 1974.

403.3.51 MUENCH, L.H. The Private Burden of Urban Social Overhead:
         a study of the informal housing market of Kampala, Uganda.
         Ph.D. thesis, University of Pennsylvania, 1978.

         See also 4.0.6, 4.0.7, 4.0.25.

Lira (District headquarters. Population at 1969 census: 7,000.)

403.4.1 DAHLBERG, F.M. "The provincial town (Lira)." Urban
         Anthropology, 3, 1974, 171-183.
             The small provincial town as a distinctive worldwide
         type of urban society is analyzed, using Lira as an
         illustration. The existence of separate Langi, other
         African, and non-African social subsystems is noted.

403.4.2 DAHLBERG, F.M. "The Asian community, with special reference
         to Lira (Uganda)." Sociologus, 26, 1976, 29-42.
             Discusses the historical process of Asian settlement
         in Lira, continuing ties with India, links with other
         Uganda Asians, and Asian community life within the town.

Unpublished thesis:

403.4.3 DAHLBERG, F.M. A plural community: Lira, Uganda. Ph.D.
         thesis, Cornell University, Ithaca, New York, 1970.

Mbale (Eastern regional center. Population at 1969 census: 24,000.)

403.5.1 HANNA, W.J. and HANNA, J.L. "The political structure of
         urban-centered African communities." In Miner, H. (ed.),
         The City in Modern Africa. Praeger, New York; Pall Mall,

London, 1965, 151-184.
Describes the political structures of Mbale and of Umuahia in Nigeria, emphasizing ethnic differentiation, ineffectiveness of local administrative authorities, and importance instead of influential individuals.

403.5.2 HANNA, W.J. and HANNA, J.L. "Influence and influentials in two urban-centred African communities." Comparative Politics, 2, 1969, 17-39.
Develops the third theme from the paper noted above.

403.5.3 HANNA, W.J. and HANNA, J.L. "Polyethnicity and political integration in Umuahia and Mbale." In Daland, R.T. (ed.), Comparative Urban Research. Sage, Beverly Hills, Calif., 1969, 163-202.
On the basis of surveys of relationships among ethnic groups, the extent and nature of social and political integration in the two towns is examined.

403.5.4 JACOBSON, D. "Friendship and mobility in the development of an elite African social system." Southwestern Journal of Anthropology, 24, 1968, 123-138. Reprinted in Gugler, J. (ed.), Urban Growth in Subsaharan Africa. Makerere University, Kampala, 1970, 52-59.
Examines friendship interaction as part of the social organization of the elite in Mbale, noting that it is much influenced by their position as migrants and by the high degree of interurban mobility.

403.5.5 JACOBSON, D. "Culture and stratification among urban Africans." Journal of Asian and African Studies, 5, 1970, 176-183.
Analyzes the values, beliefs, and expectations of friendship among the elite of Mbale, to shed light on the emergence of class structures in African towns.

403.5.6 JACOBSON, D. Itinerant Townsmen: friendship and social order in urban Uganda. Cummings, Menlo Park, California, 1973, 150 pp.
Provides a background account of the history and geography of Mbale and discusses its social structure, before presenting the results of intensive 1965-1966 fieldwork on patterns of friendship and how these influence the ordering of this urban society.

403.5.7 TWADDLE, M. "The founding of Mbale." Uganda Journal, 30, 1966, 25-38.
Argues that while Mbale town dates only from 1902, its origins depended as much on African as on European initiatives.

South-Central Africa

5.0.1 BARBER, W.J. "Urbanisation and economic growth: the cases of two white settler territories." In Miner, H. (ed.), The City in Modern Africa. Praeger, New York; Pall Mall, London, 1967, 91-125.
Examines the nature of urban development in relation to the dual economies of Zambia and Zimbabwe, suggesting that it may be both generative within the European-controlled sector and parasitic in terms of the indigenous economy, and that massive urban growth may reflect failure in rural development.

5.0.2 DOTSON, F. and DOTSON, L.O. The Indian Minority of Zambia, Rhodesia and Malawi. Yale University Press, New Haven, 1968, 444 pp.
Various chapters examine the arrival, economic role, religious beliefs, social organization, and political relationships of this group, which is overwhelmingly concentrated in the towns of these countries.

5.0.3 FEDERATION OF RHODESIA AND NYASALAND. Census of Population 1956. Central Statistical Office, Salisbury, 1960, 167 pp.
Covered the non-African population and African employees, giving the numbers of these for all towns in 1951 and 1956, and employees by industry for the main towns in 1956.

5.0.4 FEDERATION OF RHODESIA AND NYASALAND. Preliminary Results of the 1961 Federal Censuses of Population and of Employees. 3 vols. Central Statistical Office, Salisbury, 1962.
Provides detailed data on the distribution of non-Africans in 1956 and 1961 and data on employees by race and industry for each town in 1961.

5.0.5 MADU, O.V.A. "Problems of urbanization in Central Africa." Présence Africaine, 86, 1973, 20-37.

321

A broad outline of some social aspects of urbanization in Malawi and Zambia and of the relationships between towns and rural societies.

5.0.6   NORWOOD, H.C. "Informal industry in developing countries." Town Planning Review, 46, 1975, 83–94.
With reference mainly to Zambia and Zimbabwe, the paper examines the nature of small-scale industry, its relationships with the large-scale or "formal" sector, its potential, and appropriate planning responses.

See also 0.2.26, 4.0.20.

ANGOLA

General

501.0.1   AMARAL, I. do. "Note sur l'evolution de la population urbaine d'Angola." In CNRS, La Croissance Urbaine en Afrique Noire et à Madagascar. Paris, 1972, 247–253.
Describes the growth of the urban population from 1940 to 1960, especially in Luanda, and discusses some of the problems arising.

Publications in Portuguese include:

501.0.2   ALBUQUERQUE e CASTRO, E.G. de. Angola: portos e transportes. Obra Politica-Economica de Consulta e Divulgaçao. Luanda, 1974.

501.0.3   AMARAL, I. do. Ensaio de um Estudo Geografico da Rede Urbana de Angola. Junta de Investigações do Ultramar, Lisboa, 1962, 99 pp.

501.0.4   AMARAL, I. do. "Contribuição para o conhecimento do fenómeno de urbanização em Angola." Finisterra, 13, 1978, 43–76.

501.0.5   ANGOLA. Recenseamento Geral da População, 1960. 4 vols. Luanda, 1964.

501.0.6   SOARES, A.C. "Introdução a um estudo do urbanismo em Angola: bairros indigenas nos centros urbanos." Estudos Ultramarinos, 1, 1960, 119–155.

Huambo (Chief inland town. Population at 1970 census: 62,000.
        Former name: Nova Lisboa.)

501.1   No publications have been found, even in Portuguese.

Lobito (Third town of the country and major port. Population at
        1970 census: 60,000.)

Nothing substantial appears to have been published since:

501.2.1 HANCE, W.A. and VAN DONGEN, I.S. "The port of Lobito and
            the Benguela railway." Geographical Review, 46, 1956,
            460-487.

Luanda (Capital city. Population at 1970 census: 475,000.)

*501.3.1 BOXER, C.R. Portuguese Society in the Tropics: the
            municipal councils of Goa, Macao, Bahia and Luanda.
            University of Wisconsin Press, Milwaukee, 1965, 240 pp.

501.3.2 DAVEAU, S. "La croissance et les caractères de la ville de
            Luanda." Cahiers d'Outre-Mer, 22, 1969, 430-435.
            Outlines the growth and structure of the city, summar-
            izing the 1968 study by I. do Amaral, noted below.

501.3.3 JOHNSON, L.L. "Bibliography of Luanda, Angola. African
            Urban Notes, 5 (4), 1970, 90-100.
            An alphabetical listing, mainly of items in Portuguese.

501.3.4 MONTEIRO, R.L. "From extended to residual family: aspects
            of social change in the musseques of Luanda." In
            Heimer, F. (ed.), Social Change in Angola. Weltforum,
            Munich, 1973, 211-234.
            An analysis of changing family structures, including
            rules of descent, inheritance, etc., in spontaneous
            settlements that are becoming the eastern suburbs of
            Luanda.

501.3.5 SAMPAIO, M. "Luanda." Revue Française d'Etudes Politiques
            Africaines, 69, 1971, 62-75.
            Largely a historical account, tracing the city's
            growth from sixteenth-century origins to the 1960s.

501.3.6 VAN DONGEN, I.S. "The port of Luanda in the economy of Angola."
            Boletim da Sociedade de Geografia de Lisboa, 78, 1960, 3-43.
            Mainly on the development, facilities, and traffic of
            the port and on transport links with its hinterland, but
            with a brief discussion of the growth of the city.

Publications in Portuguese include:

501.3.7 AMARAL, I. do. Luanda: estudo de geografia urbana. Junta de Investigações do Ultramar, Lisboa, 1968, 152 pp.

501.3.8 AMARAL, I. do. "A 'baixa' de Luanda, como area de centralização de actividades economicas." Jornadas de Engenharia e Arquitectura do Ultramar, 2, 1969, 257-267.

501.3.9 AMARAL, I. do. "Nota sobre a evolução da população de Luanda e dos sus 'innuceques'." Jornadas de Engenharia e Arquitectura do Ultramar, 2, 1969, 269-285.

501.3.10 BETTENCOURT, J. de S. "Subsidio para o estudo sociologico da população de Luanda." Boletim do Instituto de Investigação Cientifica de Angola, 2 (1), 1965, 83-130.

501.3.11 MONTEIRO, R.L. A Família nos Musseques de Luanda. Junta de Acção Social no Trabalho de Angola, Luanda, 1973, 492 pp; and in Trabalho, 36-40, 1971-1972 (5 issues).

501.3.12 OLIVEIRA, M.A.F. de. "Aspectos sociais de Luanda, inferidos dos anuncios publicados na sua imprensa." Boletim do Instituto de Angola, 17, 1963, 99-110.

501.3.13 SANTOS, A. de S. "Quitandas e quitandeiras de Luanda." Boletim do Instituto de Investigação Cientifica de Angola, 4 (2), 1967, 89-112.

501.3.14 SANTOS, J. de A. Luanda d'Outros Tempos. Centro de Informação e Turismo de Angola, Luanda, 1965, 150 pp.

501.3.15 VALENTE, A. and OLIVEIRA, J.C.F. "Alguns aspectos socio-economicos da Ilha do Cabo (Luanda)." Boletim do Instituto de Investigação Cientifica de Angola, 3 (2), 1966, 261-286.

Unpublished theses include:

501.3.16 JOHNSON, L.L. Luanda: development of internal forms and functional patterns. Ph.D. thesis, University of California, Los Angeles, 1970.

Lubango (Provincial town in the south. Population at 1970 census: 32,000. Former name: Sa da Bandeira.)

*501.4.1 GUICHONNET, P. "Sa da Bandeira: une ville portugaise du haut-plateau d'Angola." In Mélanges Offerts à C.P. Terrier, Université de Genève, 1968, 105-128.

Publications in Portuguese include:

501.4.2   VALENTE, A.   "O problema habitacional e suas implicações em
          Sa da Bandeira (Angola)." Trabalho, 7, 1964, 72-121; 8,
          1964, 85-120.

                              MALAWI

General

502.0.1   AGNEW, S. and STUBBS, M. (eds.) Malawi in Maps. University
          of London Press, 1972, pp. 110-129.
               Maps and accompanying text depicting the development
          of the urban system, urban services, urban spatial struc-
          ture, Blantyre, Zomba, Lilongwe, and the capital city
          plan.

502.0.2   HUMPHREY, D.H. and OXLEY, H.S. "Expenditure and household-
          size elasticities in Malawi: urban-rural comparisons."
          Journal of Development Studies, 12, 1976, 252-269.
               Presents the results of a 1968 survey showing that as
          urban incomes rise the proportion of income spent of food,
          fuel, and clothing falls, while that spent on housing
          rises.

502.0.3   MALAWI. 1967 Housing-Income Survey for Major Urban Areas.
          Department of Census and Statistics, Zomba, n.d.
               Presents a fifteen-page summary and then full tabulated
          results of a detailed survey of housing conditions, em-
          ployment, and income in Blantyre, Zomba, Lilongwe, and
          Mzuzu, with supplementary tables covering birthplace,
          length of residence in town, etc.

502.0.4   MALAWI. Population Census 1966. Zomba, 1969.
               Includes data on age and sex structure, race, and
          educational level for the population of each town.

502.0.5   MTHAWANJI, R. "Urbanisation in Malawi." In Oliver, P. (ed.),
          Shelter in Africa. Barrie & Jenkins, London, 1971,
          190-199.
               Contrasts economic organization, social structure, and
          housing types in rural and urban areas, and considers
          ways to avoid excessive divergence between them.

502.0.6   PACHAI, B. "The story of Malawi's capitals old and new,
          1891-1969." Society of Malawi Journal, 24 (1), 1971,
          35-56.

Discusses the adoption of Zomba as the first capital, the repeated debates about a shift to Blantyre, and the 1965 decision to move the capital to Lilongwe.

502.0.7 PIKE, J.G. and RIMMINGTON, G.T. Malawi: a geographical study. Oxford University Press, London, 1965. Chap. 9 "Urban Settlement," 167-172.
Describes the origin, growth, and present form of Blantyre, refers briefly to Zomba and Lilongwe, and notes the nature of the very limited amount of urban development elsewhere, with a map of Dedza as a typical minor township.

Blantyre (Chief city. Population at 1977 census, including adjacent Limbe: 226,000.)

502.1.1 BETTISON, D.G. "Changes in the composition and status of kin groups in Nyasaland and Northern Rhodesia." In Southall, A.W. (ed.), Social Change in Modern Africa. Oxford University Press, London, 1961, 273-285.
Demonstrates the persistence of traditional kin and village organization in the settlements adjacent to Blantyre, compared with the changes around Lusaka, where most peri-urban settlement is new.

502.1.2 BETTISON, D.G. and APTHORPE, R.J. "Authority and residence in a peri-urban social structure--Ndirande." Nyasaland Journal, 14, 1961, 7-39.
Examines the system of village headmanship in this settlement on the fringe of Blantyre and its effects on the integration of new settlers.

502.1.3 BETTISON, D.G. and RIGBY, P.J. Patterns of Income and Expenditure, Blantyre-Limbe. Rhodes-Livingstone Institute, Lusaka, 1961, 153 pp.
Presents results from 1957-1958 household surveys in both the urban area proper and peri-urban areas.

502.1.4 BROWN, C.P. "Marketing of food crops in Blantyre, Malawi." African Social Research, 12, 1971, 111-128.
Presents results from a 1969-1970 survey of 1400 market sellers in and around Blantyre, covering crops sold, average income, distance travelled, and seasonal variations. Most produce moves directly from farmers to retailers, with few middlemen.

502.1.5 CHILIVUMBO, A.B. "The ecology of social types in Blantyre." In Parkin, D.J. (ed.), Town and Country in Central and Eastern Africa. Oxford University Press, London, 1975, 308-318.
Distinguishes four types of residential area, notes

the population characteristics of each, and considers relationships among them.

502.1.6   MALAWI. Blantyre City Population Sample Census 1972. Government Printer, Zomba, 1974, 117 pp.
           Provides details of the demographic structure, educational levels, and occupations of the population and data on house ownership, quality, etc. Includes some data for small subdivisions of the city.

502.1.7   NORWOOD, H.C. "Ndirande: a squatter colony in Malawi." Town Planning Review, 43, 1972, 135-150.
           Describes the main squatter settlement on the edge of Blantyre and discusses official policies towards it.

502.1.8   UNIVERSITY PRESS OF AFRICA. Welcome to Blantyre: A Handbook to Blantyre and Limbe. University Press of Africa, Nairobi, 1969, 109 pp.
           Compendium of information on the city's history, amenities, industries, etc.

Slightly earlier studies include:

502.1.9   BETTISON, D.G. The Demographic Structure of Seventeen Villages in the Peri-urban Area of Blantyre-Limbe, Nyasaland. Rhodes-Livingstone Institute, Lusaka, 1958, 93 pp.

502.1.10   BETTISON, D.G. The Social and Economic Structure of Seventeen Peri-Urban Villages, Blantyre-Limbe, Nyasaland. Rhodes-Livingstone Institute, Lusaka, 1958, 95 pp.

502.1.11   NYIRENDA, A.A.; NGWANE, H.D.; and BETTISON, D.G. Further Economic and Social Studies, Blantyre-Limbe, Nyasaland. Rhodes-Livingstone Institute, Lusaka, 1959, 49 pp.

Lilongwe   (Former Central Province headquarters, now being developed as the national capital. Population at 1977 census: 103,000.)

502.2.1   COLE-KING, P.A. Lilongwe: a historical study. Department of Antiquities, Zomba, 1971, 53 pp.
           Examines briefly the prehistory of the Lilongwe area and, more fully, its nineteenth-century history and the growth of the town from its 1902 origin up to the 1940s.

502.2.2   CONNELL, J. "Lilongwe: another new capital for Africa." East African Geographical Review, 10, 1972, 89-93.
           Brief and somewhat skeptical account of the decision to establish a new capital, of its proposed form, and of its economic prospects.

*502.2.3 GERKE, W.J.C. and VILJOEN, C.J. Master Plan for Lilongwe, the Capital City of Malawi. Purnell, Johannesburg, 1968.

502.2.4 LAVRIJSEN, J. and STERKENBURG, J.J. The Food Supply of Lilongwe, Malawi. Geografisch Instituut, Utrecht, Netherlands, 1976, 71 pp.
    Examines the demand for food, the marketing structure, and the pattern of supply sources prior to the main period of growth as capital city, largely based on an extensive survey of traders.

502.2.5 MALAWI. The Establishment of a New Capital. Government Printer, Zomba, 1965, 12 pp.
    Reviews the reasons for moving the capital from Zomba to Lilongwe, the costs involved, and the anticipated developmental consequences.

502.2.6 LMIA, J.N. "Malawi's new capital city: a regional planning perspective." Pan-African Journal, 7, 1975, 387-401.
    Examines the background to the decision to develop Lilongwe as a new national capital, especially in terms of the need to correct regional imbalances in economic and social development.

502.2.7 RICHARDS, G. From Vision to Reality: the Story of Malawi's New Capital. Lorton, Johannesburg, 1974, 63 pp.
    A well-illustrated booklet publicizing the new capital, providing some information on the plans and the early stages of implementation.

MOZAMBIQUE

General

503.0.1 GUEDES, A. d'A. "The caniços of Mozambique." In Oliver,
         P. (ed.), Shelter in Africa. Barrie & Jenkins, London,
         1971, 200-209.
              Describes the spontaneous settlements found on the
         fringes of Mozambique towns, stressing that many houses
         are well built and that the quality of life is superior
         to that in many squatter settlements elsewhere. Numerous
         illustrations are provided.

Publications in Portuguese include:

503.0.2 MOCAMBIQUE. IV Recenseamento Geral da População 1970. 10
         vols. Instituto Nacional de Estatistica, Lourenco
         Marques, 1973.

503.0.3 OLIVEIRA, M. de. Problemas Essenciais do Urbanismo no
         Ultramar: estruturas urbanos de integração e convivencia.
         Agencial Geral do Ultramar, Lisboa, 1962, 58 pp.

Beira (Second city and important port. Population at 1970 census:
       114,000.)

No study in English has been produced since:

503.1.1 HANCE, W.A. and VAN DONGEN, I.S. "Beira, Mozambique gateway
         to Central Africa." Annals of the Association of
         American Geographers, 47, 1957, 307-355.

Publications in Portuguese include:

503.1.2 AMARAL, I. do. "Beira, cidade e porto do indico."
         Finisterra, 4 (7), 1969, 76-93.

502.1.3 RODRIGUES, R. "A cidade da Beira." Geographica, 4 (14),
         1968, 76-95.

Maputo (Capital city, formerly named Lourenco Marques. Population
        at 1970 census: 348,000.)

503.2.1 DE BLIJ, H.J. "The functional structure and Central Business
         District of Lourenco Marques, Mozambique." Economic
         Geography, 38, 1962, 56-77.
              A brief outline of the evolution and functions of the
         city, followed by a detailed study of the spatial struc-
         ture of its central business district.

503.2.2   DELEMOS, V. "Lourenco Marques." Revue Française d'Etudes
           Politiques Africaines, 81, 1972, 58–91.
               A full account of the city's origins and growth, its
           demography and social structure, its economy, and its
           role in political affairs up to 1972.

503.2.3   MITCHELL, H.F. Aspects of Urbanisation and Age Structure
           in Lourenco Marques, 1957. Institute for African Studies,
           University of Zambia, Lusaka, 1975, 49 pp.
               Outlines the growth and physical form of the city and
           reports on a 1957 survey of its African population con-
           cerned with demographic structure, duration of residence,
           and extent of stabilization.

503.2.4   SILVA, C.A.V. da (ed.) The City of Lourenco Marques Guide.
           2nd ed. Tipografia Academica, Lourenco Marques, 1964,
           216 pp.
               A profusely illustrated account of the city's history,
           administration, and amenities.

An earlier publication was:

503.2.5   HANCE, W.A. and VAN DONGEN, I.S. "Lourenco Marques in
           Delagoa Bay." Economic Geography, 33, 1957, 238–256.

Publications in Portuguese include:

503.2.6   AZEVEDO, M. de. "O plano director de urbanização de
           Lourenço Marques." Urbanizacao, 5, 1970, 239–314.

503.2.7   LOBATO, A. Lourenço Marques, Xilonguíne: biografia da
           cidade. Agência-Geral do Ultramar, Lisboa, 1970, 309 pp.

503.2.8   MENDES, M.C. Variação Espacial da Densidade de População
           Urbana em Lourenço Marques. Centro de Estudos Geográficos,
           Universidades de Lisboa, 1976, 93 pp.

503.2.9   PACHECO, A. "Lourenço Marques na ultima decada do seculo
           XIX." Boletim da Sociedade de Estudos de Moçambique,
           31, 1962, 7–58.

503.2.10   PINHEIRO, V. and NORTON, M.A. "Evolução demographica de
           Lourenço Marques: contribuicao para o estudo da sua
           urbanização." Centro de Estudos Demograficos, Revista,
           17, 1966, 43–78.

ZAMBIA

General

504.0.1 DANIEL, P. <u>Africanisation, Nationalisation and Inequality:
mining labour and the Copperbelt in Zambian development</u>.
Cambridge University Press, 1979, 202 pp.
Primarily a study of changing labor supply and demand
in the copper mining industry, rather than of urbanization; but all is relevant to the Zambian urban situation,
while chapter 2 examines the general employment situation
in the Copperbelt towns.

504.0.2 DAVIES, D.H. (ed.) <u>Zambia in Maps</u>. University of London
Press, 1971, pp. 80-89.
Maps and brief accompanying texts on the distribution
of towns; the towns of the Copperbelt; the site and
morphology of Lusaka; and Kabwe, Kafue, and Livingstone.

504.0.3 DUFF, C.E. (ed.) <u>First Report on a Regional Survey of the
Copperbelt</u>. Government Printer, Lusaka, 1960, 133 pp.
Surveys existing conditions and future needs with regard to mining, industry, power, transport, water supplies,
etc. Includes notes on economic prospects and housing
needs in each Copperbelt town.

504.0.4 GARDINER, J. <u>Some Aspects of the Establishment of Towns in
Zambia during the 1920s and 1930s</u>. Institute for Social
Research, University of Zambia, Lusaka, 1970, 33 pp.
Examines processes of public administration and physical planning with respect to urban growth in this period,
dealing individually with Ndola, Luanshya, and Kitwe,
and referring more briefly to other towns.

504.0.5 HARRIES-JONES, P. "The tribes in towns." In Brelsford,
W.V. (ed.), <u>The Tribes of Zambia</u>. 2nd ed. Government
Printer, Lusaka, 1966, 124-146.
Examines the origins of the urban labor force up to
the 1960s and discusses the decline of tribal institutions
and the extent of intertribal marriage.

504.0.6 HEISLER, H. "The creation of a stabilized urban society."
<u>African Affairs</u>, 70, 1971, 125-145.
Examines the influx of population to the towns in the
1930s and 1940s and the factors encouraging people to
settle permanently from that period onwards.

504.0.7 HEISLER, H. "The enclave society and nation-building in
Zambia." In INCIDI, <u>Urban Agglomerations in the States
of the Third World</u>. Brussels, 1971, 412-435.

Contrasts Zambian urban society with traditional and
commercialized rural communities, examines factors favoring more permanent residence in town, and stresses the
consequent need for efforts to integrate town and country
as parts of one nation.

504.0.8   HEISLER, H. "The pattern of migration in Zambia." Cahiers
          d'Etudes Africaines, 13, 1973, 193-212.
             Shows that rural-urban migration in Zambia has become
          longer-term and now involves women to as great an extent
          as men and discusses various factors affecting the chang-
          ing character of Zambian migration.

504.0.9   HEISLER, H. Urbanisation and the Government of Migration.
          Hurst, London, 1974, 166 pp.
             A study of the migration processes that have created
          the urban centers of Zambia, with special reference to
          policies of government and employers. Examines rural
          pressures for movement to town and government fears of
          overurbanization up to the 1940s. Analyzes the early
          recruited labor system and the later free flow of labor
          and also the increased movement of women from the 1950s.
          Investigates the transition from mere labor camps to
          authentic African towns, with a permanently settled
          population.

504.0.10 JACKMAN, M.E. Recent Population Movements in Zambia: some
          aspects of the 1969 census. Institute of African Studies,
          University of Zambia, Lusaka, 1973, 66 pp.
             Examines the changes in population distribution be-
          tween the 1963 and 1969 censuses, emphasizing the extent
          of rural-urban movement and consequent rapid increase of
          urban population.

504.0.11 KAY, G. "The towns of Zambia." In Steel, R.W. and Lawton,
          R. (eds.), Liverpool Essays in Geography. Longmans,
          London, 1967, 347-361.
             Reviews the growth, functions, and present form of
          Zambian towns, emphasizing their colonial origins, their
          concentration along the "line of rail," and the continu-
          ing influence of Europeans on their character.

504.0.12 MAIMBO, F.J.M. and FRY, J. "An investigation into the
          change in the terms of trade between the rural and urban
          sectors of Zambia." African Social Research, 12, 1971,
          95-110.
             Shows how government fixing of agricultural prices
          increases the attraction of urban employment and how
          new prices and incomes policies, urban and rural, could
          be beneficial.

504.0.13 MARTIN, R. Self-Help in Action: a study of site-and-
          service schemes in Zambia. National Housing Authority,
          Lusaka, 1975, 168 pp.
              Reports in detail on a survey of the building pro-
          cesses, housing conditions, housing costs, and occupiers'
          perceptions on site-and-service schemes in Lusaka (Kaunda
          Square and Mtendere), Kafue (Chamwama), and Ndola (Luboto).

504.0.14 MIRACLE, M.P. "African markets and trade in the Copperbelt."
          In Bohanan, P. and Dalton, G. (eds.), Markets in Africa.
          Northwestern University Press, Evanston, Ill., 1962,
          698-738.
              Examines the extent and nature of the marketing of
          agricultural produce in the Copperbelt towns of both
          Zambia and Zaire.

504.0.15 MITCHELL, J.C. "Differential fertility amongst urban
          Africans in Zambia." Central African Journal of Medicine,
          10, 1964, 194-211: and Rhodes-Livingstone Journal, 37,
          1965, 1-25.
              Presents fertility data collected in several towns in
          1951-1954 and investigates their relationships to data
          on tribe, religion, and socioeconomic status.

504.0.16 MITCHELL, J.C. (ed.) Social Networks in Urban Situations:
          analyses of personal relationships in Central African
          towns. Manchester University Press, U.K., 1969, 378 pp.
              A set of symposium papers, focused on theory and on
          methodology, but drawing on field studies in Zambia in
          the case of papers by Boswell (Lusaka), Epstein (Ndola),
          Harries-Jones (Luanshya), and Kapferer (Kabwe).

504.0.17 MITCHELL, J.C. "Africans in industrial towns in Northern
          Rhodesia." In Mangin, W. (ed.), Peasants in Cities.
          Houghton Mifflin, Boston, 1970, 160-169.
              A broad outline of demographic structures reflecting
          male in-migration, and of social relationships much in-
          fluenced by kinship and ethnicity, in Zambian towns in
          the 1950s.

504.0.18 MITCHELL, J.C. "Distance, transportation and urban
          involvement in Zambia." In Southall, A.W. (ed.), Urban
          Anthropology. Oxford University Press, New York, 1973,
          287-314.
              A quantitative analysis of data from 1950-1954 social
          surveys in Copperbelt towns shows some negative correla-
          tion between the distance of a migrant's home and the
          extent of his or her involvement in urban social rela-
          tionships, and points to some special cases with unusually
          high or low involvement.

504.0.19 OHADIKE, P.O. Development of and Factors in the Employment
          of African Migrants in the Copper Mines of Zambia,
          1940-1966. Institute for Social Research, University of
          Zambia, Lusaka, 1969, 24 pp.
             Presents data on the source areas of mine labor and
          considers factors such as distance and intervening oppor-
          tunities that affect regional variations in migrant flow.

504.0.20 OHADIKE, P.O. "The nature and extent of urbanization in
          Zambia." Journal of Asian and African Studies, 4, 1969,
          107-121.
             Analyzes some 1963 census results, providing a broad
          view of the extent of urbanization in each province, the
          size distribution of urban centers, and the demographic
          and economic characteristics of the urban population.

504.0.21 ROTHCHILD, D. "Rural-urban inequities and resource
          allocation in Zambia." Journal of Commonwealth Political
          Studies, 10, 1972, 222-242.
             Shows that there is genuine concern in government
          about rural-urban inequalities, but that constraints on
          action to redistribute resources are such that disparities
          widened as a result of development in the 1960s.

504.0.22 SIMMANCE, A.J.F. Urbanization in Zambia. Ford Foundation,
          New York, 1972, 52 pp.
             Reviews rural-urban migration and the urban housing
          situation, official and unofficial, but also discusses
          rural development strategies and concludes that these
          are at least as important as urban planning.

504.0.23 SIMMANCE, A.J.F. "Urbanization of Zambia." Journal of
          Administration Overseas, 13, 1974, 498-509.
             Summary of above paper, noting that the Second
          National Development Plan emphasizes rural development
          and reduced rural-urban migration.

504.0.24 SIMONS, H.J. et al. Slums or Self-reliance? Urban Growth
          in Zambia. Institute for African Studies, University
          of Zambia, Communication No. 12, Lusaka, 1976, 128 pp.
             Comprises a broad historical review of urbanization
          in Zambia by H.J. Simons; a substantial discussion of
          the growth and causes of squatter settlement in Lusaka
          by T. Seymour; a brief paper on the policy of upgrading
          such settlement by R. Martin; and an account of self-
          help water supply projects by M.S. Muller.

504.0.25 VAN VELSEN, J. "Urban squatters: problem or solution."
          In Parkin, D.J. (ed.), Town and Country in Central and
          Eastern Africa. Oxford University Press, London, 1975,
          294-307.

Notes the critical views of most officials towards
squatters in Zambian towns and shows that many such
squatters are long-term urban dwellers in regular wage
employment, who also contribute to the urban economy by
their house-building efforts.

504.0.26 YOUNG, C.E. "Rural-urban terms of trade." African Social
Research, 12, 1971, 91-94.
Reviews an index of producer prices that suggested
that Zambian towns were enriching themselves at the ex-
pense of the rural economy.

504.0.27 ZAMBIA. Final Report of the 1961 Census of Non-Africans
and Employees. Central Statistical Office, Lusaka, 1965,
70 pp.
Provides data on the numbers of non-Africans in each
town by race and the numbers of employees in each town
by race and industry.

504.0.28 ZAMBIA. Census of Population and Housing, 1969. Final
Report, vol. 2, Provincial Reports. Lusaka, 1974.
Provides data on population by sex, age, household
size, ethnic group, birthplace, education, and housing
conditions for each of the major towns.

504.0.29 ZAMBIA. Census of Population and Housing, 1969. Final
Report, vol. 4(i), Urban Districts. Lusaka, 1975.
Provides data on population by sex and age for each
polling district within each town.

An important earlier paper is:

504.0.30 MITCHELL, J.C. and EPSTEIN, A.L. "Occupational prestige
and social structure among urban Africans in Northern
Rhodesia." Africa, 29, 1959, 22-30. Reprinted in Van
den Berghe, P.L. (ed.), Africa: social problems of
change and conflict. Chandler, San Francisco, 1965,
198-220.

Other major works relating to urbanization include:

504.0.31 BATES, R.H. Unions, Parties and Political Development.
Yale University Press, New Haven, 1971, 291 pp.

504.0.32 BATES, R.H. Rural Responses to Industrialization: a study
of village Zambia. Yale University Press, New Haven,
1976, 380 pp.

504.0.33 BERGER, E.L. Labour, Race and Colonial Rule: the Copperbelt
from 1924 to Independence. Oxford University Press,
London, 1974, 257 pp.

504.0.34 BURAWOY, M. The Colour of Class on the Copper Mines.
          Institute of African Studies, University of Zambia,
          Lusaka, 1972, 121 pp.

504.0.35 PERRINGS. C. Black Mineworkers in Central Africa: industrial
          strategies and the evolution of an African proletariat in
          the Copperbelt, 1911-41. Heinemann, London, 1979, 302 pp.

Unpublished theses include:

504.0.36 NGWISHA, K.J. Urbanization and Family Structure: a study
          of the family on the Copperbelt of Zambia. Ph.D. thesis,
          Brandeis University, Waltham, Mass., 1978.

Kabwe (Provincial town between Lusaka and the Copperbelt. Population
       at 1969 census: 66,000. Estimate for 1975: 100,000. Former
       name: Broken Hill.)

504.1.1 KAPFERER, B. The Population of a Zambian Municipal
         Township. Institute for Social Research, University of
         Zambia, Lusaka, 1966, 66 pp.
             Presents and analyzes the results of a 1964 social
         survey in the main residential areas of the town.

504.1.2 KAPFERER, B. Strategy and Transaction in an African
         Factory. Manchester University Press, U.K., 1972,
         366 pp.
             Primarily an analysis of worker-management relations
         in one factory, but all is relevant to the urbanization
         process, while chapter 1 includes an outline of the
         demographic, social, and economic structure of the town.

504.1.3 KAPFERER, B. "Structural marginality and the urban social
         order." Urban Anthropology, 7, 1978, 287-320.
             Examines the evolution of two shanty areas in Kabwe,
         tracing their emerging social order and their inhabitants'
         links with people elsewhere in the town, and discussing
         whether they can properly be termed "marginal."

An unpublished thesis is:

504.1.4 TURNER, A. A History of Broken Hill, Northern Rhodesia.
         Ph.D. thesis, University of California, Los Angeles,
         1975.

Kitwe (Largest of the Copperbelt mining towns. Population at 1969
       census: 180,000. Estimate for 1975: 260,000.)

504.2.1 ELGIE, I.D. (ed.) Kitwe and its Hinterland. Zambia

Geographical Association, Lusaka, 1974, 168 pp.
A wide-ranging set of papers on the physical and human geography of the area around Kitwe, with three concerned specifically with the city (listed below).

504.2.2 KAJOBA, G.M. "Some aspects of land tenure in Kitwe." In Elgie, I.D. (ed.), Kitwe and its Hinterland (above), 77-90.
Outlines the pattern of land ownership in Kitwe District, noting mine-owned land, state land, and individual freehold and leasehold; and includes a map of land use in the city.

504.2.3 KAY, G. A Social Geography of Zambia. University of London Press, 1967. Chap. 7 "Nkana-Kitwe," 133-145.
Discusses the origins of Nkana mine and Kitwe as a government township, their fusion into a single urban entity, the total land-use pattern, and the 1963 distribution of the European and African sectors of the population, then still very distinct.

504.2.4 SONAWANE, D.B. "The city of Kitwe: a general appraisal." In Elgie, I.D. (ed.), Kitwe and its Hinterland (above), 113-124.
Outlines the physical growth of the city, its present infrastructure, and current plans for its expansion.

504.2.5 TIPPLE, A.G. "Self-help housing policies in a Zambian mining town." Urban Studies, 13, 1976, 167-169.
Notes that since independence government housing has fallen far short of needs, squatter settlements have developed, and government has had to adopt more positive policies towards these.

504.2.6 TIPPLE, A.G. "The low-cost housing market in Kitwe, Zambia." Ekistics, 41, 1976, 148-152.
A slightly fuller version of the paper noted above.

504.2.7 TIPPLE, A.G. "Mufuchani - a squatter settlement in Zambia." Habitat International, 2, 1977, 543-546.
Describes a squatter settlement on the edge of Kitwe and argues that its self-help schemes have been successful enough to justify a positive approach by the authorities.

504.2.8 VAN DEN BERG, L.M. "Kitwe: the growth of a mining town." In Elgie, I.D. (ed.), Kitwe and its Hinterland (above), 99-112.
Examines the origins, population growth, present economic activities, residential areas, and planning problems of the city.

See also 504.0.4.

Livingstone   (Provincial town on the southern border.   Population at
              1969 census: 45,000.   Estimate for 1975:   60,000.)

Nothing appears to have been published since:

504.3.1   McCULLOCH, M.   A Social Survey of the African Population of
              Livingstone.   Rhodes-Livingstone Institute, Lusaka, 1956,
              96 pp.

Luanshya   (One of the Copperbelt towns.   Population at 1969 census:
           96,000.)

504.4.1   HARRIES-JONES, P.   "Marital disputes and the process of
              conciliation in a Copperbelt town."   Rhodes-Livingstone
              Journal, 35, 1964, 29-72.
                  Examines some activities of the Roan Township Citizens
              Advice Bureau, showing largely through case studies how
              it has settled marital disputes.

504.4.2   HARRIES-JONES, P.   Freedom and Labour: mobilization and
              political control on the Zambian Copperbelt.   Blackwell,
              Oxford, 1975, 256 pp.
                  A detailed study of political activity in Luanshya
              in 1963-1965 as a case study of the operation of the
              United National Independence Party at the local level.
              Focuses upon how the people were mobilized politically,
              how local leadership emerged, and how it then exercised
              control.

504.4.3   POWDERMAKER, H.   Copper Town: Changing Africa.   Harper &
              Row, New York, 1962, 391 pp.
                  An extensive discussion of African life and attitudes
              in Luanshya in the early 1950s, set against an account of
              the rural "tribal" background, of the arrival of the
              Europeans, and of the consequent migration process.   The
              focus is upon the mining compound, but comparisons with
              the government township are also made.

A notable earlier study is:

504.4.4   EPSTEIN, A.L.   Politics in an Urban African Community.
              Manchester University Press, U.K., 1958, 254 pp.

          See also 504.0.4.

<u>Lusaka</u> (Capital city. Population at 1969 census: 240,000. Estimate
        for 1975: 430,000.)

504.5.1 ANDREWS, P.; CHRISTIE, M.; and MARTIN, R. "Squatters and the
          evolution of a life-style." <u>Architectural Design</u>, 43 (1),
          1973, 16-25.
              Studies the mechanisms adopted by squatters, the types
          of neighborhood that they have created, and the lessons
          of this experience for urban planners. Includes several
          maps and plans.

504.5.2 BEVERIDGE, A.A. and OBERSCHALL, A.R. <u>African Businessmen
          and Development in Zambia</u>. Princeton University Press,
          1979, 382 pp.
              An intensive study of small-scale businesses in post-
          independence Zambia, largely focused on Lusaka and in-
          corporating much material from Beveridge's 1973 doctoral
          thesis. Specific chapters deal also with historical an-
          tecedents, with expatriate enterprise, and with rural
          traders, but the primary concern is with Zambian entre-
          preneurs in the city, not only in economic terms but also
          in regard to their role in social and political change.

504.5.3 BOSWELL, D.M. "Kinship, friendship and the concept of a
          social network." In Kileff, C. and Pendleton, W.C. (eds.),
          <u>Urban Man in Southern Africa</u>. Mambo Press, Gwelo, 1975,
          145-197.
              Provides information on ethnic composition, household
          structure, religion, occupations, and income in different
          parts of Lusaka, but focuses on elite interpersonal re-
          lationships as exemplified by one individual.

504.5.4 COLLINS, J. <u>Lusaka: the myth of the garden city</u>. Institute
          for Social Research, University of Zambia, Lusaka, 1969,
          32 pp.
              Argues that the form of the city is rooted in the
          single planning concept of the "garden city," largely
          misapplied before independence, and even more inappropri-
          ate since. Calls for new approaches in future planning
          for the city.

504.5.5 COLLINS, J. "Home ownership aspects of low cost housing in
          Lusaka." In Kanyeihamba, G.W. and McAuslan, J.P.W.B.
          (eds.), <u>Urban Legal Problems in Eastern Africa</u>.
          Scandinavian Institute of African Studies, Uppsala,
          Sweden, 1978, 104-125.
              Reviews attitudes towards home ownership over the
          1966-1974 period in relation to the 1974 Housing Act,
          focusing on misunderstandings over the ownership of land
          versus buildings and over land-tenure on new serviced
          sites.

504.5.6   DAVIES, D.H. Lusaka: some town planning problems of an
           African capital city. Institute for Social Research,
           University of Zambia, Lusaka, 1969, 20 pp.
               Investigates the origins of the city's morphology,
           which now provides an unsatisfactory base for a fast-
           growing national capital. Stresses the urgency of bold
           new planning policies.

504.5.7   DOXIADIS ASSOCIATES. "Zambia: the Lusaka peri-urban area
           and Kafue new town." Ekistics, 36, 1973, 193-204.
               Summarizes a report on service provision in the peri-
           urban zone and a plan for the physical expansion of the
           satellite town of Kafue.

504.5.8   HANSEN, K.T. "Married women and work: explorations from
           an urban case study." African Social Research, 20,
           1975, 777-799.
               Shows how few of the married women in Mtendele, on
           the eastern fringe of Lusaka, have paid employment or
           are self-employed and discusses the socioeconomic struc-
           tures responsible for this.

504.5.9   KAY, G. A Social Geography of Zambia. University of London
           Press, 1967. Chap. 6 Lusaka, 190-132.
               Describes the origins and physical growth of the city,
           discusses and maps its pattern of land-use, and examines
           with large-scale maps and photographs its contrasting
           residential areas--European, planned African, and spon-
           taneous African.

504.5.10   LEESON, J. and FRANKENBERG, R. "The patients of traditional
           doctors in Lusaka." African Social Research, 23, 1977,
           217-234.
               For a sample of 3000 patients, those attending tradi-
           tional doctors and a modern doctor are compared in terms
           of age, ailments, etc: and reasons for many moving from
           modern to traditional doctors are considered.

504.5.11   McCLAIN, W.T. "Legal aspects of housing and planning in
           Lusaka." In Kanyeihamba, G.W. and McAuslan, J.P.W. (eds.),
           Urban Legal Problems in Eastern Africa. Scandinavian
           Institute of African Studies, Uppsala, Sweden, 1978,
           63-84.
               Discusses postindependence urban land policies in
           Zambia and reviews laws affecting rural-urban migration,
           urban planning, and especially processes of and responses
           to squatter settlement in Lusaka.

504.5.12   MARTIN, R.J. "Housing in Lusaka." In Hawkesworth, N.R.
           (ed.), Local Government in Zambia. Lusaka City Council,
           1974, 53-93.

Examines the evolution of government low-cost housing
projects, the range of self-help and site-and-service
schemes, patterns of squatter settlement, and the provision of higher-cost housing, with many photographs of
housing types.

504.5.13 MARTIN, R. "The evolution of a traditional morphology in
an urban setting: Greater Lusaka." Zambian Geographical
Journal, 29/30, 1975, 1-20.
Shows how Lusaka's squatter settlements reflect
initiatives in local planning and self-government, con-
stitute viable urban systems, and can be provided with
amenities without undue disruption.

504.5.14 MARTIN, R. "Housing options, Lusaka, Zambia." Ekistics,
44, 1977, 88-95.
Reviews the housing problem in Lusaka and discusses
the relative merits of site-and-service schemes and upgrading of squatter settlements, favoring the latter.

504.5.15 MIHALYI, L. "The pedlars of Lusaka." Zambian Geographical
Journal, 29/30, 1975, 111-126.
Examines the activities of pedlars, mainly trading
from bicycles, in Lusaka streets, discussing the economics of their businesses and their role as agents of
socialization for new in-migrants.

504.5.16 MIRACLE, M.P. "Apparent changes in the structure of African
commerce, Lusaka, 1954-1959." Northern Rhodesia Journal,
5, 1962, 170-175.
Presents the results of a 1959 survey of market
vendors and market trade and compares these with results
of a similar survey undertaken in 1954 by A.A. Nyirenda.

504.5.17 MUNYANGWA, P.M. "The planning and growth of Lusaka
1900-1970." In Hawkesworth, N.R. (ed.), Local Government
in Zambia. Lusaka City Council, 1974, 33-52.
Outlines the origins of the city, its later selection
and growth as the national capital, its postwar expansion,
and the present town planning organization.

504.5.18 OBERSCHALL, A. "Lusaka market vendors: then and now."
Urban Anthropology, 1, 1972, 107-123; and Journal of
Social Science, University of Malawi, 1, 1972, 28-41.
Reports the findings of a 1970 study of Matero market,
with information on each trade, an assessment of the
place of market traders in the total consumer goods distribution system, and a discussion of changes since the
studies of Nyirenda and Miracle in the 1950s.

504.5.19 OBERSCHALL, A. "African traders and small businessmen in

Lusaka." <u>African Social Research</u>, 16, 1973, 474-502.
Examines the nature of small-scale African retail
businesses in various parts of the city, partly through
individual case studies, with a view to contributing to
theories of entrepreneurship.

504.5.20 OHADIKE, P.O. "The evolving phenomena of migration and
urbanization in Central Africa: a Zambian case." In
Parkin, D.J. (ed.), <u>Town and Country in Central and
Eastern Africa</u>. Oxford University Press, London, 1975,
126-144.
Presents the results of a 1968-1969 survey of a large
sample of households in Lusaka, focusing on the origin,
age, permanence, and residential pattern of migrants to
the city, and noting changes in migration patterns by
distinguishing between the most recent and longer-settled
migrants.

504.5.21 PASTEUR, D. "The management of squatter upgrading: the
case of Lusaka." <u>Institute of Development Studies
Bulletin</u>, 10 (4), 1979, 52-55.
Shows how the execution of squatter upgrading projects
in Lusaka has exemplified effective institutional innovation in response to new types of social need.

504.5.22 PASTEUR, D. <u>The Management of Squatter Upgrading</u>. Saxon
House, Farnborough, U.K., 1979, 232 pp.
A detailed case study of the upgrading program in the
Chaisa, Chamwama, and George areas of Lusaka, concerned
essentially with matters of organization, management, and
public participation, and suggesting that many other
cities might benefit from the Lusaka experience.

504.5.23 ROTHMAN, N.C. "Urban administration and African organizations
in colonial Central Africa: a case study." <u>African Urban
Notes</u>, B 1 (2), 1975, 75-94.
Traces the evolution of administrative structures in
Lusaka and their long failure to adapt to the situation
in which the African population were becoming long-term
residents.

504.5.24 ROTHMAN, N.C. "The liquor authority and welfare administration in Lusaka." <u>African Urban Studies</u>, 1, 1978, 27-38.
Examines the effects of colonial policies to control
drinking in Lusaka and to use profits from the government
liquor undertaking to finance welfare services.

504.5.25 ROTHMAN, N.C. "Housing and service planning in Lusaka,
Zambia." In Obudho, R.A. and El-Shakhs, S. (eds.),
<u>Development of Urban Systems in Africa</u>. Praeger, New
York, 1979, 272-287.

Reviews the process of urbanization through the colonial and postcolonial periods, emphasizing government
policies towards housing and public services and their
social and economic consequences.

504.5.26 SCHUSTER, I.M.G. New Women of Lusaka. Mayfield, Palo Alto,
Calif., 1979, 209 pp.
The published version of a 1976 Sussex doctoral thesis,
examining the life-style of educated young women in
Lusaka. Individual chapters consider childhood, school
life, single women at work and leisure, marriage and
married life, and images of women projected in the media.

504.5.27 SEYMOUR, T. "Squatter settlement and class relations in
Zambia." Review of African Political Economy, 3, 1975,
71-77.
Outlines the growth of squatter settlement in Lusaka
and suggests that World Bank interest in upgrading since
1973 constitutes an attempt to forestall revolutionary
political movements.

504.5.28 SNADEN, J.W. "Locational factors in Lusaka's primary
business district." Kenyan Geographer, 1, 1975, 45-53.
The eccentric location of the business center in the
west of the city is noted and the factors causing it are
considered, physical features being of most significance.

504.5.29 TODD, D.; MULENGA, A.; and MUPIMPILA, C. "Markets and
vendors in Lusaka, Zambia." African Urban Studies, 5,
1979, 45-70.
Reports on a study of five Lusaka markets, summarizing
the results and making comparisons with previous studies
by Nyirenda, Miracle, and Oberschall.

504.5.30 UNITED NATIONS ECONOMIC COMMISSION FOR AFRICA. Human
Settlements in Africa. United Nations, New York, 1976.
Pp. 112-120, "The programme for the upgrading of squatter
settlements in Lusaka."
Indicates the needs for urban housing in Zambia, the
types of squatter settlement existing in Lusaka, the
scope for upgrading these, and issues involved in imple-
menting such a policy.

504.5.31 WILSON, E. "Lusaka: a city of tropical Africa." Geography,
48, 1963, 411-414.
A brief outline of the origin, site, form, and function of the city.

The most substantial pre-1960 study is:

504.5.32 BETTISON, D.G. Numerical Data on African Dwellers in

Lusaka, Northern Rhodesia. Rhodes-Livingstone Institute, Lusaka, 1959, 118 pp.

Unpublished theses include:

504.5.33 BEVERIDGE, A.A. Converts to Capitalism: the emergence of African entrepreneurs in Lusaka, Zambia. Ph.D. thesis, Yale University, 1973.

504.5.34 HANSEN, K.T. The Work Opportunities of Married Women in a Peri-Urban Township: an exploratory study. Ph.D. thesis, Arhus University, Denmark, 1973.

504.5.35 ROTHMAN, N.C. African Urban Development in the Colonial Period: a study of Lusaka, 1905-1964. Ph.D. thesis, Northwestern University, Evanston, Ill., 1972.

504.5.36 SEYMOUR, A. Squatters, Migrants and the Urban Poor. D.Phil. thesis, University of Sussex, U.K., 1976.

504.5.37 WILEY, D.S. Social Stratification and Religion in Urban Zambia. Ph.D. thesis, Princeton University, 1972.

See also 504.0.13, 504.0.24.

Ndola (Third city of Zambia and chief service center for the Copperbelt. Population in 1969: 150,000. Estimate for 1975: 240,000.)

504.6.1 EPSTEIN, A.L. "The network and urban social organization." Rhodes-Livingstone Journal, 29, 1961, 28-62. Reprinted in Mitchell, J.C., Social Networks in Urban Situations: analyses of personal relationships in Central African towns. Manchester University Press, U.K., 1969, 77-116.
     Explores the networks of social relationships in Central African towns through the experience of one in-dividual resident of Ndola.

*504.6.2 NDOLA. City of Ndola. Ndola City Council, 1971, 48 pp.

See also 504.0.4, 504.0.13.

ZIMBABWE

General

505.0.1   ASHTON, E.H. "The economics of African housing." Rhodesian
Journal of Economics, 3 (4), 1969, 29-37.
    An analysis of the total costs of municipal housing
provision at different standards, with a discussion of
the prospects of low-income urban dwellers meeting these
costs.

505.0.2   BOURDILLON, M.F.C. "Labour migrants from Korekore country."
Zambezia, 5, 1977, 1-29.
    Investigates the circumstances, attitudes, and home
ties of fifty-eight migrants from a rural area in the
northeast, most working in towns.

505.0.3   CHAVUNDUKA, G.L. "Rural and urban life." Zambezia, 4 (2),
1976, 69-78.
    Discusses the reasons for urban migrants' retaining
close ties with rural areas and the problems for these
areas caused by male labor migration.

*505.0.4   CUMMING, E.E. The Spheres of Influence of Urban Service
Centres in Southern Rhodesia. Town Planning Department,
Salisbury, 1963.

*505.0.4a   DAVIES, D.H. "Primacy, decentralization and the evolution
of an urbanization strategy for Zimbabwe Rhodesia: an
exploratory discussion." Geographical Association of
Rhodesia Proceedings, 11, 1978, 13-23.

505.0.5   DAVIES, R. "Informal sector or subordinate mode of
production?" In Bromley, R. and Gerry, C. (eds.), Casual
Work and Poverty in Third World Cities. Wiley, Chichester,
U.K., 1979, 87-104.
    Drawing on a survey in the small town of Hartley, a
model of the informal sector as a subsidiary, peripheral,
and dependent mode of production is presented as being
applicable to Zimbabwe-Rhodesian towns in general--and
beyond.

505.0.6   FEDERATION OF RHODESIA AND NYASALAND. Final Report of the
1962 Census of Africans in Southern Rhodesia. Central
Statistical Office, Salisbury, 1964, 91 pp.
    Records the African population by age and sex for
each town and for areas within each and provides other
data, e.g., on education for whole towns.

505.0.7   GARBETT, G.K. "Circulatory migration in Rhodesia: towards a decision model." In Parkin, D.J. (ed.), <u>Town and Country in Central and Eastern Africa</u>. Oxford University Press, London, 1975, 113–125.

Examines the nature of labor circulation, partly but not exclusively rural–urban, with theory formulation as the primary aim.

505.0.8   GARGETT, E. <u>The Administration of Transition: African urban settlement in Rhodesia</u>. Mambo Press, Gwelo, 1977, 104 pp.

Examines the nature of African urban settlement and government responses to it, with special reference to Bulawayo. Includes a brief general account of African urban life, covering household structure, education, income, etc., and fuller discussions of housing, welfare services, and African participation in local government.

505.0.9   KAUFMAN, R. "Shona urban music: a process which maintains traditional values." In Kileff, C. and Pendleton, W.C. (eds.), <u>Urban Man in Southern Africa</u>. Mambo Press, Gwelo, 1975, 127–144.

Examines Shona music and how it changes in urban situations as a result of European influences.

505.0.10   KAY, G. <u>Rhodesia: a human geography</u>. University of London Press, 1970. Chap. 7 "Mining, manufacturing and urban development," especially pp. 158–166.

Describes and maps the urban hierarchy and urban spheres of influence. Discusses the morphology of Salisbury, with several maps.

505.0.11   McEWAN, P.J.M. "The urban African population of Southern Rhodesia." <u>Civilisations</u>, 13, 1963, 267–293.

Presents the results of a 1960–1961 survey in Salisbury, covering income, education, religion, life-styles, and attitudes to town and to Europeans.

505.0.12   MASSER, I.F. "Changing patterns of African employment in Southern Rhodesia." In Steel, R.W. and Prothero, R.M. (eds.), <u>Geographers and the Tropics</u>. Longmans, London, 1964, 215–234.

Reviews pre- and postwar labor policies and draws on a survey of the 1950s labor situation in a Salisbury tobacco factory to show the increasing stability of the urban labor force.

505.0.13   MITCHELL, J.C. "Structured plurality, urbanization and labour circulation in Southern Rhodesia." In Jackson, J.A. (ed.), <u>Migration</u>. Cambridge University Press, 1969, 156–180.

Examines the establishment and growth of urban centers,

colonial attitudes to African settlement in them, the
resulting labor circulation system, and the factors influencing the decision to migrate to town.

*505.0.14 O'CLEARY, C.S. "Informal employment in urban Zimbabwe."
South African Labour Bulletin, 3 (6), 1977, 72-82.

505.0.15 RHODESIA. 1961 Census of the European, Asian and Coloured
Population. Central Statistical Office, Salisbury, n.d.
The final report on the Rhodesia portion of the 1961
federal census, giving data on urban population and
housing for 1956 and 1961, and some population data
from earlier censuses.

505.0.16 RHODESIA. Report on the Urban African Budget Survey in the
Midlands: Gwelo, Que Que and Gatooma, 1970. Central
Statistical Office, Salisbury, 1971, 25 pp.
Presents the results of household sample surveys of
income and expenditure in the African townships of these
three urban centers, with data also on socioeconomic
characteristics.

505.0.17 RHODESIA. Census of Africans, Europeans, Asians and Coloured
Population, 1969. Central Statistical Office, Salisbury,
1976, 210 pp.
Includes much data on the population of each of the
towns.

505.0.18 SMOUT, M.A.H. "Urbanisation of the Rhodesian population."
Zambezia, 4 (2), 1976, 79-91.
Discusses the origins of the country's urban centers,
the steady growth of their non-African population, and
the recently much more rapid, yet still constrained,
growth of the African population.

505.0.19 SMOUT, M.A.H. "Urbanization and development problems in
Rhodesia." Journal of Tropical Geography, 45, 1977,
43-51.
Outlines the national pattern of urbanization, noting
the increasing dominance of Salisbury and Bulawayo, and
the powers to limit African urban settlement; and argues
for accelerated urbanization as an appropriate path to
development.

*505.0.20 SMOUT, M.A.H. "Urbanization in Sub-Saharan Africa, with
special reference to Rhodesia." Geographical Association
of Rhodesia Proceedings, 11, 1978, 7-12.

505.0.21 TANSER, G.H. (ed.) The Guide to Rhodesia. Winchester Press,
Johannesburg, 1975. Pp. 161-223, "Cities and towns."
Describes the history and principal present-day

features of Salisbury (pp. 161-183), Bulawayo (pp. 183-197), and fifteen smaller towns.

*505.0.22   WHITTLE, A.C.   "The role of Rhodesia's government town planning department viewed in historical perspective." Geographical Association of Rhodesia Proceedings, 8, 1975, 19-24.

Bulawayo   (Second city, rivalling Salisbury as a commercial and industrial center. Population at 1969 census: 250,000. Estimate for 1975: 340,000.)

505.1.1   NEHWATI, F.   "The social and communal background to 'Zhii': the African riots in Bulawayo, Southern Rhodesia, in 1960." African Affairs, 60, 1970, 250-266.
          Includes a general review of the social characteristics of the city's African population, as well as showing how common interests can outweigh sectional ones in providing a basis for communal political action.

505.1.2   PEEL, H.A.   "Varied approaches to delimiting the C.B.D. of Bulawayo." Journal for Geography, 3, 1972, 1021-1031.
          Examines and maps several characteristics of the city's central business district, including height of buildings, land values, employment intensity, and vehicle parking, as alternative criteria for its delimitation.

505.1.3   PHIMISTER, I. and VAN ONSELEN, C.   "The political economy of tribal animosity: a case study of the 1929 Bulawayo location 'faction fight.'" Journal of Southern African Studies, 6, 1979, 1-43.
          Reconstructs from contemporary documents a major incident in the social history of the city and discusses ways in which it reflected the social and economic conditions of the African population.

505.1.4   RANSFORD, O.   Bulawayo: historic battleground of Rhodesia. Balkema, Cape Town, 1968, 182 pp.
          An illustrated account of the history of the Bulawayo area, primarily concerned with the late nineteenth century, including as chapter 5 "The modern city takes shape" and also a five-page postscript on the period from 1918 to 1968 and an appendix of photographs showing the same sites in 1900 and 1968.

505.1.5   RHODESIA.   Report on the Urban African Budget Survey in Bulawayo, 1968. Central Statistical Office, Salisbury, 1970, 19 pp.
          Presents the results of a household sample survey of income and expenditure, with data also on socioeconomic characteristics.

505.1.6 WOLCOTT, H.F. The African Beer Gardens of Bulawayo.
         Rutgers Center of Alcohol Studies, New Brunswick, N.J.,
         1974, 261 pp.
              Surveys patterns of African drinking in Bulawayo, re-
         viewing relevant social and cultural factors, the attitudes
         and involvement of administrators, welfare workers, doc-
         tors, and churchmen, and diverse individual adaptations
         to the general patterns.

An unpublished thesis is:

505.1.7 GARGETT, E.S. Welfare Services in an Urban African Area
         (Bulawayo). Ph.D. thesis, University of London, 1971.

         See also 505.0.8.

Fort Victoria (Provincial town southeast of Gwelo. Population at
               1969 census: 11,000. Estimate for 1975: 20,000.)

505.2.1 WEINRICH, A.K.H. Mucheke: race, status and politics in a
         Rhodesian community. UNESCO, Paris, 1976, 278 pp.
              An intensive study of the African residential area
         that houses the majority of Fort Victoria's population,
         based mainly on intensive 1968-1969 surveys. Individual
         chapters deal with Mucheke's relationship to the rest of
         the town; demographic, educational, and occupational
         structure; economic conditions; social stratification;
         voluntary associations; local and national politics; and
         distinctive local neighborhoods. A further study of peo-
         ple in domestic service elsewhere in Fort Victoria is
         appended.

Gwelo (Provincial town between Bulawayo and Salisbury. Population
        at 1969 census: 46,000. Estimate for 1975: 64,000.)

505.3.1 DAVIS, P. "The history of Gwelo." Rhodesiana, 34, 1976,
         9-20, and 35, 1976, 4-15.
              An illustrated account of the origins of the town in
         1894 and its early growth up to 1902.

505.3.2 SCHWAB, W.B. "Social stratification in Gwelo." In Southall,
         A.W. (ed.), Social Change in Modern Africa. Oxford
         University Press, London, 1961, 126-144.
              Shows that the key themes of Gwelo social life in the
         late 1950s were the racial cleavage and the urban/rural
         dichotomy for Africans, the latter causing new forms of
         stratification based on the values of Western industrial
         society.

505.3.3   SCHWAB, W.B. "Urbanism, corporate groups and cultural
           change in Africa." Anthropological Quarterly, 43, 1970,
           187-214.
               After a general discussion of African urbanization,
           the relationships between corporate groups and social
           communities are examined for Gwelo and for Oshogbo in
           Nigeria, towns of sharply contrasting character.

       See also 505.0.16.

Salisbury   (Capital city. Population at 1969 census: 386,000.
            Estimate for 1975:   550,000.)

505.4.1   CHAVUNDUKA, G.L. "A social survey of the Dzivaresekwa
           Township, Salisbury." Zambezia, 2 (2), 1972, 67-72.
               Presents the results of a 1966-1967 survey of the
           demographic structure, household composition, education,
           religion, occupations, and earnings of the population of
           this African housing area.

505.4.2   CHRISTOPHER, A.J. "Salisbury 1900: the study of a pioneer
           town." Journal for Geography, 3, 1970, 757-766.
               Examines in detail the physical structure of the city
           in 1900, mapping patterns of land-use and land values
           and discussing factors influencing these.

*505.4.2a CHRISTOPHER, A.J. "Air photo interpretation and urban
           sprawl: a case study of Mount Pleasant, Salisbury."
           Rhodesia Science News, 6, 1972, 207-212.

505.4.3   CHRISTOPHER, A.J. "Land ownership in the rural-urban
           fringe of Salisbury." South African Geographer, 4,
           1973, 139-156.
               Reviews and maps the evolution of European land
           ownership within 32 km of Salisbury from 1895 to 1970
           and discusses the factors affecting it and its implica-
           tions both for agriculture and for urban sprawl.

*505.4.3a HARDWICK, P.A. "Salisbury's urban transport problems in
           the light of current overseas trends." Geographical
           Association of Rhodesia Proceedings, 6, 1973, 20-30.

505.4.4   HARDWICK, P. "Journey-to-work patterns in Salisbury,
           Rhodesia: the contrast between Africans and Europeans."
           Journal of Transport Economics and Policy, 8, 1974,
           180-191.
               Shows how the sharp separation of workplace and resi-
           dence involves much movement to work and how racial resi-
           dential segregation produces contrasting travel patterns,
           although journeys for low-income Africans are as long as
           those for high-income Europeans.

*505.4.4a HARDWICK, P.A. "Salisbury's urban transport problems:
          how severe are they and is rapid transit the answer?"
          Rhodesia Science News, 8, 1974, 33-38.

505.4.5   HARDWICK, P.A. "Progress towards transportation planning
          in Salisbury." Zambezia, 4 (1), 1975, 77-93.
               Provides information on the journey to work by the
          Europeans and shows how their interests have been para-
          mount, with municipal efforts at transport planning fail-
          ing to respond to the needs of the African majority.

505.4.6   KAY, G. "A socio-geographic survey of Salisbury."
          Zambezia, 3 (2), 1974, 71-88.
               Examines the distribution of the European and African
          population within the city, using the 1969 census, and
          reviews contrasting residential patterns in relation to
          the economic circumstances of each group.

505.4.7   KAY, G. and SMOUT, M.A.H. (eds.) Salisbury. Hodder and
          Stoughton, London, 1977, 119 pp.
               A thorough geographical survey of the city at the
          end of the period of white rule, with numerous maps and
          photographs. The individual essays cover site and situa-
          tion (R.W. Tomlinson and P. Wurzel); early settlement
          (A.J. Christopher); the physical form of the city (M.A.H.
          Smout); the population (G. Kay and M. Cole); the city
          center (Smout); suburban shopping centers (Smout);
          industrial areas (J. Trinder); transport in the city
          (P.A. Hardwick); and a brief review of problems and
          prospects (Kay). The book's value will probably lie
          partly in the basis that it provides for future studies
          of change in the city.

505.4.8   KILEFF, C. "Black suburbanites: an African elite in
          Salisbury, Rhodesia." In Kileff, C. and Pendleton, W.C.
          (eds.), Urban Man in Southern Africa. Mambo Press, Gwelo,
          1975, 81-97.
               Describes the life-styles, family structures, and
          social relationships of African professionals and busi-
          nessmen living in two small upper-class African residen-
          tial areas, noting environmental influences upon them.

505.4.9   LUKHERO, M.B. "The social characteristics of an emergent
          elite in Harare." In Lloyd, P.C. (ed.), The New Elites
          of Tropical Africa. Oxford University Press, London,
          1966, 126-138.
               Shows how an elite was emerging in Salisbury's largest
          "African Township" in the early 1960s, stressing the cri-
          tical importance of education at that early stage.

505.4.10 MITCHELL, J.C. "The meaning of misfortune for urban Africans."

In Fortes, M. and Dieterlen, G. (eds.), <u>African Systems of Thought</u>. Oxford University Press, London, 1965, 192-203.
 Examines attitudes in Salisbury largely through case histories, arguing that many people continue to interpret misfortune in terms of witchcraft.

*505.4.11 MOLLER, V. "Some aspects of mobility patterns of urban Africans in Salisbury." <u>Geographical Association of Rhodesia Proceedings</u>, 7, 1974.

505.4.12 MOLLER, V. "Migrant labour in Harare hostels, Salisbury." <u>Zambezia</u>, 5, 1977, 141-159.
 Presents the results of a 1973 survey of migrants in wage employment, covering age, marital status, origins, home visits, kinship reliance, and aspirations, as a contribution to the study of continuing circulatory migration in southern Africa.

505.4.13 MOLLER, V. <u>Urban Commitment and Involvement among Black Rhodesians</u>. Centre for Applied Social Sciences, University of Natal, Durban, 1978, 473 pp.
 Examines in depth many aspects of the African population of Salisbury, drawing on the results of a 1975 survey and of sophisticated quantitative analysis of these. Individual chapters provide much background information on the city's African townships and its rural hinterland, as well as discussion of topics such as family status, migration history, continuing rural contacts, and commitment to urban life.

505.4.14 RHODESIA. <u>Report on the Urban African Budget Survey in Salisbury, 1963/4</u>. Central Statistical Office, Salisbury, 1965, 32 pp.
 Presents the results of a household income and expenditure survey, with data also on socioeconomic characteristics.

505.4.15 RHODESIA. <u>Report on the Urban African Budget Survey in Salisbury, 1969</u>. Central Statistical Office, Salisbury, 1970, 24 pp.
 Presents the results of a further survey, similar to that noted above.

505.4.16 RHODESIA. <u>Report of the Greater Salisbury Local Authority Commission 1970</u>. Government Printer, Salisbury, 1970, 98 pp.
 The report of a Commission of Inquiry set up to define the area of greater Salisbury, to investigate the effects of its fragmented local government structure, and to consider a new unified structure.

505.4.17 RHODESIA. <u>Report on the European Family Budget Survey in
          Salisbury 1969/71</u>. Central Statistical Office, Salisbury,
          1973, 29 pp.
               Presents the results of a sample survey of income and
          expenditure among the European population.

505.4.18 SEAGER, D. "The struggle for shelter in an urbanizing
          world: a Rhodesian example." <u>Zambezia</u>, 5, 1977, 83-90.
               Investigates the nature, origins, and motivations of
          a squatter community established on the edge of the city
          in 1976 and reviews government action in resettling the
          squatters on serviced plots elsewhere in the peri-urban
          area.

*505.4.19 SEAGER, D. "A Salisbury squatter settlement." <u>South
          African Labour Bulletin</u>, 3 (6), 1977, 83-93.

505.4.20 SMOUT, M.A.H. "Suburban shopping patterns in Greater
          Salisbury." <u>Geographical Association of Rhodesia
          Proceedings</u>, 3, 1970, 41-49.
               Reports on a study of shopping patterns in non-African
          residential areas and maps where people move for small-
          scale purchases among the suburban shopping centers.

505.4.21 SMOUT, M.A.H. "Shopping centres and shopping patterns in
          two African townships of Greater Salisbury." <u>Zambezia</u>,
          2 (1), 1971, 33-39.
               Examines the extent of shopping facilities in Harari
          and Highfields, the use made of these, and people's de-
          pendence on the facilities of the city center.

505.4.22 SMOUT, M.A.H. "Townscape description and synthesis: the
          case of central Salisbury." <u>South African Geographer</u>,
          4, 1972, 33-44.
               Analyzes the evolution of the physical fabric of the
          city center and the resulting pattern of buildings in
          terms of age, size, and the visual images produced by
          them.

*505.4.23 SMOUT, M.A.H. "Recent commercial growth patterns in
          suburban Salisbury." <u>Geographical Association of
          Rhodesia Proceedings</u>, 5, 1972.

*505.4.23a SMOUT, M.A.H. "Comments on planning proposals for central
          Salisbury." <u>Rhodesia Science News</u>, 6, 1972, 201-206.

*505.4.24 SMOUT, M.A.H. "Service centre development in greater
          Salisbury." <u>South African Geographical Journal</u>, 55,
          1973.

505.4.25 SMOUT, M.A.H. <u>Commercial Growth and Consumer Behaviour in</u>

Suburban Salisbury, Rhodesia. University of Rhodesia, Salisbury, 1974, 70 pp.

*505.4.26 STOPFORTH, P. Survey of Highfields African Township, Salisbury. Department of Sociology, University of Rhodesia, Salisbury, 1971, 55 pp.

*505.4.27 STOPFORTH, P. Two Aspects of Social Change: Highfield African Township, Salisbury. Department of Sociology, University of Rhodesia, Salisbury, 1972, 120 pp.

505.4.28 STOPFORTH, P. "Some local impediments to social change among urban Africans." Zambezia, 5, 1977, 31-40.
Argues that political domination by whites has exacerbated the normal social problems of African urbanization, with special reference to increasing elite/mass differentiation, drawing upon the social surveys noted above.

505.4.29 TANSER, G.H. A Scantling of Time: the story of Salisbury, Rhodesia, 1890-1900. Pioneer Head, Salisbury, 1965, 276 pp.
An historical narrative, largely concerned with personalities, but including discussions of the origins of the city, its early phase of physical growth, and the establishment of a municipal administration.

505.4.30 TANSER, G.H. Sequence of Time: the story of Salisbury, Rhodesia, 1900-1914. Pioneer Head, Salisbury, 1974, 299 pp.
A further historical narrative, covering the period of consolidation of the settlement as a European town transplanted to this part of Africa.

505.4.31 VAN HOFFEN, P. "The City of Salisbury report on the African Affairs section of the urban plan." Rhodesian Journal of Economics, 9, 1975, 147-154.
A review article on an unpublished report that is said to contain useful material and to reflect City Council views quite clearly, but to offer few solutions to the city's most urgent planning problems.

Unpublished theses include:

505.4.32 KILEFF, C. Black Suburbanites: adaptation to Western culture in Salisbury, Rhodesia. Ph.D. thesis, Rice University, Houston, Tex., 1970.

505.4.33 SMOUT, M.A.H. Service Centres in Greater Salisbury. Ph.D. thesis, University of London, 1972.

See also 505.0.10, 505.0.11.

Umtali   (Provincial town near the eastern border. Population at
         1969 census: 46,000. Estimate for 1975: 62,000.)

505.5.1 RHODESIA. Report on the Urban African Budget Survey in
             Umtali, 1963. Central Statistical Office, Salisbury,
             1965, 24 pp.
             Presents the results of a household survey of income
         and expenditure, with data also on socioeconomic charac-
         teristics.

505.5.2 RHODESIA. Report on the Urban African Budget Survey in
             Umtali, 1971. Central Statistical Office, Salisbury,
             1973, 25 pp.
             Presents the results of a further survey, similar to
         that noted above.

Indexes

Index of Place Names

ABA   111.1
ABECHE   204.1
ABEOKUTA   111.2
ABIDJAN   106.1
ACCRA   103.1
ADDIS ABABA   302.1
ADO EKITI   111.3
AGBOVILLE   106.2
AGEGE. See Lagos
ARUSHA   402.1
ASMARA   302.2

BAMAKO   108.1
BANGUI   203.1
BANJUL   102.1
BATHURST   (now Banjul)
BAWKU   103.2
BEIRA   503.1
BENIN   111.4
BISSAU   105.1
BLANTYRE   502.1
BO   113.1
BOBO DIOULASSO   115.1
BOUAKE   106.3
BRAZZAVILLE   205.1
BROKEN HILL   (now Kabwe)
BUEA   202.1
BUJUMBURA   201.1
BUKAVU   209.1
BULAWAYO   505.1

CALABAR   111.5
CAPE COAST   103.3
CONAKRY   104.1
COQUILHATVILLE   (now Mbandaka)
COTONOU   101.1

DAKAR   112.1
DALOA   106.4
DAR ES SALAAM   402.2
DJIBOUTI   301.1
DODOMA   402.3
DOUALA   202.2

ELISABETHVILLE   (now Lubumbashi)
EL OBEID   304.1
ENUGU   111.6

FORT ARCHAMBAULT   (now Sarh)
FORT LAMY   (now N'djamena)
FORT VICTORIA   505.2
FREETOWN   113.2
FRIA   104.2

GAGNOA   106.5
GAROUA   202.3
GONDAR   302.3
GULU   403.1
GWELO   505.3

HARAR   302.4
HARGEISA   303.1
HO   103.4
HUAMBO   501.1

IBADAN   111.7
IFE. See Ile Ife
IJEBU ODE   111.8
IKEJA. See Lagos
ILE IFE   111.9
ILESA   111.10
ILORIN   111.11
ISEYIN   111.12

359

Index of Authors

Index of Authors

Index of Authors

ZAHIR AL ZADATY, F.   304.2.39.

ZALACAIN, V.   115.0.8.

ZARHY, M.   203.0.5, 204.0.6.

ZE NGUELE, R.   202.7.13.